George Crook

George Crook as a brigadier general, probably in 1863. Courtesy of Brigham Young University Library.

George Crook

From the Redwoods
to Appomattox

by Paul Magid

Paul Magid

University of Oklahoma Press : Norman

Library of Congress Cataloging-in-Publication Data

Magid, Paul, 1940–
    George Crook : from the redwoods to Appomattox / by Paul Magid.
        p.   cm.
    Includes bibliographical references and index.
    ISBN 978-0-8061-4207-4 (hardcover : alk. paper) 1. Crook, George, 1829–
1890. 2. Generals—United States—Biography. 3. United States—History—Civil
War, 1861–1865—Biography. 4. United States—History—Civil War, 1861–1865—
Campaigns. 5. United States. Army—Biography. I. Title.
    E467.1.C86M34 2011
    355.0092—dc22
    [B]
                                                                    2011008976

Contents

Illustrations

FIGURES

MAPS

George Crook

Prologue

Oakland Station, March 1890

In the Alleghenies, where they spill across the panhandle of western Maryland, March does not necessarily depart like a lamb. A traveler through these mountain valleys learns to expect the unexpected—chill winds, icy rain, even a sudden snow squall. But in Oakland, this twenty-fourth day of March, 1890, holds all the promise of a lovely spring day. The large crowd that has been gathering since dawn mills quietly about the town's distinguished redbrick railway station and fills the narrow streets. It is still too early in the season for the trees to bud, and the town's surrounding slopes have not yet lost winter's grays and browns, but the sun, shining benevolently in a clear sky, fills the air with brightness and warmth. So there are few complaints when, at 10 A.M., the stationmaster announces that the train bearing Major General George Crook's body from Chicago will be four hours late.[1] Many who live in town or on nearby farms simply return to their homes to wait. Those coming here for the first time take advantage of the interlude to explore and enjoy the bucolic surroundings that have made Oakland, Maryland, a popular summer resort.

The military officers present wear civilian dress for the occasion, both at the widow's request and in deference to Crook's well-known dislike of military show. They mingle easily with congressmen and industrialists who have also come to pay their last respects. Among them are Captain John Bourke and Lieutenant Lyman Kennon, both aides to the general at different times in his career.[2] Only a year from now, Bourke, a noted

3

The railroad station in Oakland, Maryland, as it appeared in 2001. Here, Crook's body was received for burial after it arrived by rail from Chicago, where he died in March 1890. Photo by author.

anthropologist and prolific writer, will publish *On the Border with Crook,* describing his commanding officer's campaigns against the Apaches and the Sioux. Kennon will do his part in preserving Crook's memory by collecting many of the general's papers that now reside in the U.S. government's archives.

William F. Cody, popularly known as "Buffalo Bill," who scouted for Crook in the Powder River country of Wyoming in August 1876 following the Custer fight, has come to Oakland for the funeral. But he has a small problem. In his haste to catch the westbound train from Washington on Sunday afternoon, he has failed to bring sufficient funds. He uses the extra time to call at local businesses to see if they will cash a check. Most establishments have closed for the day to honor the general, but the proprietors of those few that remain open are only too happy to oblige the famous showman.[3]

Congressman William McKinley also has come here to honor the general. McKinley served on Crook's staff toward the end of the Civil War, when the general was commander of the Army of West Virginia and McKinley a twenty-one-year-old brevet major. In the intervening years, he has gone into politics, now represents Ohio in Congress, and in only six more years will be elected the twenty-fifth president of the United States. The train's delay affords McKinley the opportunity to visit the spacious grounds of the Oakland Hotel, the most prestigious in town, and to see its historic gazebo. From the station siding, across the tracks and through the bare trees, he can glimpse the elegant gingerbread façade of the rambling inn, built against a steep hillside on the opposite bank of the Little Youghigeny River, a gently flowing stream that runs through the community, paralleling the railroad. A ten-minute stroll over the track and across a narrow bridge brings him and a companion, George Washington Dorsey, veteran of the Sixth West Virginia Infantry Regiment during the war and now congressman from Nebraska, to the hotel grounds. They follow a narrow path along the riverbank and quickly come to the gazebo, a simple structure composed of an umbrella-like shingled roof resting on four upright posts perched atop a rocky spring at the confluence of three Indian trails. McKinley's gaze rests on a spot George Washington visited in the early fall of 1784 on the president's return from a tour of his landholdings in the Allegheny Mountains. It is a moment Washington recorded in his diary.[4]

Other mourners linger about the town's Queen Anne–style station, built only six years earlier by Francis Baldwin, an architect who constructed many stations for the Baltimore and Ohio Railroad.[5] It is the pride of the town. The station's eclectic design, the subject of much comment, features a bell-shaped cupola on a distinctive tower that would seem more at home on a chateau in the Loire Valley than adorning a railway depot in western Maryland.

Well before two o'clock, the crowd, swollen by an influx of Oakland's citizens, begins to drift back to the station. The Crooks have had a strong attachment to the area since the Civil War. Mary, the general's widow, is native to the area, and Crook was headquartered in nearby Cumberland during the winter of 1864–65. Mary's late father, John Dailey, owned the Glades Hotel, a modest establishment on one of Oakland's main streets. The couple stayed there during their visits, the general signing the register with characteristic reticence, "George Crook, USA," the standard abbreviation noting military service; Mary more pridefully identifying herself as "Mrs. General George Crook, Oakland." During their days in Oakland, Crook hunted the surrounding hills with locals, and he and Mary socialized with their families in the evenings, their presence bringing some measure of fame to the area. The attendance by a large number of Oakland's residents and the town's air of mourning—flags at half-staff and stores closed, their windows draped in black—testify to the respect and affection in which the couple are held.[6]

The Civil War has been over less than twenty-five years, and not a few of the men waiting at the station are veterans of either the Union or Confederate army, a fact that surprises no one in this border region. Among those who wore gray are Ira Mason, John Faye, and George Johnson, members of McNeill's Rangers, a rebel partisan unit that operated behind Union lines, attacking targets of opportunity in the Maryland and Virginia countryside.[7] On a frigid night in the last winter of the war, the three took part in a raid on Cumberland, capturing Crook, then commanding general of the Army of West Virginia. Seizing him, the highest-ranking Union officer taken prisoner during the war, was widely regarded as a great coup for the Rangers and the Confederacy. Locally, the incident inspired considerable interest and speculation as the raiders included the brother of the general's future wife, and the hotel from which he was abducted belonged to her father. Characteristically, Crook enjoyed the humor inherent in the moment and won the admiration of his captors. Mason, Faye, and Johnson have come, like the others, to pay their last respects.

There are no Indians present on this spring day. Two of the most prominent—warriors who successfully opposed Crook on the battlefield and cast long shadows of controversy over his otherwise unblemished reputation as an Indian fighter—cannot attend. Crazy Horse, the Sioux war leader who outfought Crook at Rosebud Creek just days before the Custer massacre, is dead. And Geronimo, symbol of Apache resistance, languishes as a prisoner of war at Mount Vernon Barracks in Alabama. Others who knew the general are on reservations far to the west. In any case, they would not have the resources to attend the funeral, though they mourn his passing because of the honesty and fairness he displayed in dealing with them and his attempts to ameliorate their captivity during the last years of his life. John Bourke will write that when the Indians at Fort Apache heard of Crook's death, they "let their hair down, bent their heads forward on their bosoms, and wept and wailed like children." On a reservation far to the north in Dakota Territory, Red Cloud, leader of the peace faction of the Oglala Sioux, will sadly confide to a missionary: "General Crook came; he, at least, had never lied to us. His words gave the people hope. He died. Their hope died again. Despair came again."[8]

As the appointed hour approaches, the mourners fill the station platform and line the tracks to the east and west of the depot. Except for the light hum of conversation, the crowd stands quietly in anticipation of the train's arrival. Across the track, facing the station, stand forty aging veterans, members of Oakland's Grand Army of the Republic (GAR), Post no. 35, an honor guard for the funeral cortege.[9] Standing at ease in open ranks, they exchange a few words in subdued tones and from time to time glance impatiently westward like old war horses eager for the action to start.

At exactly two o'clock, B&O engine no. 6 chuffs into the station, pulling two cars, hung with black crepe, that have been specially provided by the Pullman Company to carry Crook on his last journey east. The funeral car is shunted onto a siding where the coffin will be unloaded onto a small platform for viewing prior to being borne to the cemetery.[10] The clatter of the engine and squeal of brakes die out in a swath of steam. A solemn silence falls on the waiting crowd.

Mary Crook, ponderous in her heavy black dress, tiredly follows the conductor onto the platform. She is assisted by her sister, Fanny Read, and one of the general's aides. While the two sisters are the only surviving members of the Dailey family, Mary recognizes many close friends in the crowd. Although she has expressly asked that attendance at the graveside be limited to the family, she cannot help but feel gratified by the size of the throng that has turned out to honor her husband.[11]

Webb Hayes, the general's godson, follows her onto the platform. His father is former president Rutherford B. Hayes, who commanded the Twenty-Third Regiment of Ohio Volunteers, part of Crook's Army of West Virginia. The two veterans remained close following the war. Just days earlier, the former president had served as an honorary pallbearer at a funeral ceremony for Crook in Chicago, where the general had died suddenly from heart disease.[12]

Although Webb officially represents his father at the interment, he is here very much in his own right, having been almost a surrogate son to the childless Crook; their annual hunts in the West had become a ritual. Without hesitation, Webb agreed to accompany the casket, together with a few of Crook's friends and fellow officers and one of his surviving brothers, Walter. The latter had suffered a stroke at his brother's memorial service but chose to accompany the body to Oakland despite his infirmity.[13] The small group quietly greets old friends, mostly hunting companions and the general's fellow officers, on the platform.

Six soldiers from Fort Sheridan have escorted the body from Chicago and are the only troops in uniform for the occasion. They ease the casket, covered with a cloth of army blue, on to the platform and place it on a temporary catafalque. The casket is opened, and a crowd, later described by *The New York Times* as "fully a thousand persons," files past in silent tribute. It takes some time, but after the quiet multitude has paid its respects, the six soldiers stiffly bear the coffin to a waiting hearse. Oakland's GAR contingent proudly takes its position at the head of the procession, followed by the hearse and a cart overflowing with floral tributes. With the mourners on foot bringing up the rear, the cortege winds slowly through the town, past the closed shops and flags at half staff, and up Quality Hill to the Odd Fellows Cemetery. There the man characterized by William Tecumseh Sherman as America's "greatest Indian fighting General" is lowered into the earth near a stand of hickories overlooking the wooded hills where he spent many hours as a soldier and hunter.[14]

Though the general was not a churchgoing man, Mary has asked the Reverend J. E. Moffat of the First Presbyterian Church to read a few passages from the Bible. Afterward a squad of Civil War veterans from surrounding Garrett County fires a final volley over the grave. Its echoing crack fades over the hills, and the crowd gradually disburses. Some on their way back to town will pass by a roomy but unpretentious house standing unfinished on a ridge not far from the cemetery. Locals among them know it as Crook Crest, the home the general was building for his retirement but now will never occupy.[15]

Nine months after the funeral, John Bourke, who knew Crook better than most, would write grimly to his publisher of the massacre of Indian men, women, and children along Wounded Knee Creek at the Pine Ridge Agency in South Dakota. In a single sentence he would sum up what Crook's death meant to the army and to Native America: "Now that he is dead and we have taken to slaughtering women and suckings [*sic*] with Hotchkiss guns, the nation feels that it has lost one of its greatest sons."[16]

Though widely recognized and admired in his lifetime, George Crook has since slipped into semi-obscurity. Most writers of western history have in large measure passed him by, perhaps deterred by the extreme reticence that in life made him such a private figure and in death so inaccessible. Crook left no known cache of letters, and the only diary he is known to have kept, during the 1880s, contains for the most part the names of visitors and reports of the weather.[17]

An autobiography that the general dutifully put to paper some few years before his death provides few clues to his true nature. Several drafts exist, roughhewn documents narrowly confined to the facts of his public life and almost devoid of reflection, though occasionally spiced with unanticipated flashes of self-deprecating humor and acid comments about officers who disappointed his expectations. The tale he chose to tell begins following his graduation from West Point and ends on the eve of the disaster at the Little Big Horn, revealing little of his personal life while foregoing the opportunity to give his perspective on the more controversial aspects of his career.

Upon its completion, he deemed the work of so little interest that he stowed it in a desk drawer, where it remained until his death. The papers then passed to his wife and subsequently to a former aide, Colonel Walter Schuyler, whose widow eventually donated them to the Military History Institute (then in Washington, D.C.), a repository for military records of all kinds. There Martin Schmitt, a professor at the University of Oregon then serving in the army, discovered them in 1942.[18] Schmitt subsequently published the work with a brief commentary describing the missing portions of the general's life. Though sketchy, the autobiography has become the primary, and in some cases only, source for authors who reference Crook, particularly regarding his early career.

The memories of Crook's contemporaries shed some light on the general's character. But their recollections are of a controversial and eccentric figure who made vivid, though often contradictory, impressions on others. Some idolized him, while others found him difficult, exasperating, and perhaps a bit of a sham, thus leaving it to the historian to sort truth from bias.

Much that is fascinating about George Crook, both as a person and as a historical figure, stems from the elusive, fragmented, and sometimes contradictory nature of the documentation about his life, which makes it a challenge to discern the inner man and his motivations. This work has been fueled by that quest. By providing detail and context to the spare and often one-dimensional image that Crook chose to present and that others have drawn of him, it is my objective to paint a more complete picture of his multifaceted and complex character and of his role in American history. This volume begins that story and carries it through to the end of the Civil War.

CHAPTER ONE

On the Ohio Frontier

1828–1847

George Crook was born on the 28th of September 1828. Taciturn by nature and almost fanatical about his privacy, he was famously closed-mouth about the details of his personal life, including his childhood. At the height of his career, Crook received a letter from a boy named Daniel Farrington of Massachusetts who had written in the hope of learning something of the early years of the great Indian fighter. The general's curt response was all too typical. It read in toto: "My boyhood was passed exactly like that of all boys on a farm—my home was six miles from Dayton, Ohio."[1] His family seems to have been equally reserved, sharing very little information that would shed light on their lives or interaction with their famous relative. Thus, most of what we know of Crook's early years has been gleaned from secondary sources— local histories, the writings of contemporaries, and government records, notoriously scanty in the early years of the Republic.

There was little in George Crook's background that foretold a career as a soldier. His father, Thomas Crook, was born on a farm along the Middle River in Baltimore County, Maryland, into a family that immigrated to America in the seventeenth century from East Renfrewshire, in the southwest corner of Scotland. Members of the Crook family may have fought in the Revolution, but Thomas's father (George's grandfather), James, was a farmer, not a soldier. He had been modestly successful, amassing some two hundred acres of bottomland and five slaves to help him work it.[2]

Families were large, making it unlikely that Thomas would inherit the farm, so he apprenticed as a tanner at age twenty. In February 1812, just before the outbreak of war with Britain, his prospects seemed sufficiently hopeful that he proposed marriage to Elizabeth Matthews, daughter of a prosperous Baltimore family. She accepted. A little over a year later, she gave birth to their first child, a daughter, who was given her mother's name.[3]

Thomas, meanwhile, enlisted in a Baltimore militia company to fight the British. But his military career was short-lived and disappointing. He served for roughly a year during a period when the militia's primary task was the construction of defensive works at Fort McHenry in preparation for an anticipated British attack. Then he was discharged for ill health.[4]

Returning to civilian life with a wife and infant to care for, Thomas found his situation precarious, both economically and politically. The British blockade of the Maryland coast had depressed the local economy, making it uncertain whether the young man could support his family. In addition, many Americans in southern Maryland favored the British cause, raising the distinct possibility that some neighbor might inform the invaders of his militia service. And as long as he remained in the state, he could be recalled into the militia and once again forced to leave his young wife and infant daughter for the unpleasantness and danger of military service.

At the time, a substantial number of economically distressed and war-weary Marylanders turned their gaze toward the Northwest Territory, their attention particularly focused on the western frontier of what would become Ohio. The Shawnee and Miami tribes, the former occupants of these rich hunting grounds, had been driven west after half a century of warfare so fierce that the area had become known as the "Miami Slaughterhouse." Now land speculators sold acreage in the region to land-hungry eastern farmers, a number of whom immigrated from Maryland. Glowing reports sent back east to friends and relatives described cheap, fertile land available for the taking. These accounts attracted the attention of Thomas and his wife's two brothers, Elias and John Matthews.

For Thomas, the notion of immigration as a means to a fresh start was deeply embedded in his family heritage. His ancestors had sought new horizons from their earliest origins in medieval Scandinavia. Men

bearing variations of the Crook name had left Denmark as Viking raiders to settle in Norman France and, from there, later accompanied William the Conqueror to England, fanning out to the remotest reaches of
the British Isles. In the case of Thomas's family, a descendant, one Robert
de Croc, established an estate that became known as Crookston in East
Renfrewshire. For five hundred years Crooks lived in the county's towns
and villages. Economic reasons, or perhaps the desire to practice their
religion freely, enticed some of the more adventurous members of the
family to sail for the New World in the 1640s.[5]

Like his forebearers, in the spring of 1814, Thomas too turned his face
west toward the outer limits of his familiar world in hopes of a fresh
start. He rode alone, guiding his horse along Indian trails through the
primeval forests, following the broad Ohio River into the far reaches of
the Northwest Territory. Finding what he was looking for in the fertile
bottomlands of the Miami River valley, the young tanner returned to
Maryland to fetch his family and in-laws. Selling most of their possessions to raise cash for the trip, the extended family set off by boat down
the Ohio. In October they arrived at their destination, Montgomery
County, on the east bank of the Miami River about four miles from the
growing town of Dayton. There Thomas purchased "a hundred acres
more or less" of timbered land for one thousand dollars.[6]

The new Crook homestead was old-growth forest—hickories, butter-
nuts, elms, maples, and oaks—trees of enormous girth. These Thomas attacked with only an ax and a stolid persistence that his son would come
to mirror in his own life. Despite the pain and inconvenience of an
improperly healed fracture of his right thigh bone, he eventually would
clear land for a farm that, through a series of small purchases made over
the years, would total 340 acres, again "more or less." From the enormous trees that he felled, Thomas built a two-story log home for his
family, so solid that it remained standing for almost 150 years.

With hard work, perseverance, and luck, the family prospered. In 1827
their land multiplied in value after construction began on a canal connecting the Ohio River to Lake Erie. Running directly across the property, the waterway provided easy and cheap access to markets to the
north and east.[7]

The Whig Party, forerunner of the present Republican Party, supported the construction of canals (and other internal improvements) and

favored enterprising landowners like Thomas; so it was natural that he would become active in local Whig politics. As the result of his political activities and his growing prominence in the community, Crook was eventually appointed justice of the peace and acquired the honorary title of "squire."[8]

As his farm and standing in the community grew, so did his family. He fathered ten children. Elizabeth, the eldest, was joined by Maria, his second daughter, in 1815, followed by Catherine in 1817, Oliver in 1819, John the next year, and then, at two-year intervals, Thomas Jr., Walter, James, George, and finally Charles. As soon as they were old enough, the boys went to work in the fields. But aware that his holdings would not provide a livelihood for all of them, and placing great value in education, Thomas did not keep them there, taking great care to provide for their schooling. Of the older boys, Oliver, Thomas, and James went on to study medicine; Elizabeth married a physician. Each of the boys became highly respected in his profession and a valued member of the community in his own right. Only Walter and Charles became farmers, with Charles inheriting the family farm. But Walter, in addition, was elected to the state senate and appointed postmaster. He became the only other sibling beside George to serve in the Civil War, raising a company of volunteers and advancing to the rank of captain. John, who may have been mentally challenged, worked as a tailor, living with his sister Maria and her husband, a well-to-do businessman.[9]

The children had a religious upbringing thanks to their mother, a practicing Methodist who attended services at the United Brethren church. The brethren were a conservative offshoot of the Dutch branch of the Methodist faith, a strict and intolerant sect noted for its opposition to earthly pleasures. Every Sunday, Elizabeth scrubbed the children, dressed them in their Sunday best, and led them off to the local church, yet another rude log cabin in the woods. Here George and his siblings endured interminable sermons blasting the sins of drink, profanity, sex, gambling, tobacco, and every other vice available on the frontier.

Though married in the Methodist Episcopal church in Baltimore, Thomas was not himself a churchgoer. Probably he shared the skepticism of his frontier neighbors, one in five of whom chose not to affiliate themselves with a particular sect. These holdouts were dubious of the competing claims to religious truth put forward by a proliferation of Protestant sects and denominations and uncomfortable with the intolerance they preached. But like his neighbors, Thomas firmly accepted the existence of a supreme deity, "was moral in his deportment," and saw social value in organized religion. This became evident in 1852, when he donated land and the sum of one hundred dollars toward the construction of a modest church building. But he and his fellow donors, in a notable expression of their own tolerance, deeded the structure to the United Brethren in Christ with the stipulation that it would be "open and free to all other Christian denominations."[10]

At the time of George's birth in 1828, farmers on the Ohio frontier were a generation removed from the fear of imminent attack by Indians or the odd bear or mountain lion. But though the backbreaking labor of clearing primeval wilderness was behind them, theirs continued to be a struggle for subsistence that fully occupied the time and energy of all family members, including the children.

The tract purchased by Thomas Crook had been "entirely in the woods," requiring a tremendous effort to clear and improve it. Although he performed much of the labor himself, he relied heavily on help from those sons of sufficient age and physical strength to withstand the rigors of nineteenth-century farming. Boys began their active participation in the economic life of the farm as early as five or six years of age, helping the women around the house. As they grew older, they moved to the fields. The need for George's labor was probably acute because the oldest children were girls and two of his older brothers had already left the farm to pursue medical studies.[11]

Hard labor proved agreeable to the younger Crook. He soon grew into a strapping, self-sufficient youth able to participate in heavy work—plowing, planting, and harvesting as well as helping with the slaughter of livestock and the mending of fences. By the time he entered his teenage years, George was tall and muscular, with unusual strength and stamina for his age.

Whenever the opportunity presented itself, the boys hunted, both for the pot and to rid the area of wildlife that preyed on their stock and consumed their crops. For George, hunting became a lifelong passion. Though school and chores left scant free time, he took every opportunity to slip off into the surrounding forest. His brother Walter awakened one chilly morning at dawn to the sound of ducks flying overhead. George "was up in a minute, dressed in a hurry, never stopping to slip his braces over his shoulders and away he went. After breakfast we went out to hunt for him. We found him pretty soon, and there he was banging away with his trousers slipping down around his ankles." In later years he would acquire "a familiarity with the habits of wild animals possessed by but few naturalists," augmenting his own observations with the works of the most eminent ornithologists and naturalists.[12]

George's mother, Elizabeth, had her hands full with ten children and an impressive list of household chores. She was fondly described as "a woman esteemed by a large circle of friends [who] treated everybody that came under their roof with kindness and respect."Yet the exigencies of frontier life did not leave her much time to lavish on her large brood except on Sundays, when she attended to their religious education. With respect to George, her efforts to impart religion achieved only moderate success. Throughout his life he did adhere to the strict lifestyle tenets required by his mother's faith, abstaining from the use of profanity, strong drink, and tobacco. But like his father he would join no denomination and was not a regular churchgoer. In an army characterized by the extremes of hard drinking, profanity, and the use of all forms of tobacco on the one hand and ostentatious piety on the other, Crook was known for his avoidance of immoderation at either end of the spectrum.[13]

With mothers heavily occupied, the older girls in frontier families often took responsibility for childrearing until their younger siblings were old enough to work. In the Crook family, the eldest daughter, Elizabeth, assumed this role. Only fifteen when George was born, she cared for five boys with only the assistance of her two sisters, eleven and thirteen. After the birth of Charles two years later, the number of boys increased to six, all under the age of ten.

Raised by sisters little older than themselves, necessity dictated that the boys learn early to do for themselves, developing rapidly into self-reliant and confident youngsters. For George, maturity may have even come earlier than it did for his older siblings. His mother died in 1844 at fifty-seven, when he was only sixteen. He never publicly gave voice to the emotions that must have overcome him at such a vulnerable age. But death was a constant and accepted presence in pioneer families, and the grieving process necessarily brief. With such a large family and a farm to run, Thomas could not go it alone. In the fall of the following year, he took a second wife, Anna Gallahan, a widow in her middle years who had also emigrated from Maryland. The marriage would survive until Anna's death in 1874 only months before Thomas also passed on.[14]

As George matured, he took on the traits that he observed in his father: the adventurous spirit that had drawn Thomas west; a tolerance for the habits and beliefs of others; the stoicism and silent determination that characterized his father's daily battle with the land; and like all his siblings, he imbibed Thomas's commitment to public service, appreciation of the value of education, and the ambition to excel in his chosen vocation.

Along with the lessons absorbed at home, Crook's youth was immersed in the lore of the Ohio frontier. Every turn in its woodland trails and bend of its rivers offered reminders of the Indian wars that had raged in the region. The Crook farmstead on the banks of the Miami was no longer wilderness, and the Miami and Shawnee Indians who lived there had long since been driven west, though they remained a tangible presence. Major General "Mad" Anthony Wayne's climactic defeat of the Shawnee at Fallen Timbers, which secured the Ohio frontier for the United States, was fought only thirty-four years before George was born. Indian trails still criss-crossed the remaining forest; arrowheads and other artifacts regularly appeared in the turn of a furrow or rose from the mud after a heavy rain. Most immediately, memories of the Indians lingered vividly in the minds of many of Montgomery County's older settlers who had participated or lost friends and relatives in the fighting.

John Cuppy, a frontiersman of local note, was a veteran Indian fighter and a friend and neighbor of the Crooks. He had moved west in 1779 at the age of eighteen. Before long, his growing reputation as a hunter and woodsman prompted his selection as one of the founding members of Brady's Rangers, an elite corps of frontiersmen handpicked to act as scouts and guardians for the settlements on the Ohio frontier. Regularly patrolling the Ohio River, these men served as the settlers' first line of defense against attack, warning farmers of war parties in their vicinity and ambushing and driving off hostile bands. Cuppy scouted for General Wayne during the frontier wars that ebbed and flowed up and down the length of the river. Passing through the Miami Valley in 1794, he fell in love with the land and purchased 320 acres not far from the Crook farm, living there until his death in 1861 at the age of one hundred.[15]

For a time, George and his brother Charles attended the one-room log schoolhouse built on the Cuppy farm and presided over by Cuppy's son, Henry. Old John undoubtedly had occasion to regale the wide-eyed youngsters with tales of the Indian wars. He had been a close friend of

Simon Kenton, often compared at that time to the legendary Indian fighter Daniel Boone. As Kenton lived in nearby Urbana and visited Cuppy from time to time,[16] George likely met him and heard his wondrous tales of battles and great hunts in the primal wilderness. Kenton had an encyclopedic knowledge of Native American customs and lifeways and deeply admired the Indians with whom he had lived and fought. He was also a consummate woodman. Later Crook's life would in many ways come to mirror Kenton in his attitudes and abilities, resulting in many interesting parallels between the lives of the two men.

George may have learned eagerly at the knees of these and other larger than life heroes who visited his classroom, but mastering academic subjects took more effort. Lyman Kennon, the last in a long line of loyal aides to the general, would quote one former classmate, who described Crook as "a farmer's boy, slow to learn, but what he did learn was surely his."[17] George's later writings indicate that he mastered penmanship and spelling but showed distinct deficiencies in grammar and punctuation, a failing common for the era. He was notably lax in capitalization, commas, and even periods; run-on sentences and dangling participles abounded. The son of a frontier farmer usually left school after four or five years once having learned to read and to do simple mathematics. But despite the brevity and rudeness of his elementary education, Crook had sufficient grasp of these skills to give him a firm foundation for future learning.

While average in the schoolroom, in the schoolyard he demonstrated the first signs of a lifelong devotion to the underdog. "He was older, somewhat, than his comrades, and was good natured, stolid, and was like a big Newfoundland dog among a lot of puppies. He would never permit injustice or bullying of smaller boys."[18]

The future general's only youthful exposure to things military came during the annual community military muster, a holdover from the days of the frontier militia, usually held after the completion of the harvest. It provided the one occasion when frontier farmers assembled for what passed for military drill. Their arms consisted of little more than squirrel rifles, shotguns, canes, or, if nothing else was available, wilted cornstalks. With these at shoulder arms, the motley crowd, usually in various states of inebriation, marched up and down the stubbled fields to the ragged beat of a drum and the shrill call of a fife, struggling to obey the shouted commands of their citizen-officers. The latter were resplendently attired in uniforms of unusual flamboyance, each representing their wearer's highly individual concept of military dress.[19] While these rambunctious and farcical events could hardly inspire a young boy to seek out a career steeped in martial glory, they may well have shaped George Crook's life-long contempt for frontier militia forces and his marked indifference to all types of military show.

CHAPTER TWO

West Point

1847–1852

In the spring and summer of 1847, the shops and taverns of Ohio were alive with talk of the war with Mexico—America's first full-scale involvement in hostilities with a foreign power since the British defeat in 1814. Phil Sheridan, then a sixteen-year-old dry-goods clerk in the small town of Somerset, Ohio, later wrote that he was so stirred by the war that "my sole wish was to become a soldier and my highest aspiration to go to West Point as a cadet from my Congressional district."[1]

If George Crook was similarly inspired, he never admitted to it. Unlike Sheridan, he had little interest in the fame and glory of a military career. Devoted as he was to hunting, fishing, and roaming the woods—and devoid, at least in his youth, of higher ambition—he would probably have become a farmer like his father. Like him, George would have undoubtedly achieved some measure of local prominence and passed his life quietly in rural western Ohio but for the intervention of Robert C. Schenck, a third-term Whig congressman from Ohio's Third District.

Schenck, like every member of Congress since 1828, had the privilege of annually nominating a candidate from his district for enrollment in the U.S. Military Academy at West Point. Despite the war with Mexico, Schenck later recalled, he had difficulty finding a suitable nominee that year. Finally, he remembered Squire Thomas Crook, a loyal Whig in nearby Wayne Township. The squire had seven sons. Surely one of them would be suitable. "I sent word for him to come into town," he later told a reporter, "and I inquired if he had a spare boy he'd like to send off to West Point. After studying awhile, he said he didn't know but he had."[2]

Five sons had already embarked on their professional careers, and his last born was still too young to move away from home. That left George. Since both father and son were men of few words, it is safe to assume that when he drew George aside to broach the subject, their conversation was brief and to the point. Ulysses Grant, upon learning of his father's wish that he attend the academy, initially refused because he lacked confidence in his academic prowess. George, by contrast, appeared untroubled by the prospect.[3] He agreed to meet with the congressman and traveled to Dayton without delay.

Schenck remembered the young man as being "exceedingly noncommunicative. He hadn't a stupid look but was quiet to reticence." The congressman could discern neither interest nor anxiety in young Crook's demeanor when he laid the proposal before him. After Schenck had fully explained the requirements and work involved, he inquired, "Do you think you can conquer all that?" Crook responded simply, "I'll try." And, Schenck triumphantly concluded, "so I sent him, and he came through fairly."[4]

Having committed himself to accept the appointment, Crook sought to supplement his meager frontier education so that he could pass the academy's entrance exam and survive its rigorous course of instruction. In the fall of 1847, he entered the nearby Dayton Academy, a private school run by Milo G. Williams, a self-described "instructor in Math, Natural Philosophy, Natural Science, etc." The school advertised that it taught poor children without charge, a policy sure to appeal to the son of a cash-poor Ohio farmer.[5]

The course of instruction was brief, and Crook appeared a quick study. By December Williams was able to inform Representative Schenck that the boy's "application and improvement satisfies me that he has a mind, which will sustain him honorably in the required courses at West Point." On receiving Williams's assurances, Schenck promptly sent a letter to Joseph Totten, then inspector of the military academy, requesting that George Crook's name be placed on the list of applicants for cadet. With it he enclosed a brief testament written by Squire Crook the previous August, tersely informing anyone concerned that his son, George, was "18 years, health good, body perfect, height 5 feet 8 inches and is a good English scholar."[6]

In March Schenck formally nominated "George W. Crook," adding a middle initial that George had casually given himself and would soon, just as casually, discard.[7] Ten days later Crook received his conditional appointment. For a boy who had never traveled farther from his farm than the frontier town of Dayton, this was heady stuff.

In 1848 the young Crook was able to travel from Ohio to West Point with relative ease and dispatch thanks to an elaborate system of interconnecting waterways like the Miami and Erie Canal. As the canal providentially crossed his father's farm, he commenced his journey almost at his front doorstep. A small barge brought him to the bustling Lake Erie port of Toledo, where he boarded a steamer headed east on the lake to Buffalo, New York. Though the voyage was brief, it gave Crook his first taste of the seasickness that was to plague him throughout his life. On the crowded steamer, he made the acquaintance of several other young men on their way to enroll at the academy. Two of them, Phil Sheridan and David Stanley, were also from Ohio, and both would record their impressions of what for them was a historic journey.[8]

From Buffalo, the future cadets traveled by barge on the famous Erie Canal to Albany to connect with the steamer that would carry them down the Hudson River to West Point. The barge, long and narrow, was crammed with upward of a hundred passengers. At night the boys slept in rows on narrow wooden berths that pulled down from the sides of the vessel like beds on a Pullman car. During the day, when it was too hot and stuffy to remain below, they lounged on deck, watching the scenery of upstate New York pass by slowly, occasionally ducking their heads to avoid decapitation as the barge passed beneath one of the many low bridges that spanned the canal.[9] The subsequent steamboat journey down the Hudson carried them past some of the most beautiful scenery in North America. But the natural splendor of the Hudson Valley was lost on Crook and his fellow cadets, too absorbed in anticipation of their arrival at the academy to enjoy it.

At last the school's austere battlements came into view, poking above the trees on an escarpment looming above the river. The steamer eased alongside a small wharf known as North Dock, where Crook and the others disembarked. They were met by the provost of post and, without further ceremony, led up the steep road to the campus and assigned to barracks for the night.[10]

The next morning the first-year cadets, or plebes, were herded into the academy library to be officially enrolled by the post adjutant's clerk, "Old Tim" O'Maher, a West Point institution. Depending on his mood, Old Tim could be kindly or overbearing. Unfortunately, Crook's small group found him disgruntled. He savagely berated David Stanley for failing to come up with the ninety dollars required for the purchase of uniform and kit. As the academy simply deducted such funds from the future pay of those unable to produce the cash, this humiliating exercise was entirely superfluous. O'Maher then turned to Crook. As the young Ohioan still had one hundred and fifteen dollars in his pocket left over from his trip, he was spared the tirade but was summarily ordered to surrender the entire sum since cadets were forbidden to keep any funds upon their person during their four years at the academy.[11]

After registration the plebes were issued the furniture and equipment they would need. With a sinking feeling, Crook watched as the costs of these items were recorded one by one in his expense book, to be deducted from his future pay of $28 per month: $10.37 for a chair, $0.25 for a laundry bag, and so on, including $0.55 for the expense book itself.[12] Heavily laden with his purchases, he was briefly introduced to an upperclassman assigned to help him and others in his section prepare for the entrance exam they would be taking in fourteen days. Then the new cadet staggered off to the barracks.

Having lived all his life in a log cabin with ten siblings, Crook probably was not daunted by the austere thirteen-by-thirteen-foot room he shared with three roommates, whose names the academy never recorded. He stowed his meager possessions on one of the shelves that bracketed an open fireplace and on wooden pegs that lined the walls. A rifle rack behind the door, a fireplace, iron bedsteads, a triangular shelf holding a bucket for drawing water, and several small cast-iron tables completed the decor.[13]

Though there are no records to confirm that Crook and Sheridan roomed together during the first year, by all accounts they became good friends from the outset. Neither fit in very well with the cosmopolitan world of the southern and eastern aristocrats who dominated cadet society. Crook—awkward, reticent, an Ohio farm boy—and Sheridan—Irish, Catholic, also from rural Ohio—may well have drawn together for mutual protection from the wealthy scions of the plantation South and the better-educated and snobbish New Englanders.[14]

George Crook, Philip Sheridan, and John Nugen as West Point cadets. This is the only known photographic image of Crook in his youth. Courtesy of the U.S. Military Academy Library.

A photograph taken during their time at the academy documents their early camaraderie. A boyish George Crook and John Nugen, another cadet from Ohio, both in blue uniform coats, flank the irrepressible Sheridan, clad in cadet gray. Sheridan has draped his long arms over their shoulders in a proprietary manner and glowers at the camera from under heavy brows. To his left, Nugen stares impassively into the lens, hands crossed, in the stiff pose favored at the time, while Crook, on Sheridan's right, sits stolidly, mirroring Nugen's pose, his hands also crossed in his lap; his eyes are so close together they almost appear crossed. Crook appears a broad-shouldered, guileless young man with hair slicked forward across a high forehead. His jaw is prominent, his mouth wide. His expression suggests a slight uneasiness, as though he considers the camera—and perhaps Sheridan's proprietary hand on his shoulder—an intrusion on his beloved privacy.

For Crook, the first two weeks at the academy were dominated by the total strangeness of his new life, compounded by concerns about whether he would pass the physical and academic exams that would determine his future there. A sturdy farmboy, he had no problem with the physical. The most rigorous element, the eye test, required him to determine whether a dime was turned to heads or tails at a distance of fourteen feet. This he did with ease—his eyesight was exceptionally keen and would remain so throughout his life.[15]

The academic exam, though no one explained this to the plebes, was intentionally easy. The administration of the academy and Congress, aware that many cadets like Crook had received only the most rudimentary education, had no intention of losing a high percentage of their potential officer corps at the outset by imposing stringent academic entry qualifications. So the examination consisted of only a few simple mathematical questions. The cadets also were asked to read several lines from a book and given four or five lines of dictation to test their spelling and writing ability. George, like 93 percent of all antebellum cadets, passed with ease and was officially enrolled as a member of the class of 1852.[16]

No longer civilians, the cadets, addressed as "plebes" or "animals" by upperclassmen, were now eligible to draw the school's tight-fitting gray uniform with white summer pantaloons. Newly uniformed, they were organized by height into four companies, A through D, two companies of taller men ("flankers," A and D) and two of shorter ones ("runts," B and C). Crook, standing almost six feet tall, was assigned to Company D, a flanker. Sheridan, an unimpressive five foot, five inches in height, could only have been a runt.[17]

Crook's military education then began in earnest. Every summer, from June until the end of August, the entire school, except for the entering fourth-year class, camped on the academy grounds and learned the rudiments of soldiering in the field. In the fall the instruction moved into classrooms. There cadets were taught from a curriculum that for the most part had been designed by Sylvanus Thayer, superintendent from 1817 to 1833. To Thayer, mathematics and French were the twin pillars of a military education. Mathematics was essential to the study of military engineering, the raison d'être of West Point in the nineteenth century; French because, in Thayer's opinion, all great books on military strategy and tactics since Napoleon were written in that language.

As a consequence of Thayer's biases, Crook's first two years were dominated by these two subjects. Only in his third and fourth year, would he round out his course of study with chemistry, drawing (to aid in mapmaking and field observation), mineralogy, physics, rhetoric, and moral and political philosophy. And only in his last year did he receive training in military engineering, which almost as an afterthought included tactics and strategy.

Were it not for Dennis Hart Mahan, an eccentric and charismatic teacher who taught the course Engineering and the Science of War, the academy would have completely neglected to impart to its students the practical principles of warfare, conventional or otherwise. Mahan, who graduated from West Point in 1824 and taught there for almost forty years, emphasized engineering. But he did devote 6 out of the 112 lessons in the course to the "science of war." Even these focused primarily on strategy, tactics, and military usages more suited to the set-piece battles fought by the European powers in the nineteenth century than to the type of partisan warfare his pupils would be likely to encounter on the frontier.[18]

But during the period from 1836 to 1840, well before Crook's enrollment at West Point, Mahan, influenced by events during the Seminole Wars, briefly introduced a single lesson on Indian warfare. He borrowed from Roman military teachings that advocated the adoption of tactics used by one's foes for use by one's own troops—in this case those of the Seminoles modified to suit the American soldier. To this Mahan added lessons learned from guerrilla warfare in Spain and from the American Revolution, relying heavily in the latter instance on the recommendations of George Washington, himself a veteran of the French and Indian War (1754–63). Washington's advice that "war should be carried . . . into the heart of the enemy's country," destroying his food supplies to force him to come to terms, introduced Mahan's pupils to the concept of total war in partisan conflicts. Drawing upon the Seminole Wars (1818, 1835–42), Mahan added several additional tenets, among them that marches should be undertaken in force and with "the extreme of prudence;" campsites should selected with care and be well fortified; friendly Indians and trappers should be employed as scouts; and tribes at odds with the enemy should be enlisted as allies.[19]

Though Mahan dropped Indian warfare from the curriculum in 1840, these tactics, which now seem self-evident, had become basic military lore by the time Crook reached the frontier. Officers returning from the West to teach at the academy reinforced these lessons based on their personal experiences and passed them on to the young cadets.[20] But aside from these informal exchanges and Mahan's short-lived efforts, West Point graduates assigned to the frontier would have to find their way by trial and error, learning Indian fighting from their more senior officers or from observing the Indians themselves. Some, like Crook, would be more successful than others.

George's grades were posted weekly and sent each month to his parents in Ohio. Grades were weighted based on the importance attached to each course, with mathematics having the highest value, and courses like drawing and political philosophy having the lowest. The value assigned to a course was then multiplied by a cadet's grade to assign overall academic rank.

Class standing, critical because it determined the branch of service to which a cadet would be assigned, was not solely determined by grades, however. Conduct also factored into the equation through a system of demerits meted out for violations of regulations. These demerits and resultant punishments were detailed for each cadet on conduct rolls published monthly. One hundred demerits earned within a six-month period would result in a cadet's expulsion, as could a single serious infraction.

Extra guard duty or confinement to quarters were the usual punishments for such minor offenses as "throwing a missile in mess hall at dinner" or spitting tobacco juice out barrack windows. But some, like Cadet Sheridan, who committed serious infractions were dealt with more severely. In the spring of his third year while on parade, the hot-blooded Sheridan lost his temper at a fancied insult delivered by a cadet officer, broke ranks, and charged him full tilt, bayonet at the ready. Drawing back at the last instant, he retired to his position in ranks and hurled pungent epithets at his tormentor. For his "insubordinate conduct" and use of "highly insulting and disrespectful language," Sheridan was suspended for a year and thus failed to graduate with Crook in 1852.[21]

Crook's own record reflects his conservative, retiring nature, and, probably not inconsequentially, the fact that he was too overwhelmed by academic work to engage in the usual collegiate shenanigans. During his first term, he received demerits on only two occasions: for making or allowing boisterous noise in quarters during study hours and for smoking, a rare departure from his usual abstemious habits. In his second year he committed a far more serious infraction when he was discovered "offering a composition to his instructor as his own which was not original." Fortunately for Crook, cheating was not regarded as a serious matter at the pre–Civil War academy and in fact was common—recognized by a perhaps too tolerant administration as the consequence of inadequate secondary education and the academic pressure imposed on cadets. Consequently, he was simply confined to quarters on four successive Saturdays and required to take two extra turns at guard duty.[22]

The combined result of Crook's academic performance and his conduct was recorded on the "Merit Roll." Published upon graduation, this document would establish his class standing and the branch of the service to which he would be assigned. If he stood among the top of the roll, he knew that he would be appointed to the Corps of Engineers, the elite of the army; if among the lowest, the infantry. Students in between went into the artillery or the mounted service, the dragoons or mounted infantry; the cavalry did not become a recognized military arm until 1855, after Crook had graduated.[23]

Despite hard work and diligence, Crook failed to shine as a student. Major General Oliver Howard, who was two years his junior at the academy, found him "not very quick at learning; . . . but he was persistent, and what he learned stuck to him." At the end of the first term, Crook stood fifty-second in a class then numbering sixty-two. By his third year, possibly more comfortable with the work, he managed to make his way up to thirty-seventh in a class that had dwindled to forty-seven members. Ultimately, he would graduate thirty-eighth in his class, not a brilliant showing, but commendable in light of his limited academic background.[24]

In his senior year, now fairly certain that he would graduate and aware of his future social obligations as a member of the officer corps, Crook began to pay attention to the social graces. For the princely sum of $3.50, he bought himself dancing shoes and arranged for the services of a dancing master.[25] Suitably attired in the dress uniform he had purchased for his only furlough, in the summer following his third year, he attended at least some of the cotillions, parties, and balls to which upperclassmen received invitations. Being painfully shy around women, these formal, well-chaperoned occasions did not result in any romantic interests—or if they did, he certainly never mentioned them.

Though romance might not have been foremost in his mind, Crook evidently sowed a wild oat or two. On February 7, 1852, he was confined to his room for two weeks as the result of "absenting himself from quarters after taps," an indication that he had given himself a break from the puritanical and monotonous routine of academy life.[26]

Accounting for his absence that evening is not difficult since there were few distractions to attract a cadet after lights out. The academy went to great lengths to ban almost all forms of pleasure that might lighten the cadets' burden. Gambling, drinking, musical instruments, smoking, and playing cards or any other sort of games were prohibited. And the food was awful. To relieve both the boredom and their colorless diet of boiled beef and potatoes, cadets mounted nocturnal foraging expeditions, cooking their booty in their fireplaces, a practice known as "hashing," at which William Tecumseh Sherman was said to excel.[27] If hashing did not strike Crook's fancy, there is a remote possibility that a trip to the notorious Benny Havens tavern in nearby Buttermilk Falls may have drawn him. There upperclassmen could eat a prepared meal, consume strong drink, and even vie for the attention of a comely barmaid before sneaking back to the barracks in the early hours of the morning.

While Benny Havens provided some cadets with momentary relief for their physical appetites, the school library offered recreation for the mind, though Spartan ideals prevailed there too. The type and number of books one could read was severely limited, as was access to the library, open only on Saturday afternoons; even then a student could borrow only one book for the week. A record of the reading materials that cadets signed out over the years has been preserved in the academy library, now a much more welcoming and well-stocked institution than in Crook's day. These handwritten book lists provide a narrow window into a cadet's personality.[28]

Initially Crook, a serious student under considerable pressure to achieve success in his chosen profession, selected reading material with potential for intellectual improvement rather than escape. He focused on history and works of travel and exploration, practical works that might offer insights useful to a professional soldier. He began his literary explorations in the spring of his second year. His initial selection was J. Quinn Thorton's history of Oregon and California in two volumes, a practical choice for a cadet who knew that the Pacific Coast could well be his first assignment. He then plunged into Charles Rollin's eight-volume treatise on ancient history, tenaciously plowing through volume after volume in an effort that carried him well into the winter of the following year.

Having evidently sated his appetite for knowledge of the ancients, Crook moved on to medieval and modern Europe, with a bias toward the history of Scotland, his ancestral home. By the spring of 1851, he was signing out almost a book a week, and his subject matter, while remaining primarily focused on history and exploration, began to broaden. His choices ranged from a volume on Alexander von Humboldt's travels in the New World, replete with its numerous references to natural history; to Adolphe Thier's work on the French Revolution; to readings on the Mexican War; and even to a history of the Jews. Unlike his friends Nugen and Sheridan, Crook avoided both fiction and poetry.

Early in his last year, he discovered the works of Washington Irving, devouring twelve titles in rapid succession, many of which dealt with the exploration of the West. Approaching graduation, he allowed himself the frivolity of reading the Waverly novels, fiction based on Scottish history written by Sir Walter Scott, evidencing his continued interest in his ancestral roots. Scott was the lightest reading available in the West Point library.

At last, in June 1852, he graduated. His class standing earned him an assignment in the infantry. But because of the downsizing of the military following the end of the Mexican War, for the time being, there were no permanent second-lieutenant positions available. So he received only a brevet, or temporary, appointment to the rank.

Despite an academic record that would later mark him as the lowest-ranking graduate to ever become a major general, Crook had reason to be proud of his performance at the academy.[29] He had overcome the disadvantages of sporadic schooling and minimal academic exposure on the Ohio frontier to successfully complete an extremely difficult and demanding course of study. He absorbed the lessons that West Point had to offer and looked forward to the three-month furlough granted to graduates, followed in due course by his first assignment as an officer in the U.S. Army.

CHAPTER THREE

An Entirely New Experience

October–December 1852

On an unusually balmy early November day in 1852, Brevet 2nd Lieutenant George Crook, neatly attired in his dark-blue uniform with contrasting sky-blue infantry facings, stood on the deck of the *Prometheus*. The steamer would carry him to Nicaragua, the first stage of his journey to California and his first assignment as an officer in the U.S. Army. As the ship cleared New York harbor and entered the Atlantic, wallowing lightly in the ocean swells, he experienced the dreaded surges of inner turbulence that usually heralded the onset of seasickness.[1]

A month before, on October 1, after bidding farewell to their families, Crook and three former classmates reported to Governors Island, off the southern tip of Manhattan, to receive their first assignments.[2] This was the moment that Crook would choose, some thirty years later, to begin his narrative of his military career.

Governors Island was the recruitment and training center for the army's infantrymen as well as the point of departure for ships ferrying troops to posts in the Southwest and the Pacific Coast.[3] The term "training center" was something of a misnomer, actually. Neither here nor elsewhere in the 1850s did the army pay much attention to the training and orientation of new arrivals. Crook and his comrades, the equally green John Nugen, John Mullan, and August Kautz, were left pretty much to their own devices.

By the end of October, all four had received orders to report to commands on the West Coast. Crook, Kautz, and Nugen were each assigned

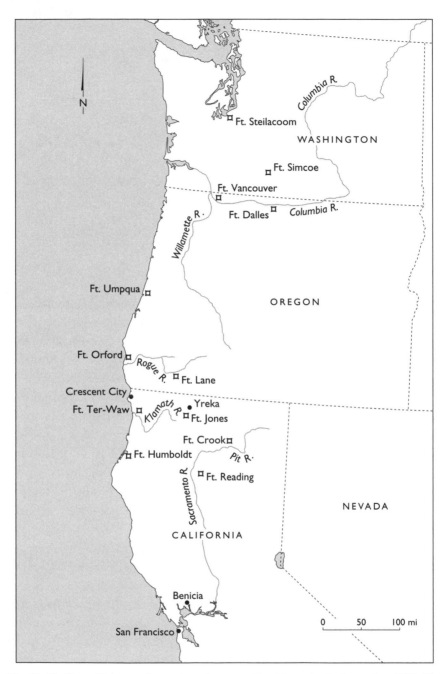

N

Ft. Steilacoom

WASHINGTON

Ft. Simcoe

Columbia R.

Ft. Vancouver

Ft. Dalles   Columbia R.

Willamette R.

Ft. Umpqua

OREGON

Ft. Orford

Rogue R.   Ft. Lane

Crescent City

Ft. Ter-Waw   Yreka

Klamath R.   Ft. Jones

Ft. Crook

Pit R.

Ft. Humboldt

Sacramento R.

Ft. Reading

NEVADA

CALIFORNIA

Benicia

0   50   100 mi

San Francisco

The Pacific Coast. This map shows sites relevant to Crook's service in the region, 1852–60.

to one of the eight companies of the Fourth Infantry that had preceded them to California five months earlier; Mullan, whose class standing was somewhat higher, received an appointment to the First Artillery Regiment.[4] The young lieutenants joined a growing contingent of troops dispatched over the past four years to the West Coast to garrison the Division of the Pacific, a sprawling command covering the entire region west of the Rocky Mountains except for the territories of Utah and New Mexico. Their primary duties would involve keeping peace between the thousands of immigrants seeking riches in the goldfields and fertile lands of the Pacific Northwest and any Indians who might find themselves in their path.

In 1852 travel to the Pacific Coast was a major undertaking. Prior to the construction of either the Transcontinental Railroad or the Panama Canal, most travelers faced the choice of a tortuous overland journey across the trackless expanse of the American West or a long and dangerous voyage by steamer around Cape Horn. A third possibility, one the army found the most economical and expeditious, required a trek across the isthmus connecting North and South America. Ulysses Grant had crossed at Panama five months before Crook's departure.[5] Traveling during the rainy season, he found himself mired in a sea of mud amid a jungle rife with disease. One out of every seven soldiers who made that journey with him died of cholera along the way. Perhaps as a result of this experience, Crook and his comrades aboard the *Prometheus* had been routed through Nicaragua, a comparatively healthier region.

After a monotonous and bilious voyage from Governors Island, Crook greeted his arrival at the tiny harbor of Grey Town on Nicaragua's Caribbean coast with relief, shortly replaced by wonder. Herded off the steamer, he and his fellow passengers boarded several small steam-powered river launches that would carry them ninety-one miles up the muddy San Juan River to Lake Nicaragua. There was scarcely room to stand on the decks of the ramshackle boats, and the weather was hot and sticky, broken intermittently by drenching showers. But most passengers, entranced by the passing scene, hardly noticed. The farmboy from Ohio was particularly taken. He wondered at "the dense, impenetrable jungle of trees, with vines intertwining their branches," and thrilled to the sight of alligators "watching their chances for prey, lizards, climbing in the branches of trees, at least four feet long, [and] flights of parrots screaming at the tops of their voices."[6]

But the idyll soon turned dangerous. The boats did not put in for the night but continued upriver in total darkness. The occasional shower had become a continuous downpour, and the only illumination came from the blurry yellow glow of oil lamps fastened to the prow and stern of the launches, barely penetrating the blackness. At about ten o'clock the lead boat struck an overhanging branch that violently tore the smokestack from her deckhouse, killing her captain and disabling the craft. Fearing the boat might sink, the crew hastily transferred the passengers to another launch. In the darkness, frightened men and women felt their way over a shaky gangplank made slippery by rain. One elderly lady, traveling west to meet her husband, lost her footing and disappeared into the swirling waters, never to be seen again.[7]

On the second launch, the chilled passengers, packed tightly on the slick decks, were unable to lie down or even sit for the remainder of the night. One man dozed off and slipped into the river. Fortunately, his screams caught the attention of fellow passengers who plucked him from an overhanging limb before he could be snatched by an alligator or pulled under by the turbulent currents.[8]

Finally, the terrible night drew to a close, the rains abated, and by mid-morning the steamers arrived at the Castillo Rapids, a portion of the river where passage was blocked by immense stones that looked to the young Crook as if they had been hurled into the riverbed by careless giants. On the river bank above the rapids loomed an ancient, crumbling citadel that gave this treacherous stretch its name. Beneath the castle's walls sprawled a squalid hamlet of bamboo-and-mud huts, into whose inhospitable streets the shaky passengers were discharged.

They were soon accosted by the sort of "enterprising Yankee" who, in Crook's words, "is ever willing to sacrifice himself for his fellow man by dispensing bad whiskey and poor fare," a type of entrepreneur the young lieutenant would encounter all too often during his service on the frontier. As the proprietor of the town's sole accommodations, this avaricious expatriate made available a single large room adjacent to a bar from which it was separated by only a thin partition. In that room, for one dollar, those passengers with hammocks could sling them from the rafters for the night. For the same amount, those without were welcome to wrap themselves in blankets on the floor. At nightfall, having no alternative, Crook found a spot on the floor, folded himself into his blanket, and promptly fell into exhausted slumber.

Sometime during the night, he abruptly awakened to a chorus of frantic screams punctuated by the menacing click of pistol hammers and cries of "Don't shoot!" Crook hugged the floor and feared the worst, "knowing that pretty much all were armed with pistols or knives— and some with both." But the innkeeper, accustomed to such nocturnal alarms, calmly lit a lantern and identified the root of the disturbance: a passenger's hammock rope had given way, catapulting him onto a sleeper below whose terrorized howls had unleashed bedlam in the darkened room.[9]

The next morning the dazed passengers resumed their river journey on boats moored below the rapids, by evening reaching the broad, calm expanse of Lake Nicaragua. The trip across the 110-mile long lake could be dangerous during the winter, when sudden squalls and even water-spouts were not uncommon. But Crook's crossing was uneventful, under a full moon that cast its shimmering image on the water's glassy surface. He later remembered the voyage as "one of the grandest of my life."[10]

In contrast, the final twelve miles by mule from a squalid village on the lakeshore to San Juan del Sud on the Pacific coast was "just one mud hole from one end to the other." Another traveler, who followed the same route some years earlier, wrote that the mud was of "a soft slippery, clayey character," so soupy in fact that "very frequently, I have seen mules dashing along, their backs covered by the mud, and their heads only vis-ible. Really it was a swim through a muddy sea."[11]

Mules were beasts with which Crook had become familiar from life on the farm. The Nicaraguan variety he described as "poor, weak, and stubborn." He might have added "abused," for their plight was truly moving. Overloaded with baggage and passengers, many of whom had never ridden a mule, the hapless creatures struggled to make progress through the mire. Some simply sank under the weight of their burden and were abandoned to their fate, their decomposing carcasses adding the stink of death to the miserable ordeal. Despite the poor quality of these particular animals, Crook knew the breed to be hardy, courageous, and possessed of more stamina than most horses. The farmer's son had a talent for their management sadly lacking among his fellow travelers. "Having a pretty fair mule, and getting off and leading him when I came to any very bad place," Crook crossed the muddy stretch in fair time and was among the very first to reach the Pacific shore. There, after tending to the welfare of his mount, he gratefully rinsed the mud from his own body and clothing in the rolling surf and settled back on the beach to await the others. To his amusement, his friend Kautz did not arrive until midnight, filthy and played out. Setting down his luggage, Kautz wearily complained that the last time he could recollect seeing *his* mule, only its ears were showing above the mud.[12]

The next evening the exhausted passengers once more took to the sea, this time on the steamer *Brother Jonathan,* bound for San Francisco. Their captain was in such a great hurry to depart—he carried the first news of James Buchanan's election as president—he left some of the passengers and much baggage stranded on shore.[13] Fortunately, the Pacific proved considerably calmer than the Atlantic. Nevertheless Crook again suffered from acute seasickness and so was greatly relieved when, on the first of December, the ship docked at the Long Wharf in San Francisco Bay. Disembarking on wobbly legs, he and his fellow officers found themselves immersed in the jostling crowd that met every ship in eager anticipation of news and mail from the States.

Four years earlier, gold had been discovered at Sutter's Mill, and the ensuing flood of would-be miners turned San Francisco from a sleepy village into a bustling city that overwhelmed the young lieutenant: "I never saw so much life in so small a compass before. . . . Everything was so different from what I had ever seen before that I could hardly realize that I wasn't in a foreign country." Riches from the gold fields had so inflated prices that the common unit of currency was the fifty-dollar gold piece, a locally minted octagonal coin called a slug. Eggs cost one dollar each, half a dozen potatoes were nine dollars a sack, and a small apple went for five dollars. Crook's pay as a second lieutenant was sixty-four dollars a month, supplemented by a meager two-dollar per diem authorized by a niggardly Congress for officers serving on the West Coast. But he fared well compared to the enlisted men, who received from seven to thirteen dollars a month and no supplement. From his meager pay, an officer was supposed to feed and clothe himself, making it frighteningly clear to Crook that he would be hard pressed to make ends meet.[14]

Under these circumstances, it was hardly surprising that the troops, filled with fanciful tales of easy wealth in the goldfields, deserted in droves. In 1853 alone, 1,500 men in an army totaling only 10,000 soldiers, went "over the hill," undeterred by the prospect of draconian punishment should they be caught. To ameliorate this problem, the army moved its newly arrived troops away from the temptations of San Francisco as swiftly as possible. So Crook and his fellow brevet second lieutenants were quickly whisked out of the city in wagons headed for Benicia Barracks, forty-five miles up the coast, where they were warehoused pending transfer to units stationed throughout the department. Here Crook received his assignment to Company F, Fourth Infantry Regiment.[15]

At Benicia, Crook became aware that the army also had a serious problem with alcohol abuse. Raised in the strict tenets of Methodism and recently imbued with the monastic traditions of West Point, the young lieutenant was shocked by the conduct of the officers he now met. With few exceptions he found them drunk every day, sometimes carousing until the small hours of the morning. The revelry was led by none other than the post commandant, Major Hannibal Day. To Crook's amazement, Day's bizarre antics when intoxicated included a fondness for piling up his furniture in the center of his room and setting it afire.[16]

The day after his arrival, Crook found himself assigned as the file closer at the funeral of a Major Miller, who has just died from "the effects of strong drink." Aghast, he watched as Day called the men together around the corpse, raised his glass, and proposed, "Well, fellows, old Miller is dead and can't drink, so let's all take a drink."[17]

CHAPTER FOUR

Assignment to Fort Humboldt

Winter–Fall 1853

Mercifully, Crook's tenure at Benicia Barracks was short. In late January 1853, orders arrived assigning the Fourth Regiment's Companies B and F to a new military post to be constructed at Humboldt Bay on the northern California coast.[1]

Just days before his scheduled departure, the young lieutenant's prospects suddenly dimmed when he was stricken with a severe streptococcal infection known as erysipelas. The disease, which in its more virulent forms can cause gangrene and death, usually manifests itself in painful swellings on the arms and legs, particularly in the region of the joints. In Crook's case it attacked both his shins and ankles. Overcome with fear that he would miss the ship transporting his company to Humboldt Bay, he turned in desperation to the medical officer, a callous practitioner who painted the infected area with iodine and creosote. When this treatment appeared ineffective, a second doctor dosed Crook with calomel and jalap, purgatives that made him violently ill.[2]

Despite this treatment, within two days Crook recovered sufficiently to embark on schedule with his troops, demonstrating an amazing recuperative power that time after time allowed him to survive illness and injury with little medical intervention. He was fortunate to have such an iron constitution, for the health care available in the frontier army offered little hope of recovery from any but the mildest of infirmities. But as he prepared to board the boat for Humboldt, the second surgeon who had treated him approached in an inebriated condition. Before being allowed to depart, the young man was forced to stand rooted to the dock while, without a flicker of irony, the drunken physician berated him for daring to recover without his permission, thereby depriving the good doctor of an interesting case study.[3]

Crook had learned a second lesson. Like drunkenness, indifference by officers to the welfare of their troops was endemic in the nineteenth-century army. Inherited in part from European military traditions and class divisions, in America such callousness was reinforced by the yawning social and educational chasm between officers and enlisted men. The former were usually educated sons of the middle class—78 percent of Crook's fellow officers were West Point graduates—while the latter were recruited predominantly from the ranks of newly landed immigrants or the desperately poor.[4] Crook's egalitarian frontier background and his empathy for the underdog appeared to have inoculated him against the cruel indifference displayed by many fellow officers, including his new commanding officer, Brevet Lieutenant Colonel Robert Buchanan.

The steamer *Goliah,* transporting the soldiers from Benicia to their new duty station, was an overcrowded old tub of questionable seaworthiness, so packed that soldiers were unable to find space to lie down at night. The wind picked up as they proceeded north, blowing rain in sheets across the rolling decks that soaked the troops to the bone. Desperate, some huddled against the bulkhead on the lee side of the bridge near Buchanan's cabin. As Crook watched helplessly, the colonel drove the men away from even this token shelter, sarcastically demanding if they expected an invitation inside for dinner.[5]

Fort Humboldt, which Companies B and F were tasked to build and garrison, was the most recent outpost constructed in response to the unrest that roiled the West Coast following the discovery of gold in California. The heavy influx of miners and settlers into the region quadrupled the white population in two years from an estimated twenty-six thousand to over one hundred thousand. The onslaught devastated the indigenous Indian populations. Most miners and settlers considered the Indians vermin to be pushed aside or exterminated. Even where the two cultures managed an uneasy coexistence, whites drove off game, exhausted firewood, and dammed or polluted streams. Deprived of their traditional means of subsistence, the Indians responded by stealing stock to replace depleted fish and game, raided immigrant wagon trains for supplies, and revenged their dead by ambushing isolated travelers. Action and reaction provoked an endless cycle of murder and revenge, its victims usually the innocent who were simply in the wrong place at the wrong time.[6]

It was not uncommon to find officers in the antebellum West sympathetic to the plight of the Indian. Many perceived them to be the weaker of the two cultures, victims rather than perpetrators, and thought it the army's duty to protect them.[7]

Ultimately, the government intended to separate the two antagonistic populations, taking possession of the land and forcing the Indians onto reservations representing a fraction of their original holdings. This appears a draconian solution, but in the nineteenth century, it was considered a humane alternative to extermination, the option favored by many whites on the frontier. Maintaining the Indians on reservations was expensive, though, and in the 1850s, Congress saw no pressing need to appropriate the necessary funds, leaving it to the army to maintain order. Yet the military, reduced by the legislature to a bare minimum in peacetime, did not have sufficient resources for the task. The army had a force of only thirteen hundred officers and men to garrison the entire Pacific Division, an area with a 1,600-mile frontier, home to an Indian population of approximately 134,000 souls.[8] With such limited resources, division commanders relied on a strategy of satellite outposts, like Fort Humboldt, to protect the settlers and Indians from one another. Patrols from these small posts were supposed to cover the surrounding area, responding to settler complaints about depredations and protecting the Indians from civilian attacks.

Brevet Lieutenant Colonel Buchanan, a West Pointer and veteran of the Seminole, Black Hawk, and Mexican wars, would command at Humboldt Bay. Prior to the Civil War, brevet, or honorary, ranks were used to reward outstanding service. During the Mexican War, Buchanan had earned brevet promotions to major and then lieutenant colonel for bravery and meritorious conduct. In deference to his brevet rank, he was addressed as colonel, though after twenty-two years in the army, he still held the permanent rank of captain. Normally, an officer of his rank would command a single company, but because the Fourth Infantry's companies were understrength, and perhaps in consideration of his brevets, Buchanan commanded two companies, ninety-one men and four junior officers.[9]

George Crook was second in command of Company F under a more senior second lieutenant, Edmund Underwood, an enlightened and competent Pennsylvanian. As one of four junior officers of similar views and abilities in a locale noted for its scenic beauty, Crook should have anticipated a pleasant tour. It was marred, however, by Buchanan's difficult disposition. The colonel had such a self-important and supercilious manner that local residents nicknamed him "Jesus Christ Jr." Inevitably, relations between Crook, described by a contemporary as "a sweet-tempered fellow, about twenty years old and brimful of fun and laughter," and the overbearing Buchanan would not be amicable.[10]

Having to deal with Colonel Buchanan, as with the antics of the drunken Major Day, contributed to Crook's growing disillusionment with the army's senior officer corps. Looking back on his years of service, he would later record his disdain for "petty tyrants" like Buchanan, who "lost no opportunities to snub those under them and prided themselves in saying disagreeable things." Crook observed: "Most of them had been in command of small posts so long that their habits and minds had narrowed down to their surroundings, and woe unto the young officers if his [sic] ideas should get above their level and wish to expand." Buchanan's "mode of discipline," he further opined, "consisted in trying to break down men's self respect and make a machine of them instead of appealing to their better feelings and judgment." The colonel ignored unsolicited suggestions from subordinates, even if he knew them to be correct. And, Crook wryly observed, he followed this rule faithfully, "judging from the number of mistakes he made."[11]

Because Crook was frequently critical of other officers who failed to meet his exacting standards, his commentaries can often be taken with a grain of salt. But in this instance, his opinions had some corroboration. A civilian residing near the post who knew the commanding officer well related that "Colonel Buchanan was an efficient officer, but strict in petty details to the verge of absurdity." This characteristic, exacerbated by old grievances, caused him to focus unwonted attention on Captain Ulysses Grant, who arrived at Humboldt shortly after Crook. Having known, and disliked, each other since serving together at Jefferson Barracks, Missouri, Buchanan and Grant were at odds from the moment the latter reported for duty. Like Crook, Grant had a casual approach to military protocol and a careless manner of dress. But unlike Crook, he was bored and lonely, seeking solace in alcohol. On a small post like

Humboldt, the two younger officers found it hard to escape the notice of their martinet commander. Grant's informality and the effects of alcohol on his demeanor touched a raw nerve in the spit-and-polish colonel, who seemed to take a special delight in abusing him.[12]

Despite their shared antipathy toward their commanding officer, Crook and Grant did not become close at Humboldt. Grant, the older of the two and a veteran of the Mexican War, was a solitary man, not prone to confide his woes. And Crook's natural taciturnity undoubtedly would have discouraged intimacy with such a man.

Humboldt was Grant's Elba. He missed his family terribly and feared that he would never be able to afford to bring them to California to join him. Unlike Crook, he took no interest in hunting or fishing, nor in the dancing, gambling, and billiards that absorbed others of his fellow officers. He drank and, unfortunately, seemed unable to hold his liquor, showing the effect of even moderate amounts of alcohol.[13] Ultimately, he succumbed to homesickness and resigned from the service after being threatened by Buchanan with a court-martial for drunkenness on duty.

Crook resolved to deal with Buchanan's prickly personality by avoiding him as much as possible. Unfortunately, his intention was thwarted when the colonel appointed him post adjutant, forcing the two officers into constant proximity. But Crook obtained some relief from this oppressive arrangement through frequent forays into the surrounding countryside, where he indulged his growing passion for hunting and fishing. The young lieutenant found the country a paradise, and years later he could still recall it in lyrical detail:

> the country abounded in game, both large and small. . . . [D]ucks rose before us from the adjacent marshes in clouds. The flapping of their wings sounded like distant thunder. Back from the bay a few miles were what was known as the bald mountain, the tops of which were denuded of timber, evidently by fires, and were then covered with grass running off into a dense forest of redwood toward the ocean. In this [forest], elk, deer, and bear abounded, arriving in the evenings and mornings to graze, remaining hid in the timber in the day time. Blue grouse in the spring time could be heard drumming in all directions about these mountains. Salmon ran up all streams of any size, while the speckled trout were plentiful in some of the streams.[14]

John Bourke, who would become Crook's aide and a sort of Boswell to the general's Johnson, thought that Crook's lifelong love for hunting and fishing "received its greatest impetus in those days of service in Oregon and Northwest California." But at this early stage of his life, Crook frankly admitted, while many species of game abounded, "my inexperience in hunting made it more difficult to take them than I at first supposed." He learned quickly, however, and soon kept his mess well supplied with game. His prowess made an indelible impression on the settler population, one local resident recalling years later that Crook had tracked and killed a bear, apparently a momentous event that "created no small excitement at the fort."[15]

Crook's woodland ramblings became the occasion for his first recorded contact with local tribes. The Wiyots, an Algonquian tribe, occupied the coastal plain on which the fort was constructed. They subsisted primarily on fish and local roots and berries, like most Indians living on the Pacific coast. Few in number, they tried to coexist with the forty-niners, but their efforts at accommodation failed, and they were soon driven off their lands. By the time of Crook's arrival, the Wiyots had become impoverished refugees, dependent on other tribes and settlers for survival.[16] Though sympathetic to their plight, Crook thought them "scroffolitic" and degraded without giving much thought as to how they might have come to such a state. He much preferred the prouder and more aggressive Athabascan-speaking peoples, hunters who lived in the nearby mountains, ascribing the differences in the two tribes to climate and diet.

The Athabascans were more numerous and thus could actively defend their lands. They also raided settlements and stole livestock. Their depredations angered the miners and settlers, who retaliated by attacking the defenseless and more accessible Wiyots. From the beginning, Crook was disgusted and outraged by these retaliatory strikes. In his autobiography he bitterly described an all too common incident in which local settlers had "worked themselves up to the pitch of going in force one night to a village of poor defenseless people and brutally massacring large numbers of them, mostly women and children."[17]

Buchanan, for all his arrogance, subscribed wholeheartedly to the army's policy of trying to protect the Indians wherever possible. He sent patrols into Wiyot and Athabascan country to establish communications with the tribes, hoping to influence them to move away from white settlements and into the proximity of the fort. Here they could be protected and fed, decreasing the temptation for young warriors to steal livestock and prey on isolated miners and settlers. Initiating a dialogue proved difficult, though. Whites in the community who benefited from this conflict spread rumors among the Indians that Buchanan was only trying to trap and kill them. So they fled his patrols.[18]

Buchanan's task was further complicated by the fact that a major part of the army's mission was to protect the settlers and miners from Indian depredations. The post was subject to a steady stream of reports about stock theft. Crook's first military patrol required him to pursue a band of Indians suspected of stealing cattle. The soldiers had mild success, capturing one of the perpetrators, who was incarcerated in the Humboldt stockade, a facility so porous that the prisoner immediately escaped.[19] Crook's second expedition, designed to open up communications with the surrounding tribes, came to nothing when the Indians, aware that he had previously arrested one of their number, understandably avoided contact. Eventually, mounted patrols, led by Crook and other junior officers, succeeded in opening a dialogue between the wary bands and the army, which successfully induced some of them to move their camps to the military post.

But soldiering on the frontier involved more than acting as a buffer between whites and local tribes. In the 1850s army engineers mounted a number of topographical expeditions that explored and mapped America's newly acquired western territories. These missions, staffed by military and civilian personnel, required army escorts as the engineers' work often led them into Indian country. In the summer of 1853, Crook was placed in charge of an escort for a surveying party commanded by Colonel Henry Washington, deputy surveyor of California. Washington's expedition mapped the northwest corner of California, traveling up the coast as far as the mouth of the Klamath River. The work provided Crook with valuable experience in the management of men and logistics in the field while providing an opportunity to enjoy the exotic scenery of northern California.

CHAPTER FIVE

Fort Jones

October 1853–Spring 1855

In early October 1853, after a full year on active duty, Crook's brevet appointment was converted to permanent rank. That month he also received orders transferring him from Humboldt to Fort Jones, constructed the year before in the Scott Valley near the Oregon border.[1] Troops stationed at Fort Jones had been called out to suppress an uprising of tribes in the nearby Rogue River valley, and additional officers and men were required to reinforce the garrison in their absence.

To Crook, the causes of the Rogue River War of 1853 and other such uprisings were obvious. "It was of no infrequent occurrence for an Indian to be shot down, or a squaw to be raped by some brute. Such a thing as a white being punished for outraging an Indian was unheard of. . . . The consequence was that there was scarcely a time that there was not one or more wars with the Indians somewhere on the Pacific Coast."[2]

This particular conflict began in June after a mob from the mining town of Jacksonville hanged a Rogue River subchief and three others whom they believed had murdered seven whites the previous winter. Their blood up, the men then proceeded to a nearby camp and murdered six more innocent Indians. The Indians swiftly retaliated on a scale that enraged and frightened white residents. The *Yreka Herald* gave voice to their general mood: "We hope that the Government will render such aid as will enable the citizens of the north to carry on a war of extermination until the last Redskin of these tribes has been killed.

Extermination is no longer a question of time—the time has arrived, the work has commenced."[3]

The citizenry of northern California demanded assistance from the troop commanders at Fort Jones and Fort Vancouver, who responded quickly. The regulars, reinforced by local militia, soon overwhelmed the Indians, who were then required to sign a harsh, one-sided agreement, known as the Table Rock Treaty. Under its terms, they ceded title to the entire Rogue River valley to the federal government in return for compensation in cash and farm implements, blankets, and trade goods totaling $60,000. Of this amount, $15,000 was deducted to compensate settlers for losses they claimed to have incurred during the uprising. The Indians were then temporarily confined to the Table Rock Reserve, a 100-square-mile area on the Oregon coast, pending congressional appropriations that would finance their removal to a permanent reservation at a site to be selected at a later date.[4]

Though peace reigned for a short while, the treaty did nothing to resolve the causes of the uprising. The Indians, crammed into their small reservation, nearing starvation, and plagued by disease, became increasingly restless, which in turn made whites fearful. Talk in area towns was of preemptive strikes, and in several instances the local citizenry made good on their threats. The cycle of violence resumed.[5]

Fort Jones was only about one hundred miles from Fort Humboldt, but the mountainous geography of northern California and a still-primitive transportation system required Crook to take a circuitous route that consumed the better part of a month. The uprising had ended by the time he arrived to assume his duties as second in command of E Company, Fourth Infantry.

Fort Jones was little more than a scattering of rude log huts built along the low hills rimming the verdant Scott Mountain valley. But Crook was immediately taken with the physical beauty of the place. The valley was green and well watered by a meandering stream, shaded along its banks by overhanging cottonwoods and willows. Rolling hills rose from the valley floor covered with dark forests of ancient pines teeming with game, while snow-covered mountain peaks, etched against a cloudless blue sky, provided a striking backdrop for the scene.

To Crook's delight, he recognized his new post commander, Captain Bradford Alden, as the former commandant of cadets during the

Fort Jones as it appeared in 1855. The post is portrayed here in a mural painted on the side of the Scott Valley Bank in Fort Jones, California, by Loree Di and Mary Carpelan, members of the Scott Valley Artists Guild, Fort Jones, California. Photo by author.

young man's tenure at the academy, an officer he had greatly admired. Alden was a soldier of great promise. He had served with distinction as aide-de-camp to Major General Winfield Scott before the Mexican War and had taught at West Point for some years. Though a stern taskmaster at the academy, in the field he was relaxed and good tempered, occasionally bursting into song, which so surprised young Crook that he "would just as soon thought of hearing a mule sing."[6]

Unfortunately, Alden remained at Fort Jones only a short time. As the result of a wound received during the Rogue River fighting, one of the captain's arms became paralyzed. Though he appeared undaunted by the injury, on hearing of it, his wife had submitted his resignation from the service on his behalf. It was accepted, and having no alternative, he soon left Fort Jones to face an uncertain future as a civilian in the East. In 1870 he would die of his lingering wounds.[7]

Alden's replacement was his second in command, Brevet Major (Captain) G. W. Patten, known behind his back as "He! He! Be God!"

G. Washington Patten. The mocking nickname derived from his afflic-
tion as a stutterer and his unusual habit of prefacing every sentence with
a grimace and the words "He! He! Be Jesus" or "Be God." Crook cal-
lously dismissed him as ill suited to command, describing him as "one of
the curiosities of the Army." In reality Patten was a distinguished officer
who had received brevets during the Mexican War and an accomplished
poet as well as author of military manuals.[8]

Patten's tenure at Fort Jones was equally short-lived. In January 1854
he rotated back east with his command, troops from the Second Regiment of Infantry. Crook's Company E, which he referred to without
explanation as the "Forty Thieves," replaced Patten's men and soon received a new commanding officer, Captain Henry M. Judah. Judah's
career had been distinguished prior to his arrival in California. An 1843
graduate of the academy, he had served in Texas and earned two brevet ranks for gallantry during the Mexican War.[9] Recently promoted
to captain, Judah had brought his wife and daughter with him to Fort
Jones. Shortly following his arrival, his conduct deteriorated due to a
losing struggle with alcoholism, which began to erode his character and
judgment.

From his letters and reports to the adjutant general in San Francisco,
Judah emerges as an insecure, thin-skinned man, rigid, defensive, and
overly concerned with the prerogatives of rank. Crook bluntly characterized him as a drunk, an incompetent, and a coward who sought to
avoid danger to himself while unhesitatingly putting others' lives at risk.
This harsh assessment would be validated during the Civil War, when the
captain, who by then had risen to the rank of brigadier general, became
notorious for the callous treatment of his troops and incompetence in
battle.[10] However much Crook may have disliked and disrespected the
man, Judah, like Buchanan, demonstrated a humane and, for the time, innovative approach in his dealings with the Indians that may have served
as a model of his young subordinate. The captain understood the plight of
the local tribes, and his mediation skills and willingness to use his troops
as a buffer between the settlers and miners and the native population
enabled him to peacefully resolve several tense situations, earning him
plaudits from his superiors. Over time he was so successful in gaining the
trust of the tribes that, on at least one occasion, he convinced a chief to
apprehend and punish a few of his own people for crimes against whites,
a technique later employed by Crook in the Southwest.[11]

Henry Judah, Crook's commanding officer and nemesis at Fort Jones, California. This image was taken during the Civil War, after Judah had been promoted to brigadier general of volunteers. As was the case during his time in the Pacific Northwest, Judah's Civil War service was problematical, probably a result of his alcoholism. Courtesy of the National Archives.

Though they may have agreed on policies regarding the Indians, Crook and Judah shared little else in common. If Crook found Judah to be an alcoholic incompetent, the captain thought the young lieutenant insufferably presumptuous and insolent. Nevertheless, he recognized his subordinate's value. Shorthanded like all post commanders in the Northwest, Judah relied on Crook to perform a number of critical duties, giving the young man frequent opportunities to improve his military and administrative skills.

A month after his arrival, Judah appointed Crook acting assistant quartermaster and acting assistant commissary service for the post. When the captain departed on detached service, remaining away for several months, Crook assumed both functions and for a time was designated post commander in Judah's absence.[12] As a young officer at an isolated fort, he exercised a high degree of independence, which served to strengthen his already burgeoning self-confidence. Though he undoubtedly found poring over accounts and dealing with the remote military bureaucracy irksome, he seemed to have a facility for the work.

Crook's correspondence with headquarters at Benicia Barracks, source of funding and supplies for Fort Jones, give a good indication of the tediousness and frustrations of the job.[13] The frontier army was grossly underfunded by Congress, and the lack of appropriations was especially keenly felt at small posts like Fort Jones. Because of the fort's remoteness and headquarters' inefficiencies, even when funds were available, the cash often arrived months after being requested. As a consequence, local contractors, who provided the post with livestock, forage, wood, and supplies, went unpaid for months at a time, leaving them angry and distrustful of the military. The young officer bore the brunt of their ire.

But while Lieutenant Crook could cope with such difficulties, Captain Judah, by his own admission, had neither the desire nor the ability to do so. During one of Crook's extended absences, the commander was forced to take on his lieutenant's duties. Overwhelmed, Judah wrote in desperation to the chief quartermaster at Benicia: "The amount of outstanding debts I am unable to state. Indian affairs are in such a precarious state that I cannot leave the post for more than an hour. . . . I have no one at the post who understands quartermaster papers. I do not myself and have no desire to learn beyond what is actually necessary. Neither do I have the time to do so. . . . I trust . . . you will send some officer to relieve me of the duties."[14]

In addition to Crook's official duties, he and many of his fellow junior officers were, of necessity, preoccupied with matters of personal finance. Inadequate pay and the inflated cost of living inspired an ongoing quest for additional sources of income. Those at Fort Jones dealt with the problem by starting a business supplying meat to local miners and settlers. Pooling their funds, they ordered powder and shot from San Francisco, which Crook then used to hunt game, which the post physician, Dr. Francis Sorrel, marketed in the nearby towns. As Crook's skills as a hunter improved with practice and guidance from local Indians, he was able to bag so much game that, he proudly declared, "the mess was enabled to declare a dividend."[15]

While Crook adjusted to life at Fort Jones, in the surrounding countryside, tensions with the local tribes increased. On January 14, 1854, miners from the town of Cottonwood on the Klamath River north of Fort Jones drafted a petition to Captain Judah demanding his help in recovering horses they claimed had been stolen by hostile Indians.[16] Their own attempt to recover the stock had failed, they said, when they were ambushed and four of their number killed.

On this occasion, Judah quickly responded. Accompanied by his entire command, including Lieutenant Crook, and a contingent of twenty-four volunteers from Cottonwood, he set out on the trail of the Indians. A blizzard commenced during their first night in the field and continued throughout the next day, reducing visibility to near zero. To keep his men together, Judah organized them into three units. The advance guard was commanded by 1st Lieutenant John C. Bonnycastle, who had transferred with Crook from Fort Humboldt and was now the Ohioan's immediate superior. The main body of troops under Crook followed, while a third contingent, composed primarily of the volunteers under a Captain Geiger, the militia commander, brought up the rear. Judah assigned himself the task of moving from one element to the next to maintain contact between the three groups.[17]

Mounted on mules, Crook's men floundered through deep drifts all that day. Absorbed in their effort to keep to the trail of the advance party before it was obscured by the driving snow, they soon lost all contact with the militia to their rear and saw nothing of Captain Judah. As darkness fell, the advance guard and the main body made camp on the bank of a mountain stream about four miles from the cave where the miners had said the Indians were located. As the hour grew late and Judah and the rear guard failed to appear, Crook and Bonnycastle became increasingly alarmed. In response to their call for a volunteer to backtrack and locate the missing men, a militiaman named Ward and one of the regulars stepped forward. The two rode off on mules down the trail, disappearing into the still-falling snow across a nearby stream.

Within a short time, a great commotion emanated from the bushes on the opposite side of the stream, and before long Ward, sans mule, stumbled out of the brush. Floundering into the firelight, the militiaman breathlessly informed the open-mouthed soldiers who rushed to his side that he had heard the ghastly shrieks of Indians just down the trail. They were "exulting over their victory," he announced, having just massacred the entire rear guard. When Crook inquired about his companion, Ward heatedly responded that it was every man for himself. He had abandoned the mule because it slowed him down; of the soldier he knew nothing.

As the agitated troops milled about, the missing soldier rode serenely into camp. Closely questioned by the two officers, he admitted to having heard a noise, but who made it he was unable to say. He appeared far more concerned about the loss of Ward's mule, having chased it through the brush for some time, fearing that he would be held responsible for its loss.[18]

Bonnycastle, by now seriously concerned about the fate of the rest of the command, ordered Crook down the back trail with ten men to investigate while he followed with the main body. To the young lieutenant, the situation looked extremely perilous. A hard crust had formed on the snow, and the men made an unholy racket as they crunched through the drifts. Riding in the van and armed only with a pistol, Crook feared for his life should they run into a large party of Indians.

His worst fears appeared realized when "a tremendous uproar" echoed through the woods to their front. The sound soon resolved itself into the yelling and whooping of a large body of men. The bemused lieutenant soon realized that the noise came not from wild Indians, but from the rear guard, roaring drunk and strung out along the trail for a distance later determined to be more than ten miles. Among the straggling revelers was Captain Judah, so besotted that he was unable to dismount from his mule without assistance.[19]

It took the better part of the night to get the entire party bedded down, and it was almost morning before Crook had the opportunity to snatch a little sleep for himself. He wearily wrapped himself in a soggy blanket covered with an India-rubber dropcloth to keep off the snow. He then lay down, feet toward the fire to thaw out his ice-encrusted boots. But having placed his bedding too close to the embers in his fatigued state, he soon awoke with a start to find his blanket ablaze. In his haste to beat out the flames, drops of hot rubber from his melting dropcloth singed the back of his hand, causing an ugly scar, a lifelong reminder of a particularly miserable night on the campaign trail.[20]

After a day spent nursing hangovers, the company resumed its exhausting march through ice, knee-deep snow drifts, and thick brush. About two miles from the cave, they came upon the bodies of the four miners killed in the original ambush. Stripped of their clothing, frozen stiff, and partially torn apart by wolves, they were a terrible sight. They buried the men as best they could, and the next morning proceeded to a point about 150 yards short of the cave, where they halted to assess the situation. The cave mouth was clearly visible: a black opening in the perpendicular face of a cliff that Crook estimated to be well over 100 feet in height. The entrance was small and blocked with a breastwork of logs and rocks. To the junior officers, the position appeared almost impregnable since the only approach to the cliff face was up a steep, rocky incline strewn with rubble washed down by a mountain torrent.[21]

Candidly, Judah later reported, "I deemed it my duty to propose to Captain Greiger (commanding the volunteers) to storm the cave, a proposal to which I think for good reasons he did not consider it safe to accede." Since Geiger refused to put his men in such jeopardy, Judah sent a company of volunteers to reconnoiter the cliff top to see if they could flush out the Indians from above. This proved impossible—an overhanging ledge prevented the volunteers from getting a clear shot into the cave. Judah then turned to his regulars, ordering Lieutenants Crook and Bonnycastle to lead a frontal assault up the slope toward the cave mouth, intending, as Crook sarcastically put it, to himself "stand at a safe distance and view it." Bonnycastle sensibly sized up the situation and agreed to move forward. But he informed Judah that if he survived, he intended to prefer charges against his commander. Judah promptly rescinded his order.[22]

Since a direct assault on the cave was out of the question, the captain decided to send for artillery. He directed Crook to ride to Fort Lane, across the border in the Rogue River valley in Oregon Territory, to fetch a mountain howitzer to bombard the barricaded Indians into submission. The company medical officer, Dr. Sorrell, by now a good friend of Crook and an adventurous soul, volunteered to accompany him. The trip turned out to be an exhausting two-day journey across a mountain range through snow drifts that at times reached above the bellies of their horses.[23]

Fort Lane was under the command of Captain Andrew Jackson Smith of the First Dragoons, a bearded, stern-faced West Pointer from Pennsylvania. Like his namesake, Smith, a thoroughgoing professional, could be as unbending and decisive as the situation required. On being apprised of the situation, he provided not only the howitzer but also decided to accompany Crook and Sorrell back to cave with a detachment of dragoons.

Smith shared the army's prevailing belief that whites could usually be found behind any Indian troubles. So he was open to information that he learned en route to the cave concerning the true origins of this fray. According to his informant, whom he regarded as reliable, a company of ne'er-do-wells from Cottonwood had learned that a band of Shastas had established themselves in a cave not far from town. The men set out for the site, intent upon kidnapping Indian women for their amusement. Chief Bill, leader of the band, was away at the time, and the raiders managed to catch the remaining Indians unawares, killing three men, two women, and two children before being driven off. The whites had then returned to Cottonwood and recruited reinforcements to renew their attack under the pretext of retrieving stolen stock. Chief Bill, having returned, ambushed this group, killing four. With this version of events in mind, Smith arrived at Judah's camp with distinctly mixed feelings about the legitimacy of their undertaking.[24]

There he found the captain confined to his tent by "illness." As ranking officer, Smith assumed command of the force. Meanwhile, Captain Geiger, who had been reconnoitering the cave mouth from above, leaned too far over the overhanging ledge and received a mortal wound from an Indian bullet. A popular leader, his death fanned the vengeful mood of the volunteers, already stoked by the deaths of their ambushed comrades. To placate the miners and hopefully intimidate the Indians into surrendering, Smith ordered his men to fire two howitzer shells at the opening. But owing to the angle of fire, the shells did little damage.[25]

The noise and smoke from the howitzers succeeded in frightening the Indians, however, and they offered to surrender and lay their case before Captain Smith. In the ensuing discussions, the commander discovered that their story corresponded with the information provided by his informant. Concerned that the vengeful miners would massacre all of the Indians—men, women, and children—if they left the cave, he directed Chief Bill to remain where he was and ordered all of the assembled troops to withdraw. The militiamen, deprived of an opportunity for revenge and plunder, angrily abused the soldiers for failing to assault the cave and for protecting the Indians. Crook contemptuously observed that, while unwilling to risk themselves in a fight, they were fully prepared to expose the regulars to danger: "They didn't care how many of us were killed, and they said it was our business to be killed."[26]

After returning to Fort Jones, the troops would learn that the militia's attitude was widely shared by the local community and the frontier press. A typical editorial, this one from the *Yreka Herald,* declared, "Captain Smith drew off and returned to Rogue River Valley, contrary to the wishes, advice, and urgent solicitations of the volunteers and citizens of Cottonwood generally, thereby virtually acknowledging himself whipped by a small party of Indians and leaving our citizens and their property wholly unprotected from the ruthless and murderous incursions of these savages."[27]

Shortly after this expedition, Judah departed Fort Jones under an unwritten agreement with Bonnycastle that the lieutenant would drop charges against the captain for his conduct at the cave providing he apply for a transfer to another post. Judah eventually ended up at Fort Humboldt, where he replaced Captain Grant and, by all accounts, performed credibly. Checking white vigilantism and protecting innocent Indians from slaughter, he managed to redeem himself in the eyes of his superiors. Unhappily, in August 1855 he would return to Fort Jones, where he and Lieutenant Crook would resume their fractious relationship.[28]

In the meantime Crook and Bonnycastle worked well together. Bonnycastle proved to be courageous and innovative in his efforts to maintain peace in the Yreka area. Among other actions, in defiance of the army's decision to avoid the creation of "feeding stations" for the Indians, he brought Chief Bill's band onto the post for their protection, supplying them with subsistence rations that allowed them to avoid contact with hostile miners and settlers. For Crook, the remainder of 1854 and the early months of 1855 passed relatively peacefully, with the exception of what he dismissively described as "an occasional Indian scare."[29]

For most soldiers, garrison life during such periods of relative calm left yawning voids that many, including officers, filled with liquor, fights, and gambling. For Crook, hunting and fishing filled his spare time, while he continued to explore means to supplement his meager income. To that end, in the fall of 1854, he and a fellow lieutenant, John Bell Hood, a young Kentuckian, who later fought for the Confederacy as a general in the Army of Northern Virginia and as commander of the Army of Tennessee, hunted extensively in the nearby mountains. To further augment their pay, they tried their hand at ranching and wheat farming. Unfortunately, throughout his military career, Crook demonstrated a lack of business acumen. On this occasion, as he succinctly described it, Hood "sold out in the spring [of 1855] and made money, while I held on and lost money."[30]

What Crook had dismissed as "an occasional Indian scare" portended a full-scale uprising—the Rogue River War of 1855–56—that would erupt the following year. The closing months of 1854 were marked by a steady escalation of violence by individual Indians or small groups of warriors and savage reprisals by settlers and miners that frequently claimed the lives of innocent third parties rather than the actual perpetrators. The situation was exacerbated by criminal elements in the mining community, who used the atmosphere of fear and hatred to conceal their own acts of theft, rape, and even murder. The army once again found itself squarely in the middle, scorned by whites for protecting the Indians whom they were simultaneously expected to punish for their depredations. The troops' standing in the settler community was not helped by the lack of diplomacy exhibited by Major General John Ellis Wool, who assumed command of the redesignated Department of the Pacific that year. A veteran of the Mexican War, Wool was a man of short stature but towering ego. He had a caustic tongue and spoke his mind bluntly and without regard to the sensitivities of the civilian population. Like Crook and other officers, he had little use for volunteer militia, blaming them loudly and often for many of the troubles with the Indians.[31]

CHAPTER SIX

Exploring the Country and the Williamson-Abbot Expedition

June–November 1855

As the snow melted from the mountain passes in June 1855, the War Department mounted an expedition into the area between the Sacramento Valley in northern California and the Columbia River near Portland, Oregon Territory. Aimed primarily at finding suitable routes for railroad construction in the region, it was led by Lieutenants R. S. Williamson of the Corps of Topographic Engineers and Henry Abbot, a young engineering officer. The venture was well staffed, with a civilian geologist, a botanist, a civil engineer, and a draftsman among others.

As the path of the column would lead it through the Pit River country, where a previous expedition had been attacked several years earlier, officials deemed it prudent to provide a military escort of one hundred soldiers. The escort was commanded by Lieutenant Horatio Gibson, an artillery officer and veteran of the Mexican War.[1]

Crook accompanied the column as commissary and quartermaster. In this role he supervised the procurement of supplies and the activities of the eighteen packers and one hundred mules assigned to transport them. It was to be his first experience with the art of pack-train management, which was to become a lifelong avocation. He evidently performed his role so well that Lieutenant Abbot would commend him in his report for contributing, "to a high degree, to the success and harmony of the expedition."

The technicians and scientists departed Benicia on July 10, joined Crook and the military escort at Fort Reading along the Sacramento River on the twenty-first, and then ascended into the Sierra Nevada

Mountains. Almost from the start, as the expedition wound its way through the heart of the rugged Pit River country of northeastern California, their progress was marked by columns of light smoke drifting upward from the summits of surrounding hills. Their presence had been "discovered by watchful savages."[2]

Whites had named the country and its inhabitants, who called themselves Achomawi, for the pits the Indians dug at intervals along the trail. About six feet deep, lined at the bottom with sharpened stakes and carefully covered over with brush and dirt, these holes were the tribe's chief means of procuring game and their first line of defense against enemies. Though shy at first, the Achomawi, eventually satisfied that the party meant them no harm, visited the expedition's campsites, scavenging leftover food and possibly appraising the strength of the military escort. They appeared an impoverished lot, described by the ethnocentric Abbot as "very treacherous, bloody in their dispositions and disgusting in their habits." Without access to firearms, they carried only bows and arrows tipped with obsidian points that were, as Crook would soon learn, dipped in a witches' brew of decomposed deer liver impregnated with rattlesnake venom. The points were fastened to the shafts with hide sinews that softened when they entered the body, allowing the head to detach and remain in the wound when the shafts were removed. There they caused the wound to fester, usually resulting in eventual, painful death by infection.[3]

Not long after the Indians appeared, Crook was pleasantly surprised one evening when his old friend and West Point classmate Lieutenant Philip Sheridan rode into camp. He had come from Fort Reading to relieve Lieutenant Hood, who commanded the mounted escorts, as the latter had orders to return to California. Though tired from the ride, Sheridan entertained the column with a hair-raising account of his adventures en route.

Accompanied by only two troopers, he had followed the expedition's trail from Fort Reading. He soon came upon the moccasin tracks of a party of Achomawi, who appeared to be shadowing the column. Following the tracks through hilly country, he suddenly spied a band of about thirty Indians a half mile to his front. Though they appeared friendly, Sheridan, ever suspicious of Indians, believed that they were up to no good. Vastly outnumbered and fearful of the tribe's reputation for treachery, he made a run for it, only to find his way blocked by the sheer, high bank of a broad river.

The three soldiers wheeled to face the Indians, who instead of attacking them, continued to signal their friendly intent, walking their ponies into the river to demonstrate where it could be safely forded. Still suspicious, Sheridan rode cautiously through the gesturing warriors, crossed the stream, and mounted the next rise. Much to his relief, he crested the hill and spied Williamson's camp in the valley below. He would later attribute the Pit River Indians' failure to attack to their awareness of the proximity of the expedition's camp.[4]

Despite their fearsome reputation, the Achomawi continued to refrain from attacking the column, perhaps deterred by the large military escort. Instead they limited themselves to desperate acts of petty theft that underscored their sorry state. The Indians' food supply had been badly depleted by the numerous prospectors who had come through their lands, scaring off the game and poisoning the salmon in the streams with the tailings from their gold mines. Their extreme want became painfully evident whenever the expedition broke camp. The soldiers would no sooner mount their horses before the Indians would make a mad scramble into the abandoned site, scavenging voraciously among the ashes of the campfires for castoff food scraps.[5] The officers who recorded the expedition's progress (Abbot, Sheridan, and Crook) appeared oblivious to the connection between the miner's destruction of the Pit Rivers' food supply and their hostility toward whites who invaded their territory.

By August 11 the party reached the lake region of southern Oregon just north of the California border, the country of the Klamath tribe. A shy and elusive people, they built their villages in close proximity to the lakes common to the area, scattering into the bulrushes (tules) at the approach of strangers. As was their habit, when Williamson's expedition came into view, the Klamaths took to the water and, from the safety of the swamp, howled imprecations at the whites, shaking their weapons angrily in the air. Ultimately, perceiving that the soldiers meant them no harm, they emerged cautiously from the tules and hesitantly entered the expedition's camp. Abbot thought the members of this tribe "intelligent and in every way superior to those of the Pit River." They spoke Chinook, the trade language of the Pacific Northwest. With Crook, who had developed an interest in and facility with local Indian languages, acting as translator, the soldiers were able to converse with them. As he learned more of the tribe's language, the lieutenant also assisted William-son in compiling a short Klamath vocabulary.[6]

Throughout August and September, the expedition moved north at a leisurely pace, exploring and surveying valleys and streams along their route. Thus occupied, they had no contact with the white-settler com-munity until they encountered a party of volunteer militia from Jack-sonville. The volunteers were hunting for hostile Indians, whom they claimed had committed depredations in the area, and brought news of an uprising by the Rogue River Indians along the expedition's return route south to Fort Reading. Apparently untroubled by this information, perhaps discounting the source, Williamson released Lieutenant Gibson and his men from their escort duties, allowing them to return south to Fort Lane, while the surveyors and scientists, accompanied only by Crook, Sheridan, and a handful of dragoons, continued their explora-tions in the north.[7] A little over a week later, the Yakimas around nearby Fort Vancouver turned hostile.

Initially, the tribes in that area, among whom the Yakimas were prom-inent, had been slow to recognize the threat that white civilization posed to their culture and ultimate survival. Their first contact had been with traders from the Hudson's Bay Company. These men had provided the tribes with guns and other valuable trade goods in return for furs; their interest in land was limited to small plots on which to build their trading posts. But the traders were followed by men who pounded long sticks into the ground, peered through shiny three-legged instruments, and made mysterious marks on large sheets of paper. And after them came the settlers and miners, hungry for land and gold.

In the winter of 1854–55, whites manipulated the Yakima chiefs into signing away some 22 million acres of their lands east of the Cascades in exchange for reservations representing a fraction of their former hold-ings and promises of money and supplies. The tribes' discontent, fu-eled by this one-sided deal, intensified when the promised compensa-tion, already deemed inadequate, failed to arrive, delayed by a dithering Congress. Dissatisfaction turned to bitter anger when the discovery of gold near the Canadian border unleashed a stream of miners who used the Yakima reserve as a shortcut to the goldfields. They left behind the usual trail of devastation—polluted rivers and forests depleted of wood and game. At last, the tribes understood that their very existence was imperiled.

Led by an intelligent and physically imposing chieftain, Kamiakin, the Indian peoples of the Columbia River basin (the Yakima, Walla Walla, Cayuse, Umatilla, Palouse, Upper Columbia Salishan, Klikitat, and scattered smaller bands) were not the weak and fragmented clans Crook had encountered in California but the representatives of a proud warrior culture akin to the horsemen of the Great Plains. As Crook's expedition wound its way through northern Oregon, these Indians rose in a last desperate struggle to preserve their institutions and beliefs; their declared objective, to exterminate or drive out every white man who occupied their lands.

The attacks, at first haphazard, grew in frequency, and by the time a well-regarded Indian agent was murdered, the territorial government realized that it had a full-scale uprising on its hands and requested immediate assistance from the military. The army responded promptly, though inadequately. On October 6, while Abbot and Crook made their way toward Oregon City, an expedition numbering 150 regulars was soundly defeated by a superior force of Yakimas and forced into an ignominious retreat back to the protection of their forts.[8]

This victory heartened Indian resistance and sowed panic among the region's settlers. When Abbot's small party emerged into the Columbia River valley a week after this battle, they were greeted with "the rare pleasure of reading in the newspapers an account of our own massacre in the mountains."[9] Undeterred by premature stories of their demise, the small group pushed on to Fort Vancouver, where they learned further details of the uprising. They also heard chilling confirmation that the Rogue River Indians had risen to the south at about the same time.

Lieutenant Abbot turned for help to Major Gabriel Rains, commanding officer of Fort Vancouver. But his request for an escort through the troubled area fell on deaf ears. With too few troops to put down an uprising that had spread all across the Northwest, the major needed every man he could lay his hands on. While recognizing Abbot's predicament, Rains refused his request and instead commandeered Lieutenant Sheridan and his dragoons, integrating them into the force he had assembled to fight the Yakimas and their allies.[10]

Stripped of Gibson's infantry, now well on their way south, and the dragoons, Abbot's fighting manpower was reduced to one officer—

twenty-seven-year-old 2nd Lieutenant George Crook—three civilian surveyors, a hunter, and some twenty packers. Abbot later estimated that he had "only 5 rifles in the whole command."[11] Despite the obvious danger, the expedition chose to ride south out of Fort Vancouver. And their luck held. Passing safely through the Willamette Valley without incident, they proceeded down the Umpqua River into the Rogue River country, which only days before had turned into a war zone.

The causes of this second Rogue River conflict so closely resembled those of the Yakima outbreak that many at the time suspected a conspiracy between the two tribes. But in fact the two uprisings were separate and spontaneous reactions to similar, though unrelated, circumstances.

In the Rogue River valley, the native peoples nursed unresolved grievances stemming from their defeat in the first conflict. Their lands at Table Rock Reserve, only a fraction of the size of their traditional hunting grounds, were inadequate to support the population. Hunger and disease soon began to decimate their families. To add insult to injury, the proud Rogue Rivers were forced to share their meager space with a number of small tribes, with whom they did not get along. Many of the young warriors, restless and resentful, left the confines of the reservation daily to hunt and buy liquor from the whites, occasionally venting their anger and frustration in random acts of theft or violence.

The situation smoldered throughout the late summer and into the fall. In early October it flared into full-scale warfare, ignited by an unprovoked attack by miners from Jacksonville, home of those who had precipitated the Rogue River War of 1853. The raid, on the campsite of peaceful Indians from Table Rock, resulted in the deaths of twenty-three Indians, eighteen of whom were women and small children, the remainder, old men. The next day the Table Rock Indians vengefully swept down the Rogue River valley, leaving behind them twenty-seven settlers dead in the ruins of their burnt-out cabins. In only a few days, the conflagration spread to all of the tribes, with few exceptions, in an area stretching from Yreka, California, north to the upper reaches of the Umpqua Valley in Oregon, and from the coast to the lands of the Modocs in the northeastern corner of California. As the bands were small and fragmented in this region, despite the number of tribes involved, only about 400 Indians of fighting age actually participated in the uprising.[12]

The army, its troops spread out thinly over a vast, mountainous area, was unprepared to put down such a widespread rebellion. Available manpower included only two companies of dragoons (about 120 men) stationed at Fort Lane, a small garrison under Crook's West Point classmate Lieutenant Kautz at Fort Orford on the Oregon coast, and Lieutenant Gibson's 64-man infantry detachment in the Umpqua Valley, just returned from its escort duties with the Williamson-Abbot expedition.[13]

To supplement this force, Oregon's territorial governor, George Curry, authorized the formation of a number of militia companies, enlisted for three-month terms, to deal with the emergency. Bent on revenge and unable or unwilling to distinguish between friendly and hostile Indians, this ill-disciplined force would create more problems than it resolved, particularly as their orders read, "In chastising the enemy, you will use your discretion provided you take no prisoners."[14] As one would expect from such a force, they performed poorly, incurring heavy casualties despite the inferior weaponry of their enemy. The army fared little better at the outset, suffering a major defeat at a place called Hungry Hill under the redoubtable Captain Andrew Jackson Smith, whom Crook had last met during the cave fight.

Unaware of the fighting, Crook and Abbot made camp at the entrance to Umpqua Canyon at the head of the Rogue River valley, just a few miles north of Hungry Hill and only two days after the battle. They pitched their tents near a local inn known as the Six Bits House, linking up in the dubious hope of protection with two companies of volunteers marching to join Smith's forces on the Rogue. Reflecting his contempt for militia, Crook derisively referred to these men as a "Falstaffian Army."[15]

To reach Smith's regulars, Crook, Abbot, and their militia escort would have to pass through an eleven-mile-long narrow gorge whose steep, wooded slopes rose a thousand feet above the river. Since the gorge was an ideal spot for an ambush, Abbot wanted to start at daybreak to get through it before nightfall. To that end, he told the militia commander to prepare to leave at first light.[16]

But as the sun rose the next morning, Abbot discerned no movement in the volunteer camp. He went to investigate and found the men still asleep while their cooks baked beans for breakfast. Knowing this was a lengthy process, Abbot turned to the commander and nervously suggested that the delay might cause problems. The commander agreed and suggested to the cooks that beans were not really essential for breakfast. The lead cook, "placing his hand upon his stomach, replied gravely:

'Major, when I'm going into battle I likes to have my belly full of beans.' There was nothing more to be said and we waited for the beans.'"[17]

If, after this incident, the regulars needed further evidence of the buffoonish nature of the militia, their leader was ready to provide it. After beans had been consumed, the major, brandishing a short sword over his head, assembled his men with cries of "Tenshun the company!" His men responded "Go to hell!" or "Hold it, Cap until I go to the rear," according to their individual inclinations. Apparently unfazed, the major then attempted to mount his horse, whereupon his "foot slipped out of the stirrup and his chin struck the pommel of the saddle and his corporosity [*sic*] shook like a bag of jelly."[18]

Abbot was amused to note that the volunteers tethered their horses in a line so close together that the men were unable to mount them. But he found them willing learners. They responded gratefully when he suggested that they adopt the army's method of moving every other horse back a step or two from the horse next to it, permitting each rider to swing himself into the saddle without planting a foot in the horse or rider next in line.[19]

When the column finally moved out, Crook, riding in the rear through the narrow canyon, contemplated what would happen in the not unlikely event that this comic-opera company was ambushed. In a loud voice he sarcastically remarked that he would prefer to be in the front of the column as the Indians might miss him, whereas if he continued in the rear, in the event of an attack, he would surely be trampled to death by panicked volunteers.[20] His comment did nothing to smooth the already frayed relations between the militia and the regulars.

Fortunately, the column reached Captain Smith's command without incident. With Smith was August Kautz, whom Crook had last seen in San Francisco two years earlier. The two men exchanged tales of their experiences, Kautz relating an account of several narrow escapes from the Indians. (In a demonstration of how time had eroded Crook's memory by the 1880s, his version of these incidents materially confused the facts.)[21]

As Abbot was impatient to complete his journey to Fort Reading, he remained only briefly in Smith's camp before resuming his journey through the Rogue River country to northern California. The expedition's path led them past scenes that provided vivid testimony to the widespread and savage nature of the uprising. "Blackened and smoking ruins, surrounded by the carcasses of domestic animals, marked the places where, but a few days before, the settlers had lived. We passed a team on the road; the oxen lay shot in the yoke, and the dark bloodstains upon the seat of the wagon told the fate of the driver. Even the stacks of hay and grain in the fields had been burned."[22] But the expedition's extraordinary good luck held. Without incident, they made their way through the area of devastation and into California, arriving in the mining town of Yreka on November 7.

Abbot had planned only a brief stop at Fort Jones, Crook's post, before heading to Fort Reading. But on the trail from Yreka, the party encountered Captain Judah headed in the opposite direction, toward Oregon to participate in the Rogue River fighting. The reunion was not a happy one. Judah, irritated by Crook's long absence from the post, peremptorily ordered him to detach himself from Abbot's command and remain at Fort Jones, presumably to carry out the duties of quartermaster, which Judah had found so onerous. Abbot was furious, noting in his report that Crook's reassignment now required that he, Abbot, serve as his own quartermaster, making it impossible for him to leave the column, as he had planned, to explore the Sacramento River valley as part of his survey.[23]

Crook too was incensed. The official complaint he lodged with department headquarters has been lost, but he did submit one, withdrawing it only under pressure from Judah.[24] The captain had won this round, and Crook grudgingly resumed his labors as quartermaster at Fort Jones, traveling only briefly later in the fall to Fort Reading, where he completed his accounts for the expedition.

CHAPTER SEVEN

Indian Removal and the Rogue River War

Winter 1855–June 1856

In December 1855, while Lieutenant Crook labored over his paperwork at Fort Jones, Captain Judah and Company E marched to Fort Lane to join A. J. Smith's dragoons and a force of volunteers on an expedition against the Rogue River tribes; Judah appointed Crook post commander in his absence. The mountainous terrain into which the Indians fled, the severity of the weather, and the ineptitude of the volunteers turned the foray into a dismal failure. Declaring further operations impossible, Judah returned to Fort Jones and spent the remainder of the winter guarding peaceful Indians who had sought shelter at the post from attack by vengeful settlers.[1]

While hostilities continued throughout the winter, one atrocity begetting another, Crook chaffed over his accounts under Judah's jaundiced eye. Then, abruptly, his prospects took a turn for the better. In February 1856 he received orders to march his company to Fort Lane, a post established two years before near Jacksonville to protect and guard the Indians on the Table Rock Reservation.[2] The infantrymen were to aid Captain Smith's troops in quelling continuing unrest among the Rogue River tribes.

Crook's arrival at Fort Lane coincided with preparations for a spring offensive against the hostile bands. But before this campaign could begin, Smith had other pressing business. During the winter months, Joel Palmer, Oregon's superintendent of Indian affairs, had decided to remove the four hundred Indians at Table Rock to the Grand Ronde Reserve, where they could be better controlled and, at least in theory, protected from the Oregon militia.

Removing four hundred destitute Indians, mostly elders, women, and children, in the dead of winter was a daunting proposition. Grand Ronde Reserve, seventy thousand acres in the lower Willamette Valley on the northwest Oregon coast, was more than 250 miles over mountain trails from Table Rock. Many of the Indians were barefoot, and some were virtually naked. The Indian agent, Dr. D. H. Ambrose, unable to obtain money from the government in time for the move, used his own funds to purchase shoes and rudimentary clothing for the people in an attempt to mitigate their suffering.[3]

Settler hostility toward Indians in southern Oregon was virulent. The tribesmen slated for removal were the remnants of villages already attacked by white militia. So when an Indian was slain from ambush by a volunteer just prior to the scheduled departure date, Ambrose asked Captain Smith to furnish a military escort to provide security for the march north.[4] As one of the officers assigned this unenviable duty, Crook was to accompany the Indians as far as the upper Umpqua Valley, where Smith believed they would no longer be in danger of attack. Crook and the bulk of his escort would then return to Fort Lane to participate in the upcoming spring campaign, while the remaining soldiers continued with the Indians to Grand Ronde.

This was Crook's first exposure to the government's policy of forced removal, a standard practice in its management of Indian affairs. He quickly perceived the obvious, that the Indians were "very loathe to leave their country and go to a land they knew nothing of. There was great weeping and wailing when the time came for them to go." Their departure presented a heart-rending scene: a gathering of destitute and frantic old men, women, and children herded along by armed soldiers. Some thirty of their number, too sick to walk, had to be loaded onto carts hired for the purpose. By the time the escort finally delivered the Indians to Grand Ronde after a thirty-three-day, 263-mile winter trek, eight of their charges had died of exposure or disease.[5] Yet this was a relatively successful move in light of other Indian removals Crook would witness during his career.

By the time Crook returned to Fort Lane, preparations were almost complete for the final campaign of the Second Rogue River War. The rebellion had been led by a chief known to whites as Old John or

Applegate John, who had sworn never to leave his homeland. With his surviving warriors, he had retreated into the densely wooded mountains near the big bend of the Rogue River to make his final stand. General Wool, the department commander, chose Lieutenant Colonel Buchanan, Crook's former superior at Fort Humboldt, to lead the forces against Old John, hoping to force a climactic engagement that would end the war. Crook was to participate, commanding a detachment of thirty infantrymen in support of Captain Smith's dragoons. But before he could assume command, the lieutenant was unexpectedly stricken with a severe attack of rheumatism in his left shoulder and a disabling recurrence of erysipelas, this time in his left arm. Too ill to ride, he was replaced by Lieutenant Nelson Sweitzer of the First Dragoons.[6]

The recurrence of erysipelas was far more serious than his initial bout at Benicia Barracks three years earlier. Stoic by nature, Crook did not often complain of illness or hardship, but in this instance he admitted, "For some time, it was thought that I would not live." The disease caused him to lose control over his left arm while the flesh wasted away, leaving "mere skin and bones." An abscess formed just above the elbow, so deep that he "could move a probe clear to my shoulder when it was lanced."[7]

The gravity of his condition was brought home to him one afternoon when an Indian woman entered his room and asked who would get his possessions when he died. Shocked by this bland assumption of his imminent demise, Crook dismissed the post physician, who appeared to take no interest in his illness (and in any event was rarely sober). Taking charge of his own cure, he first tried brandy, but believing it aggravated his rheumatism, he turned to his old remedy of calomel and jalap. When the arm began to show signs of improvement, he augmented the treatment with a primitive form of hydrotherapy: each day Crook poured a pitcher of ice-cold water over his shoulder, stoically ignoring the pain. His arm soon began to regain its strength as the erysipelas was apparently flushed from his body. For a year afterward, however, Crook was unable to raise the affected arm above his head, and he never regained full use of it.[8]

Though the disease was cured, before he could return to duty, the lieutenant had to overcome an addiction to the morphine that had been administered during his illness to numb the pain. Understating the horrors of withdrawal, he summed it up with the comment, "it was some time before I could sleep well without [morphine]."[9] By May, having surmounted this last hurdle, his recovery was complete. But the joy and relief Crook experienced upon his return to good health was tempered by news of the fate that had befallen his troops during his absence.

While Crook had waged his battle against erysipelas during March and April, federal troops under Buchanan marched up the Rogue River valley to link up with Captain Smith's column from Fort Lane in a maneuver intended to envelope the Indians between the two commands. Outnumbered and exhausted, Old John's forces staged a last-ditch surprise attack against Smith's dragoons and the thirty infantrymen who would have been under Crook's command but for his illness.

The fighting raged for two days. with the regulars bottled up on a hilltop surrounded by screaming warriors. On the second day, outnumbered and worn down by fatigue and casualties, the troops grimly prepared to meet a final charge that seemed destined to overrun them. At the last moment, though, reinforcements from Buchanan's column came to their rescue. Attacking Old John's men from behind, while the survivors of Smith's force met them head on, the troops broke the Indian charge, sending the warriors fleeing into the thick brush. The battle was won, but a third of Smith's command had been either killed or wounded. Among the dead were Lieutenant Sweitzer, Crook's replacement, and two-thirds of his men.[10]

Crook joined Smith's column immediately following the battle. Years later he blandly recorded the losses in his autobiography in a single sentence that neither referred to Sweitzer's death nor mentioned any of the emotions that he must have experienced on receiving the casualty report.[11] Always committed to the welfare of his troops, his silence in this regard likely reflects his private nature more than a lack of sensitivity. It must also be recalled that Crook wrote of these events after service as a combat officer for many years, by which time death in combat had become commonplace. Given his profession and the fact that he faced his own imminent demise on a regular basis, he could hardly afford to view it otherwise.

For the Rogue River Indians, Old John's defeat and subsequent surrender ended their war. Within days, 1,200 Indians from southwestern Oregon were sent off to the Grand Ronde to join their fellow tribesmen. On the reservation many would succumb to a combination of inadequate food, diseases, and pure homesickness. Of the 600 Rogue River and Cow Creek Indians removed to the Siletz Agency (part of the Grand Ronde Reservation) in 1856, only 385 survived into the next year. The long-range consequence was even grimmer. By 1871, 6,000 Indians would die each year on the Oregon reservations.[12]

CHAPTER EIGHT

Campaigning in the Pit River Valley

January–August 1857

In March 1857 Crook was promoted to first lieutenant and reassigned as second in command of Company D, Fourth Infantry. While advancement in rank must have pleased him, he cannot have welcomed the prospect of returning to Fort Jones and Captain Judah's authority. But unknown to him, his new assignment would provide his first opportunity to independently command troops in combat.

The brief peace that followed Old John's surrender had ended on a wintry evening in early February. Two young men named Fowler and Whitman (or Whitney, according to some accounts), overcome with exhaustion, cold, and hunger, staggered out of the snow-covered mountains into Yreka, carrying news of an Indian massacre in the Pit River country. Their shocking tale swept like an icy wind through the small community.

Two weeks earlier, after a six-day trek over the mountains from California, the two men had arrived at the upper ferry landing on the Pit River to find the ferryman gone, his house burned to the ground, and the ferry destroyed. As they hurried downriver to the lower ferry to learn if it too had been attacked, they were shadowed by a band of Indians, hovering just out of rifle range like wolves circling their prey. At the lower ferry they found a similar scene of devastation: the buildings had been reduced to charred ruins, the ferry destroyed, and the livestock, both horses and cattle, slaughtered or carried away. No sign remained of the five white men who wintered in the valley, but Fowler and Whitman supposed that they had been murdered. That night the two badly frightened men eluded the Indians and made their way back to Yreka with the news.[1]

The Achomawi had become increasingly restive over the months since Crook had ridden through their country on the Williamson-Abbot expedition in 1855. Their hunting grounds had become an important transportation route for miners and settlers, with the usual destructive effect on the tribe and a consequent escalation in the number and gravity of clashes between Indians and whites.

In early 1856 a white entrepreneur named Lockhart built two ferries, which became the focus of the Indians' attention when a small settlement grew up around them. While the increasing white presence caused uneasiness among the Achomawi, Lockhart's behavior precipitated open hostilities. That summer the ferryman and his employees murdered several Indians—one for stealing a box of matches—and raped several Indian women; Lockhart had even bragged to a local newspaper of poisoning several others with strychnine. Enraged, the Achomawi attacked during the winter, when the valley was isolated by heavy snows, leaving behind the devastation found by Fowler and Whitman.[2]

Trouble in the Pit River country fell under the jurisdiction of Captain Judah at Fort Jones, and the papers in Yreka freely advised him on how to handle this latest incident. "Now is the time to strike," one editor wrote. "[T]he snow is deep in the mountains and the Indians cannot escape. If it is put off till [sic] spring it will be an utter impossibility . . . to successfully cope with them."[3]

Judah's response must have disappointed the paper. He reported Fowler and Whitman's tale to the adjutant general at Benicia and then bustled off to San Francisco to brief General Wool on the nuances of the situation. But the department commander did not require a briefing. He bluntly instructed the captain to force the chiefs to turn over those responsible for the killings to the proper authorities "as soon as it can be done." If they fail to do so, he directed, "fit out an expedition against them and chastise them." As a precaution against future outbreaks, Wool ordered Judah to leave an outpost in the Pit River country during the summer and fall to protect travelers and residents.

Upon his return to Fort Jones, the captain continued to delay, fearing an expedition in the deep snow would come to nothing. To his chagrin, faced with his inaction, a mob of Yreka's citizens took matters in hand and mounted their own campaign. Soon they reported with considerable satisfaction that they had killed some fifty-nine Indians and captured sixteen children, whom they carried back to town to sell into slavery.[4]

It was not until May 18 that Captain Judah deemed the route through the mountains clear of snow and suitable for military activity. Only then did he mount his campaign, assembling a force of sixty-five regulars that included Lieutenant Crook and Company D. Having missed out on the fighting in the Rogue River, the young lieutenant had chaffed all winter under his commander's dithering and was spoiling for a fight. In his autobiography he sardonically describes the campaign, making no attempt to conceal his lack of respect for Judah or his growing confidence, bordering on cockiness, in his own abilities.[5]

By now an aficionado of mule power, Crook was amused by Judah's efforts to mount his troops on the fractious beasts. The mules issued to the troops (many of whom were drunk) were unbroken, and soon "the air was full of soldiers. . . . [For] the next two days," he wryly observed, "stragglers were still overtaking the command." Though the troops and their mounts would eventually come to terms, the route to the Pit River country proved difficult for both. Snow still lay two to five feet deep in the passes and in places collected in drifts from ten to fifteen feet in depth. Fortunately, freezing weather caused a hard crust to form on top of the snow that held the wagons and allowed them to make fairly good time.[6]

Just before reaching the Pit River, Judah received an express dispatch from an officer identifying himself as Captain John Gardiner of the First Dragoons. The communiqué announced that Gardiner was making a reconnaissance of the Pit River valley to identify a site for the establishment of a permanent post.[7] Though neither captain realized it, this brief and seemingly innocuous message became the opening salvo in a absurd altercation that would preoccupy both men over the next few months.

On the twenty-second, Judah's command came upon the charred ruins of the cabins described by Fowler and Whitman, now occupied by Sam Lockhart and other survivors who had returned to the valley for the summer. Lockhart was particularly bitter, having lost his brother in the attack, and hungered for revenge. He eagerly pointed to a nearby marsh where he believed the Indians had concealed themselves. The following day, from a rise near the river, the soldiers sighted Indians making their way through the tules, their black hair sharply contrasting with the green background of tall bulrushes. Judah ordered Crook in pursuit, but the warriors easily eluded the regulars, who were forced to content themselves with the destruction of several rancherias.[8]

For two days the soldiers waded through water up to their knees, searching vainly for their quarry in a maze of head-tall bulrushes that obscured their view in every direction. On occasion they would catch a tantalizing glimpse of an Indian popping up for an instant above the reeds, only to disappear well before the troops could reach him. Finally, Judah called off the exercise and left the tules to search the rest of the valley.

On the fourth day in the area, the command spied a small rancheria in the distance. Among the wickiups several dark figures were observed strutting about, which Judah solemnly identified as Indians. With his legendary eyesight, Crook quickly perceived that they were birds, specifically crows.[9] Knowing that correcting his captain's assumptions could be counterproductive and seeing the humorous possibilities of the situation, he did not argue the matter, observing in silence Judah's preparations to charge the village. Fortunately for the troops on their unbroken mounts, the village had been abandoned for some time. The potential tragedy that might have ensued thus became a farce. As the soldiers rode full tilt across the rough, stony ground, the mules began to stumble and buck, throwing men in all directions. To the amused lieutenant, the scene was "as good as a circus."[10]

At this point an embarrassed Captain Judah decided to conclude the campaign. Omitting mention of the charge on the crows, he optimistically reported to headquarters that "the most important practical results of the expedition having been accomplished, the road being now traveled with impunity by many solitary individuals, while thousands of heads of cattle are grazing safely over the entire valley." Having completed his mission to his satisfaction, he expressed his intention to return to Fort Jones, though he had spent little more than a week in the valley. Learning of Judah's decision, Crook cynically concluded that the captain, recently married for the second time, was anxious to get back to his bride.[11]

Though contemptuous of his commander's conduct, Crook was delighted by one aspect of his hasty departure. Before leaving the valley, Judah, in compliance with Wool's order, directed the lieutenant to remain behind with a small detachment to garrison an outpost at the ferry crossing on the Pit River.[12] Judah's instructions permitted Crook latitude to scout the surrounding area as "your judgment may dictate or necessity requires, taking care to leave during your absence a small force for the protection of the ferry." The detachment was to stay in the valley until the present order was "countermanded or further orders are received from headquarters of the Department or myself."[13] Neither man foresaw the problems that this seemingly innocuous language would create.

Almost before Captain Judah had rounded the first bend in the trail back to Fort Jones, Crook put into motion plans to mount an aggressive campaign against the Achomawi, whom he firmly believed were still in the area. He was not so immodest as to think that he was already a seasoned Indian fighter, and only too well aware of his ignorance of the countryside, but he knew enough about his enemy to understand that they were keeping a careful eye on the camp to avoid unwanted contact with his troops. Relying solely on this assumption, he devised a plan to seek out and destroy them.[14]

Crook stole out of camp with two of his men, concealing his movements from the watching hostiles. Returning to the area where Judah had made his notorious charge, he discovered an occupied rancheria. When spotted by some warriors, Crook claimed to be a miner from Yreka and so was able to return to his camp without arousing their suspicion. Waiting until nightfall cloaked his movements, he again set out for the rancheria, this time with his entire contingent, and somehow located it in total darkness. But the planned night attack failed. Having gone ahead to scout out the camp, Crook lost touch with his men in the inky blackness and did not reunite with them until daybreak. Though he then led them to the rancheria, by the time they arrived, the Indians had fled.[15]

Undaunted and without pause, Crook led his troops to cover under a nearby range of bluffs and set off alone on his mule in search of the Indians' trail. Before long he came upon a woman's moccasin prints. He had become sufficiently proficient as a tracker to know that the tracks were fresh and that the woman was moving rapidly, as she probably had spotted Crook or his soldiers. If he could capture her, she might lead him to her village.

As the trail became fresher, Crook picked up the pace, and soon he was riding at a gallop. Passing a spot where some Indian belongings lay strewn on the ground, he saw that the woman's tracks had been joined by others, men by the size of their moccasins. Though aware that following this trail alone at a headlong pace was dangerous, like a hound on the scent, he could not restrain himself. Suddenly he glimpsed Indians running through the trees ahead, and putting spurs to his mount, in moments he found himself among them.[16]

Years later Crook recalled his first combat experience in vivid detail:

> I carried an old-fashioned muzzle loaded rifle. When I got in their midst, I dismounted and shot a buck, when Indians I had not previously seen rose up all around me and commenced closing in. . . . I at once sprang into the saddle and drew my pistol. Now, as the most dangerous time with an Indian is when he is wounded, I aimed at the one whom I had wounded with my rifle. The first barrel snapped. The second barrel killed him. My rifle was empty and I only had four barrels in my pistol loaded, and there was no certainty that they would go off. There was but one thing left for me to do and that was to make my escape by flight. There was but one gap of about 100 yards left open to me and for this I made my run. I shall never forget the looks of a big buck with his hair tucked behind his ears. He seemed ten feet high, running at the top of his speed to close this gap. He kept an arrow in the air all the time. Besides, a dozen others were doing the same thing. As they flew past my head, [the arrows] didn't seem much more than a couple of inches long, they sped so swiftly.[17]

Somehow escaping from the Indians, he rejoined his troops and rushed them to the site of the fight. But by then the Indians had gone, leaving behind only the body of the warrior Crook had slain, a grieving elderly woman, his mother Crook supposed, by his side. Questioning the old woman proved fruitless, and the soldiers left her to mourn in peace. After further efforts to follow the Indians' trail in the rough country failed, Crook led his disappointed men back to camp.[18]

Combat left Crook elated and with no remorse for the dead warrior. He summed up the incident laconically with the statement, "[t]his was my first Indian."[19] But the detail and immediacy with which he recounted the tale spoke volumes about its importance for him.

The incident was indeed a milestone for Crook, both as a military officer and as an individual. By killing the warrior, he had shown that he could carry out his professional duties without hesitation. More importantly, he had demonstrated that he possessed the requisite courage and sangfroid to stand up under fire. Based on his description of the incident and later experiences in combat, it is evident that it also proved that he had a taste for combat and a desire to close with the enemy that, on occasion, could override his instinct for self-preservation. For an officer, such eagerness could be both a blessing and a curse. While it might allow him to act boldly and decisively under the most horrendous conditions, it could also expose him to great danger. Yet almost miraculously, Crook survived a career filled with deadly combat without ever suffering a life-threatening wound. Such would also be the case with Phil Sheridan, who seemed equally fearless under fire.

Crook's contemporaries often ascribed his effectiveness as an Indian fighter to his ability to think like an Indian. To some degree, he cultivated this quality through careful observation of Indian customs and habits. But on a more fundamental level, as this incident shows, he shared with his foe many of the attitudes and characteristics of their hunter-warrior culture.

In war Indians fought as individuals rather than in coordinated units. While self-preservation and revenge were motives for combat, an Indian's primary objective was not to kill the enemy, but to demonstrate prowess and courage, thereby achieving status in his community, even at the cost of his own life. Similarly, the hunt, while providing meat required for survival, furnished an additional opportunity to display courage and prowess.

Crook too hunted for food and fought his enemy because it was his duty as a soldier. But his ambition for advancement—status in the military community—was also a spur that drove him to excel in battle. And like an Indian warrior, he seems to have relished opportunities to match wits with a worthy quarry, going after the largest bear or the most elusive and fierce Indians, as a test of courage and skill. He killed without animus. On the contrary, he often expressed admiration for his foe's strength, ability, and cunning, knowing that only by defeating a worthy adversary could he earn the accolades he sought. Though he might have been the last to admit it, he clearly shared many of the values of the tribes it was his job to suppress.

If, during that spring of 1857, Crook paused to reflect on the implications of his first combat experience, it was not for long. On June 10, after only the briefest respite, settlers complained to him that a band of Achomawi had stolen eighty head of their cattle. The lieutenant set out after them immediately, this time accompanied by a detachment of ten men. From the back of his mule, picking his way along the rim of an escarpment, Crook peered down at a fast-flowing river that coursed through a canyon far below. His vantage point and keen eyesight gave him an uninterrupted view for a considerable distance downstream, and he soon spotted an Indian campsite by the river's edge. At almost the same moment, the Indians became aware of the soldiers' presence and scattered into the brush.[20]

Again, swept up in the heat of the moment, Crook threw himself off his mount and hurtled along a steep trail down the side of the escarpment. Before he could consider the consequences of his impetuosity, he found himself alone on the riverbank near the encampment. From where he stood, he sighted a warrior swimming for the opposite shore, holding his bow and arrows and a wolf robe above his head. Crook carefully aimed at the warrior's head, dark against the swirling waters, and fired. The Indian sank into the foaming water, his bow spinning downstream in the current.[21]

By now a number of Indians had taken positions behind huge boulders and were launching volleys of arrows in Crook's direction. A shouted warning from one of his troopers on the cliff came too late—an arrow struck him in the right hip. Seizing the shaft, Crook pulled it out, in the process leaving the obsidian head buried deep in his flesh.

As other arrows continued to hiss around him, he realized that if he remained on the bank, he would be struck again, perhaps fatally. Faced with this inevitability, he began a hasty retreat up toward the canyon rim. Though in great pain, he struggled up the sheer slope, grasping tufts of grass, and at one spot arrow shafts imbedded in the ground, to pull himself upward. The arrowhead in his hip had been poisoned, and as he climbed, Crook began to sweat profusely, overcome by waves of nausea. By the time he reached the safety of the cliff rim and examined the wound, the flesh around it had already turned blue and green.[22]

Though aware that he needed medical attention, Crook was initially reluctant to send a message to Fort Jones, fearing that on learning that he was wounded, Judah would relieve him of command. After suffering in silence for a day, the pain and the gravity of the wound finally forced him to capitulate. Penciling a brief note to the captain, he struggled to express his need for medical assistance while minimizing the seriousness of the wound. Ultimately, in his spiky scrawl he wrote: "I . . . received an arrow wound in my thigh, the arrow penetrating some 3 only inches, as well as I can judge. The arrow point is still in the wound, and I wish you would have the kindness to send out someone to extract the flint." But he added, "I feel confident that if it was out, I would be able to ride in 3 or 4 days and return to my duty."[23]

The note was delivered to Fort Jones on June 13 by Dick Pugh, a civilian scout assigned to Crook's command. To his credit, that same day Judah dispatched not only Dr. C. C. Kearney, the post surgeon, but also a twenty-five-man detachment under Lieutenant Hiram Dryer to his subordinate's aid. In his report to headquarters, the captain attempted to make light of his lieutenant's "collision with the Indians." Knowing that it conflicted with his claim to have pacified the valley, he characterized Crook's encounter as "quite accidental," assuring his superiors that, "anticipating nothing further of a serious nature from that quarter, I did not deem my personal presence with the expedition . . . necessary."[24]

Judah was aware that Captain Gardiner was en route to the valley to take charge of the garrison. So in his mind this obviated the need for Crook's continued presence. Anxious to have his lieutenant back under his control as soon as possible, he instructed Dryer to bring the entire Fort Jones contingent back to the post as soon as Gardiner determined they were no longer needed. He anticipated that this meant their return in short order.[25]

While Dryer rode to his rescue, Crook, never one to miss an opportunity for outdoor activity, went fishing. Though still unable to paddle a canoe, he had a soldier take him out to a fork in the river, where he cast his line, catching "some magnificent trout weighing several pounds."[26]

When the post surgeon arrived at the camp on June 16, he found the young officer much recovered. A cyst had formed around the arrowhead, and the wound was healing nicely without infection. Under the circumstances, the doctor saw no reason to remove the point; Crook would carry this piece of sharpened obsidian to his grave. With his strong constitution and amazing recuperative powers, only two weeks passed before the lieutenant was back in the saddle, with only some stiffness in his leg to show for his wound.[27]

While Crook recuperated, Lieutenant Dryer conducted several patrols in the area without turning up any Indians. But on June 26, sixteen days after Crook had been wounded, the detachment received information that twenty head of cattle had been stolen, probably by Modocs. Crook asked Dryer for permission to go after them, which he granted.[28]

Crook and twelve troopers tracked the thieves for several days into a rough area to the east known as the lava beds. This country was a forbidding moonscape of sharp, broken volcanic rock, cut with numerous outcroppings, fissures, and caves, the entire area overgrown with thick brush. The Modocs found it ideal for concealment and ambush.[29] Before attempting to engage the cattle thieves, Crook returned to camp to consult with Dryer. The latter had just received an order from Judah to return to Fort Jones, leaving Crook in charge of the command, which now included thirty-three men, counting the soldiers from Dryer's detachment. Following the lieutenant's departure, Captain Gardiner, contrary to Judah's expectations, approved Crook's request to continue his campaign against the Modocs.[30]

Returning to the lava beds, Crook launched an early morning attack on the thieves. Maneuvering his troops through the tangled vegetation toward a column of smoke that marked the Indian campsite, he divided his men into three groups to surround it. At a prearranged signal, the soldiers opened fire. "The pandemonium let loose beggared all description," Crook wrote. "There must have been two or three hundred of them all told, yelling, screeching, scolding, [with] war whoops imitating different wild beasts in their most hideous sounds. What with our firing and the yelling of the soldiers, it made one's hair stand on end." Reporting the fight to Judah, he stated that he and his men had killed eighteen Indians in the fray "and wounded as many more (most of the latter mortally)." He proudly noted that his troops had not lost a man and "but one squaw [was] killed."[31]

Crook duly noted the profound effect that the sudden and unexpected appearance of troops in their midst had on the Modocs. It was graphic proof for him of the efficacy of the surprise attack in Indian warfare, usually executed at dawn to maximize the shock value of the tactic.

The troops discovered quantities of beef at the campsite, convincing Crook that he had correctly identified the guilty parties and providing him with the justification he felt he needed to destroy the camp. He then rounded up the women and children who had taken refuge in nearby lava caves, fed them, and released them the next morning. After spending several more days in a fruitless search of the area for more of the perpetrators, he returned to Gardiner's post to rest and refit.

Crook and Gardiner got on well together. The latter, a New Englander with some twenty years of military experience, seventeen years with the dragoons, was so impressed with Crook's efforts that he named his outpost after the young lieutenant. In addition, though he had not yet communicated his intentions to Judah, he had decided to ask that Crook and his detachment remain with him at the Pit River for the rest of the summer. As Gardiner informed his superiors, his own men were fully occupied trying to complete the post and cutting hay to feed the livestock before the onset of winter. He therefore needed Crook's troops to mount patrols to protect settlers and travelers in the area from the depredations of Indians, whom he wrote, were both "more numerous and more hostile than I had supposed."[32]

For his part, Crook was thoroughly enjoying himself. When he was not out on patrol, Gardiner had him hunting game to feed the post, which he vastly preferred to the onerous and boring duties of quartermaster that awaited him at Fort Jones. So with perhaps more arrogance and less commonsense and tact than was appropriate for a junior officer, he intervened personally in the matter of his reassignment. Rather than wait for the two commanders to work matters out, Crook, flush with his victory in the lava beds, wrote to Judah. "Captain G is going to recommend the stationing of another company at this post, so I feel quite confident I will be stationed here if they get your recommendation to that effect at Hd. Qtrs." So far so good. But then, with unwarranted presumption, Crook breezily informed his captain that he had already sent a wagon back to Fort Jones to pick up his clothing. He then concluded with a gratuitous jab. Judah had previously asked that Gardiner appoint Judah's brother as post sutler at Fort Crook. The lieutenant now responded on Gardiner's behalf—and certainly without his knowledge or consent—that the captain had "appointed his sutler before he arrived here, (some gentleman from Bavaria). I don't know his name."[33]

Predictably, the thin-skinned Judah was infuriated by Crook's brashness and, undoubtedly, by the reference to the sutler's position. He fired off a response to Gardiner in which he quite properly referred to Crook's request for temporary reassignment as "unofficial," blaming the captain for Crook's failure to follow protocol. Warming to his subject, Judah then accused the captain of a breach of courtesy in failing to communicate with him directly. At this point his anger got the better of him, and Judah overstepped the bounds of military propriety, asserting that Crook's men were "surplus and unnecessary to the protection of the residents of the Pit River Valley." In an accompanying letter, he peremptorily ordered Crook to report immediately to Fort Jones for duty since his presence was no longer required in the valley. Failure to promptly comply, he threatened, would "subject you to the process indicated in General Regulations for enforcing the accountability of officers from their superiors."[34]

Gardiner read these letters as a slur on his military judgment and an insult from a fellow officer. Further, since Gardiner outranked Judah by virtue of having an earlier commission date, Judah's refusal to detail Crook to him was (to Gardiner) an attempt to undermine the authority of a superior officer. Consequently, he demanded that charges be preferred against Judah for "conduct subversive of good order and discipline" and "conduct unbecoming an officer and a gentleman."[35]

Both officers proceeded to direct a lengthy and peevish correspondence to Major William W. Mackall, the assistant adjutant general in San Francisco, who had no wish to see this petty argument escalate into formal legal proceedings. Ultimately, when Judah demanded a court of inquiry to vindicate his honor, the commanding general intervened. Tired of the bickering, Brevet Brigadier General Newsome S. Clarke, who had replaced Wool in May, dismissed all charges and countercharges in stern tones that made it clear that the junior captain had not done his career much good.[36]

While Judah and Gardiner feuded, Crook, pursuant to Gardiner's orders, continued his aggressive campaigning against the fractious Pit River tribes. At the end of July, while on a scout, he stumbled across the tracks of a single Indian leading into a mountain valley. Suspecting the presence of an Indian village, he climbed a rocky ridge to get a better view of the valley floor. The sight of smoke and several warriors moving about in the high grass below confirmed his suspicions, and he returned to his command to prepare a dawn attack on the encampment.

At midnight the men assembled for a hasty meal of hardtack and water. Then, mounting their mules, they picked their way gingerly in total darkness over a rough trail that descended into the valley. Just after daybreak they were spotted by an Indian, who swiftly disappeared in the opposite direction. Moments later they saw a swarm of Indians, scattering like quail in all directions across the valley floor.

Ordering his men in pursuit, the young lieutenant leapt once more into the forefront of the action. Dismounting in order to shoot more accurately, he killed one warrior and, as he reloaded his weapon, saw a second attacking a trooper whose rifle appeared to be empty. Aware that the Indian would kill the soldier unless he intervened, Crook decided to go after the warrior himself. The veteran Indian fighter recounted the scene years later:

> I at once mounted, and put spurs to my horse, and when I had gotten within one hundred yards of them, the Indian, evidently judging that my rifle was loaded, left the soldier and came at me.
>
> I dismounted and ran ahead, so he would not shoot my horse, to within sixty yards of him. He was half bending and half squatting, with his breast toward me, jumping first to one side and then to the other, evidently trying to draw my fire, keeping an arrow pointed at me all this time. . . .
>
> He was singing his death song. I took a rest on my knee, and moving my rifle from one side to the other, following his movements, I got a good aim, when I pulled the trigger, and broke his back. In this condition, while lying on the ground, he shot five arrows into the soldier's mule, three of them going through the saddle and three thicknesses of blankets into the mule before I killed him with my pistol.[37]

Reporting the engagement to Captain Gardiner, Crook wrote admiringly that the Indians had fought bravely, losing "23 warriors dead and

9 wounded on the field," before the remnants of the band disbursed into the hills beyond the reach of his men. He had not, he declared, lost a single soldier.[38]

After the fight ended, the soldiers located and burned the village. Ordinarily, Crook carefully documented evidence establishing the involvement of "chastized" Indians in depredations against the white population. In this case he mentioned no such proof, leaving open the possibility that, in his haste to do battle, he may have launched an attack on an innocent community. To his further discredit, he ordered the destruction of the encampment though fully aware that "about all they had to eat were grasshoppers and a few grass seeds."[39] By burning their few material possessions, Crook certainly knew that he was condemning these people to a winter of destitution and possibly death. Yet at this point in his career, he appeared untroubled by the consequences of his actions and disinclined to temper his behavior to ameliorate the suffering of his adversaries.

As the summer wore on, Crook's aggressive patrolling, though performed under orders from Gardiner, began to concern department headquarters in San Francisco. General Clarke, Wool's replacement, shared his predecessor's empathy with the Indians and his opinion that settlers' provocations were to blame for most of their depredations. Consequently, he was unwilling "to continue to destroy longer than duty to the whites makes it imperative," implying that he considered Crook's campaigns to have gone beyond what was required. As an alternative to the killings and the destruction of property, he urged Gardiner to attempt negotiations with the Indians. If his efforts bore fruit, "Lieut. Crook [was to] cease his operations at once; and under any circumstances, stop his operations the moment you are satisfied that this may be done with safety to the inhabitants."[40]

Gardiner defended Crook's activities—which after all were carried out under his orders. Endorsing the lieutenant's attacks, he pointed out that in the face of the Indians' hostility, such aggressiveness was necessary to impress them with the military's great power and willingness to use it in order to convince them of the need to make peace.[41]

Gardiner's argument reflects a widespread belief among military officers on the frontier, including Crook, that a warrior culture could only be induced to make peace if convinced of the overwhelming martial superiority of their foes. To bring this lesson home to the tribes, they believed, it was necessary not only to administer a decisive defeat on the battlefield but also to destroy the food supply and shelter the Indians needed to survive during the winter months. The destruction of their food sources would force them to become dependent on the government for rations, which would only be available if they settled on the reservations set aside for them. The more ruthlessly these policies were carried out, the argument ran, the quicker the tribes would accept confinement to the reservations, thereby shortening the period of their own suffering.

As Crook continued to implement this strategy, his sense of honor and fairness and his natural sympathy for the underdog warred with his belief that such harsh measures would bring about a swifter, more humane result. His compromise was to attempt to ensure that these measures were carried out within the confines of certain humanitarian bounds. Soldiers under his command had strict orders to spare noncombatants—elders, women, and children (not as obvious a moral imperative as it would seem today)—treat prisoners humanely, and provide food and medical care to the wounded. In later years, after the tribes had been consigned to reservations, his humanitarian impulses and sense of honor would put him in the forefront of the effort to ameliorate the harsh conditions and rampant corruption that plagued the reservation system. For Crook, fair treatment of the Indians had both moral and practical consequences. It became axiomatic to him and other officers that unfair treatment invariably led to violent uprisings. Moreover, a hostile Indian who knew that his women and children would be spared and that he would be treated decently in captivity would be more likely to surrender than fight to the death.

But aggressive military tactics aimed at crushing Indian resistance were just coming into favor in the Department of the Pacific in the mid-1850s, and peaceful negotiations were still preferred by it commanding officers. So, though Gardiner defended Crook's tactics to his superiors, he also reassured them that aggressive patrols were only a means to get the Indians to treat with him and would not continue "a moment longer than necessary" to achieve that end. In line with these assurances, when the government's Indian agent for the area arrived at Fort Crook in mid-August to negotiate peace with the Indians, Gardiner assigned Crook to escort him through the country.[42]

For their part, the Indians were wary but receptive to these peacemaking efforts, and soon the officers induced them to come into the fort to receive rations.[43] This had the salutary affect of reducing Indian raids, which were in any event largely directed at procuring food, and drawing the Indians into the vicinity of the fort, where they could be better protected from settlers. By late summer, peace had been restored in the valley.

As the month of August drew to a close, Crook's career was on the rise. Gardiner requested that the lieutenant be retained at Fort Crook for at least two months, if not permanently, as he found him to be "a very active and efficient officer, and thoroughly acquainted with the country."[44] And General Clarke, perhaps reconsidering his earlier criticisms of Crook's tactics, had decided that this was not the time to send him back to Fort Jones. So Crook remained with Gardiner into the fall, when word came that his services were required elsewhere.

In the Pit River valley, Crook had gained valuable experience in Indian warfare, had established a reputation as a competent and effective combat officer (though not an Indian hater), and perhaps most pleasing to him at the time, had escaped Captain Judah's authority. Even the notoriously fickle press had bestowed accolades on his accomplishments. In the fall of 1857, as Crook was preparing to depart from the valley, the *Sacramento Union* published a short article lauding what they regarded as his accomplishments. "Already he has induced a number [of Indians] to come in and sue for peace and it is expected that what remains of the tribe will surrender. He has pursued them into their rugged mountain fastnesses, through brakes and tules, and routed them with great loss, on the part of the Indians: and the severe lesson—the first that they have ever received—has taught them that a peace is worth keeping. It is believed that Lt. Crook's small command has killed as many Indians in the present campaign, as were killed . . . on Rogue River in 1856, and he merits a like honorable recognition."[45]

CHAPTER NINE

Fort Ter-Waw

September–October 1857

For Crook, fall in the Pit River country was idyllic. In company with his men, he roamed at a leisurely pace through the towering pines that blanketed the mountainsides and across tallgrass prairies dotted with blueberry bushes heavy with ripened fruit. Wherever he went, he was surrounded by game—grouse; deer; the occasional elk, mountain lion, or bear; and mountain sheep peering down imperiously from rocky out crops. When they tired of hiking and hunting game, the men fished in cold, clear streams abounding with trout. Pitching their tents wherever their fancy took them, they wandered as if in a dream through scenes that, in Crook's words, had an "almost fairy-like" quality.[1]

In mid-September the lieutenant returned from one such ramble to find a dispatch from Major Mackall. A long letter explained that Company D, under Crook's command, was being transferred to an Indian agency recently established near the mouth of the Klamath River not far from the coastal town of Crescent City, California. The Tolowa, a tribe transplanted there from its traditional lands along the Smith River on the coast, had become restive. Crook was to ascertain the reasons for the unrest and make "every effort to ameliorate the condition of these people and remove [any] just cause of dissatisfaction." At the same time, he was to provide protection for the Indian agent, avoiding violence "except in self-defense or a violent necessity." The job would require "firmness united with prudence," qualities that, Mackall emphasized, "Brigadier General Clarke hopes to find as conspicuous in this new field as were your energy, perseverance, and activity on that from which you are now removed." Not incidentally, since the army expected to maintain a long-term presence in the area, Crook also was expected to construct a military post at the agency.[2]

As was usually the case when liberated from the constraints of superior authority, Crook found the travel to the Klamath delightful. From Fort Jones, where he stopped briefly to "clean up some unfinished business," he marched his men through countryside laced with "streams full of fish and the mountains full of game." The salmon were running, and the troops lingered for a time by a creek roiling with fish struggling upstream to their spawning grounds. Removing their boots and rolling up the bottoms of their trousers, they joined their lieutenant in the icy water, grabbing at the slippery salmon, unmindful of the spray thrown off by their splashing quarry.[3]

After passing through Crescent City, the column moved south through majestic redwoods to the Klamath River. The flow of the river had carved its way between steep hills that reached down to the water's edge, leaving no room for a trail. So the detachment completed the six-mile journey up the Klamath by canoe, soon arriving at a narrow strip of fertile land, extending upriver for twenty miles, where the Indians had been resettled.

On arriving at the agency, known to the Indians as Waw-kell, Crook found a large contingent of Tolowa preparing to decamp for their homes on the Smith River. While the Indian agent and his few civilian employees had been powerless to stop the exodus, Crook's arrival with some ninety soldiers put an abrupt end to the plan.[4]

The lieutenant soon learned the reasons for the Tolowas' dissatisfaction. The tribe, known to whites as the Smith River Indians, had been transported against their wishes to a location that was already home to the Klamaths, a tribe hostile to the Tolowas with a different language and different customs. The fact that they were provided with insufficient food only added to the Tolowas' discontent. After a brief investigation, Crook informed his superiors that "low, unprincipled whites" from Crescent City played upon these resentments, hoping to encourage the Tolowas to return to the Smith River, where they would be exploited as a source of cheap labor.[5] As was soon to become apparent, the presence of troops only temporarily calmed the situation but did nothing to resolve it.

The day after his arrival, Crook selected the site for his new post, a meadow of about twenty-five acres amid a stand of redwoods along the bank of Ter-Waw Creek, a narrow tributary flowing into the Klamath. About a mile upstream from the agency, it was far enough away to avoid friction between his soldiers and the Indians but close enough to be able to intercede quickly if circumstances required. In a departure from tradition, which mandated that military posts be named after military officers, he asked permission, quickly granted, to name the fort Ter-Waw, a Klamath word meaning "pretty place" or "nice place."[6]

While the soldiers set about building the rudimentary structures necessary to protect them from the elements during the coming winter, the Tolowas, who had not given up hope of returning to their traditional homeland, began slipping away from the reservation in small groups. Those who remained behind formulated a plot to murder Crook, reasoning that leaderless troops would do nothing to prevent a mass escape. A Klamath Indian uncovered the plot and warned the agency. That same day Crook, by now aware of the conspiracy, was visited at his tent by a group of Tolowas who expressed an undisguised interest in his sleeping arrangements: Did he sleep alone? Where did his soldiers sleep? He must have watched with some amusement as they fingered the tent canvas to determine its thickness and otherwise carefully examined the encampment, noting that Crook had pitched his tent some fifty yards away from the rest of the troops.[7]

Characteristically, the cocky young lieutenant decided on a risky plan. Rather than tell his men of the threatened attack, he prepared to meet it on his own, declaring himself "more than a match for" the Indians. "That night I fastened my tent doors well and put a box of brass accoutrements just inside the door of my tent so that anyone entering would strike the box and the rattling of the brass would wake me up. I had lain my rifle on one side of my bed with my shotgun on the other, with my pistol and bowie knife under my head. Any object standing over me would be between me and the sky light and would give me an advantage over them."[8]

Fortunately, he never had to test the feasibility of his hazardous plan. Instead of trying to murder Crook, at the last moment the Tolowas decided to kill the Indian agent instead. Telling him that he was needed to attend a sick Indian, they lured him to their camp, where they attacked him and another agency employee with knives and bows and arrows.

The two whites held their attackers at bay long enough for a guard to come to their rescue and then dispatched a runner to fetch Crook. It took Crook some time to gather his troops and get them to the agency. When he finally arrived, the Indians fled, and he "could only get an occasional shot into the bush." Yet he reported killing about ten of the attackers in the fracas, while the rest escaped to the Smith River.[9]

On Christmas Day Crook reported to the assistant adjutant general that the situation with the Tolowas had been defused. The superintendent of Indian affairs had wisely allowed the remaining Smith River people who had fled Waw-kell to remain with their friends and families back in their home territory. In the same letter, Crook expressed the opinion that white settlers had fomented the unrest among the Indians. He described a plot to incite the Tolowas in the hope of starting an uprising that would allow local whites to enlist in volunteer companies that would be used to suppress it. Then, following the cessation of hostilities, they would submit inflated claims for reimbursement from the government for services rendered, a type of fraud common during the Rogue River and Yakima wars.[10]

Crook's correspondence from Fort Ter-Waw indicates his growing concern with the plight of the Indians on the reservation. They also provide a picture of a remarkably self-assured young officer, fully confident that he and his men could handle any problems that might arise without the need for outside assistance.

Peace now reigned at the agency, allowing Crook to concentrate on the immediate task of getting his troops under roof before the chilly downpours of a northern California winter began in earnest. "In those days," Sheridan later observed, "the Government did not provide very liberally for the sheltering of its soldiers; and officers and men were frequently forced to eke out parsimonious appropriations by toilsome work or go without shelter."[11] So, under Crook's direction and using redwood timber as their chief building material, his men constructed a series of rude structures that would serve as storage sheds, barracks, and a mess hall, laboring in rain that at one stretch fell steadily for six weeks.

Fort Ter-Waw's location on the Klamath River placed it along a major trade route from the interior to the coast. Indians were a constant presence, dropping by to trade, to talk, or simply to watch the whites go about their business. The demands of post administration were not time consuming, leaving Crook ample opportunity to socialize with them.

Curious by nature, he soon picked up enough of the local language to "carry on an ordinary conversation" with his informants.[12] His growing familiarity with their tongue earned their trust, while he in turn began to appreciate them as individuals and learn from them. There can be no question that many of his skills as a tracker, hunter, fisherman, and woodsman for which he later would become famous derived in large measure from the Indians with whom he frequently associated during this period.

While he was learning wood lore from the Indians, he was also forming opinions based on his observations of their character and beliefs. He recorded these in his autobiography years later. Though they often reflect the superficial, ethnocentric views common to most white Americans of the time, his conclusions demonstrate an unusual and genuine interest in Indian culture, a desire, as he put it, to get to know "the inner Indian."[13]

Crook freely admitted that before this time, like most whites, he "never really got any insight into Indian character before." On one hand, he wrote, "[i]t is an easy matter for anyone to see the salient points of Indian character, namely that they are filthy, odoriferous, treacherous, ungrateful, cruel, and Lazy." On the other hand, he noted, "they had another side to their character than that seen in public. . . . [T]hey had other features which were as a rule latent, but were more or less well defined and by a little stimulation could be made quite as prominent as those of the savage nature. When we stop to think about him, his life is a constant battle with all the rest of mankind and the elements for existence. [Therefore] we must expect him to show that part of [himself] which is in readiness to defend himself."[14]

He found Indian religion incomprehensible, an amalgam of legend, which he found "interesting and touching," and superstition. From his observations Crook concluded that Indians "believed firmly in the marvelous. Nothing that occurred, it made no difference how insignificant, but what they had some [supernatural] reason to account for it." Using western logic, he tried unsuccessfully to undermine their confidence in witchcraft. Failing to make an impression, he concluded that many of their notions were "so inconsistent with their activities that [their beliefs] could hardly be called a religion." Though well aware of the iniquitous behavior of his fellow whites toward the Indians, Crook was so thoroughly wedded to his belief in the superiority of Christian civilization that he saw no irony in this statement.

Viewing the Indians through that same ethnocentric prism, he described their social interactions as "made up of little tempests in teapots, of . . . jealousies and gossip." He further observed: "Their food supply gives them but little concern usually. . . . Their troubles, therefore, are mostly imaginary, but notwithstanding this fact, sometimes they get into feuds which result in death."[15]

Despite his judgmental tone, Crook refused to accept the prevailing wisdom that the Indian was inherently inferior. Nineteenth-century ethnologists, whose views he seems to have adopted, held that societies developed along a continuum from savagery upward to civilization, which they unfortunately defined in terms of their own Euro-American culture. The corollary of this belief was that "primitive" societies had within them the capacity to mature and progress. Crook intended just this point in a speech to West Point cadets in 1884, perhaps shocking them by declaring: "[The Indian] is cruel in war, treacherous at times, and not overly cleanly. But so were our forefathers."[16]

Crook, and those who shared his views, believed that Indians were "brutal and pitiless" because their "life is a constant battle with all the rest of mankind and the elements for existence."[17] By exposing them to education and white culture, they could be brought up to the level of western civilization. Upon achieving that plateau of development, Indians could be fully assimilated into white society.

The weakness in the theory of the perfectibility of human cultures is, of course, that it dismisses the value systems and beliefs of nonwhite societies. As Euro-American culture was held to be the gold standard at the time, the only path to societal maturity lay in adopting western civilization and, conversely, eschewing the values and beliefs of "less developed cultures."

Nevertheless, these ideas would become the philosophical underpinning of the assimilationist policies to which Crook ascribed and that the government would ruthlessly impose on the Indians from the 1880s, following their consignment to reservations, up to modern times. The often-brutal implementation of these policies ultimately would have horrific consequences for the tribes and erode the social and economic foundations of Indian cultures. But in nineteenth-century America, they represented a humanitarian alternative to the racially charged violence, neglect, and even extermination advocated and sometimes practiced by many in the frontier West.

CHAPTER TEN

The Coeur D'Alene War

1857–1858

In June 1858, military necessity brought Crook's ethnological explorations to an abrupt, if temporary, halt. To the north, war erupted again in Washington Territory.

The outbreak of the Yakima War in 1855 had caught Crook and the Williamson-Abbot expedition unawares as they passed through the region. At the time, the departmental commander, General Wool, accurately placed the blame for the unrest on white settlers and miners. For that reason he had insisted on a negotiated peace rather than the decisive battlefield victory that most of his officers advocated as necessary to convince the warring tribes of the futility of further resistance. The resulting peace left the Yakimas in possession of their traditional hunting grounds but did little to prevent white settlers and miners from invading their land, thus failing to address the reason for the original hostilities.

A little more than two years later, when gold was discovered on the Canadian border, the shortest route to the goldfields lay through Yakima land, and the army was unwilling or unable to stop the miners who used it. When the Yakimas and their neighbors reacted with predictable hostility, the military attempted to cow them with a show of force. The results were embarrassing. A small command of 130 dragoons sent from Fort Walla Walla to overawe the Indians found themselves confronting a party of more than a thousand painted warriors from the Spokane, Coeur d'Alene, and Palouse tribes. Facing annihilation, the troops hastily retreated under cover of darkness to their post.

General Clarke, though he shared his predecessor's desire for a peaceful settlement, was angered by the humiliation of his dragoons and abruptly ended his policy of restraint and accommodation, opting instead for a strong military response. The Coeur d'Alene War (1858), actually a resumption of the Yakima War, thus began.

Like most of his officers, Clarke had little use for volunteer militia. He planned to fight this war using only regulars under his senior officers, Colonel George Wright and Major Robert Seldon Garnett, the latter commander of Fort Simcoe, one of the posts built after the Yakima War ostensibly to protect the Indians. Clarke reinforced Garnett's force with two companies of the Fourth Infantry from California—Captain Judah's E Company and Lieutenant Crook's D Company.

Garnett, Crook's new commanding officer, was yet another veteran of the Mexican War and the recipient of two brevet promotions for bravery while fighting under Zachary Taylor. A southern aristocrat to the core, he would resign his commission in 1861, enlist as an officer in the Confederate army, and was the first general to die during the Civil War, killed at Corrick's Ford in western Virginia.[1] Not one to lavish praise on his superiors, Crook considered Garnett a fair and able commander.

The decision to withdraw Crook and his men from Ter-Waw was not welcomed by the local settlers. A petition signed by 118 citizens from the area requested that Company D remain at the post, claiming that the soldiers knew the area well and were held in such terror by the Indians that their removal would diminish the security of the agency. Their petition was ignored, and Crook and his men departed Fort Ter-Waw on June 28. They were in high spirits, happy to be relieved of their construction duties and spoiling for a fight.[2]

Company D marched to Fort Simcoe by way of Vancouver, Washington Territory, joined along the way by elements of the Ninth Infantry. On the trail Crook and Captain John W. Frazer, commander of the Ninth's detachment, compared notes on their respective arms. Crook's men carried the rifled musket, issued to the infantry in 1855. A .58-caliber muzzle-loading weapon refitted with a rear sight and a grooved barrel, it was far more accurate than the old smooth-bore muskets previously issued to their regiment. The Ninth was armed with the Yeager, a smaller-caliber rifle used to great effect by mounted riflemen during the Mexican War. As they rode side by side, the captain regaled Crook on the virtues of the Yeager. The lieutenant had tried the rifle and, in his opinion, found it wanting in comparison to his rifled muskets. While at Ter-Waw, he had drilled his men in marksmanship using the musket and further sharpened their skills by taking them hunting whenever possible. Though he was confident of their state of readiness and the quality of their rifles, for the time being he held his tongue.

But when he arrived at Simcoe in late July and learned that the custom of the post was to excuse any trooper from guard duty who could score a bull's eye, Crook saw an opportunity to put the captain in his place and secure a benefit for his men. Prudently, he first observed the Ninth at target practice before deciding to demonstrate his own troops' superiority on the rifle range. He characteristically told no one of his plan but selected several men from the company to shoot and let their rifles do the talking. Observing that Crook's men scored repeated bull's eyes while his own did not, the chagrined Frazier ruefully allowed that it might be time to turn his Yeagers in for rifled muskets.[3]

With the arrival of the California reinforcements, General Clarke was prepared to launch his campaign. Mounted on mules, Garnett's force of 306 men and eight officers, comprised of three companies of the Ninth and Crook's single company of the Fourth, rode out of Fort Simcoe on August 10. The column was guided by friendly Indians, Crook's first exposure to Indian scouts. To his delight, Judah did not join the expedition, having arranged to stay behind with his company. According to Crook, the captain remained drunk during the entire time Garnett was in the field.[4]

Following the route used by the miners to the goldfields, Garnett's path took his column into Yakima territory north of the Columbia River, while Colonel Wright with a second column of regulars moved along a different route into the country of the Palouse, Spokane, and Coeur d'Alene. Abandoning the concerns that led him to criticize Crook for being overly aggressive during the Pit River campaign, Clarke ordered his officers to attack the Indians "with vigor; make their punishment severe and persevere until the submission of all is complete."[5] Garnett's objective was the apprehension of approximately twenty-five Palouse warriors suspected of murdering miners the previous spring and thought to be hiding with their Yakima relatives.

The campaign began on a tragic note. On the fifteenth Garnett's men discovered an Indian village on the Yakima River where some of the Palouse suspects were reputed to be hiding. A young second lieutenant,

Jesse Allen, only two years out of West Point, begged to be allowed to lead an attack on the village. During the assault, in the dim light of dawn, he was shot by one of his own men. Though Allen's death cast a pall over the troops, the attack was successful. A number of Indians were taken captive, among them three warriors recognized as having participated in the miners' murders. Garland had them summarily shot pursuant to his orders.[6]

The column continued north to the Wenache River, where Crook's company was ordered to split off and proceed sixty miles upriver to another village thought to be harboring more of the suspected murderers. Leaving the main force at nightfall, his troops soon were caught in a heavy downpour that left their mules stumbling blindly along a tortuously winding trail through swampy woodlands in total darkness. The effort so exhausted both man and beast that when Crook finally called a halt, the troops simply tethered their mules and threw themselves down in the muck to snatch a few hours of rest before daylight.

Dawn brought little relief. The soldiers now saw that they were in the midst of a heavily forested bottomland strewn with the trunks of huge redwoods and dotted with bogs so deep that, Crook speculated, they could swallow a mule. The trail doubled back on itself repeatedly as it wound around the giant logs, making progress slow and tedious. To add to their misery, the troops were plagued by swarms of yellow jackets and hornets that sent the mules into a frenzy of bucking and kicking, causing soldiers to fly in all directions.

Around midafternoon they spied three saddled ponies grazing in an open field. Moments later they came upon a young warrior standing motionless by the trail, a trade musket in his hand, staring off into the distance, still as a statue. Employing his knowledge of Chinook, the trade language of the Northwest, Crook drew the young man into conversation and learned that the horses belonged to three of the Palouse warriors they had been seeking. Having spotted the troops, the fugitives had fled on foot, hoping to ambush the soldiers farther along the trail. The young warrior, it developed, was the son of the chief of a sizeable Yakima village about five miles upstream where a number of the Palouse had taken refuge.[7]

Crook considered his options. In the Pit River valley he would have undoubtedly launched a dawn attack on the village. But the inhabitants of this country had not yet demonstrated open hostility toward whites.

An assault on their village might cause them to join the uprising and could result in the deaths of a number of innocent Indians, which he felt would have been "morally wrong." Leaving aside ethical considerations, the lieutenant reasoned that it would be impossible to pick out the miscreants from the innocents in the heat of an open attack. Further, the Yakima greatly outnumbered his own force, were probably well armed, and certainly possessed an intimate knowledge of the countryside, all of which made them formidable opponents.[8] So an attack would not only be immoral but also foolhardy.

After considering these factors, he devised a plan to involve the Yakimas in the capture of the suspects. About a mile from the village, he had his men make camp and again conferred with the chief's son. Emphasizing that his mission was to capture the Palouse murderers and not to harm any others, Crook suggested that the warrior bring his father to the soldiers' camp so they could discuss the best means of bringing about this result. He asked that no one in the village be told of his presence. As usual he played his cards close to his chest, concealing his strategy even from his own men.

Crook had no idea whether the young man accepted his plan and no means to compel him to follow his suggestion. So he awaited the Indian's return in an agony of suspense. When the son finally reappeared, Crook was startled to see that he had brought not only his father but also many warriors from the camp. The lieutenant's pulse rate must have leapt when he learned that among the Indians warily edging into his camp were three of the accused Palouse. Still not sure about the Yakimas' intentions and not wanting to tip his hand until all the guilty parties were present, he took the chief aside and outlined a plan to capture the wanted men the next day. The chief appeared amenable, even agreeing to Crook's request that he and his son keep the plot secret.

That evening the Indians returned to their village amid a downpour that would last until dawn. Crook posted his sentries, still unsure whether the chief's assurances were real or simply a ruse to enable his warriors to catch the soldiers unaware. He prepared his bedding beside a fallen log. Then, after night fell, he moved to another location to foil would-be assassins, fashioning a tent from his saddlebag. The makeshift structure proved ineffective, "for it seemed to conduct water on [Crook] instead of the ground." Given the uncertainty of the venture and the fact that he had spent the night in a puddle of water, it is a tribute to his youthful hardiness and sangfroid (or perhaps his skill as a teller of tall tales) that Crook would later recall that he "never had a sweeter sleep or felt more refreshed in the morning."[9]

At dawn the Indians returned to the camp as promised. Crook, using a method he would later employ against the Apaches, had asked the chief to covertly identify the Palouse warriors, which he did. The lieutenant then stationed a noncommissioned officer and a private behind each with instructions to seize the man at his signal.

The plan went off without a hitch. The chief had been so secretive that when his people saw the Palouse being seized and bound, they scattered into the bush, fearing white treachery. Crook's troops, with the exception of those actually involved in the arrests, were equally surprised. Swift action netted four men and soon snared a fifth, a medicine man, who was apparently their leader, when he came forward, curious to see what was going on.[10]

General Clarke had ordered the immediate execution of any of the wanted men who were captured, a responsibility that Crook found "exceedingly distasteful." But unable to ignore a direct order, he turned the task over to his second in command, Lieutenant T. E. Turner, a young officer who, Crook wrote, "rather enjoyed that kind of thing." Turner was apparently not the only member of the company who relished the idea of killing Indians. Crook wryly noted that in accordance with army procedure intended to spare the feelings of a firing squad, he had arranged for some of the members of the firing squad to shoot muskets primed with powder but with no bullets. But this bit of military sentimentality was wasted on his men, particularly "one little music boy [who] cried because he wasn't allowed to shoot." After giving the miscreants the opportunity to confess their guilt—which, Crook records, all did—they were allowed to sing their death songs and then were shot.[11]

Without further incident, Company D rejoined Garnett's force on the Columbia River. The reunified command then proceeded upriver toward Canada. After reaching the border, the column then returned downstream. On Garnett's orders, Crook commandeered several Indian canoes and, with twenty men of his company, paddled down the Columbia, scouting the river ahead of the major's command. While the Indians whose boats had been taken may not have been charmed by their loss, for the soldiers the voyage downriver proved a pleasant relief from the frustrating work of stumbling through the thick, insect-infested redwood forests. Aside from an aborted attempt by the canoes' owners to reclaim their crafts, the trip was largely uneventful. For Crook the journey was a pure delight, allowing him to act on his own, demonstrate his skill with the unstable native canoes, and revel in the beauties of the virginal countryside.[12]

When Garnett's command finally reached Fort Simcoe in late September, they learned that Colonel Wright had won a signal victory over a large force of Spokanes, Coeur d'Alenes, Palouse, and Pend d'Oreilles. Stunned by their overwhelming defeat, the dazed Indians had laid down their arms.

In compliance with Clarke's orders, Wright imposed a draconian peace. He signaled his intent by first slaughtering over 800 Indian ponies he had captured during the fighting. At a stroke this brutal deed deprived the enemy of much of their wealth and their means to hunt and make war, at the same time impressing them with the army's willingness to employ extreme measures to pacify them. The practice was so effective that it would become common practice during the Indian wars of the 1860s and 1870s and was adopted by Crook without apparent hesitation. After completing this task, Wright forced the demoralized chiefs of the defeated tribes to surrender the warriors identified by the army as leading "trouble-makers." These men were summarily hanged. Other men who had been active in the fighting were led away in chains.

Wright's brutal tactics broke the back of Indian resistance and opened the mountain valleys of the Pacific Northwest to white settlement. Within a year the tribes east of the Cascades were herded onto reservations that represented only a fraction of their former lands. As happened elsewhere, their already shattered people were quickly overcome by malnutrition and disease.

When Major Garnett returned to Fort Simcoe, he received the devastating news that in his absence, his wife and infant son had died of bilious fever. The distraught colonel immediately returned to the East to inter their remains.[13]

Crook and his men, no longer needed at Fort Simcoe, returned by sea to Crescent City, where they boarded the freight boat up the Klamath to Fort Ter-Waw. The leisurely voyage afforded the lieutenant an opportunity to reflect on not only the effect of the measures Wright had used to subjugate the Indians but also matters of military leadership. In Major Garnett, one of the few officers whom he would later recall with unreserved admiration, Crook had found an example to emulate: "strict, but just, and those who did their duty well were certain to be rewarded, while those who failed to do their duty were made to feel it."[14] It was a prescription for command that could readily be applied to the Ohioan in future years.

CHAPTER ELEVEN

Return to Fort Ter-Waw

1858–1860

Company D returned to Fort Ter-Waw in October 1858, eagerly anticipating a rich harvest from a truck garden planted prior to their departure in June. Unfortunately, the garden was a failure. But the men were cheered to learn that the Fourth Regiment's Company B, which had garrisoned the post in their absence, had completed the construction of the fort, freeing the men of their duties as laborers. Crook also welcomed his return to the small, isolated post. Liberated from the constraints of superior authority and petty military protocol, he later looked back upon this period, extending up to the outbreak of the Civil War, as "the happiest part of my life." He felt "free from care and responsibility. My rank and position did not interfere with the ambition and excite the jealousies of others who were in a position to make me feel it."[1]

If his men thought that the completion of the post signaled a life of leisure, they were mistaken. For their commanding officer, it simply meant that his troops now had more time to concentrate on improving their military skills. In an army known for its indifference to preparing its enlisted men for war, Crook was unusual in the high priority he gave to training, particularly in the use of firearms. His service in the Pacific Northwest led him to believe that proficiency with a rifle was essential to a soldier's effectiveness. He established a regimen of daily target practice, commencing at 7 A.M.—moved to 5 A.M. as soon as the seasons permitted—followed by an hour of bayonet exercises.[2] He supplemented the time spent on the shooting range with extensive hunting forays into the surrounding mountains, as much for his own pleasure as for the benefit of his men. These outings honed their skills as woodsmen, built up their endurance, and not incidentally, added fresh meat to their otherwise monotonous diet of salt pork and occasional beef.

While training was a primary concern, the general health and welfare of his men were never far from his mind. Worried about the sad state of his men's' clothing, he complained to department headquarters that a requisition for uniforms submitted to the quartermaster the previous month had been only partially filled. Footwear was of particular concern. "I have to state that my men's shoes were nearly all worn out when I returned from last summer's campaign[,] and not being able to obtain any further at Vancouver, they are now in shameful condition."[3]

Due to the remoteness of the post, the procurement of supplies was a complex exercise. Anything at Ter-Waw that could not be grown or taken from the forests and streams had to be transported from Crescent City. But heavy snow closed off this avenue of supply during the long winter months. So careful planning was needed to ensure that the post was amply provisioned for the winter months, which in this clime extended from December through April.

But dealing with the myriad of small details that comprised his responsibilities as post commander, even when interspersed with frequent hunting forays, did not fully occupy the attentions of the energetic young post commander. He continued to devote time to his study of local tribal languages begun during his first days in the region. By the end of his time at Fort Ter-Waw, Crook had succeeded, in collaboration with some of his fellow officers, in compiling short vocabularies of the Hupa, Tolowa, Aliquah, and Arra Arra Indians. These he submitted to the Smithsonian Institute's Bureau of Ethnology, where they repose today.[4]

For the pragmatic lieutenant, studying local languages was not merely an academic exercise but a tool he used to meet and learn from the area Indians. With the help of the post trader, Andrew Snider, he became known to many tribesmen residing near the river. Though his fluency was only moderate, it was sufficient to gain the confidence of local Indians and give the lieutenant access to their homes and ceremonies. It also allowed him to join them on hunting and fishing trips, during which a free and relaxed atmosphere prevailed. As a consequence, he soon found himself learning much more about Indian beliefs, practices, and habits than he had previously imagined possible.

In June 1859, possibly due to his expanding relations with local tribesmen, Crook learned that the Indian agent on the Klamath Reservation had been forcibly removing Indians from their fishing grounds. Whatever the reasons for doing so, his action coincided with the tribe's spring salmon harvest, their only opportunity to gather the supply of fish needed to survive the winter. Crook quickly intervened. In what may have been his first foray as an advocate for Indian rights, he forcefully asserted his authority on their behalf, using the rationale that only by doing so could future conflict be avoided. "These Indians, and the Indians generally on the river," he wrote the agent, "are much dissatisfied and clamorous at your cruel and unjust treatment of them, and I am fully convinced that if such treatment is continued, the eventual result will be an outbreak. No Indian must be taken from this flat hereafter unless by my permission."[5] His tone, a mix of personal outrage and imperious exercise of military authority, would soon become familiar to Interior Department bureaucrats charged with oversight of Indian affairs at the agencies.

Though peace now generally prevailed between whites and Indians in Crook's corner of California, it was an uneasy truce punctuated by isolated bursts of violence. In the spring of 1859, a small group of warriors from the Klamath Lake country killed a party of whites whom the Indians claimed had inflicted what Crook termed "indignities" upon them.[6] In response, the lieutenant was ordered to send a small detachment to the confluence of the Klamath and Salmon Rivers, where they were to remain for a month to protect the whites in that area from further depredations. Anticipating trouble, the troops brought along 1,100 cartridges. But in late July Crook reported that the Indians in the area had taken control of the situation and resolved it themselves. Noting that the killings that spring had been the work of a band of "renegades," he nonchalantly informed Major Mackall that the local chief had already brought in the heads of three of the murderers and had convinced Crook he would "eventually bring in the remainder."[7]

At Fort Ter-Waw, Crook's most serious problem was not the Indians but a local liquor merchant who set up shop near the post during the late summer and began dispensing his wares to the troops. The old guard house had burned down shortly before, and the lieutenant now built a new and larger one to accommodate the increasing number of soldiers confined on charges stemming from inebriation.[8]

In the early fall, following an inspection visit to his Klamath outpost, Crook reported that the Indians were "perfectly peaceable." But he like many in the military believed that whites in the area continued to foment trouble in order to profit from the unrest. He had it "on good authority" that certain white businessmen had manufactured rumors of a threatened uprising in order to attract troops to their area "for the personal benefit they would derive from them," intending to take advantage of the military presence by selling food, forage, and whiskey to the troops at exorbitant prices. As part of their plan, the men had burned several buildings in the vicinity and blamed the Indians for it.[9] The army, perhaps as a result of Crook's reports, did not rise to the bait.

While 1859 remained a period of relative calm in California, Crook was beset by a series of personal misfortunes. Though usually in excellent health, in September, while on a mission to the Rogue River area, he was stricken with severe pains that felt like "a ball of fire" igniting in his stomach. At first attributing the malady to indigestion, he endured it until his return to Fort Ter-Waw. There the doctor, who diagnosed the problem as a liver ailment, gave him strong medicine that eventually relieved the symptoms. Not long afterward, while hunting in the mountains, the lieutenant injured his throat and chest, probably in a fall. The pain remained with him for some time, but as was his habit, he bore it stoically and did not allow it to interfere with his duties.[10]

Barely recovered from these difficulties, Crook then nearly succeeded in drowning himself. He recounted the tale in an early version of his memoir. Though the story did not make it into the final work, it is worth recording as an example of his self-deprecating brand of humor, which turned a potentially life-threatening incident into a yarn suitable for the campfire.[11]

Crook had been duck hunting at the mouth of a river amid a driving autumn rainstorm when his canoe capsized in the choppy water. Before he could get a handhold on the overturned boat, he was dragged under by the weight of his waterlogged clothing and the powder and lead shot stuffed in his pockets. Thrashing about in the icy river, he struggled to keep his head above water as wind-whipped waves repeatedly pushed him down, choking him each time he came up for air. Finally, taxed to the limit by the exhausting struggle, he went under for what he supposed was the last time. To his amazement, his feet touched bottom and he discovered that he could easily stand. It did not take him long to figure out that he had been floundering about in only three feet of water while his Indian guide watched, bemused, from his perch on the bottom of the upturned canoe. That night, in the chilly fall weather, the miserable lieutenant lay on the bare, wet ground in a fireless camp— the wood was too wet to burn—wrapped only in his sodden cloak. But for his extraordinary constitution, he might well have died of pneumonia. As it was, he survived the incident with only the loss of his hat and musket to show for it.

CHAPTER TWELVE

A Trip East

1860–1861

Crook spent the spring and summer of 1860 at Fort Ter-Waw sharpening the skills of his men and, whenever possible, hunting and fishing. In September he took an extended leave, the first since his graduation from West Point. He planned to take care of "some business," as he vaguely states in his autobiography, and to visit his family, whom he had not seen since his assignment to the Pacific Coast in 1852.[1]

His route took him south to Los Angeles and then east on the Butterfield stage line across the Desert Southwest and on to Missouri, where he would board a train for Dayton. He later recalled the journey by stagecoach as "the severest ordeal I have ever experienced of this kind." Clouds of dust, temperatures furnacelike by day and freezing cold at night, and the proximity of his fellow passengers on the filthy seats of the jolting coach all made sleep impossible. Crook and his companions soon lapsed into an exhausted stupor, oblivious to the magnificent landscape through which they passed.[2]

But in southern Arizona Territory, lucidity returned with a jolt. Their trail ran through country in the throes of a tumultuous Apache uprising led by Cochise, chief of the Chiricahuas. Arriving at one of Butterfield's way stations, they found it in ruins, smoke still rising from its burned-out shell. Fortunately, the Apache raiders had already departed, leaving Crook to contemplate his first exposure to the tribe with whose fate he would become intimately involved a little more than a decade later.

From Arizona the coach rattled onward through New Mexico Territory and into Texas, stopping at the town of Sherman, where the "business" that demanded Crook's attention apparently transpired. Crook had spent most of the past decade in close proximity to some of the most vicious and degraded men in the West, the criminals and gamblers who drifted through the gold camps and mining towns of the Pacific Northwest. But in Sherman, he claimed, "I had never in all my life seen so many hard cases assembled in one place before."[3] Completing his business as quickly as possible, with relief he clamored back aboard the stage for the remainder of its run.

In the fall of 1860, Syracuse, a small Missouri hamlet that even today boasts fewer than two hundred residents, briefly held the distinction of being the western-most terminus of the Transcontinental Railroad. Here Crook transferred to a commodious rail coach, allowing him to complete his journey to Ohio in comfort and at speeds he could not have imagined when he had first traveled to the West Coast only eight years previous. Disembarking at Dayton, he set off to see the family he had not seen for almost a decade.

Crook did not record the details of his visit, but it is not hard to imagine what it was like for him to be home after so much time on the frontier. His father and stepmother, both in their late sixties, were still in good health, but during his absence, two of his six brothers, John and James, had passed away. At the same time, his family had grown, as other siblings married and sired a new generation of nephews and nieces, all of whom were undoubtedly eager to hear their uncle's accounts of fighting wild Indians and hunting bears in the Far West. These were moments of intense enjoyment for Crook. Others who knew him later in life commented on the fact that, though he had none of his own, he was very fond of children and could often be found wrestling on the floor with the young sons or daughters of his fellow officers. The family farm that provided the setting for this reunion must have seemed quite small and the surrounding countryside tame compared to the towering redwood forests of the Pacific Northwest.

His visit coincided with the momentous election campaign of 1860, which was just drawing to a close. On the first Tuesday in November, the nation voted for the candidate whose victory would determine the outcome of the great issues of the day—slavery and secession. Crook noted with some pride that he traveled to St Louis, where he " cast my first vote for President of the United States."[4] He chose not to reveal his ballot choice. But his family's deep involvement in Whig politics and his own solidly western background and plainspoken character indicate that he likely voted for Abraham Lincoln, the candidate of the Republican Party, successor to the Whigs, and a fellow westerner.

Nor did he comment on the political issues that drove Lincoln's election. Stationed in the remote reaches of northern California and preoccupied with local Indian concerns, matters that held the East in thrall had commanded little interest for Crook. Now visiting family in Ohio, he was suddenly exposed to the nation's feverish absorption with the preservation of the Union and the issue of slavery. Saving the Union was a principle that did not resonate with him. So far as we know, he did not address the issue in writing. But Brigadier General Jacob D. Cox, who would become Crook's first commanding officer, would later describe the young officer as "one of those who had, at the beginning, no deep sympathy with the National cause, and had no personal objection to the success of the Rebellion."[5]

Crook appeared to view the great debate over slavery with similar indifference, though he was certainly exposed to the issue from childhood. His father's farm was not far from the Ohio River, the border between a free and a slave state, an active area for the Underground Railroad, and the setting for *Uncle Tom's Cabin*. As the grandson of Maryland slaveowners, he was only a generation removed from having a personal stake in the issue. As a youth he had attended a church strongly opposed to slavery. While at West Point, where the Corps of Cadets reflected the sectionalism that infected the country, particularly after the Mexican War, he certainly had been exposed to heated discussions on the topic. Yet he had little or no first-hand experience with slavery or, for that matter, with blacks. In addition, his long tenure in the West had further removed him from the issue. So the controversy held little personal relevance, leaving him neither an advocate for abolition nor for slavery.

Despite his indifference to the issues that would underlie the conflict, as a career officer and West Point graduate, the approach of war was far from meaningless to Crook. His interest lay not in high principles but in the down-to-earth knowledge that, if war came, it would bring with it both heartbreak and personal opportunity, an eventuality to be contemplated with distinctly mixed emotions. On the one hand, many of his former classmates, as well as those with whom he had served in the Northwest, were southerners, men whom he liked and admired such as Garnett and Hood. It would be against men like these, rather than for some higher cause, that he would be fighting if war erupted. On the other hand, he was thirty-two years of age and still a first lieutenant in an army with severely limited prospects for promotion in peacetime. The officer corps was small, meaning that few positions were available at the higher ranks, and those that did exist had to be vacated by death or retirement before younger officers could be promoted. As there was no system of retirement benefits available, officers habitually served into advanced age, blocking the advancement of younger men. A war, requiring a substantial expansion of the army, would offer new opportunities for promotion, particularly for an academy graduate. For that reason Crook and many other junior officers anticipated the coming conflict with ambivalent feelings of hope. But war was still a dim cloud on the horizon for a young officer preoccupied with family and friends.

Crook's visit was all too brief, and taking leave of his family was not easy. His reticence did not permit him to discuss the subject openly, but he felt a strong attachment to his kin. Such partings as this carried with them the very real possibility that he might never see some family members again, or they him. At a later time, during a visit to Dayton on the occasion of his fiftieth birthday, Crook revealed the wrenching nature of these partings to one of his brothers: "The fact is . . . it is easier for me to stay away from here than to get away if I come here. It hurts less."[6]

But leaving loved ones behind was, and remains, an accepted, though unhappy, feature of military service, and Crook had duties to perform. His orders required that he report to New York, pick up a contingent of new recruits, and shepherd them to the West Coast, this time traveling via the Isthmus of Panama.

The return journey was without mishap until the lieutenant boarded a steamer to carry him up the California coast from San Francisco to Crescent City. The ship encountered "a fearful storm" that turned the last leg of the voyage into a harrowing nightmare. Huge waves, some fifteen feet in height, crashed down upon the deck, sweeping overboard everything that was not tied down. Fortunately, due to the captain's skill, the ship remained afloat, but the battering waves caused the vessel's hull to leak. For the remainder of the voyage, the miserable passengers huddled in their cabins with several inches of water sloshing back and forth about their feet. Crook, who had little fondness for sea travel, heralded his safe return to Fort Ter-Waw on Christmas Day 1860 with the brief comment, "I was glad to get back."[7]

The following spring, Crook's sojourn on the Pacific Coast ended. Civil war had broken out, and the Fourth and Ninth Infantry were gathered at the Presidio in San Francisco, pending transfer to the East. While there, Crook received word of his promotion to captain and orders to report to the Fourteenth Infantry, then stationed in New York.[8]

Crook's tour in the Pacific Northwest had lasted a little over nine years, marked at times by privation, danger, and inevitable periods of loneliness and boredom. On the West Coast he had grown to maturity, tested himself under fire, and familiarized himself with the skills needed to command small units in combat. He had also become as close to an expert on Indian warfare as anyone in the U.S. Army of the time. His study of Indian languages had unlocked doors to their methods of warfare, beliefs, customs, and habits, information that would make him a more formidable, though more sympathetic and understanding, foe. His love of hunting had spurred him to acquire an almost encyclopedic knowledge of the wilderness, leading a future aide to compare him to Daniel Boone—no small compliment at a time when the old frontiersman was an American icon.[9] His duties at several posts and on expeditions in the field had fostered in the maturing officer an intimate knowledge of military logistics and the management of livestock, mules in particular, skills that would stand him in good stead as he advanced through the ranks.

Absorbed in his military duties and his love affair with the wilderness, and perhaps fortified by his Methodist upbringing, Crook avoided the soldier's pitfalls—tobacco, liquor, and gambling. Of women, his own reticence and the general Victorian reluctance to discuss sex ensured that his activities in this area would remain forever in shadow. Most young, single officers on the frontier keenly felt the deprivation of female society. Many sought relief in the company of prostitutes or Indian women, and perhaps Crook was no different. But that is pure speculation.

Sadly, Crook concluded his narrative about this chapter in his life, one he regarded as among his happiest, upon a peevish note. At the time he set his memories to paper, he was consumed with bitterness, obsessed with the thought that he had been robbed of proper recognition for his achievements during the Civil War and later in Arizona. As a metaphor for his discontent, he seized upon the fact that his transfer to the East had forced him to leave Fort Ter-Waw before he and his men could harvest the crops they had sown earlier that spring. He wrote: "Shortly after I left [California], Capt. L. C. Hunt was ordered to Fort Ter-Waw to reap the fruits of my sowing, and, strange to say, it has been ever thus through my life. I have had to do the rough work for others afterwards to get the benefits from it."[10]

CHAPTER THIRTEEN

A Colonel in the Volunteers

September 1861–March 1862

Undeterred by the blanket of humid air that enfolded the nation's capital, men in uniform crowded Washington's dusty streets on an early September day during the first year of the war. Two officers, hardly noticeable among the throng of blue-clad troops, emerged from the Executive Mansion and walked purposefully toward the War Department. The older of the two, a stout man with squinting eyes and an imposing mustache, was dressed in a well-tailored uniform with the insignia of a brigadier general on his shoulders. The younger, a tall officer of about thirty, wore a full sandy beard and mustache that partially obscured his youthful, tanned features. His recent promotion to captain in the regular army was obvious to even the most casual observer due to the contrast between his dark shoulder straps and the faded blue of his uniform shirt.

From the opposite direction, a tall gentleman approached the two officers. His coarse black hair, gaunt features, and gangling frame made him instantly recognizable as Abraham Lincoln, the new president. He courteously, if somewhat wearily, paused to greet the two men, and the general introduced him to the young captain, rapidly outlining the purpose of their visit.

The president heard him out before explaining that when the cabinet had met the previous day, its members had indeed agreed that one hundred officers in the regular army would be released to serve in the new volunteer regiments being formed by the northern states. Nevertheless, he would not instruct the War Department to allow the captain

Robert Schenck. As a congressman from Ohio, Schenck nominated Crook to West Point. During the Civil War, he obtained a commission as a general and lost an arm at the Second Battle of Bull Run. Courtesy of the National Archives (College Park).

to be included among the hundred officers. To do so, he said, directing a kindly smile toward the visibly disappointed younger man, would be to interfere in the operations of the government, something he would as soon do as try to mend a watch. "For if he was to put his foot in it," the president told him, "it would never run again." The self-deprecatory humor in Lincoln's words took some of the sting out of his refusal while drawing the captain's eyes to the president's feet. They were, he decided, immense. Rather than being overawed by his commander in chief's august presence, Crook thought that overall, he presented a decidedly peculiar appearance. "Over six feet tall, arms and legs very long, . . . his legs most lean and limber, his pantaloons fit as though they were on a bean pole."[1]

Crook had arrived in New York only days earlier, following a long sea voyage from San Francisco via the Isthmus of Panama. It had been a stressful journey. In Panama he and his fellow passengers had learned with dismay of the Union's defeat in its first major battle with Rebel forces. Unexpectedly and thoroughly whipped at Bull Run, Federal troops had been driven in panic almost to the gates of Washington. Added to this distressing news, the anxious passengers were bombarded with rumors of Confederate privateers roaming just off the Atlantic coast in search of prey. Reflecting on his fellow travelers' mood, Crook wrote, "when we landed in New York, everything was very blue."[2]

But within hours of docking, he had recovered sufficiently to pen a note to the War Department accepting his promotion to captain in the Fourteenth Infantry Regiment. In reply the department sent him a brief message offering him the option to remain instead with his old regiment, the Fourth. Upon reflection, he preferred this alternative.[3]

The advent of war had aroused in Crook a thirst for advancement that his recent promotion had failed to slake. Promotion in the peacetime army had been excruciatingly slow. Nine long years of frontier service had passed before he had achieved his present rank. Though not an unusual length of time—Ulysses Grant, for example, had waited eleven years for his appointment to captain—it had been long enough to stir Crook's impatience. Ironically, though his experiences in California and Oregon had given him a low opinion of militia units, he now seriously considered a request for release from the regular service to accept appointment in one of the volunteer regiments now being raised.

The need for experienced officers to command these units offered an opportunity to achieve a senior position with attendant possibilities of rapid advancement. The Fourth Infantry was still stationed on the West Coast, far removed from the theaters of war. As the need for his services would be less acute there than in an eastern regiment directly involved in the fighting, the Fourth would be more likely to release him to the volunteers.

With a volunteer appointment in mind, Crook had traveled to Washington to seek out the man who had nominated him to West Point, Robert Schenck. Since serving in Congress, Schenck had gone on to serve as ambassador to Brazil and, when war broke out, had secured himself an appointment as a brigadier general in the Ohio volunteers on the strength of his political connections. He had most recently commanded a brigade in one of five green divisions that had fought so ineptly at Bull Run.[4]

Schenck had advanced the idea of going to the White House to ask for Lincoln's assistance. When the president refused to intercede, straightaway the general marched the young captain down the street to the War Department to speak to Brigadier General Lorenzo Thomas, adjutant general of the army. Thomas might have proved a tough nut to crack, as he bore a West Pointer's contempt for volunteer regiments. For his part Schenck may not have been the most diplomatic advocate, for he nursed a grudge against the regular army. Nevertheless, after the two generals had indulged themselves in a brisk exchange of insults, Thomas conceded that if Crook received a request for his release from the governor of any loyal state, then the adjutant would arrange a leave of absence for the duration.[5]

Crook wasted no time. Without delay, he telegraphed Ohio's governor, William Dennison, of his availability to accept command of a regiment, a position that carried with it the rank of colonel, three steps above his current grade. Dennison promptly responded, offering him command of the Forty-Third Ohio Infantry, a regiment currently being organized.[6]

Anxious to lead men in the field and uninterested in taking on the tiresome business of recruiting and organizing a new unit, Crook decided to plead his case personally with the governor. A day's train ride to Columbus and a short wait in Dennison's anteroom found the captain pointing out to the busy politician that after nine years of field experience, he would be far more useful overseeing an already operational unit than organizing a new one. Dennison not only agreed but also happened to have such a regiment immediately in need of a commanding officer. And so on September 17, 1861, only six weeks after his departure from San Francisco as a newly promoted captain, George Crook arrived in the town of Summersville in Unionist western Virginia a colonel, ready to assume command of the Thirty-Sixth Regiment of Ohio Volunteer Infantry.[7]

The Ohio volunteers did not find their new commander "very pre-possessing," dressed as was his habit in "half military, half civilian" attire. Several men, observing him lounging about the camp, mistook him for an officer from a company of "Union bushwhackers." By that, they later claimed, they meant no disparagement, for "it required a smart man to fill such a post at that time."[8]

Nor was Crook impressed by the men of his new command. The Thirty-Sixth, like so many volunteer regiments during the early months of the war, was a disorganized band of raw recruits hurriedly formed at Camp Putnam in Marietta, Ohio, the previous month. It numbered about a thousand men who had been enlisted fresh from the farm by Lieutenant Colonel Melvin Clarke, a prominent local attorney in civilian life, and Major E. B. Andrews, formerly a professor of natural sciences. As yet unaccustomed to military discipline, the recruits had been marched from Marietta through the western Virginia mountains to their present site by Major Adam Slemmer, famed for his stubborn refusal to surrender Fort Pickens to Florida secessionists in early 1861, and now temporarily assigned to the regiment. Slemmer was a spit-and-polish regular who made no allowance whatsoever for the men's lack of experience. He pushed them as hard as he would professional soldiers, arousing in them a palpable hostility toward regulars of which Crook became aware the moment he arrived.[9]

Crook was not one to compromise his principles for the sake of popularity, however, and his first action did little to endear him to his men. He promptly abolished the time-honored militia custom of democratically electing officers, a practice that had divided the men into factions since the regiment's inception. Henceforth, he announced, all officers would be appointed by their commander on the basis of merit, not popularity.[10]

As he had at Fort Ter-Waw, Crook made the training and welfare of his raw recruits his first priority. Under Lieutenant Colonel Clarke's supervision, the men had repaired an old sawmill and were cutting lumber for the construction of barracks to house themselves during the coming winter. Crook ordered them to build an additional structure, a seven-hundred-foot-long wooden building in which, regardless of the weather, he could instruct them in the fundamentals of military drill.[11]

Contemporary tactics and weaponry made drill the heart of military training in the nineteenth-century army. Though soon rendered obsolete by a revolution in firepower that began just before the Civil War, Napoleonic concepts of warfare—moving military units in close-order formations about an open battlefield—still lay at the heart of military tactics. To successfully execute these movements, officers had to be able to direct large bodies of men, often under fire, through a series of complicated maneuvers, a practice demanding intensive training and rigid unit discipline.

The parade ground was the soldier's classroom. On it he learned how to handle his weapon—a muzzle-loading musket requiring a complex nine-step process to load and fire. More importantly, he was taught to act and think as part of a larger military unit, precisely executing commands—first within his squad, then his company, and finally his regiment—with a precision that had to become second nature. So "the fearsome passage to and from the drill house," as one soldier termed it, became a daily ritual, commencing before breakfast and absorbing from four to six hours of each day, ending only when it became too dark to see.[12]

While training was obviously critical, Crook was all too aware of the need to properly equip and clothe his men, particularly with a harsh Allegheny winter coming on. The regiment's gear being in deplorable condition, the colonel moved quickly to resolve this problem, aided by the competent Major Andrews. Much to Crook's delight, the latter succeeded in procuring Enfield rifles for the entire unit.[13] The Enfield, a British-made weapon much in demand because of its superiority in both accuracy and range, was normally unavailable in the early days of the war. Andrews's ability to obtain them in quantity was a recognized feat of ingenuity.

The officers were as green as the men—"rare as a piece of beefsteak," as Crook put it. But rather than berate them for their ineptitude, he counseled that while he realized they could not become professionals overnight, he did require that they apply themselves earnestly to the business of soldiering or give way to those who would. To aid in their preparation, each evening, six days a week, he assembled his officers for two hours of instruction in the art of war—tactics, strategy, map reading, and other military skills. He found them a willing group.[14]

For their part, his troops discovered Crook to be a strict, but just and competent, officer. Unlike Slemmer, he avoided playing the martinet. One of his soldiers described him as "firm and [with] as much decision as any man ought to have, yet . . . agreeable and pleasant to his officers and men."[15] Brigadier General Jacob D. Cox, commander of the division to which Crook's regiment was attached, thought him

> rather diffident and shy, his whole style quiet and reticent. His voice was light, rather than heavy, and he was so laconic of speech that this, with his other characteristics, caused it to be said of him that he had been so long fighting Indians on the frontier that he had acquired some of their habits. His system of discipline was based on these peculiarities. He aimed at a stoical command of himself as the means of commanding others, and avoided noisy bluster of every sort, going perhaps to excess in brevity of speech and in enforcing his orders by the consequences of any disobedience. His subordinates recognized his purpose to be just, and soon learned to have the greatest confidence in him as a military officer.[16]

Mutual confidence between the troops and their leaders was essential for morale during that first difficult winter. The officers and men of the Thirty-Sixth, packed together in unventilated, overcrowded quarters, suffered from typhus, dysentery, and a host of other diseases typical of military camps at the time. Deaths occurred with startling frequency, "[a]s many as three were laid away in a day, some fifty all that winter."[17] Crook kept the men busy, plugging away at training and conditioning despite their illness and homesickness. He marched them daily in the drill house and, ignoring the harsh winter weather, sent them on extended scouts into the surrounding mountains. These patrols soon became more than mere training exercises, for the area around Summersville was infested with pro-Confederate bushwhackers.

Virginia had seceded from the Union in April 1861. A month later the state's mountainous western counties, which in June 1863 would become the state of West Virginia, voted to remain in the Union, a decision that split the region, pitting neighbor against neighbor. The hills and hollows on the west side of the Alleghenies soon became the scene of intense partisan warfare as Unionists and secessionists struggled for political and strategic dominance. Strategically, the region functioned as a vital communications link for both North and South, its turnpikes and two important railroads—the Baltimore and Ohio and the Virginia and Tennessee—were the supply conduits between the eastern and western theaters of the war. Politically, the dissident counties, only tenuously in the Union camp, became a battleground on which both sides hope to win control of the allegiance of all the border states.

In the struggle for western Virginia, the Kanawha Valley was a particularly coveted prize. Situated northeast of the confluence of the Kanawha and New Rivers, the valley was a potential invasion route for the Confederacy into Kentucky and Ohio, for the Union, into southern Virginia. Federal forces moved quickly at the outset of the rebellion to consolidate their control of the area, garrisoning troops at critical points in the countryside. The Thirty-Sixth Ohio's camp at Summersville was one of these control points, situated in the heart of the valley.

The surrounding countryside had a well-deserved reputation as some of the most difficult terrain in North America. Crook described it as "heavily timbered, with thick underbrush, rocky and broken, with dense laurel thickets here and there. The thoroughfares and country roads that traversed this country were like traveling through a box canyon with the forest and underbrush for walls." Even before the war, this forbidding landscape, ideal for ambush and concealment, had been a haven for bandits and highwaymen. After the outbreak of hostilities, many of these outlaws took on a convenient political coloration and, together with authentic secessionists, preyed on Unionist families and Federal troops. Yankee soldiers referred to them as "bushwhackers," and though holding them in low regard, feared their ferocity. In these Unionist counties guerrilla ranks were so diluted with thieves and murderers that they were not considered part of the Confederate army; as such, they were not subject to the rules of war. Consequently, if captured, they could be summarily executed—though in the beginning this typically was not the case.[18]

Crook was confident that he could handle the bushwhacker problem. "Being fresh from Indian country, where I had more or less experience with that kind of warfare," he wrote, "I set to work organizing for the task." His men shared his optimism. One of his captains wrote to his wife, "Colonel Crook is a regular old Indian fighter; I reckon he will 'Bushwhack' some of the Bushwhacking cusses in regular Bushwhacking stile if they venture across his war path."[19]

Crook began his campaign in outlying Nicholas County and its environs. Relying on local Unionist sympathizers, he developed information about guerrilla activities, the location of their camps, and the paths that they followed through the mountains. Using this intelligence, his men laid ambushes into which the bushwhackers were driven like so many deer.

Though partisans were not subject to the rules of war, in the early days of the conflict, the Union military sent captured bushwhackers to Camp Chase in Columbus, Ohio, for internment. Crook followed this practice in the winter of 1861–62. Major Andrews destroyed a bushwhacker camp near Meadow Bluff and captured two prisoners, whom Crook duly shipped off to Camp Chase. But soon afterward they were paroled, "fat, saucy, with good clothes, and returned to their old occupation with renewed vigor." After this pattern repeated itself several times, and disgusted by the brutal acts of some of these outlaws, the colonel turned a blind eye when some of his subordinates adopted a more ruthless approach. "[W]hen an officer returned from a scout he would report that they had caught so-and-so, but in bringing him in he slipped off a log while crossing a stream and broke his neck, or that he was killed by an accidental discharge of one of the men's guns, and many like reports. But they never brought back any more prisoners."[20]

Guerrilla activity extended to neighboring Webster County, a region populated by pro-secessionist folk who, if they were not outright bushwhackers themselves, regularly provided such men with shelter and food. Crook moved decisively to cow the locals into ending this practice. With some hyperbole, he claimed that he was forced to "burn out the entire county to prevent people from harboring [the bushwhackers]." His policies seemed effective, at least in the short term. When his men killed three guerrillas in an ambush in nearby Greenbrier County, a month passed before anyone summoned the courage to fetch the bodies for burial.[21]

But how permanent these results were remained to be seen. Before winter ended, Crook reported that "these people were either destroyed

[or] out of the country." Yet by mid–April 1862 he was complaining to the adjutant general: "[I]t is impossible for any body of troops to march on [bushwhackers] without their being apprised of it, and it is impossible to force them to fight unless they want to, for they carry little or no baggage, and can live on little or nothing. When approached they disintegrate and hide in the mountains until all danger is over, when they again reassemble for fresh depredations."[22] He had put his finger on the essential conundrum of guerrilla warfare.

While they may not have completely eliminated the bushwhacker menace, Crook's tactics, together with the discipline and skills he instilled in his men, paid other dividends. The colonel had set the Thirty-Sixth Ohio on a path that would make it one of the most-effective volunteer units in the war, one that regular officers often compared to their own units in terms of its soldiers' professionalism in the field. But their mettle would soon be put to the test.

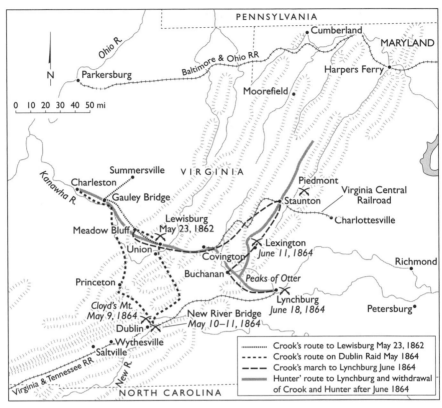

Western Virginia/West Virginia Theater of Operations. This map depicts the routes followed by Crook in his attack on Lewisburg in 1862 and in the Dublin Raid in April–May 1864 and by Hunter in his campaign against Lynchburg in June 1864.

CHAPTER FOURTEEN

Lewisburg

March–May 1862

The Thirty-Sixth Ohio belonged to one of three brigades that made up the Kanawha Division, assigned to the newly formed Mountain Department. The department, which sprawled across the hills of western Virginia and the eastern sections of Tennessee and Kentucky, was under the command of Major General John C. Frémont, whose military and political savvy had failed to match his talents as an explorer. Almost immediately after taking charge, Frémont had concocted an ambitious plan to disrupt the Virginia and Tennessee Railroad, the main communications link between the Confederate armies in Virginia and the West, and then to attack Knoxville, Tennessee.[1]

The Kanawha Division figured prominently in his plan. The division, commanded by General Cox, was headquartered at Gauley Bridge in the Kanawha Valley. Cox had served in the Ohio Senate before the war and received his commission and rank by virtue of his political connections and personal friendship with Governor Dennison. With his erect bearing, full beard, and high forehead, Cox looked every inch the general. And at least in his case, appearances were not deceiving. Though a political appointee, he was one of those amateur soldiers who adapted immediately and well to military life. Intelligent and honest, he would serve with distinction throughout the war, after which he would return to his career in politics. He went on to hold a position in President Grant's cabinet and achieved some fame as a military historian.[2] Cox appeared to like Crook and mentioned him frequently and favorably in his

Jacob Cox, commander of the Kanawha Division at South Mountain and corps commander at Antietam. Cox found Crook to be an effective, though at times difficult, officer. Courtesy of the National Archives, Washington, D.C.

dispatches, eventually promoting him to brigadier general, but the two officers had an uneasy professional relationship and crossed verbal swords on more than one occasion.

Frémont's plan required Cox to march his division south, strike the Virginia and Tennessee, and then join the rest of the army for an attack on Knoxville. So that he could carry out this operation and at the same time have sufficient manpower to leave behind a garrison to guard against a counterattack in the valley, Cox reorganized his division, adding a provisional brigade to the two already under his command. The new brigade was composed of the Thirty-Sixth, Forty-Fourth, and part of the Forty-Seventh Ohio Infantry Regiments, supported by one battery of howitzers and field pieces and the First Battalion, Second (West) Virginia Cavalry—altogether, about 2,000 men. Having noted Colonel Crook's skills in training and leading the Thirty-Sixth, Cox gave him command of the new brigade.[3]

Crook energetically threw himself into the new job. Prior to commencing the campaign, he sent scouts out along the proposed route of march, which would pass through the town of Lewisburg. They learned that the town was occupied by a Rebel force that threatened to burn all the forage in the vicinity, thus depriving the Federals of food for their horses and mules in their move south.[1] The scouts further reported that Lewisburg, which straddled a vital crossroads, was a hotbed of secessionist sentiment and served as a staging and support area for bushwhackers in Greenbrier and surrounding counties.[5]

Crook suggested to Cox that he attack and occupy Lewisburg as part of the division's move against the railroad. By doing so he would preserve forage for his division, wipe out a haven for bushwhackers, and gain control of the strategic crossroads. Cox liked the idea and incorporated it into his campaign strategy. Leaving several West Virginia residents to garrison the valley, he would take two brigades south to a temporarily fortified advance position on Flat Top Mountain west of Lewisburg. Meanwhile, Crook would march on Lewisburg with his brigade by a different route. Using the town as the division's forward observation post, Crook could then send out patrols into the surrounding countryside to ascertain the number and location of the enemy. With this information in hand, Cox could reunite the three brigades, march south, destroy the railway, and then join Frémont's troops for the thrust against Knoxville.[6]

At the beginning of May, Cox set his plan in motion, moving south to Flat Top Mountain. Crook's force, delayed by orders to hunt down a band of guerrillas north in Webster County, did not leave Gauley Bridge until two weeks later on May 16.[7] While camped at Flat Top Mountain, Cox received word from Frémont that Maj. Gen. Thomas J. "Stonewall" Jackson's Confederate army was on the march in the Shenandoah Valley to the east. Frémont called off the planned attack on Knoxville in order to meet this new threat, leaving Cox to fend for himself. Though Knoxville was no longer the objective, Cox believed that the Kanawha Division could still make a real contribution by cutting the Virginia and Tennessee and occupying Lewisburg, so he did not cancel his operation.

Lewisburg's location gave it importance disproportionate to its size. Athwart the east–west Kanawha Turnpike, which paralleled the James River, the town nestled squarely in the narrow eastern entrance to the Kanawha Valley like a cork in a bottle. A relatively small occupying force could prevent an entire army from entering the valley. A north–south road connecting Meadow Bluffs, a Federal supply depot, with Union, a village to the south, crossed the pike at Lewisburg and served as the town's main street. Lined with stores and residences, the route ran between two hills, on whose steep slopes residents had built a number of houses, many of them surrounded by board fencing.

Crook occupied the town without a fight since the Confederates had fled before his arrival. Not satisfied with simply capturing Lewisburg, he decided to mount an impromptu raid into enemy territory. Leaving a small force to garrison the town, the colonel led the bulk of his men south to Jackson's River on the Virginia Central line. Though intended primarily as a reconnaissance in force, he planned to tear up the rails if the opportunity presented itself, which it apparently did.

His men had just destroyed the railroad bridge at the depot when scouts reported that a brigade of 3,000 Confederates under Brigadier General Henry Heth, a fellow West Pointer, had been seen heading toward Lewisburg.[8] Heth had learned from the town's secessionist sympathizers that Crook had divided his forces, leaving behind only a small garrison. The general hoped to reoccupy the town before the Federals could reunite and then mount an invasion of the Kanawha Valley.

Pushing his troops hard, Crook arrived in Lewisburg before Heth. Though outnumbered by more than two to one—he had only about 1,200 effectives and no heavy artillery—and aware that Cox was too far away to reinforce him before Heth attacked, the colonel nevertheless, planned to make a fight of it. Ordering his men to dig in on the western slope overlooking the main street, he awaited the Confederates' arrival.

At dawn on Friday, May 23, Crook awoke to the distant crackle of musketry, announcing that Heth's troops had crossed the Greenbrier River south of town and driven in the Union pickets. As the Confederates moved into Lewisburg, the infantry formed a battle line along the crest of the hill to the east, reinforced with an eclectic battery of artillery pieces that included an ancient Revolutionary War 12-pounder said to have been captured from the British army at Yorktown.[9] From this position the Rebels rained shells on the Union troops on the opposite slope, their troops using the covering fire to move down the hillside into town.

To check the Rebel advance until his men could form to meet the attack, Crook led a small force through the back streets and confronted Heth's troops as they descended the hill. By keeping up a heavy fire while slowly withdrawing into town, the Federals managed to disrupt the enemy line and stall their progress. Seeing the Rebels milling about in momentary confusion, Crook ordered a spoiling charge. Sending the Forty-Fourth Ohio against Heth's left and leading his own Thirty-Sixth against the right, he moved his men up the slope, driving the Rebels before them and capturing four of the enemy's cannon, including the Revolutionary War relic, as they climbed.[10]

The going was rough, though. The Union troops had to make their way around a number of houses scattered over the hillside and in some cases clamor over board fences, behind some of which Confederate soldiers formed pockets of resistance. At times the opposing forces poured fire into each other from as close as fifty yards. The volleys of musket balls clattering against the fence boards created such a compelling illusion of hail that Crook instinctively cocked his head to one side to prevent the icy pellets from running down his neck. The ferocity of the Union attack unnerved the Rebels, many of whom were raw recruits, and less than an hour after entering town, they broke, pouring in a confused retreat over the crest of the hill, across the Greenbrier Bridge, and south toward the town of Union, with Crook's Second (West) Virginia Cavalry riding hard on their heels.[11]

During the uphill assault, Crook had felt a sudden, sharp pain in his foot; he later discovered to be a wound from a spent musket ball. Refusing to allow it to put him out of action, he continued to walk on it, his boot filling with blood. Over the next several days, the wound became severely inflamed, and he supposed the foot would have be amputated.[12] But once again the resilience of his body was such that Crook fought off the infection and recovered completely without a day of convalescence. Incredibly, considering the many engagements in which he would participate during the war, this would be his only wound in four years of fighting.

In his after-action report, Heth expressed uncertainty as to the cause of the embarrassing panic that had overtaken his men when confronted by a force numbering half their size. Lieutenant Colonel Clark, who commanded the Thirty-Sixth Ohio during the fighting, had no such doubts. "The steadiness, firmness, and determination and vigor with which the line moved on," he wrote, "together with the rapidity and accuracy of our fire, seemed to inspire the enemy—though twice our number or more—with terror." Crook's report also gives full credit to his men: "It is unnecessary to eulogize the men whom I have the honor to command. Their steady, firm advances in the face of the fire which met them, and the result will speak for itself. I need only say that not an officer or private in my command failed in doing his whole duty as a soldier." Or as he succinctly put it in his autobiography, "old veterans could not have done better." His tough training regimen had paid off.[13]

Crook's men were equally proud of their work, some gracefully acknowledging their debt to their commander's leadership. John Palmer of Company G, Thirty-Sixth Ohio, wrote to his sister, "Col. Crook has a good deal of confidence in his boys, & they have full as much in him, they would follow him to the Devil & fight him after they got there."[14]

The victory, while minor in the overall scheme of things, was complete. Crook reported thirty-eight Confederate dead and the capture of four artillery pieces, 300 stand of arms, and over 150 prisoners, while losing eleven soldiers killed and fifty-four wounded.[15]

Only one incident marred the colonel's pleasure in his triumph. After the fighting was over, as his wounded men made their way through the streets of the town, they received fire from several houses, which killed one of the wounded Federals. Outraged, Crook reported, "[t]he houses which can be fully identified as having been fired from will be burned, and if I can capture any of the parties engaged they will be hung in the main street as an example to all such assassins." Though General Cox approved his subordinate's plan, Crook paused when he learned that the fatal shot had been fired from a house belonging to an elderly widow. The assailant, a Confederate soldier and relative of the widow, had already made his escape, so there was no one to hang. But the colonel determinedly kept his word and ordered the house burned to the ground.[16]

Though successful in driving off Heth's brigade, Crook had too few men to hold Lewisburg in the event of another attack. That evening, despite considerable pain from his injured foot, he led his troops northward to a more defensible position at Meadow Bluffs. Some weeks later, by then recovered from his wound, Crook received the gratifying news that he had been awarded the rank of brevet major in the regular army in recognition of his "gallant and meritorious services at the battle of Lewisburg, Virginia."[17]

On June 21, flush with his victory and brevet promotion, Crook led his brigade in an attack against Heth's force at Salt Sulphur Spring "for the purpose of . . . driving him out of the country."[18] In his eagerness to close with the enemy, and with supreme confidence in his ability to triumph, the colonel failed to consult with Cox before going ahead with his plan. The attack came to nothing when Heth fell back across a nearby mountain and out of reach.

Cox was infuriated. The general had been husbanding supplies for an attack on the Virginia and Tennessee Railroad, but the colonel's precipitous action had frittered away some of these scarce resources, setting back the general's timetable. Though the same age as Crook, Cox managed a fatherly tone that took some of the sting out of his reprimand. "I am sincerely desirous to see you have the opportunity to win all the glory you can wish, and especially to have you win the promotion which will make your present command a permanent one. I believe this can be most certainly done by giving your energetic aid in accomplishing the result desired by the department commander [Frémont] . . . rather than by independent and unconnected movements."[19]

Crook apologized for his failure to inform Cox of his plan. But he spoiled the gesture by querulously adding that the general's dispatch had arrived in an unsealed envelope, jeopardizing the privacy of the communication. Pompously, he demanded an investigation of how this could have come to pass.[20] But the bureaucratic tempest that might have ensued was swept aside by the tide of events.

CHAPTER FIFTEEN

The Second Battle of Bull Run

August 1862

By the spring of 1862, the fighting in the mountains of western Virginia had become a sideshow. Having secured the region for the Union by victories in 1861, the War Department now focused on more strategic arenas, in particular central and eastern Virginia and the capture of Richmond. In June Lincoln consolidated Frémont's forces from the Mountain Department with the armies of Major Generals Nathanial Banks and Franz Sigel and parts of Major General George B. McClellan's Army of the Potomac, all under the command of Major General John Pope. Pope gathered his forces, which he named the Army of Virginia, for an attack on Richmond overland from the north, which he believed would end the war. As part of his plan, Pope asked the War Department to have General Cox and a major part of his division join him at Warrenton, about sixty miles west of Washington.

In preparation for the coming campaign, Cox reorganized the Kanawha Division once more into two brigades under his senior colonels, Eliakim Scammon and Augustus Moor. As Crook's brigade was thereby eliminated, he returned to command of the Thirty-Sixth Ohio, now part of Moor's Second Brigade. If the ambitious young colonel was disappointed at this reduction in authority, he masked it well. In his memoir Crook voiced only satisfaction at returning to the regiment that he considered "the pride of my heart." He declared, "I knew every man in it, and had spent so much hard work on it that I regarded it as one of my own family."[1]

Cox's brigades did not move out until August, by which time General Robert E. Lee had blocked Pope's southward advance by placing much of his army between the Union forces at Manassas, site of the North's terrible defeat the previous year, and Richmond. The Kanawha troops were quickly dispatched to reinforce Pope.

By marching the first ninety miles in three days and then completing the move by river and rail, the division reached Washington in only ten days. From there, the men were to travel by rail to join Pope at the front.[2] But for most of Cox's men, their efforts were for naught. Stonewall Jackson's "foot cavalry" detoured around the Pope's forces, marching over fifty miles in thirty-four hours, and on August 27 interposed themselves between the Union army and Washington. They destroyed Pope's supply depot at Manassas Junction, then tore up the tracks of the Alexandria and Orange Railroad, closing that conduit of supplies and troop traffic from the capital. Only two of Cox's regiments, the Thirty-Sixth and the Thirtieth Ohio, managed to reach Pope before the rails were destroyed and were thus the only units of the Kanawha Division to participate in the Second Battle of Bull Run.

Arriving at Pope's headquarters with the two orphaned regiments, Crook feared that they would be attached to a brigade that would have no interest in their welfare and needlessly expose them to danger To avoid this possibility, he contrived to have them detailed as guards to General Pope's staff.[3] Thus from the vantage point of army headquarters on a knoll to the rear of the Union lines, Crook would have an unparalleled overview of the unfolding battle and the mistakes that cost the Union victory.

He was able to observe how Pope, an arrogant and boastful man who thought he had trapped Jackson and could destroy him at his leisure, was first outmaneuvered by the Confederates and then seduced into sacrificing his men in useless charges against the well-prepared positions held by Jackson's men and Major General James Longstreet's artillery. He also witnessed the savage infighting among the top commanders of the Union army, observing how McClellan, more concerned with demonstrating his fellow general's shortcomings than with defeating the enemy, ignored Pope's frantic pleas for reinforcements from Army of the Potomac, though his troops were only a few hours to the east. The battle lasted for three days; on the last day Crook learned that General Schenck, his friend and mentor, had been severely wounded, losing an arm to the surgeon's knife.

By late afternoon of the thirtieth, overwhelmed by a massive Confederate counteroffensive, Pope sounded the retreat and fell back toward Washington. At first orderly, the withdrawal soon disintegrated into a frightened rout. Now Crook's regiment was called into action, though not in a way he would have anticipated or even wished.

After leading his young soldiers in successful battles against Rebels in the Kanawha Valley, the combative colonel was shocked by the utter demoralization of Pope's once-proud army. As the setting sun reddened the sky over the chaotic battlefield, Crook received orders to interpose his men between the fleeing troops and the army's rear in an attempt to stem the panicky stampede. In disbelief and with ill-disguised contempt, he later wrote: "we must have caught ten or fifteen thousand men without organizations trying to get to the rear. There were officers who had thrown away their shoulder straps and swords, so as to avoid detection. It was my first introduction to a demoralized army." The rout continued in a steady rain, which began shortly after sundown and continued throughout the night, on roads of red clay that quickly turned into slippery muck. Frightened and exhausted men discarded their rifles, packs, and anything else that impeded their flight and fought with wagons, artillery caissons, and ambulances filled with the maimed bodies of their comrades for access to the roads leading to Washington and safety.[4]

By dawn, Crook found himself looking at a sodden campsite filled with Union stragglers "squirming around amongst each other like so many eels," while nearby, Confederate prisoners huddled in the thick, red mud, picking the lice from the seams of their ragged uniforms. Overall, Crook sarcastically reflected, "this is one of the times when one is so glad he is a soldier."[5]

CHAPTER SIXTEEN

South Mountain and Antietam

September–October 1862

By September 12, less than two weeks after Pope's disastrous defeat, Crook had recovered his good spirits and was once again on the march, leading his regiment in the vanguard of the Army of the Potomac as it closed in on Lee's forces at the market town of Frederick, Maryland.

After the latest debacle at Bull Run, a reluctant Lincoln had restored George McClellan to command of the principal Union army. McClellan, incapable of fighting an aggressive campaign but a genius at preparing for one, was much beloved by his men, and his appointment had swiftly rekindled their ardor. On September 6 the general led them northward across the Potomac River.

Lee had invaded Maryland to feed and clothe his ragged and malnourished troops on the rich plunder of the state's countryside, as yet untouched by war. More important, he hoped to draw the Union army into a climatic battle and provide the Confederacy with the victory it needed to secure foreign recognition.[1] On September 4 Lee had marched his forces unopposed into Frederick.

In the general reorganization following McClellan's reappointment, Cox's Kanawha Division, including Crook's Thirty-Sixth Ohio, was incorporated into the army's IX Corps under Major General Jesse Reno. On September 11, as the IX Corps closed in on Frederick, Reno had observed the Kanawha men striding past in well-drilled formation. General Cox, standing close to his commander, noted with pride that "the easy swinging step, the graceful poise of the musket on the shoulder, as if it were a toy and not a burden, and the compactness of the columns were all noticed and praised with a heartiness which was very grateful to my ears." Reno was so impressed that he ordered the division to march in the lead, figuring that their mile-eating stride would set a fitting pace for the rest of the army as it pushed forward.[2]

The division's two infantry brigades alternated in the forward position. On September 12, approaching the town, Colonel Moor's Second Brigade, which included Crook's regiment, marched in the forefront in support of Brigadier General Alfred Pleasonton's cavalry. The men were in a confident mood, having successfully engaged Brigadier General Wade Hampton's cavalry brigade, Lee's rear guard, at the Monocacy bridge. These western troops had missed out on the fighting on the Peninsula and at Bull Run and now were eager to prove their worth to the predominantly eastern soldiers of the Army of the Potomac.

Bolder residents of Frederick, drawn to their upper-story windows by the boom of cannon fire and the flurry of activity below, could make out Union cavalry and long lines of blue-clad infantry rapidly approaching through thick clouds of lime dust billowing up from the road east of town. As the Federals neared the town's outskirts, ragged Rebel troops, who had occupied Frederick for the past week, could be seen hurriedly assembling in columns and then moving swiftly westward toward Catoctin Mountain. The hour of liberation appeared close at hand.

To his front Crook could see Moor, a heavyset, gray-haired German, nudging his fine black mount forward. The senior colonel mingled sociably with the western Virginia and Illinois cavalrymen he had been assigned to support, creating the impression that he was far more interested in playing the role of horse soldier than infantry colonel. The illusion was fostered by Moor's annoying habit of inserting himself into the cavalrymen's chain of command.[3]

The Rebel rear guard retreated before the superior Union force, leaving only a small contingent at the west end of town to hold back any pursuers, their position concealed from view by a bend in the road. Impatient at the slow pace set by the cavalry, Moor surged forward, eager to be the first to enter the town. General Cox attempted to check his progress until scouts could confirm that the way was clear of enemy forces. But, perhaps goaded by one of General Reno's staff officers or simply imprudent, Moor ignored his commander.[4] To the amazement of Cox and his officers, the German colonel impetuously ordered the men beside him, two cavalry companies and a horse-drawn artillery piece, to charge into town.

Taking the lead, Moor dashed down Patrick Street, waving his saber over his head and shouting, "Come on boys, come on. Let's give 'em hell!" But Hampton's Rebels were waiting for him, with the advantage of complete surprise and numbers. The Yankees had no alternative. Seeing the Confederates to their front, they wheeled their mounts in an attempt to escape. While Moor's judgment certainly was questionable, nobody could fault his courage. When a South Carolinian slashed at him with his sword, the older man fended off the strike and lunged at his assailant with his own blade but missed. The Confederate then grabbed the colonel by the collar and yanked him off his horse, sending him crashing into the street as Federal horsemen streamed past in full retreat.[5]

Moor's reckless charge cost the division five men killed, about fifteen wounded, and five captured, including the colonel, thus depriving his brigade of its commander. Cox immediately appointed Crook, already recommended for a brigadier's star due to his leadership at Lewisburg, to replace Moor. For Crook the timing was auspicious. He was about to lead his new command through one of the most important and bloodiest campaigns of the war.

The next day, as Crook's brigade led the army west in pursuit of the Confederates, McClellan received a document that confirmed his messianic belief that he alone was destined by God to save the Union. Casually wrapped around three cigars, a paper, henceforth known to history as the "Lost Order," was discovered by a Union soldier at a former Rebel campsite. It turned out to be nothing less than a general order from Lee to his generals laying out the operational plans for his entire Maryland Campaign, including the location and disposition of all of his troops.

McClellan now knew that Lee planned to cross South Mountain, west of Frederick and, once on the other side, divide his army into smaller units for a short period to forage for much-needed supplies. The Confederates would then reunite and engage McClellan's army in what Lee envisioned as a climatic battle. The site he would select, as events unfolded, was the rolling hill country that lay between the town of Sharpsburg, where five strategically important roads came together, and a rambling stream known as Antietam Creek.

The order stipulated that Stonewall Jackson and Major General Lafayette McLaws were to march to Harpers Ferry to capture arms and ammunition stored at the Federal arsenal there. Meanwhile, Lee and Longstreet would move north to Hagerstown, thirteen miles from Boonsboro on the National Road, positioning the majority of Lee's forces for an invasion of Pennsylvania.[6] Major General D. H. Hill would remain at Boonsboro at the foot of the western slope of South Mountain to hold McClellan in the unlikely event he crossed the mountain before the Confederate forces could reunite.

Lee had devised his plan confident that McClellan's cautious nature would give the Confederates ample time to reunite before the Federals attacked. Discovery of the Lost Order allowed McClellan to overcome his natural reluctance to risk his troops in combat and, momentarily, his conviction that Lee had an overwhelming numerical advantage. It also gave him a unique opportunity to attack the divided segments of the Army of Northern Virginia separately.

While McClellan planned his offensive, Crook's brigade followed the National Pike toward Catoctin Mountain, its bulk shimmering in the humid haze, filling the horizon. Beyond Catoctin, across a stunningly beautiful six-mile-wide valley, lay South Mountain. Running north to south across the path of the Union army and composed of steep, wooded ridges, South Mountain could only be crossed at three passes: from north to south, Turner's Gap, Fox's Gap, and Crampton's Gap. Beyond South Mountain lay Sharpsville, nestled in another scenic vale ironically named Pleasant Valley.

By the evening of the thirteenth, Pleasonton's cavalry had pushed the Confederate rear guard slowly up one side of Catoctin Mountain and down the other. The army's advance, Cox's Kanawha Division still in the lead, followed close on their heels and proceeded to Middletown, midway between Catoctin Mountain and South Mountain, where it bivouacked for the night.

The next morning the cavalry had orders to lead the way through Turner's Gap. The Lost Order said nothing about units defending the passes on the mountain itself. Consequently, McClellan assumed the crossing would meet little resistance. For once Little Mac had underestimated (rather than overestimated) his enemy, though it did not seem so at first. Pleasonton had reconnoitered Turner's Gap the previous afternoon and had found it lightly defended. That evening he sought out Cox in his tent to arrange for infantry support for the next day. As he did not anticipate much resistance at the gap, he requested only one brigade.

Since Crook was an old acquaintance, Pleasonton requested that the Second Brigade be assigned the task despite the fact that under division protocol, Scammon's First Brigade was scheduled to take the lead. He also specified that to get an early start, the infantry should be prepared to move out at 6 A.M. Cox saw no problem in giving the cavalry Crook's brigade and sought out Scammon to inform him of the plan.[7]

Colonel Scammon, though a brave and competent soldier, had a prickly nature and an excessive fondness for military rules and protocol. Not surprisingly, he flatly refused to accept second place to Crook's brigade. As the colonel was within his rights, Cox rescinded his original order. Crook appeared unfazed by the reversal of his orders, but Pleasonton, no less a martinet than Scammon, attempted to pull rank to get his way. Cox, his patience exhausted, refused to be bullied and pointedly denied Pleasonton's request: Scammon was given the lead, with Crook's brigade marching in the second position. Putting a good face on it, Cox told Pleasonton that he hoped placing Scammon in the vanguard would put his infantrymen "on their mettle" the next day.[8]

At daybreak the next morning, while seeing off Scammon's brigade on the National Road, Cox was startled to come upon Colonel Moor standing by the side of the road. Paroled by Hampton, Moor had been making his way on foot toward Union lines. When he heard that Scammon's men were en route to Turner's Gap, the colonel involuntarily blurted out, "My God! Be careful!" Then, realizing that he had been about to violate the terms of his parole by revealing the enemy's movements, he hurriedly moved on.[9]

As it happened, late the night before, Lee had learned from a secessionist sympathizer of McClellan's discovery of the Lost Order. The Virginian correctly surmised that its contents would galvanize the normally overcautious Union general into action, but he assumed that McClellan would march to attack McLaws and Jackson in order to relieve Harpers Ferry.[10] To block this move, Lee had ordered D. H. Hill to hold the passes across South Mountain at all costs. He also had sent Longstreet back from Hagerstown to reinforce Hill. Moor had realized the danger at Turner's Gap after seeing Hill's troops on the march up the west side of the mountain.

Cox immediately grasped the import of Moor's impulsive warning. Summoning Crook, whose brigade had remained in camp in reserve, he ordered him to move out in close support of Scammon's troops. At the same time, the general warned Pleasonton that he might expect the gaps to be warmly defended. Heeding Cox's warning, Pleasonton decided that rather than make a frontal assault on the main defenses at Turner's Gap, he would have Scammon's and Crook's brigades cross South Mountain on the Old Sharpsburg Road, a country lane that passed through Fox's Gap about a half mile south of Turner's, and strike Hill on his flank.[11]

Viewed across the valley in the clear, early morning light, South Mountain must have looked depressingly familiar to Crook and his men. The mountainside rose abruptly from the valley floor, and like the hills back home, its slopes were broken by ravines and knolls thickly covered with timber and the intertwining branches of mountain laurel. On the summit, where the slope leveled off, they could see patches of open land, farmsteads fenced with rails or stone connected by narrow dirt lanes that criss-crossed the crest.

Passing through rolling countryside and then up the steeply ascending slopes, Crook marched his men about a half hour behind Scammon. Turning off the National Road onto the Old Sharpsburg Road, a winding and increasingly steep incline, the men stopped frequently to catch their breath.[12]

Scammon made contact with the enemy about half a mile from Fox's Gap, forming his troops in a line along a country road in timber that provided some cover from enemy guns. The Rebels were dug in behind a stone wall at the far end of an open field backed by a thick wood, a brigade of one thousand North Carolina troops. These men had never seen combat, but their commander, Brigadier General Samuel Garland, was a seasoned veteran of the Peninsula Campaign. Though the Confederates would be outnumbered by three to one once Crook's brigade came up, they clearly had the advantage of position, firing from good cover on the Union troops, who would have to attack uphill and across the open field to get at them.

The fighting that followed was intense and bloody, fought at close quarters among the stubble of farm fields and in dense laurel thickets and stands of oak and elm. By the time Crook arrived on the field, Scammon had already closed with the Confederates, leading the Twelfth Ohio in a bayonet charge against the Rebel center. The green North Carolinians gave way in a panic, the men fleeing down the opposite slope just as Crook's brigade arrived. Under Cox's direction, the new brigade commander quickly threw his troops into the fight, supporting Scammon's attack by hitting both flanks of Garland's line, personally leading a charge by the Thirty-Sixth. One Ohio officer, who may or may not have witnessed the charge, offered a romantic image of the young colonel, "his hat held aloft in one hand, and his sword in the other," shouting, "To the command, 'Thirty-sixth, charge!'"[13] For a time the pressed Confederates on the flanks were able to rally, hold the ridgeline, and even counterattack, despite the loss of their line's center and their brigade commander, killed in the fighting. But the two Yankee brigades fought ferociously, firing volleys from their exposed positions into an enemy often less than thirty yards to their front, then closing with them and using bayonets and clubbed muskets to drive the Rebels off the ridge.

For the remainder of the day, the two Union brigades held the crest against repeated counterattacks by the Confederates, who were reenergized by the arrival of Longstreet's troops in the early afternoon. Though Crook's brigade spent much of the afternoon in reserve, two of his regiments, the Twenty-Eighth and his beloved Thirty-Sixth, participated in charges against the enemy flanks late in the day.

Shortly before dark, IX Corps commander Jesse Reno was killed while inspecting the lines not far from where Garland had been killed that morning. Passing Brigadier General Samuel Sturgis as his men carried him off the field, Reno calmly called to his old friend, "Hallo, Sam, I am dead!" And moments later, he was.[14] His death elevated General Cox to command of the IX Corps. Colonel Scammon, senior to Crook, took over the Kanawha Division.

Though the fighting at South Mountain continued with undiminished ferocity until after dark, the Rebels were too few and too exhausted to withstand the superior Union forces any longer, and McClellan's army broke through all three passes. By morning, South Mountain was in Northern hands.

While Crook's brigade had suffered relatively light losses in the action, seventeen killed and sixty-four wounded, he felt them keenly, particularly the fallen from the Thirty-Sixth. Years later, recalling his closeness to these Ohioans, he wrote: "I cannot help but shedding tears over some of my regiment who were killed. . . . I had seen so much of them for the last year, knew them all and felt as though they were my own family." Mixed with these pangs of loss were feelings of pride, both in the performance of his men under fire and in the discharge of his own responsibilities. He had performed creditably as brigade commander, displaying courage and coolness under fire. Both he and Scammon earned official mention from Cox for their gallantry and efficiency in action. After the fighting, Crook had learned of an odd coincidence: his mother, Elizabeth, had been born and raised on a farm, or at least one nearby, on which the battle had been fought.[15]

D. H. Hill's stand at South Mountain bought precious time for Lee to consolidate his scattered forces in the rolling fields around Sharpsburg. But the troops of Jackson and McLaws, a third of the Confederate army, were still en route from Harpers Ferry. Typically, McClellan failed to exploit his advantage. Instead of immediately attacking, he wasted two precious days making unnecessarily elaborate preparations to fight a sup-posedly superior force that, in actuality, he then outnumbered by over three to one.

During these two days, the Union commander made a move that greatly complicated the lines of authority in Burnside's wing and de-moralized its commander. McClellan chose this moment to detach Ma-jor General Joseph "Fighting Joe" Hooker's I Corps from Burnside's command and reassign it to the right wing of the army. This redeploy-ment left Burnside with only the IX Corps, in effect demoting him from wing to corps commander. Piqued by McClellan's apparent lack of confidence in him, he insisted on retaining the now-empty title of wing commander, assigning Cox the responsibilities of corps command. Cox vigorously, but without success, resisted the appointment since it put him in the ambiguous position of acting as corps commander in name only, for all orders affecting the IX still would be passed through Burnside.[16]

Thus the corps would go into action at Antietam with both gener-als in a resentful mood and neither fully devoted to command of the unit. This weakness manifested itself early on. Neither Cox nor Burnside assumed responsibility for thoroughly reconnoitering the terrain over which the IX Corps was to attack. Nor did either develop a battle plan that intelligently accounted for the enemy's position and strength. These failures would have a substantial effect on the outcome of the fighting, and more specifically, on Crook's role in the upcoming engagement.

McClellan deployed his army in the shape of an inverted mile-long fishhook. The barbed point (Hooker's I Corps) lay to the north of Sharpsburg, while Burnside's 12,000-man IX Corps, the southern shank

Rohrbach (Burnside's) Bridge at Antietam as it appeared during the battle. Crook attempted and failed to take the bridge, which was taken by troops from Samuel Sturgis's division later in the day. Courtesy of the National Archives.

of the hook, was anchored on the east bank of Antietam Creek opposite the picturesque Rohrbach Bridge. Named after a local farmer but soon to become famous as Burnside's Bridge, the span was a stout stone structure with three arches that supported a roadway 125 feet long and 12 feet wide. Chest-high parapets lined either side of the bridge, running its entire length and curving out for a short distance into the roadway beyond. Three-quarters of a mile west of the creek lay Sharpsburg, defended by about 2,500 Confederate troops. In front of the town, the land sloped down to the creek in a series of undulating folds, which concealed the strength and disposition of Lee's army.[17]

The creek itself bisected a narrow valley, with bluffs on the western side that loomed over the stream where Rohrbach Bridge crossed it. The heavily wooded bluffs were defended by two Georgia regiments commanded by Colonel Henry Benning, known to his troops as "Old Rock" because of his steadiness in combat. The Georgians had entrenched themselves on the steep slopes directly opposite the bridge and for a short distance on either side of it. They had cut down trees to form breastworks and placed marksmen in an old hillside quarry that had been the source of the stones used to build the bridge. Benning also assigned troops to man barricades of fence rails and fallen trees along the bank to cover the road's approach to the bridge on the opposite side.[18]

To the Union generals, the bridge appeared to be their sector's only means of crossing the Antietam, which at that point was wide and swift flowing, running about four feet deep. Any attempt to ford it at this point would be cumbersome and costly. But the creek actually had a number of fords both up and downstream of the bridge. McClellan's staff identified one shallow spot, but they had discounted it because, though the water was low at that point, the banks were too steep to afford ready access. For his part, Burnside made no effort to locate other crossing points, relying instead on these staff reports.[19]

Having failed to properly reconnoiter the terrain, Burnside made a frontal assault across the narrow bridge the centerpiece of his battle plan. The attack required Union troops to approach the span by means of a dirt road exposed to heavy flanking fire from the Georgians on the opposite bank. Then once on the narrow span, they would have to cross it quickly in the face of concentrated enemy fire.[20] To distract the Rebels in their front, the general planned to have one division cross downstream from the bridge and strike the defenders on their flank while his main force rushed the bridge. Though this diversion depended upon finding a suitable crossing for the troops somewhere to the south, Burnside's scouts would not locate such a point until the morning of the attack.

Crook's brigade was among the troops selected to make the assault on the bridge. Fresh from their victory at South Mountain, the men arrived on the field at 3 P.M. on the fifteenth and were ordered into camp in a cornfield screened from the creek by a rise. Unfortunately, the site was exposed to harassing fire from Confederate artillery on the heights around Sharpsburg.[21]

The next day, in anticipation of an immediate assault, the Ohioans were ordered forward to positions closer to the creek, bivouacking with the rest of the division in an orchard upstream from the bridge behind a ridge that blocked their view of the bridge and creek. To their left was the Union center, almost directly opposite the bridge, held by troops under General Sturgis and Brigadier General Orlando Willcox, supported by a battery of Parrott guns. Downstream from the bridge, Burnside had placed Brigadier General Isaac Rodman's division, which was to carry out the diversionary attack, providing it could find a suitable place to ford the stream.

But again McClellan delayed the army's assault, leaving his troops to nervously contemplate the coming battle, which judging from the numbers of troops on the field, would be the worst they had yet experienced. The men passed the time writing letters to their loved ones and grimly scribbling their names and units on small pieces of paper that they pinned to their coats so burial details could identify them should they be killed.[22]

While awaiting orders in the orchard, Crook's brigade was exposed to desultory shelling from a Confederate battery that lobbed case shot filled with musket balls over the ridge. Looking up, the men could see the burning fuses corkscrewing through the sky before the rounds exploded, sending cascades of hot lead and iron raining down upon them. This artillery fire produced few casualties, but it fueled the men's mounting anxiety about the coming battle. To add to their discomfort, they went to bed hungry since the wagons carrying their food supplies had not yet caught up to the army.[23]

Dawn on Wednesday, the 17th of September, was overcast. A light ground fog covered the neat fields around Sharpsburg. The rolling crackle of musketry and the deeper rumble of artillery could be heard to their north, where Hooker's I Corps and Jackson's Confederates were engaged in a vicious struggle. But huddled in the orchard behind the Rohrbach Bridge, Crook's men knew nothing of the slaughter that the gunfire signified. The Georgians to their front remained quiet enough for the colonel to attend to the hunger of his soldiers. In the cellar of a nearby abandoned farmhouse, one of his officers located a batch of unbaked bread "with plenty of nice butter and milk." The Ohioans baked the bread and dipped it in their coffee or in bacon grease, making a fine breakfast—a meal that for some would be their last.[24]

After breakfast, Cox and Burnside climbed a knoll to the north of the bridge, which afforded them an unnervingly clear view of the fighting to the north. "We looked, as it were, down between the opposing lines as if they had been the sides of a street," Cox later recalled, "and as the fire opened, we saw wounded men carried to the rear and stragglers making off. Our lines halted and we were tortured with anxiety as we speculated whether our men would charge or retreat."[25]

McClellan's plan called for the IX Corps to attack Lee's right, but he never made it entirely clear whether he intended this to be a diversion to pin down Confederate forces or a full-scale assault. By the time the commander got around to issuing orders to Burnside, events had overtaken him. The battle had developed on the Union right, and it was now clear that the IX Corps's movement would only serve to prevent Lee from shifting additional troops to reinforce Jackson.[26]

By 10 A.M., when Burnside finally received his instructions, Lee already had sent to his left as many troops as he could spare. Nevertheless, McClellan remained convinced that the Confederate right held vast reserves poised to strike the Union center. So he ordered Burnside to cross the creek and push forward to Sharpsburg.[27] Burnside responded by directing Cox to assault the bridge and naming Crook's brigade to lead the attack in recognition of its good work at South Mountain. Colonel Henry Kingsbury's Eleventh Connecticut was assigned to provide cover for the assault. Kingsbury was a personal friend of Burnside and, by a bizarre coincidence, the brother-in-law of Brigadier General David R. "Neighbor" Jones, commander of the Georgians defending the bridge.[28]

Word of the impending attack rolled through the Union lines like a wave, and the troops stiffened in preparation for the fight to come. A Captain Christ of Cox's staff delivered the orders to Crook, whose recollection of the ensuing dialogue captures the confusion of the moment. Christ announced: "'The General wishes you to take the bridge.' I asked, him what bridge. He said he didn't know. I asked him where the stream was, but he didn't know. I made some remarks not complimentary to such a way of doing business, but he went off, not caring a cent." As a result of this exchange, he claimed, "I had to get a good many men killed in acquiring the information which should have been supplied me from division headquarters."[29]

In light of subsequent events, it is understandable that Crook might have wished posterity to think that he had been totally in the dark with respect to the location of the creek and the bridge. But under the circumstances, that is difficult to believe. The Kanawha Division had been in place within a mile of Antietam Creek and the Rohrbach Bridge for two days. McClellan had visited the position the day before, and members of his staff had searched, albeit half-heartedly, up and down the creek for a ford. Given all this activity, it strains credulity to suppose that a brigade commander of Crook's experience would have been completely ignorant of such rudimentary facts as the location of the bridge and creek to his front. If he had been, one would suppose that he would have taken steps to remedy the situation. There is clear evidence that he did just that.

At 7 A.M., three hours before his exchange with Captain Christ, Crook had sent two companies from the Eleventh Ohio forward toward the creek to reconnoiter the enemy's position and drive off any Confederate pickets who might be found too close to Union lines.[30] These men moved forward to the Antietam, where they remained within a grove of trees overlooking the creek, sniping at enemy troops on the opposite side. It appears highly unlikely that they would have failed to report their location to their commander—whether he chose to heed them or not is another matter.

Local geography was not the only source of Crook's confusion that morning. In his after action report, written three days after the battle, the colonel states: "I received orders from the general commanding corps [Cox] to cross the bridge over Antietam Creek after General Sturgis had taken the bridge; but upon my arrival in the vicinity of the bridge I found that General Sturgis's command had not arrived." When he prepared his memoirs, Crook stuck to this version of events, writing: "I learned afterwards that Gen Sturgis with a division was repulsed when trying to take the bridge earlier in the morning. . . . I was expected to accomplish with my brigade what a division failed to do, and without ever getting the benefit of the knowledge he had gained in his reconnaissance." In a letter written in 1887 to a former officer in the Thirty-Sixth Ohio, Crook again reiterated that Sturgis had attempted to take the bridge, stating that as the colonel and others approached the span to reconnoiter the ground, "we came across the dead and wounded of General Sturgis's Division. I was far enough in advance to see the situation and to convince myself that the bridge could not be taken from that point."[31]

His repeated statements that Sturgis was to precede him over the bridge directly contradict Burnside's order to Cox that Crook's brigade was to lead the attack while Sturgis provided covering fire, an understanding that Cox later confirmed in his recollections.[32] Whether Crook was deliberately misrepresenting the facts to mitigate his subsequent failure to take the bridge or was the victim of a miscommunication remains unknown. Whatever the reason for it, Crook's error about Sturgis was only one of several mistakes and omissions characterizing his official and unofficial reports of the battle.

In his official report, Crook describes his role in the attack on the Rohrbach Bridge as follows: "I sent the Eleventh [Ohio] Regiment ahead as skirmishers in the direction of the bridge, and conducted the Twenty-eighth Regiment above the bridge to reconnoiter the enemy's position, leaving the Thirty-sixth Regiment in reserve. After a labor of two hours, I succeeded in establishing two pieces of [Captain Seth] Simmonds's battery in a position to command the bridge and getting five companies of the Twenty-eighth across the stream. I then intended taking the bridge with the Thirty-sixth Regiment, but soon after my battery opened [up on] the bridge General Sturgis['s] command crossed the bridge."[33] While terseness always characterized Crook's reports, in this case one suspects that brevity may have been used deliberately to obscure the events that transpired.

The fight for the bridge began inauspiciously when the Eleventh Connecticut, detailed from Rodman's division to provide fire support for Crook's assault, failed to take its position. As the regiment's men poured over a knoll onto the road running alongside the creek, they came under the raking fire of the Georgians on the opposite bank and from Rebel artillery. Some soldiers made it as far as the parapets on the Union side of the bridge, and one company even tried to ford the creek. But wading slowly through chest-high water, the men were too exposed to enemy fire and gave up the attempt after their captain fell mortally wounded. Under this withering musketry and without adequate cover, the New Englanders withdrew only ten minutes after making their initial charge, a third of them killed or wounded, including their colonel, who was mortally wounded at the bridge.[34]

As the Eleventh Connecticut withdrew, Crook mounted his own assault, which was poorly conceived and executed. Leaving his largest regiment, the Thirty-Sixth Ohio, in reserve, he sent in only four companies of the Twenty-Eighth Ohio, too few men to carry the bridge against determined and well-entrenched opposition. He either failed to adequately assess the strength of the enemy or, after his victories at

Lewisburg and South Mountain, had unreasonable expectations of his men. In any event the attack was over almost before it began. Charging over the crest of a knoll squarely in front of the bridge, the small force was overwhelmed by deadly fire from the quarry on the opposite hillside. The Ohioans retreated hastily back up the slope and dug in facing the creek.[35]

Crook then placed two Parrott guns in position to direct suppressing fire on the quarry while he mounted and personally led a renewed assault on the bridge. This time he directed the Eleventh Ohio to make a frontal assault while he guided five companies of the Twenty-Eighth through woods on the right flank, intending to come out at the bridge for a coordinated attack. But Crook and the Twenty-Eighth failed to appear at the appointed rendezvous. The Eleventh's men, pressing on alone, were overwhelmed by the volume of fire, coming no closer than a hundred yards to the bridge before losing their colonel. The Parrotts had hardly diminished the enthusiasm of the Confederate defenders nor slowed their fire. Realizing the suicidal nature of their unsupported attack, the Ohioans withdrew into the shelter of a copse of trees on the bluff overlooking the bridge, where they dug in beside the two companies that Crook had sent earlier to reconnoiter the ground.[36]

The failure of the Twenty-Eighth to join in the attack lay squarely on Crook's broad shoulders. Embarrassingly, the experienced woodsman and Indian fighter had lost his way in the hills east of the creek. After wandering through the woods, he finally emerged at the stream's edge some three or four hundred yards north of the bridge, too far away and too late to support the Eleventh Ohio.[37]

At this point, though suffering relatively few casualties compared to other units that day, Crook seems to have lost heart. The normally aggressive and self-confident officer threw up his hands and reported to Cox and Burnside that he was pinned down and unable to further contribute to the capture of the bridge. Then, with a figurative shrug of his shoulders, he positioned his men behind a crest about fifty yards from the stream, where they lay, trading fire with Georgia riflemen, for the next two hours.[38]

Only then did Burnside turn to Samuel Sturgis and his two brigades, one led by Brigadier General James Nagle and the other by Colonel Edward Ferraro, to take the bridge. Nagle's brigade went in first. His troops, regiments from Pennsylvania, Maryland, and New Hampshire, were cut to pieces, the Marylanders losing 30 percent of their men while the Sixth New Hampshire incurred a similar rate of casualties. Like Crook's Ohioans, they too fell back up the slope. The task then fell to Ferraro, a former dance instructor from New York, who chose his best men—his own regiment, the Fifty-First New York, and the Fifty-First Pennsylvania—for the assault. Fortified by Ferraro's promise to restore the liquor ration they had previously lost due to misbehavior, the Pennsylvanians and New Yorkers charged the bridge. The covering fire provided by the two artillery pieces that Crook had positioned with the Twenty-Eighth Ohio again did little to suppress the Rebel fire. The two regiments hesitated momentarily, stunned by the hail of minié balls unleashed by the dogged Georgians. But as they huddled behind the stone wall and wooden fence railings on the east bank, the firing slackened, and they saw Rebel soldiers abandon their positions and sprint for the top of the ridge.

Benning had finally run out his string. With his ammunition almost exhausted and word that Yankee troops were rolling up his southern flank (Rodman had found a ford), he withdrew toward Sharpsburg, leaving Ferraro's troops to pour across the span, bent on restoring their liquor ration. By one o'clock the bridge belonged to the IX Corps. The cost had been dear—five hundred casualties, almost half of whom had fallen during the last charge. But now Burnside held the ground needed to take Sharpsburg and with it, the Confederate right.

Sturgis's division crossed the bridge immediately after it was taken. Crook soon joined him on the west bank. Not waiting to cross the narrow bridge, his men instead waded across the stream at a ford the colonel had belatedly located upstream. Once across, the Ohioans fell in on Sturgis's right and waited for the order to move forward against the Rebel lines.[39]

A prompt assault by Burnside's troops at that moment, combined with an attack by the remainder of McClellan's troops, many of whom had yet to be committed to battle that day, might have been decisive.[40] But again the Union commanders dithered. Instead of following Crook's example and fording the remainder of his corps quickly across the creek, no problem once the Confederates had abandoned the opposite bank, Burnside insisted on using the bridge. Predictably, the narrow span soon became choked with wagons and caissons. Two hours were wasted before the corps had completed the crossing and put themselves in order to move against Sharpsburg. The delay bought time for the Confederates holding the town to rest and replenish their ammunition, and for the arrival of reinforcements under Major General A. P. Hill from Harpers Ferry.

When the IX Corps finally did commit to battle, the Confederates' thin defensive line tenaciously held its ground in front of Sharpsburg, fighting doggedly from behind every fence and dip in the rolling landscape. They delayed Burnside's troops long enough for Hill's men to flood onto the field. Burnside then sent an urgent plea to McClellan for additional troops. But though a fresh reserve of over 4,000 Union soldiers was available, Little Mac declined to send them. In their absence the exhausted and overwhelmed corps was forced back steadily until its back was to the creek from which it had mounted the assault only hours earlier.

At last darkness cloaked the blood-soaked fields and silenced the boom of the big guns and the rattle of musketry, leaving only the cries of the wounded hanging in the air. For George Crook, now huddled with his troops just below the crest of the bluff they had vainly assaulted that morning, this had not been his finest hour.

Filled with errors in judgment, his performance in many ways had mirrored the errors and misjudgments of his commanders—George McClellan and Ambrose Burnside. His lack of judgment in not properly scouting out the terrain in advance of battle echoed his superiors' failures to thoroughly reconnoiter the battlefield as well. In hindsight it seems obvious that with minimal effort, IX Corps commanders could have found the exact location of a ford that would have allowed the troops to cross the creek elsewhere and avoid the slaughter at the bridge. Had Crook properly scouted the ground to his front, perhaps he would have located the ford he later used. At least he would have gained some knowledge of the enemy's strength and sufficient familiarity with the ground to avoid getting lost in the woods. Crook's failed attempts to take the bridge with an inadequate force reflected McClellan's own piecemeal and poorly coordinated commitment of troops to the battle, a failing exemplified by his delay in ordering Burnside to take the bridge and his refusal to send his reserves to the aid of the IX Corps.

Crook's blunders may have reinforced his commanders' fundamental errors, but they did not change the outcome of the battle. More telling than his mistakes on the field was his lack of forthrightness in reporting the events of that day. His attempts at justifying his conduct reveal an unpleasant character flaw: an unwillingness to accept responsibility for his failures and a propensity to place blame on others. This would not be the last time that he displayed this tendency, an all-too-common failing among politicians and military officers.

The day after the battle, McClellan notified the War Department, "The battle will probably be renewed today." But after conferring with his staff, he changed his mind. The army had lost ten general officers, and Burnside, among others, had reported that his men probably would be unable to hold even the small patch of ground they had won the previous day. As Crook saw it, his played-out soldiers, clinging to their positions under a broiling September sun, were "all that was between the enemy and our impediments."[41]

To the consternation of Lincoln and his cabinet, McClellan opted once more to do nothing. So the two armies lay upon their arms in the summer heat, their nostrils filled with the stench of the rapidly decomposing corpses that lay unburied on the fields between them. In the late afternoon it rained, and in the darkness that once more cloaked the battlefield, Crook watched lines of fires spring up in the hills around Sharpsburg, lit by the Confederates to mask their silent withdrawal. While McClellan rested, Lee quietly slipped his bloodied, though hardly defeated, legions across the Potomac and back into northern Virginia.

October 1 found the Army of the Potomac, still encamped near Antietam Creek, playing host to the president. Lincoln had come to honor the dead and to vainly prod his lethargic general into pursuing Lee's shattered army. Though McClellan remained unmoved by the visit, Lincoln's presence did mark a red-letter day for Crook. While the president reviewed the troops, the still-new brigade commander received official notification from Cox's headquarters of his promotion to the rank of brigadier general of volunteers and his appointment to command of the Kanawha Division. The order was backdated to September 7, reflecting that the rank had been conferred as a consequence of his service at Lewisburg rather than at South Mountain or Antietam.[42]

For Crook, the promotion signaled his participation in a campaign devised by Major General Henry Halleck to drive the Confederates out of the Kanawha Valley, reoccupied by Rebel troops after Pope's defeat at Manassas. As these forces now posed a threat to Ohio, the War Department hoped to dislodge them with a concerted attack by General

Cox's IX Corps and the Kanawha Division. The plan required Crook to proceed via Hancock, Maryland, to a rendezvous with Cox at Gauley Bridge.

Entering Hancock on October 10, Crook learned that Major General J. E. B. Stuart's cavalry had just crossed the Potomac into Maryland a few miles to the southeast. The raiders were moving too fast for his infantry division to engage them, but he immediately sent out scouts to assess their strength and direction. After reporting later in the day that the Rebels were headed north toward Pennsylvania, Crook promptly received orders from Halleck to load his men onto railroad cars and be prepared to move at a moment's notice to block the raiders when they attempted to recross into Virginia.[43]

The Rebel cavalry had targeted the wealthy Pennsylvania town of Chambersburg, where Stuart hoped to destroy a railroad bridge and capture horses for Lee's cavalry and artillery. Though he failed to destroy the trestle, he did succeed in expropriating a number of fine horses. Stuart then led his troopers in a wide circle around McClellan's army and recrossed into Virginia at White's Ford, many miles to the south of where Crook's men sweated out the wait in their crowded and airless railroad cars.[44]

As Stuart had returned safely to Virginia, Crook was ordered to continue south to Gauley Bridge. There he learned that the Rebel forces in the Kanawha had fled on learning that a superior Federal force was en route to attack them.[45] Once again he and General Cox found themselves garrisoning the guerrilla-infested mountains of Unionist western Virginia.

CHAPTER SEVENTEEN

The Army of the Cumberland

January–July 1863

In the fall of 1862, Confederate forces under General Braxton Bragg occupied most of Tennessee. Headquartered in Murfreesboro, they threatened the Union army in Nashville while their cavalry and partisan allies controlled the countryside. In October Lincoln appointed Major General William Rosecrans to replace Major General Don Carlos Buell as head of the newly renamed Army of the Cumberland. The president made it known that he expected Rosecrans to go on the offensive immediately, leading Union forces out of Nashville and driving the Confederates southward out of Murfreesboro and eventually Tennessee. Rosecrans spent the next three months at his Nashville headquarters reorganizing his army and meticulously plotting his offensive.

Since he received his supplies from Louisville to the north, the general worried that as he moved southward, his supply lines would become attenuated and increasingly in danger of being cut by Confederate cavalry and secessionist guerrillas.[1] Tennessee partisans were of particular concern to Rosecrans. Recalling George Crook's valuable service against bushwhackers in the Kanawha Valley the previous year, he began a persistent letter-writing campaign aimed at convincing Major General Horatio Wright, in charge of military operations in western Virginia, to transfer the Kanawha Division to Tennessee. Confident of Crook's ability to handle the work, Rosecrans wrote: "I do not want to 'send a boy to the mill.' We must make things sure in front and rear."[2]

General Cox, Crook's immediate superior, whose own troops were thinly stretched in western Virginia, resisted Rosecrans's pressure, blocking Crook's transfer as long as he could.[3] As a result Crook's troops were spared the slaughter of the opening gambit of Rosecrans's campaign, a bloody battle fought to a stalemate at Stones River in late December 1862. Both sides suffered such terrible casualties—each losing almost a quarter of their respective troops—that Bragg withdrew his battered army south of the Duck River, which flows east to west, dividing the state roughly in the middle. Rosecrans established his new base at Murfreesboro on the other side of the Duck. There matters rested for the remainder of the winter while both armies recuperated and refitted for the campaign to follow.

The Army of the Cumberland's losses at Stones River and rumors of Confederate reinforcements flooding into Tennessee finally convinced the War Department of Rosecrans's need for additional troops and supplies. Cox at last capitulated to increasing pressure from Washington and ordered Crook, accompanied by the Eleventh, Thirty-Sixth, Eighty-Ninth, and Ninety-Second Ohio Infantry, to report to Louisville for transfer to Tennessee. On January 29, 1863, Rosecrans expressed his appreciation in a brief note to Wright. "Am very glad you sent General Crook," he scribbled. "No man could be more acceptable."[4]

At Louisville Crook's troops joined about 14,000 other reinforcements under Major General Gordon Granger onboard gunboats headed down the Ohio and Cumberland Rivers to Nashville. The voyage on the Cumberland provided some excitement when the flotilla engaged and helped drive off Confederate cavalry under Major General Joseph Wheeler at Fort Donelson, a vital strongpoint on the Federals' lines of communication. Disembarking at Nashville, Crook proceeded downriver to the town of Carthage to establish what he later described as a "most impregnable position" from which to guard the town and traffic on the Cumberland. At the same time, his men patrolled the surrounding area in search of Confederate cavalry known to be raiding at will throughout the region.[5]

Though a strong defensive force, Crook's infantry proved ineffective against the highly mobile Confederate cavalry. On foot his men even had difficulty guarding their own lines of supply and communications and were unable to react quickly enough to protect couriers and patrols sent out to secure food and forage in the area. Attacks on Crook's supply lines grew so severe that his soldiers began to suffer from a shortage of winter clothing and, more seriously, from scurvy due to the lack of fresh fruits and vegetables. Repeated requests for cavalry went unanswered, for the Army of the Cumberland as a whole suffered from a lack of horses, most of the livestock in Tennessee having been commandeered already by the Rebels. To make up for this loss, Rosecrans acquired over 42,000 additional mounts from the War Department during the coming months but husbanded them for his future offensive, sending none to Crook.[6]

Besieged by Confederate cavalry, morale plummeted, and for the first time Crook recorded disciplinary problems within his command. Particularly troublesome were two regiments of Kentuckians that had been assigned to him at Nashville, to whom he referred in his West Point French as "mauvaise sauvages." Reflecting the sectional violence that tore through border states like Tennessee and Kentucky, these men believed that wearing Union blue gave them license to wreak havoc on their secessionist neighbors, which they did with a vengeance, looting Carthage and even desecrating a local church. To add to his problems, not long after the Kentuckians' arrival, a brigade of East Tennessee volunteers and six companies of Tennessee cavalry appeared in town. Normally the general would have welcomed the cavalry, but these men were worse than the Kentuckians. Crook described them as "a lawless lot with grievances to redress against their neighbors and they now lost [no] opportunity to redress them." Among their more salient faults was a habit of shooting prisoners in cold blood.[7]

Though he ordinarily found the manner and practice of a martinet to be abhorrent, the presence of so many fractious troops convinced Crook that he could not afford to appear weak or uncertain. To assert his authority, he became a strict and uncompromising disciplinarian.

His resolve was soon put to the test. His troops were camped on the land of an openly secessionist farmer. Nevertheless, Crook issued strict orders not to destroy his property. When soldiers tore down some split-rail fences for use as firewood, a common practice, Crook promptly ordered the offending units to split new rails and repair the damage. Unhappily, the offenders were from his own Ohio regiments, including the Thirty-Sixth, one of whose officers refused to obey. From his perspective, the Ohio officer, who had an otherwise impeccable service record, was simply declining to give aid and comfort to a traitor to the Union.

In his defense he pointed out that the farmer had even donated funds to equip two companies of Confederate soldiers. Firm in his convictions, the officer simply would not back down.[8] The general now found himself confronting a possible mutiny.

Once Crook made up his mind on a course of conduct, he rarely gave ground. Stubbornly, he ordered the officer tried by court-martial. The man was acquitted, but the affair stirred such ill feeling toward Crook that some of his troops brought charges of disloyalty against him, an unimaginable scenario in any of his previous commands. Though Rosecrans ignored the charges, the incident continued to rankle Crook's men and had a decidedly negative effect on the morale of the division. Years later, with the benefit of hindsight, Crook recognized that he had used bad judgment, allowing that at the time he was "much troubled with my liver and suffered much pain, and was irritable, and really not myself."[9] Yet notwithstanding all the problems he faced during that winter and spring, Crook continued to pass on to Rosecrans helpful intelligence about the strength, movements, and intentions of the enemy in his area of responsibility.

June came, bringing with it an end to Crook's travails on the Cumberland. His force, the four Ohio regiments he had brought with him from western Virginia and the Eighteenth Kentucky Infantry, were withdrawn from Carthage and reassigned as the Third Brigade, Fourth Division, XIV Corps.[10] Under Major General George Thomas's command, the XIV Corps would play a key role in upcoming operations.

After six months of preparation, Rosecrans was finally ready to mount his campaign to drive Bragg out of Tennessee and ultimately capture the city of Chattanooga. With 87,800 effectives against Bragg's 41,680 men, he believed, and Lincoln and Secretary of War Edwin Stanton heartily concurred, that the time had come to put to use the additional troops, thousands of mules and horses, and tons of supplies and equipment the War Department had lavished upon him over the past six months. On June 24 the general sent the president a long-awaited message: "The Army begins to move at 3 o'clock this morning."[11]

Confederate forces, which had withdrawn to Shelbyville and Tullahoma, had used the six months since Stones River to prepare their positions against the Federals' anticipated offensive, which Bragg assumed would involve a frontal assault on his army. But Rosecrans wished to avoid storming these strong defenses head on, and instead he devised an elaborate strategy to draw the Confederates out from behind them. While feints to the east and west distracted Bragg's attention, Rosecrans would send Thomas's XIV and Major General Alexander McCook's XX Corps south between his decoying forces across the intervening mountains through a pass known as Hoover's Gap. Once past the mountains, they would press on to Manchester, a town on the rail line leading to Bragg's primary supply depot at Tullahoma. If successful, these maneuvers would place the main body of Rosecrans's army on Bragg's right flank, cut his supply line, and threaten him with encirclement. The Rebel general would be forced to abandon his fortified position at Tullahoma and either do battle with Rosecrans or, even better, retreat south into Georgia or Alabama.[12]

The capture of Hoover's Gap, a task assigned to the Fourth Division of the XIV Corps, was critical to the success of the plan. The honor of leading the attack on the gap went not to Crook's men but to the division's First Brigade, two thousand Illinois and Indiana mounted infantry, fervent Unionists commanded by Col. John Wilder. At midmorning on the twenty-fourth, Wilder's men poured into the north end of the gap and quickly drove the Confederates out of the three-mile-long declivity, clearing the pass for Thomas's and McCook's infantry. Establishing artillery at its southern end, Wilder's troops fought off a counterattack and held the pass open until reinforced and then relieved by Crook's brigade. Over the next two days, in an unusual driving rain that pounded both armies for the following two weeks, Crook's troops defended the mouth of Hoover's Gap. Finally, exhausted, famished, their clothing soaked and mud-slimed, the men slogged into Manchester to receive the first rations they had been issued since leaving Murfreesboro.[13]

From Manchester, Crook and Wilder became Rosecrans's eyes and ears, probing enemy lines in the direction of Tullahoma to learn Bragg's intent. On June 30 they reported that the Confederates had abandoned the town.[14]

Rosecrans had achieved a brilliant strategic victory. In a relatively bloodless campaign, his elaborate maneuvering had forced the Rebels to fall back across the Tennessee River, in effect abandoning Middle Tennessee, and to retreat into Chattanooga. It was Rosecrans's bad luck that his triumph was eclipsed by news of the simultaneous Union victories at Vicksburg and Gettysburg.

CHAPTER EIGHTEEN

In Command of Cavalry and the Chattanooga Campaign

July–September 1863

At the end of July, Crook unexpectedly received his first cavalry assignment, replacing Brigadier General John Turchin, the Union's only Russian-born general, as commander of the Second Division, Cavalry Corps. A veteran officer of the czar's Imperial Guard, Turchin had been suspect for some time because of his notorious inability to shed his Cossack mentality. The year before he had caused considerable consternation by allowing his troops to sack the town of Athens, Alabama. Most recently he had disobeyed orders from his commander, Major General David Stanley, in the face of the enemy. Stanley demanded Turchin's removal, telling Rosecrans, "If he stays then relieve me."[1]

Casting about for a replacement division commander, Stanley's gaze quite naturally fell upon George Crook, a brother cadet in the West Point class of 1852, a fellow Buckeye, and a veteran of frontier duty. His scouting activities at Carthage and again at Tullahoma, together with his defense of Rosecrans's supply lines, commended him for a cavalry posting that would require similar, if not identical, duties. The appointment advanced Crook forward once again from brigade to division command and provided an opportunity to gain experience in the management of cavalry, a skill essential to his future in the Indian Wars.

The Tullahoma Campaign had been only a preliminary move in Rosecrans's grand strategy to capture Chattanooga. Situated in the extreme southeast corner of Tennessee, not far from both the Alabama and Georgia borders, the city had long been considered the gateway to the

Deep South. It was not only a vital coal-mining and manufacturing center but also an important transportation hub, straddling rail lines that penetrated the heartlands of the three contiguous states.[2]

Bragg's army had retreated to Chattanooga, putting the Cumberland Mountains and the winding Tennessee River between it and the Federals. Though the mountains proved more a hindrance than a help to the Confederates—Rosecrans used them to screen his troop movements—the river was a formidable barrier. Wide and deep, its banks were topped by a ridge that formed a natural barrier to attack from the north. Beginning many miles to the southwest and running east to a point opposite the city, the ridge was actually four separate, steep, and elongated hills. These were Raccoon Mountain; Lookout Mountain, where Bragg established an observation post; Missionary Ridge, squarely in front of Chattanooga; and finally, Pigeon Mountain. To enhance this natural defense, Bragg had constructed elaborate earthworks as well.

To capture the prize, Rosecrans relied on the same strategy that had secured his victory at Tullahoma. Again, with the mountains screening his movements, he would feint to the southwest to disguise the main thrust of his attack, an assault by Thomas and McCook farther west. Once across the river and ridgeline, these corps would circle Chattanooga and come at the city from the south, cutting the railroad to Atlanta, Bragg's only remaining supply line. The Rebels would be trapped in the city with their backs to the river. If Bragg wished to avoid the trap, his only option would be to retreat from behind his breastworks into the open countryside, where his army could be engaged and destroyed.[3]

Diverting Bragg's attention so that Thomas and McCook could cross the Tennessee unopposed required a steady stream of accurate information regarding Rebel deployments at various points along the river. Providing that information occupied both divisions of Stanley's cavalry during the months of July and August.

When the attack was finally launched, the cavalry's First Division, together with Crook and elements of his Second Division, crossed the river with McCook's XX Corps, assigned to protect the Federals' right flank. The remainder of Crook's division, temporarily led by one of his brigade commanders, participated in the feint to the southwest, carried out under Major General Thomas L. Crittenden. The river crossing took several days but was completed without incident by September 4, after which Crook reconnoitered McCook's proposed line of march across

Raccoon and Lookout Mountains. He found Raccoon unoccupied and easily drove off the few Confederates posted on Lookout's summit.[4]

Two days later Rosecrans ordered Stanley to probe to his south to destroy railroad lines and generally disrupt any attempt Bragg might make to escape. Stanley, suffering from dysentery, made little effort to fulfill this mission and was severely criticized by Rosecrans for his lack of aggressiveness. At this point, ill and disgruntled, he relinquished his command. Crook states in his memoir, "I being next in rank present assumed command of the cavalry corps." In fact Stanley had appointed Brigadier General Robert B. Mitchell to that position.[5] In any event Crook spent the next few days probing enemy strength on the flanks of Lookout Mountain and in the valley beyond.

On September 8 Crittenden entered Chattanooga. Rosecrans's strategy seemed to have worked, for Bragg abandoned the city without a fight. But now the Federal commander could not find his quarry. The Confederate force had disappeared into the maze of mountains and valleys outside the city. Unwisely, Rosecrans relied on information planted by Rebels pretending to be deserters—tall tales of a demoralized Confederate army fleeing deep into Georgia toward the city of Rome, a substantial distance to the southeast.

In reality the Army of Tennessee had never been stronger, and it had not withdrawn toward Rome. Instead, reinforced by veteran troops sent by Generals Joseph E. Johnston and Lee, Bragg planned to go on the offensive. Rosecrans's strategy had required him to spread out his army along a fifty-mile front, divided by numerous ridges and valleys. Bragg planned to take advantage of this vulnerability by attacking the Federals in detail. In his memoir Crook records that he suspected this was Bragg's intent but that Rosecrans chose to believe reports that the Confederates were in full retreat. There is no independent corroboration of the truth of Crook's claim, but some historians think that General Thomas also smelled a trap.[6]

Bragg gathered his forces at LaFayette, Georgia, a town on the flank of Pigeon Mountain twenty-six miles south of Chattanooga. There he was joined by troops from Johnston's Army of Mississippi and James Longstreet's men from Virginia, after which he prepared to spring his trap. But on September 10 Thomas's corps made contact with Confederate forces, and by the following day, Rosecrans had decided that "the weight of the evidence" indicated the Rebels were not retreating into Georgia but assembling in LaFayette. In anticipation of this probability, he suggested that McCook's corps close up with Thomas.[7]

The XX Corps was at Alpine, a small town considerably south of Chattanooga, where McCook had positioned his men to block Bragg's supposed retreat into Georgia. From there he dispatched Crook to confirm the reports of the Confederate presence in LaFayette. On the thirteenth Crook's troops captured several Rebel pickets on the LaFayette Road. When questioned, the men admitted to being from Johnston's army, substantiating reports of Rebel reinforcements. Now Rosecrans definitely knew that he was the pursued and Bragg the pursuer. For the Union commander, the situation had become "a matter of life and death to effect the concentration of the army" or face defeat in detail. Fortunately for him, Confederate commanders were slow to take advantage of the opportunity. Their failure to move gave Rosecrans time to reunite his army along a north-south axis east of and parallel to the LaFayette Road. He now faced Bragg across a stream aptly named Chickamauga, a Cherokee term meaning "River of Blood."[8]

The Battle of Chickamauga commenced on September 19, but Crook did not arrive on the field until the morning of the twentieth, having been assigned to guard McCook's rear at a gap in the mountains about twenty miles to the south of the army's main body.[9] So he missed the first day of the battle, a bloody firestorm that resolved nothing.

An imaginative soldier awakening in the chill dawn stillness on that second morning of the engagement might have viewed the blood-red sunlight filtering through the dust and smoke that lingered from the previous day's fighting as an omen of things to come. During the night Longstreet had arrived on the field with the remainder of his two Virginia divisions, giving Bragg fresh forces to put into action.

Crook's cavalry came on the field about ten o'clock, about a half hour after the fighting had resumed in earnest. Reporting to his superior, General Mitchell, at Crawfish Spring, Crook found himself on the army's right flank, its most southerly point. Well away from the main arena of combat, his horsemen were assigned by General Mitchell to relieve the First Division, then guarding a ford on Chickamauga Creek to prevent Rebel troops from using it to flank the Federal line.

Although he had served briefly in the Mexican War, Mitchell was a "political general," characterized by Stanley as "always thinking of the votes he could make in Kansas." Crook, whose sensitivity to incompetence among senior officers, whether perceived or actual, equaled if not exceeded Stanley's, was equally contemptuous of Mitchell's abilities and had little faith in his judgment.[10] Though his formal report of the events that ensued at Crawfish Spring on the twenty-first did not reflect this attitude, the general's memoir more than made up for this oversight.

As Crook described it, the only path from Mitchell's headquarters to the First Division's position along the creek was a narrow, winding country lane that cut through a juniper thicket choked with underbrush. When Mitchell ordered him to transport his artillery down this narrow trail, Crook strongly objected. He feared that should the enemy attempt to take the guns, his men would be trapped and suffer needless casualties in an effort to save the ordnance. But Mitchell insisted, assuming at this time that the Rebels were on the opposite bank of the creek and probably thinking such an attack unlikely. Crook, without further options, reluctantly obeyed.

When he arrived at the First Division's position, Crook found that Mitchell had been wrong about the whereabouts of the enemy. The Rebels had crossed to the Union side of the creek and were massing among the pines along its western banks, evidently preparing to attack across a meadow separating the two forces. A brief Federal cannonade stirred them to action. Crook reported: "Both cavalry and infantry came charging out of [the pines] like so many hornets, completely enveloping me. I lost a hundred men in about fifteen minutes," many in defense of the guns, as he had predicted.[11]

During the melee, Crook at one point found himself surrounded by Confederate horsemen, their bullets zipping through the air, slashing the trees, and loosing clouds of leaves upon the heads of his men. Jamming his hat over his eyes, the general spurred his horse back into the junipers, moving so fast that, he admitted without embarrassment, he "didn't touch the saddle more than once in any twenty feet." Once in the thicket, Crook rallied his men and pulled back to Mitchell's position, where, he claimed, the now-panicky commander turned to him and cried, "General, you are a military man, I wish you would take charge and straighten things out and make the necessary dispositions." Crook readily complied, forming a battle line in a wooded area on the western edge of an open field. The Rebels, unwilling to risk a frontal assault, remained at bay until about 3 o'clock in the afternoon, when Mitchell received the shocking news of the Confederate breakthrough to the north.[12]

Things had not gone well for Rosecrans that day. Due to misinformation he received on the battlefield, he had moved troops to reinforce Thomas's corps, which had borne the brunt of the fighting. In doing so, he inadvertently opened a gap in the Union lines, which Longstreet quickly exploited. Rushing through and enveloping the Federal right, the Confederates threw Rosecrans's army into hopeless confusion. The bulk of his forces panicked and beat a disorganized retreat north to Chattanooga, leaving only Thomas's intrepid corps to face the surging Rebels. Rosecrans, believing that it would be impossible for Thomas's men to hold the line alone, quit the field and joined the chaotic stampede northward.[13]

But Thomas held. Known forever after as the "Rock of Chickamauga," he rallied the remaining Union troops and fought off wave after wave of Confederates bent on his destruction. The fighting continued until an hour before sunset, when the general at last conceded that his losses were too great to continue and retreated in good order up the road to Chattanooga.

Crook's troopers served as Thomas's rear guard, retiring northward in the growing darkness and well into the night, their path lit by the flickering light of burning fence rails. The exhausted men feared that the enemy would locate and attack them by the firelight, but they need not have worried. Bragg's army was too exhausted by the fighting, and the Federals completed their retreat to Chattanooga virtually unmolested.[14]

Chickamauga was the bloodiest two-day battle in American history. The Confederates lost an estimated 16,000 men killed or wounded, with another 2,000 taken prisoner. Federal casualties totaled over 11,000 killed or wounded and 8,000 captured. Crook's own losses, 136 men killed or wounded, paled by comparison but were relatively severe considering his limited participation in the fighting. His performance had been creditable, though General Mitchell, ever the politician, undoubtedly indulged in hyperbole in his after-action report when he wrote, "there was never work more opportunely done on the battlefield than the work of the cavalry on the 20th of September at Chickamauga." With a politician's knack for gilding the lily, he added a personal mention of Crook, lauding the "gallant manner in which he discharged his duty throughout the entire advance as well as on the battlefield." Crook ungraciously repaid the compliment by describing Mitchell's report as "falstaffian": "How he could have the cheek, after what had passed, surpassed my understanding. It was humiliating to see persons wearing the uniforms of general officers to be so contemptible."[15]

CHAPTER NINETEEN

The Wheeler Raid

September 30–October 9, 1863

Following his defeat at Chickamauga, Rosecrans retreated behind the fortifications at Chattanooga, where he was besieged by Bragg's forces. The Federal position was precarious. During the retreat, Rosecrans had withdrawn his outposts from Lookout and Raccoon Mountains to prevent them from being captured. Bragg had retaken these strategic heights and from them controlled the river and the railroads into Chattanooga. With these avenues of supply closed, Rosecrans could feed and reequip his forces only by wagon train through the mountains of Middle Tennessee, a circuitous route vulnerable to attack by Confederate cavalry.[1]

To safeguard his tenuous supply line, he positioned Crook's division, about 2,000 effectives, on the north bank of the Tennessee opposite Chattanooga with responsibility for patrolling the river for fifty miles in either direction.[2] The many fords and ferries available on this stretch made the task difficult, particularly with such a relatively small number of cavalry.

Crook established his headquarters at Washington, a small roadside town about twenty miles north of Chattanooga, and picketed his troops at intervals along the river. From these vantage points, his men could spot a crossing, though they lacked the manpower to oppose one should it occur.

It was not long before the Confederates discovered and exploited this weakness. On September 30 "Fighting Joe" Wheeler, Bragg's cavalry commander and an officer of considerable tactical skill and boldness, crossed the river with a force of between five and six thousand men.[3] He intended to disrupt Union supply lines through Middle Tennessee and capture or destroy as much of the enemy's stores and livestock as possible. Predictably, his men brushed aside the small contingent of Yankee cavalry guarding the ford where they crossed. Pausing only long enough to capture two wagon trains, Wheeler's column then headed north across the Cumberland Mountains in the direction of McMinnville and Murfreesboro, cutting a swath of destruction as they rode.

Crook gave chase with his only available troops—two brigades of the Second Division, each numbering about five hundred horsemen, commanded by Colonels Robert Minty and Eli Long and supported by one artillery battery. By the time the Union cavalry got underway, Wheeler had about a fourteen-hour head start and was well on the way to McMinnville. By taking short cuts over mountainous terrain and riding through the night in a heavy downpour, the column overtook the Confederate rear guard just as Wheeler's main force struck McMinnville. The skirmishing that ensued delayed Crook, and when he finally entered the town, he found to his disgust that the Union garrison had surrendered without a fight. The Confederates had sacked McMinnville and were already on their way to Murfreesboro.[4]

Crook resumed the chase and again caught up with the Rebel rear guard, which turned to confront him. Suspecting that Wheeler's main force was too far ahead to interfere, Crook ordered Colonel Long to mount a saber charge against the Rebels, an unusual tactic in the Civil War, but one that worked here. The shock of five hundred screaming horsemen, steel blades flashing in the sunlight, riding down on them overwhelmed the Confederates, who broke and ran, with Crook's energized troopers hard on their tails. But when the rear guard rejoined the main body, the Rebels turned and fought a two-hour engagement with Crook's outnumbered troopers that lasted until dark. Wheeler would later downplay this clash as "a demonstration," but the delay it occasioned forced him to abandon his plans for Murfreesboro.[5] Instead he turned south, intending to head back to the Tennessee River and safety. En route his men ripped up several miles of railroad track and also destroyed large quantities of military stores at Shelbyville.

Both raiders and pursuers, man and beast, were played out after six days of ceaseless action. The heated chase had allowed time for neither adequate food nor sleep. But on October 5, the day after Long's gallant saber charge, Crook received an infusion of fresh troops, a reinforced cavalry division under General Mitchell. The combined force, now numbering about 6,000 men, continued in pursuit of Wheeler's raiders.[6]

On the seventh outside Shelbyville, the Federals learned that Wheeler had sacked the town and then had divided his force into three columns. A civilian informed Crook that one column had gone into camp on a farm road that ran along the Duck River, some three miles away. On orders from Mitchell, Crook gathered his men and, with Long's brigade and a brigade of mounted infantry in the lead, headed for the site. Encountering Wheeler's rear guard, he again ordered Long's brigade to charge with drawn sabers. At the same time, fearing that he might be flanked by Wheeler's other columns, he sent instructions to Minty's brigade, which he supposed to be to his rear, to take positions so as to block the Confederates' retreat.[7]

Long and the mounted infantry successfully routed the Rebels, but Minty's men were not in position, allowing the defeated column to reunite with Wheeler outside the town of Farmington. Crook, in hot pursuit, suddenly found himself confronted by a Rebel force of perhaps three times his strength, drawn up in line of battle to his front, their flanks invisible in the thick woods, their artillery deployed in the center of the road. Despite long odds, Crook dismounted his men and fought an action on foot, disabling or capturing the enemy's artillery and taking several prisoners. But Wheeler's superior numbers eventually forced the Federals to withdraw. A month later Crook noted in his report of the fighting: "the absence of Colonel Minty and some five hundred men left at Murfeesborough . . . left me but about fifteen hundred effective men. . . . Had Colonel Minty with his brigade been there at the time, I should have thrown him on the left flank, and as things turned out since, I would have captured a large portion of [Wheeler's] command."[8]

When Minty finally arrived on the scene late in the afternoon, well after the engagement, he informed Crook that he had received no orders to march out that morning and so had remained in camp. After considering his statement, "together with a disposition manifested during the whole expedition to frustrate my designs in a covert manner," the general angrily relieved Minty of his command and ordered him to the rear.[9] He later preferred charges against him for disobedience to orders and conduct subversive to good order and military discipline.

Crook's report of the Farmville action was published in the War Department's *War of the Rebellion: A Compilation of the Official Records of the Union and Confederate Armies* with this footnote from the editors: "In February, 1864, Colonel Minty was tried by general court-martial on charges of 'disobedience of orders' and 'conduct subversive to good order and military discipline,' and honorably acquitted.'" When he edited Crook's autobiography, Martin Schmitt quoted this footnote, adding, "Crook admitted that he had forgotten to give Minty the orders."[10] This sentence made it appear that the general brought charges against the colonel for disobeying orders, though Crook knew full well that he had forgotten to give Minty the order in the first place.

Schmitt's aside has led historians to conclude that Crook improperly used the court-martial process to punish a man he knew to be innocent of wrongdoing—or worse, that he brought the charges in an attempt to cover up his own negligence. Either conclusion is so at variance with Crook's reputation for probity that it warrants a full exposition of the circumstances of the incident. A review of the trial transcript serves this purpose, revealing a more complicated situation than either Schmitt or Crook reported.

The court-martial proceedings took place over a two-week period, February 2–16, 1864, and involved the testimony of a number of witnesses for both the prosecution and defense. The case file contains both the trial transcript and a nine-page summation of the case written by the presiding judge advocate in his role as Minty's prosecutor.[11]

The specific allegations offered in support of the charges were that Minty received and disobeyed an unequivocal order to march out of camp with Crook's column on the morning of October 7 and that, during the two days preceding, he had acted in a manner intended to subvert his commander's authority, an intention that moved him to deliberately flout the general's orders on the seventh.[12] The latter allegation, if proved, would take on added gravity under battlefield conditions.

Detailed testimony was presented regarding events during the two days prior to the incident. On the morning of October 5, while the command was in hot pursuit of Wheeler's raiders, witnesses related that

Minty had approached Crook to ask for a halt so that his men could search for forage for their horses, complaining that they had insufficient opportunity to do so the previous night. Whether he was justified in making this request occasioned much discussion but was immaterial, for Crook testified that he refused to allow the halt due to the need for haste in the continuing pursuit. He added that he found the colonel's request "strange" and that Minty seemed resentful of Crook's refusal to grant it. The prosecutor took note of this point, commenting that the general's denial of the request could be reasonably said to have "stimulated disaffection" on the colonel's part—a polite way of saying that Crook probably ruffled the colonel's feathers, providing a motive for his subsequent behavior.[13]

The following morning, October 6, Crook left camp at daybreak to scout the road ahead, having ordered Minty's brigade to take the lead position in the column and move out promptly at nine o'clock. Minty departed at the specified time, but as his men rode out of camp, they encountered a wagon loaded with horseshoes. At the time, witnesses testified, all of the division's horses had been ridden exceptionally far and hard over the previous few days and badly needed to be reshod. Military exigency, however, dictated that no time could be spared for that purpose. Nevertheless, without authority, Minty halted the column, ordered the horseshoes in the wagon distributed among his men, and ordered that they reshoe their horses on the spot. As his brigade held the advance position, the colonel's action delayed the entire column's forward movement by almost three hours; they did not catch up with Crook until 11:30 that morning. One might suppose that the general was less than delighted at having been forced to cool his heels by the side of the road at a time when speed was crucial to the success of his mission. But no one testified that he reprimanded Minty at the time for causing the delay.

At sundown that evening, Crook and Minty had a conversation while the two men watered their horses in a creek at their campsite. In testimony that the judge advocate later characterized as "candid and careful," Crook told the court, "I gave [Minty] orders to get ready to move at daylight the next morning." He further stated that he had repeated this command at least once and perhaps twice. When asked by the court whether he had informed the colonel of what position in column his brigade would occupy, Crook frankly responded, "I do not recollect whether I told him . . . although it was my custom to do so when I gave orders in person." Any uncertainty in this regard was cleared up in subsequent testimony by the division surgeon, Dr. M. C. Cuykendall, who had also been present at the time. On the stand he recalled Crook's exact words: "The command will move at daylight tomorrow morning and your brigade will move in the rear as you had the advance today."[14]

On cross-examination Minty asked Crook whether he recollected remarking that part of the command would be going by Shelbyville and the other by Unionville, implying that there was reason for the colonel to be unclear as to the direction he was to take the next morning.[15] Crook replied that so much was going on at the time, he did not remember. He then asked whether it was the general's practice when giving a verbal order to one of his commanders to follow up with written confirmation. Crook said that it was. The two men and the judge advocate then engaged in the following exchange:

> Minty: Do you recollect that you did not send me any order to march on the morning of the 7th October?
> Crook: I think I did not.
> Judge Advocate: Was there any notification to the other brigade commanders of your division more particular than that to the accused on the morning of Oct. 7th, 1863?
> Crook: I think there was. My impression is that there were orders issued to the other brigade commanders and not to Colonel Minty by mistake.

This last comment appears to be the origin of Schmitt's statement that "Crook . . . had forgotten to give Minty the orders." But the context in which this testimony was provided shows that Crook referred only to his failure to give Minty *written* orders on the morning of the march, having already established in his earlier testimony, corroborated by the division surgeon, that he had given Minty an oral order the previous night.

According to other witnesses, on the morning of October 7, the Second and Third Brigade moved out at daylight, with Crook riding alongside the column. The horsemen passed directly through Minty's campsite, and the colonel asked one of his lieutenants to see if Crook was riding with them. But if he felt he needed information as to the direction of the march, Minty admitted that he made no attempt to seek it, even though the general passed within no more than a few hundred feet. Instead Minty remained in camp with his troops, horses unsaddled, some tents still standing, until General Mitchell rode up with his staff around noon. Mitchell asked Minty why he had not moved out with the rest of the division and noted in his report, with apparent skepticism, that the colonel "claimed" not to have received orders. The general added that Crook at the time was engaged in a fight and certainly expected the colonel's brigade to join him.[16] Only then did Minty finally move out, joining his commander at about dark—after the fight was over.

From the trial record then, it appears clear that the colonel's failure to follow the general's marching orders on the seventh was not due to a failure of communication on Crook's part but rather to Minty's decision to communicate his unhappiness with his commanding officer by engaging in a series of deliberate actions that together constituted what today we would refer to as passive-aggressive behavior. This was precisely what Crook meant when he reported that Minty manifested "a disposition to frustrate my designs in a covert manner."[17] Given the circumstances, he viewed the colonel's failure to march out on the morning of the seventh not only as insubordination but also as conduct that endangered his command.

Though Minty had a well-earned reputation as a brave and able officer, Crook determined that he should be called to account for his behavior. While the colonel's actions might have been overlooked in peacetime, in the context of Wheeler's raid, their consequences were too grave to be ignored. His pique had allowed a substantial body of enemy troops to escape the battlefield. Had the fighting gone against Crook, the results might have been far worse.

Based on his analysis of the facts, the judge advocate opined that there was a strong basis for a guilty finding. In his summation he presented a compelling argument in support of such a result and gave no indication that he considered Crook's charges improper. On the contrary, he believed that Minty was aware of his duty to march out on the morning of the seventh, dismissing the colonel's argument that the order was unclear. In considering the latter, the judge advocate wrote, "Is it not a military axiom that a soldier must seek instructions in case of doubt?" In his opinion, if an opportunity existed to clarify an order, the onus rested on Minty for failure to do so.[18]

In the end, the court-martial panel ignored the judge advocate's summation and acquitted Minty, either because they accepted his contention that he truly did not understand the orders or, more likely, to preserve the reputation of an officer with an otherwise sterling military record. Their decision offered no hint that Crook had acted improperly in bringing charges against the colonel.[19]

Following the engagement at Farmington, Wheeler's retreat became a rout. Men deserted—in one case an entire regiment—and a great many wounded were abandoned along the way. By the time the raiders finally crossed the Tennessee at Muscle Shoals, Alabama, on October 9, Crook estimated that Wheeler had lost one-third of his force, about 2,000 men, along with six pieces of artillery and innumerable horses.[20]

Reports submitted by Crook and Mitchell paint a picture of an aggressive campaign by a small number of dedicated men that hamstrung a superior enemy force, prevented much destruction, and turned the raid into a debacle for the Confederacy. For his part, Wheeler greatly exaggerated the numbers of his pursuers and minimized the severity of the engagements he was forced to fight, instead emphasizing the devastation he inflicted in Middle Tennessee. But neither side presented a complete picture. An objective assessment would have to conclude that the raid caused severe loss and damage to Union supply lines, but Crook's vigorous pursuit substantially mitigated the destruction and imposed a high cost in men and horses that the Confederate army in Tennessee could ill afford.

Crook was pleased with the performance of his command. It had borne the brunt of the casualties, 110 of the 120 Union troopers killed or wounded during the campaign. In his report he wrote, "[n]otwithstanding the fatigue and severe hardships under which the men suffered—having but three days rations in twenty days, many of them nearly naked and several times exposed to a cold drenching rain—yet they never complained, but were always cheerful and ever ready to perform all duties required of them." General Thomas characterized the entire campaign as "unsurpassed for its energy and the bravery and endurance of the officers and men engaged in it, and prevented the execution of an extensive plan of destruction to our command." Rosecrans chimed in too, praising Crook for his aggressive leadership and tactical skill, and complimented him for "inaugurating the new practice of coming to close quarters without delay," a presumed reference to his use of the saber charge.[21]

The sheer tenacity that Crook displayed in his pursuit of Wheeler's force, and the will to ignore hardship and inspire his men to do the same, would become a hallmark of his leadership in the Indian Wars. Unfortunately, so would his propensity to bring charges against officers who failed to live up to his expectations.

CHAPTER TWENTY

Blazer's Scouts

February 1864

Crook spent the winter months of 1863–64 patrolling the Tennessee River and pursuing bushwhackers and Rebel cavalry around northern Alabama. In February 1864, while preparing the Second Division to meet a threat from forces under Major General Nathan Bedford Forrest, he unexpectedly received orders transferring him back to the Kanawha Division and the hills of the new state of West Virginia (admitted to the Union in June 1863). As had previously been the case with his cavalry appointment, this abrupt reassignment was due to the ineptness of a fellow officer.

The previous year, when Crook had been transferred to the Army of the Cumberland, he had been replaced by Colonel Eliakam Scammon, the same officer who had fought beside him at South Mountain. Time had done nothing to temper Scammon's obsessive concern for military prerogatives or to soften his reputation as a martinet, for which he was not popular with his men.

At dusk on a rainy February evening, Scammon, now a brigadier general, having completed some business in Point Pleasant, a small town on the Kanawha River, had boarded a river steamer loaded with soldiers returning to division headquarters from furlough. Anxious to make all possible speed, he browbeat the captain into agreeing to depart immediately instead of taking the safer course of remaining overnight at Point Pleasant and departing in daylight. As the evening progressed, the weather worsened and with it, the visibility. Finally the situation became so bad that the captain refused to further endanger his vessel, and with Scammon's grudging concurrence, moored on the shore opposite a small village. But the general, infamous for his constant carping about security, failed to post guards ashore even though Rebels were known to be active in the area.[1]

An hour later, while Scammon and his men slumbered, a Confederate cavalry detachment swiftly and silently boarded the steamer and took the entire contingent prisoner without a fight. The cavalry, operating behind enemy lines, had no way of transporting such a large number of prisoners and so offered them parole. The enlisted soldiers readily accepted, but Scammon and a fellow officer refused and were bundled off to Libby Prison in Richmond, where they remained until exchanged in August 1864. Because of the general's pedantic penchant for security, news of his capture became widely regarded as "the greatest joke of the war" and was greeted with few regrets.[2]

With Scammon a prisoner of war, the Kanawha Division fell under the temporary command of Brigadier General Alfred Duffié, a Frenchman of limited abilities. The men, therefore, were pleased when they learned that their old commanding officer, George Crook, had been detached from the Army of the Cumberland and returned to West Virginia. Crook himself claimed to have been somewhat less enthusiastic, believing at the time that if he had remained with the Army of the Cumberland, he stood a good chance of becoming its commander of cavalry.[3] Nevertheless, he looked forward to rejoining the men whom he had molded into a fighting unit.

Crook's primary task, and the reason for his reassignment, was to quell the guerrilla war that continued to rage in the mountains of the southern part of the region since well before his departure in 1862. To aid him in this effort, he turned to a newly created unit known as Blazer's Scouts.

In his autobiography Crook would claim credit for forming the scouts and selecting Lieutenant (later Captain) Richard Blazer to head it. But the unit actually had been established several months prior to the general's arrival in Charleston, the division's West Virginia headquarters. Recognition for the concept rightfully belongs to Colonel Carr White, a Mexican War veteran who had become a physician in civilian life before rejoining the army in 1861. In September 1863 he convinced General Scammon to establish a company of scouts for the purpose of gathering intelligence about guerrillas and hunting them down wherever and whenever possible. On September 5, with Scammon's approval, White issued a call for volunteers for a unit whose headquarters would be "in the woods"—only "experienced woodsmen and good shots" need apply. Originally called Spencer's Independent Scouts after its first commander, Captain John W. Spencer, the unit quickly became known as Blazer's Scouts after the lieutenant who was appointed to succeed Spencer after the latter transferred to other duties.[4]

Richard Blazer, a thirty-year-old Buckeye, came to the scouts from the Ninety-First Ohio Infantry. On the surface he presented a deceptively unmilitary picture:"He had a far away look in one eye, and a nearly sleepy look in the other. His vest was not always buttoned straight, nor his coat collar always turned down. If he undertook to drill his company he would give the wrong command, and at dress parade he rarely placed himself in the exact position required." Despite his outward appearance and lack of military experience prior to the war—he had worked on coal boats and as a hack driver in civilian life—Blazer proved to be a natural leader, charismatic, courageous, and steady under fire.[5]

Blazer recruited his men from the western regiments of the Kanawha Division, many of them natives of West Virginia. Because of its reputation as a free-wheeling and adventurous unit, he had no trouble attracting volunteers and consequently chose only the best. By the time Crook arrived on the scene four months later, the scouts had already proven their value, and by all accounts the general was delighted by what he heard. He was particularly taken with Blazer, whose unconventional manner in many respects mirrored his own.

Indicative of the priority Crook gave the scouts, one of his first acts upon assuming command of the division was to implement several innovations to improve the effectiveness of Blazer's men. Under Scammon they had operated as infantry. Now, based on his experiences in the West and those as a cavalry commander in Tennessee, Crook turned the scouts into a mounted force to give them greater mobility. Knowing that the army would not provide horses to units officially designated as infantry, he authorized the men to obtain their own mounts "in the country, expropriating them from citizens known to be disloyal to the Union." But he added one caveat: compensation would be provided and "sufficient stock left these people to attend their crops with." Not satisfied with simply mounting the scouts, the general reorganized them like cavalry into an eighty-man company (seventy-eight men and two officers) divided into four squads. Convinced of the importance of good leadership, he specified that the officers be selected from among "such persons only as are possessed of strong moral courage, personal bravery, and particularly adept for this kind of service." Finally, Crook devoted attention to the unit's weaponry, making several attempts to secure Spencer repeating rifles, whose effectiveness as a weapon for mounted troops he had seen demonstrated in Tennessee. Unfortunately, his efforts foundered on the army's prejudice against providing infantry with repeaters, which were normally reserved for officially designated cavalry units. Not until Major General Sheridan interceded on their behalf in 1864, after deciding to deploy the unit against Mosby's men in the Shenandoah, did Blazer's men receive Spencers.[6]

Under Crook's guidance, the unit shed its ad-hoc, informal nature and became a highly organized, mounted company of handpicked men to serve not only as the general's eyes and ears but more importantly as his strike force against the guerrilla bands infesting the area. In the process he boosted the men's morale, giving them an élan that caused one of Blazer's sergeants to boast, "With a commander [Blazer] at our head, a country at stake, and such a General to instruct, you may suppose we felt sure of our success and to break down and smash all guerrillas was our delight."[7]

In March 1864 the scouts commenced their work in earnest, raiding into the counties surrounding Charleston and materially reducing the partisan threat by capturing or killing a number of bushwhackers operating in the Kanawha Valley. Their importance would increase during the coming spring campaign, when they would gather valuable intelligence about Confederate troop movements and locate and eliminate bushwhackers along Crook's line of march. Ultimately they would become seasoned practitioners of counterguerrilla warfare capable of mounting effective actions against even the legendary John Singleton Mosby in Virginia.

Crook's positive experience with Blazer's Scouts led him to appreciate the value of a well-run and disciplined scouting unit in irregular warfare. After the war he would use this experience to organize and manage units of Indian scouts on the frontier. As he had done with Blazer's men, he would introduce military organization and discipline to enhance the already superior knowledge these men possessed regarding local terrain and the habits of their quarry, making them so effective that often their mere presence cowed their enemies into surrendering.[8]

CHAPTER TWENTY-ONE

The Dublin Raid

April–May 1864

On March 9, 1864, while Crook hunted bushwhackers in the mountains of West Virginia, President Lincoln promoted Ulysses S. Grant to lieutenant general, a rank last awarded to George Washington during the Revolution. To this plainspoken, rumpled man now fell command of all Union forces and overall responsibility for the conduct of the war. Grant's strategy for victory was as simple and straightforward as the man himself. He meant, he said, "to employ all the force of all the armies continually and concurrently... so as to provide... no respite of any sort, anywhere, until absolute submission ended the War."[1]

Grant aimed not to seize or hold territory but to destroy the enemy's capacity to wage war, hence the general's interest in the fertile Shenandoah Valley of Virginia. Known as the breadbasket of the Confederacy, it was also the terminus of two railroads vital to the South's ability to wage war. To disrupt these lines, he envisioned a two-pronged campaign aimed at both the Virginia Central Railroad, which supplied Lee's army, and the Virginia and Tennessee Railroad, which linked the South's eastern and western theaters of war. Such a threat to vital communications would force General Lee to detach much-needed troops from the Army of Northern Virginia to defend the railroad, thus weakening his ability to protect Richmond.

On Union military maps, the Shenandoah lay within the Department of West Virginia, at the time under the command of German-born Major General Franz Sigel. A small man with pale blue eyes and high cheek bones set above a mustache and goatee, which gave his face an almost oriental caste, Sigel was the product of a German military education. Yet he owed his position not to his training as a soldier, but to his popularity among the German immigrant population, on whose support Lincoln relied. Though personally courageous, Sigel's record had demonstrated a greater propensity to retreat than advance, giving rise to concerns regarding his fitness to command. Accordingly, Grant decided to bypass him in his search for an officer to conduct the strike against the Virginia Central, choosing instead Major General Edward O. C. Ord, a fellow veteran of the Pacific Northwest. While Ord, leading some 8,000 men drawn from Sigel's army, attacked the Virginia Central, a second force, commanded by an officer Grant had not yet named, would fall upon the Virginia and Tennessee, severing the connection between Lee's Army of Northern Virginia and Confederate forces in the West.[2]

Grant had known George Crook since their brief service together at Fort Humboldt. Though never close friends, the two westerners had much in common—both were reserved, pragmatic men, careless of dress and military protocol but aggressive and cool on the battlefield. Valuing Crook's prior experience in West Virginia and his skills in guerrilla warfare, Grant had been instrumental in transferring him back to the Kanawha Valley. Now in late March, he summoned the general to his field headquarters in Culpepper, Virginia, "with a view of learning from him the character of the country and roads in West Virginia" and to get his opinion on the practicality of Grant's idea for the simultaneous assaults on the two rail lines.[3] While he did not mention it to Sigel, Grant may also have wanted to assess Crook's suitability to command one arm of the attack.

There is no record of the discussions held at Culpepper, but Grant emerged from them confirmed in his opinion that his plan was viable and that Crook should lead the campaign against the Virginia and Tennessee. Crook's principal objective would be a 780-foot-long covered trestle spanning the New River at the village of Central Depot. Demolition of the bridge would neatly cut the line while affording the opportunity to attack and destroy nearby Dublin, the Confederate military headquarters and supply center for southwestern Virginia.[4]

Grant informed Sigel of his plan on March 29 in a dispatch requesting him to supply 8,000 troops for the campaign and stating that Crook and Ord would be leading it.[5] Sigel, angered at being so brusquely shunted aside, immediately began raising objections to the scheme, insisting that he could not spare the men. Ord, fearing that he would get little or no logistical support from the reluctant German, soon asked to be relieved of the command. Without Ord to lead the attack and with Sigel claiming that he had insufficient forces to carry it out, Grant had to give up the idea of an attack on the Virginia Central.[6] Sigel and Crook then each offered alternative plans.

Crook proposed that he lead the Kanawha Division against Dublin and the New River Bridge as Grant had originally envisioned. Surprise was essential since, if the Confederates divined that Dublin was the objective, it would only take them a day to move reinforcements from Richmond by rail. To prevent this from happening, he proposed dispatching a small force toward Lewisburg as a diversion while his main force headed south. To further confuse the enemy, a cavalry force led by Brigadier General William Averell, but under Crook's overall command, would simultaneously mount a raid against Saltville, a town on the Virginia and Tennessee a hundred miles west of Dublin. If successful, Averell's cavalry would be able to tear up the rails east to the New River Bridge while destroying the vital Confederate salt works at Saltville. Meanwhile, he suggested, Sigel could further divert attention from New River by attacking Staunton in the Shenandoah Valley. Though Sigel objected vigorously, Grant liked the plan and ordered its immediate implementation.[7]

In asking for Averell to lead the Saltville raid, Crook was placing a great deal of trust in the abilities of this boyish-looking former Indian fighter and his 2,000-man cavalry unit. Previously a cavalry commander in the Army of the Potomac, Averell was a veteran of the Peninsula Campaign and had subsequently led several independent raids from West Virginia into Virginia. Most notable was a highly successful attack on Salem, Virginia, for which he received one of four brevet promotions earned during his career. He was a great admirer of General McClellan and, like his idol, had an arrogant and egotistical bent. Unfortunately, as he would soon demonstrate, he also shared McClellan's overly cautious nature and lack of boldness. But based on the general's extensive experience as an independent cavalry commander, Crook had no qualms about sending him off on an operation whose success depended on qualities that Averell had demonstrated in the past. Unfortunately, he would be disappointed in the results.

William Averell, Crook's commander of cavalry during the Dublin Raid. Philip Sheridan removed Averell from command for poor performance during the 1864 Shenandoah Campaign. Courtesy of the National Archives.

During April, Crook prepared for the operation and reacquainted himself with the officers and men of the Kanawha Division, with whom he had parted company shortly after the Antietam campaign. The men of its regiments, from West Virginia, Ohio, and Pennsylvania, were by now tough, battle-hardened veterans. Among them were those of Crook's old regiment, the Thirty-Sixth Ohio, often referred to by professional soldiers as "Crook's Regulars" in tribute to their disciplined performance under fire. Captain Russell Hastings, adjutant to Colonel Rutherford B. Hayes of the Twenty-Third Ohio, spoke for all when he wrote, "We knew enough of [General Crook] at this time to have great respect for his military ability." On April 26, just before the outset of the campaign, the troops demonstrated their affection by presenting the general with a dress sword they had purchased for the princely sum of seven hundred dollars, raised by contributions from the ranks.[8]

Crook's division numbered only a little over 6,000 soldiers, its ranks thinned by disease during the long winter in camp. These he organized into three brigades commanded by three competent officers, Colonels Horatio Sickel, Carr White, and Rutherford Hayes. In a gesture of confidence, recognized and appreciated by Hayes, Crook assigned his own Thirty-Sixth Regiment to that colonel's First Brigade.[9] This mark of trust launched a relationship between the two men that would ripen into close friendship over the next several months and continue until Crook's death. Though Hayes was six years his senior, at least for the period of their military service, Crook served as the colonel's inspiration, mentor, and advocate, while Hayes became one of the few officers in whom the reticent general felt he could confide.

On April 29, under a cloudless spring morning, the Kanawha Division confidently marched out of its camp near Charleston, its regimental colors snapping brightly in the sun's early rays, the martial airs of the regimental bands ringing in the men's ears, their spirits buoyed by faith in their leader's "skill and good judgment."[10] Unhappily, their carefree mood, like the fine weather, soon deteriorated. The route chosen by the general, east to Gauley Bridge at the mouth of the Kanawha Valley—which would serve as the expedition's forward base—and then south toward the Virginia and Tennessee Railroad, would take them deep into country infested with bushwhackers and removed from the possibility of resupply or reinforcement. Before them snaked 140 miles of muddy, rutted trails on which they would toil up and down mountains and across rain-swollen streams in weather that would turn wet and cold.

Crook marched the men, soft from a winter of garrison duty, slowly at first so they could become conditioned to the work.[11] As a result, they did not arrive at Gauley until May 1. Up to this point the weather had been so fair that many of the soldiers had carelessly discarded blankets and overcoats. But on May 2 a chill rain fell, changing first to sleet and then to snow, turning their path into a slippery mire. That night they bivouacked in mud rimed with ice. Before dawn, it snowed, and Captain Hastings awoke at sunrise to the sight of "innumerable hillocks of snow, each hillock representing a soldier soundly and warmly sleeping rolled in a blanket." Despite the growing cold, Crook forbade the use of fence rails as fuel for campfires. Knowing that they might have to return through this country after the raid, he saw no need to antagonize the local farmers unnecessarily. Nevertheless, the order drew complaints from the troops, who were now forced to gather damp firewood.[12]

As they moved south that day, the Federals entered bushwhacker territory, and Crook's marching orders reflect his experience with Indian warfare. Posting cavalry on his flanks, he chose the most difficult and unexpected routes to move his men, banned bugle calls, and imposed tight noise discipline on the column. Despite these precautions, guerrillas, like persistent mosquitoes, found them, and the crack of their muskets became a common feature of the march.[13] Several times during the ensuing days, sure that he had been seen by the enemy, Crook had his men set fire to the brush along the route, using the smoke to screen his numbers.

When they had advanced sufficiently southward, the general dispatched his diversionary force, the Fifth West Virginia Cavalry and Blazer's Scouts, east toward Lewisburg to draw attention away from the southward movement of the main body. Once at Lewisburg, the tiny force, following Crook's instructions, divided into two "regiments," building numerous fires and beating drums to simulate the presence of greater numbers. The stratagem worked, for Rebel scouts soon reported the presence of a division in the Lewisburg area.[14] As a result the Confederates pulled their bushwhackers off the road in front of Crook's column, leaving the Federals unmolested until they arrived at Princeton. The Lewisburg diversion and Averell's move on Saltville thoroughly confused the enemy, and Crook's true destination remained undetected except by a few Rebel partisans who continued to harass the column.

On May 6 Crook's force emerged from the still wintry West Virginia mountains into the warmer lowlands near Princeton Court House. A small Rebel cavalry detachment fired on them as they approached the town but quickly withdrew in the face of the superior force.[15]

Two days later, shrugging off pinprick partisan attacks, Crook reached Shannon's Bridge, only seven miles from Dublin. While his men made camp, he ordered the telegraph line tapped to see whether he could learn something of the disposition of Confederate troops. As soon as the operator at Dublin became aware of the tap, he greeted the eavesdroppers with a cheery "Hello, Yank" and invited the general to join him for supper. Crook promptly accepted the invitation but added regretfully that he would have to put off the visit to the next evening. After dark Crook's scouts reported a Rebel presence on the southern slope of Cloyd's Mountain, about two miles away, and barring the path to Dublin. Experienced veterans knew there would be a fight the next day. An "ominous hush" fell over the camp that night.[16]

On May 9, in the early dawn of what promised to be a beautiful Sunday morning, Crook moved his men out on the Dublin–Pearisburg Turnpike, the road leading from Shannon's Bridge across Cloyd's Mountain to Dublin. He had assumed that the Confederates would build their defenses on the summit of the mountain and so climbed it cautiously, deploying his men in two columns to flank any defenders. But caution proved unnecessary. The Rebels had stationed only a small force of forty men on the mountaintop to delay the Federals' advance.[17] They were quickly dispersed, and Crook used the heights to spy out the enemy's strength.

To the south, toward Dublin, lay a wide meadow that terminated in a series of bluffs. Running along the ridgeline of the bluffs, the general could see an imposing breastwork of logs, fence rails, and dirt. In front of these barricades and in positions running down into the meadow, he could make out the tiny gray and butternut figures of skirmishers positioning themselves against the attack. Turning to his staff, he calmly remarked: "The enemy is in force and in a strong position. They may whip us, but," he added confidently, "I guess not."[18]

Crook had disguised his route so well that the Rebel troops occupying Dublin became aware of his intended objective until only two days before. With such a short time to prepare, the Confederate commander, Brigadier General Albert Jenkins, hastily assembled a meager force of about 2,350 troops and ten pieces of artillery to face a far stronger Union command of more than 6,500 men and twelve guns. Confederate ranks had been filled by home guards and militiamen, old men and boys, some of whom would come to battle straight from church, armed with ancient shotguns and muskets but eager to repel the Yankee invader.[19]

With such a small force, rather than attempt to defend the town from the top of Cloyd's Mountain, Jenkins opted to construct his line, as Crook had observed, along the ridge between the mountain and Dublin, a position that would require the Kanawha Division to cross the open grassland, estimated to be about five hundred yards in width, under artillery and musket fire.[20] The meadow was bounded on the west by the Dublin road, to the east by wooded hills, and to the south by the bluffs below the Rebel barricades. A narrow stream ran along the foot of the bluffs, its presence revealed by the glint of sunlight reflecting off its surface. According to a black man who had guided Crook to the summit of Cloyd's Mountain, the stream was named Back Creek. It varied in width from ten to twenty feet, and in places it was waist deep. Union soldiers would have to ford this stream before charging uphill toward the enemy. The creek did offer one advantage: its far bank was high enough so that those who crossed the meadow would be afforded some cover while they regrouped for the final assault. Behind their formidable barricades, the Confederates were spread thinly over a distance of about a half mile along the ridge, their right flank curved slightly forward and their left slightly to the rear. Jenkins had placed his artillery on the left and center of the line to command the Dublin road and the meadow all the way to the base of the mountain.[21]

Crook's battle plan required White's Second Brigade to march under cover of the thick pine woods around the east side of the meadow to a point where it could turn the Rebels' right. While White got his troops into position, Hayes's First and Sickel's Third Brigades would descend the mountain and deploy in the woods along its base, their presence intended to distract the enemy from White's movement. As soon as Hayes and Sickel heard the sound of White's guns, they were to mount their assault across the meadow.[22]

White's advance seemed to take forever to the men of Hayes's and Sickel's brigades, assembled in ranks in the thick woods and staring upward at the screaming shells that tore into the treetops. Then, about 11:30 A.M., the sudden harsh crackle of musketry signaled that the Second Brigade had finally made contact with the enemy. Sickel promptly advanced his Third Brigade out of the woods and into the open meadow, confronting a perfect gale of artillery and small-arms fire. He continued to move his brigade forward through this storm until, after losing over a hundred men, including five flag bearers in rapid succession, his attack dissolved as soldiers scattered in search of cover.[23]

Hayes's First Brigade followed the Third onto the field. Though caught in the same withering fire and sustaining heavy casualties, these regiments forged ahead and succeeded in reaching the far bank of Back Creek, the men perhaps inspired by the example of General Crook, who leaving his horse behind, had enthusiastically joined them on foot in their charge across the meadow. Once across the stream, the soldiers shed their knapsacks under cover of the embankment and prepared for the assault on the breastworks. Looking about them during this brief lull, those in the lead were amazed to see their general floundering in the creek. He had leapt into the muddy water, and his high cavalry boots had promptly filled with water, becoming so heavy that he required assistance to get across the stream. The sight of him being dragged panting from the creek like some large blue fish moved a young lieutenant in the Twenty-Third to sarcastically remark that "the only objection he had to a corps commander leading a charge was that he had to be helped across the creek."[24]

But there was little time to enjoy this comic sight as the First and the remnants of the Third Brigade quickly reformed for the final push up the slope toward the enemy's fortifications. Although they suffered heavy losses, with a tremendous effort the Federals smashed their way through the breastworks in fierce hand-to-hand combat. Caught between White's brigade coming in on their right and the other two brigades to their front, the demoralized and outnumbered Rebel defenders broke and fled toward Dublin.

At this point Crook, exhausted by the sustained exertion of that long morning, fell to the ground in an apparent faint. As his concerned officers quit the field to rush to his aid, some of the troops, flushed with victory and bloodlust, killed several unarmed prisoners before anyone in authority could intervene.[25] Unusual in Crook's normally well-disciplined command, this regrettable incident may be attributed to the ferocity of the battle and the temporary absence of officers to restrain the men.

Although the Confederate defenses had been breached, the real objective, Dublin, remained to be taken. A romantic and somewhat improbable tale has Crook reviving from his faint and staggering to pick up a bowie knife lying nearby. Handing the outsized blade to a soldier, he was said to have rallied his men forward with the inspiring utterance, "Go in, boys!"[26]

With Crook hors de combat for a brief but critical period, his officers—Colonel Hayes in particular—assumed the reins of command. Recognizing the importance of denying the enemy an opportunity to regroup, Hayes gathered some five hundred men to continue the pursuit. As they raced toward Dublin, they ran headlong into a large force of Kentucky cavalry just arrived by rail from Saltsville to reinforce Jenkins. Undaunted by the odds, the colonel led a charge against the Kentuckians on foot, instructing his men to "yell like devils" to fool the Rebels into thinking they faced ten times their number.[27] The ruse worked, and aided by the timely reappearance of the now-recovered general and the remainder of his command, the Federals took the town before sundown. As darkness fell, the last of the Rebel forces evacuated Dublin, crossed the New River, and from the opposite bank watched helplessly as Crook's troops began the work of destruction they had come to perform.

Dublin was an important supply center for Lee's army, and the Union soldiers discovered numerous warehouses stuffed with provisions, clothing, and military equipment, irreplaceable to the Confederacy in this third year of the war. Troops gleefully carried away whatever booty they fancied, particularly large quantities of first-quality Virginia tobacco, highly prized by the men. What they could not carry, they put to the torch, burning any buildings essential to the war effort, including the train station and water tower. But Crook and his officers strictly enforced orders sparing civilian property not being used to support the rebellion.[28]

The original plan included the possibility that, after completing the task at Dublin and reuniting with Averell, Crook would proceed northeast along the railway to join Sigel near Staunton for a combined thrust against Lynchburg. But circumstances made this ambitious plan seem impossible. Calling at the telegraph office in town for news of the war (and possibly to rib the telegrapher about his dinner invitation), Crook found several troubling dispatches sent by Lee's army. The messages, later proven inaccurate (perhaps intentionally so), described a Rebel victory over Grant in the Wilderness. Having received no word from Sigel regarding his offensive in the Shenandoah or any indication of Averell's whereabouts, these reports made Crook uneasy. If Sigel's thrust toward Staunton had proven unsuccessful (which turned out to be the case) and Lee had indeed defeated Grant, Crook's small force would be isolated and exposed to a counterattack by Lee's entire army.

Crook was already low on provisions and ammunition, and his horses and mules were played out from the hard march south, leaving him without the means to haul the ammunition he did have as well as the rations and fodder necessary for an attack on Lynchburg. Under these circumstances, and having over 140 miles of mountain roads between his men and their supply base, he opted for caution over boldness and decided to fall back into West Virginia. But before withdrawing, he had to complete his assignment by destroying the railroad bridge over the New River and the six miles of tracks leading up to it. His soldiers were up to the task, attacking the line with great enthusiasm, ripping up the iron rails and heaving them onto great pyres fueled by ties uprooted from the railbed. The heat of the flames warped and twisted the rails into strange shapes.[29]

The following day, the regimental bands' rendition of "Yankee Doodle" ringing in his ears, Crook moved against the New River Bridge. A 780-foot wooden span that rose 500 feet above the river, it was a key point on the Virginia and Tennessee, which the Rebels felt they could not surrender without a fight. But heavy fire laid down from the far bank by infantry and a few artillery batteries scraped together failed to deter the energized Union soldiers, who swarmed onto the trestle and set fire to its wooden sides. To hasten the span's destruction, the men stuffed several freight cars with flammable materials, ignited them, and pushed them out onto the span. Fire quickly spread from the blazing cars to the dry wood of the bridge, and the structure suddenly exploded into flame. To those witnessing the scene from the river bank, the bridge "seemed to leap into the air from its piers and plunge, a mass of ruins into the river below." "A fine scene it was," Hayes commented, "[m]y band playing and all the regiments march[ing] on to the beautiful hills hurrahing and enjoying the triumph." Unfortunately, having brought no explosives with them, the Federals could not blow up the piers, allowing the Confederates to reconstruct the bridge within a month. Nevertheless, the repairs used resources that the South could ill afford to waste, and the destruction of the span denied the Rebels the use of a vital rail link for a period of several weeks.[30]

As the Union troops prepared for the long trek north back into West Virginia and safety, they found themselves surrounded by over two hundred contrabands (the term used by Union troops to describe liberated slaves), men, women, and children, most of whom owned nothing but the clothes on their backs and had nothing to eat and nowhere to go. Crook knew that taking them with him would slow down his pace and deplete his already inadequate provisions, but he was also aware that if they remained behind, they would be forced back into slavery. In the end, though not a committed abolitionist, the general decided to take them along since the drain of slave labor from the region would seriously hamper Confederate food production and other war-related activities.[31]

While breaking camp the next day, Crook finally received word from Averell. The cavalryman's diversionary attack, intended to destroy the Rebel salt works at Saltville and lead mines at Wytheville, had failed. Confederate intelligence about Averell's route and objectives had been far superior to the information the Rebels had about Crook's column. When the raiders had approached Saltville on May 9, they were met by more than 4,000 Confederates dug in to the north of town. Outnumbered two to one, Averell detoured to the east, hoping to attack Wytheville. En route his men were ambushed and, in a sharp fight, suffered over 100 casualties. Forced to abandon the field, he decided to join Crook at Dublin. When the cavalry commander notified Crook of his intention, the latter ordered him to move east from Dublin toward Lynchburg along the Virginia and Tennessee, destroying track as he went.[32]

Although the Confederates mounted one feeble attack on the column on May 12, an assault Crook easily repulsed, the real dangers during the withdrawal were the weather, terrain, and inadequate rations for both men and horses. Foul weather, cold rain, and spitting snow turned the steep, narrow mountain tracks into a viscous mud in which the heavy supply wagons sank to their beds. When the ill-fed, worn-out horses and mules died in their traces trying to pull them free, desperate soldiers shoved fully loaded wagons and dead animals off the side of the mountain to clear the road, harnessing surviving mules to the remaining carts to help with the burden.[33]

At the outset the column passed through unpopulated wilderness, so the troops were unable to forage for food to supplement their dwindling rations. After several days, however, they reached more settled terrain where poor farmers eked out meager livings. There the soldiers augmented their provisions with a little seed corn foraged from these impoverished farmsteads. Everyone worked hard to keep the wagons and troops moving forward, including Crook, whom Hayes noted worked himself "like a Turk." On the fifteenth the men stumbled into the town of Union, about two-thirds of the way in their return journey. There they rested while Crook awaited Averell's arrival. The latter had abandoned his march toward Lynchburg upon learning that Confederate reinforcements were en route to Dublin.[34]

With Averell's horsemen now in tow, Crook led his fatigued command on the final stretch to his base at Meadow Bluff. The rain-swollen Greenbrier River ran directly across their line of march, forcing the column to laboriously transport men and carts across the raging waters on a single small ferry, supplemented by wagon beds hurriedly converted into makeshift barges. For several days bushwhackers had been harassing the troops, firing at them from ambush. Now, while waiting to cross the Greenbriar, Crook was struck in the thigh by what must have been a spent bullet. Giving no sign of pain, the general continued to apply himself vigorously to the work at hand. The command's livestock had to be swum across, and the mules in particular balked at the idea of plunging into the torrent. Crook, incapable of remaining aloof, especially when the subject involved mules, threw himself into the fray with a long brush switch, "clubbing the mules into the river."[35]

On May 17 the column finally arrived, proud but footsore, at Meadow Bluff, the ordeal behind them at last. Nine grueling days had elapsed since they left New River on a trek that Crook estimated should have taken only four days under normally dry conditions. That evening Hayes penned an enthusiastic letter to his wife: "This campaign in plan and execution has been perfect. We captured ten pieces of artillery, burned the New River Bridge and culverts and small bridges, thirty in number for twenty miles from Dublin to Christianburg, captured General Jenkins and 300 officers and men, killed and wounded three to five hundred and routed utterly his army." To his uncle he wrote, "This is our finest experience in the War & Gen. Crook is the best general we have ever served under not excepting Rosecrans."[36]

Although few would argue with the conclusion that the campaign was a Union success, it is hard to accept Hayes's glowing assessment of its value to the war effort. Strategically the foray did not amount to much in the general scheme of things. As has been noted, the damage done to the railway was soon repaired, the plan to join Sigel in an attack on Lynchburg never came to fruition, and Averell's raid, other than distracting Rebel forces from Crook's column, was a complete failure. While it can be said that both Crook and Sigel tied down troops who could have been put to good use by Lee at the Battle of the Wilderness, weighing the rewards against the costs, it is doubtful that the effect on the Army of Northern Virginia was worth the body count.

The battle at Cloyd's Mountain, though short in duration—lasting only an hour and a half—was a bloody affair, particularly considering the number of troops involved. As one Yankee sergeant recorded in his diary, with indifferent spelling but palpable emotion: "There dead & wounded lay strewed over the ground very thick. O what a sight a battlefield is. I never want to see it again." Of the approximately 9,000 men who participated in the battle—about 6,000 Yankees and 3,000 Rebels—Union losses amounted to 688 dead, wounded, or missing, almost 10 percent of Crook's entire force, while the Confederates suffered 538 casualties, 23 percent of their men. Rebel casualties included 76 dead, among them General Jenkins, who survived the amputation of his arm by Union surgeons only to bleed to death two weeks later when stitches tying off a main artery were accidentally knocked loose by a careless orderly.[37]

Though the Dublin raid and the battle at Cloyd's Mountain were minor footnotes to the war, the campaign was something of a personal triumph for Crook and his command. Leading an independent operation that carried his force deep into enemy territory, the general demonstrated superior tactical and leadership skills. Through a variety of subterfuges, he had kept the Confederates in constant doubt as to his route of march and prevented Jenkins from marshalling sufficient troops at Dublin in time to meet the Union threat. He had then deployed his forces intelligently at Cloyd's Mountain and dislodged a Confederate force, which though outnumbered had the advantage in both terrain and position. In both instances and during the subsequent withdrawal of his forces into West Virginia, Crook displayed a critical quality that defines military leadership: the ability to inspire confidence in his men. The views of Captain R. B. Wilson, an officer in the Twelfth Ohio, were perhaps representative of the command: "General Crook had the nerve, the skill and the confidence in his army requisite to the undertaking, and his army had the training, the endurance, and above all, the confidence in its leader that left no question of success." Or as Captain Hastings more simply put it, "[we] grew to love him, having every confidence in him as a commander."[38]

The leadership afforded by Crook, together with his attention to training, allowed his men to emerge from their ordeal in remarkably good shape. As a unit they had compiled an impressive statistical record during the twenty-one-day campaign, marching 270 miles through eleven counties, crossing seventeen mountains and fording uncounted streams and rivers. They also endured sixteen days of rain and snow and marched on short rations for ten of the twenty-one days.[39] Nevertheless, soon after returning to camp, they would be back on the road.

CHAPTER TWENTY-TWO

The Lynchburg Campaign

May–June 1864

On May 19, even before all of his fatigued units had arrived at Meadow Bluff, Crook received a dispatch from General Sigel ordering him "to make a demonstration on Staunton as soon as possible." His men exhausted, in many cases without shoes and inadequately provisioned, and his horses also badly in need of rest, Crook delayed. Ultimately his inaction was of no consequence since Sigel failed to attack Staunton. Instead, after being soundly defeated in an engagement at New Market, the German general beat a hasty retreat back toward the Maryland line. After this debacle, General Grant, when asked by the War Department if Sigel should be replaced, promptly responded, "By all means I would say appoint Genl Hunter or any one else to the command of West Virginia."[1] So Major General David Hunter succeeded Sigel as head of the Department of West Virginia.

Because of his swarthy visage, dyed mustache, dark brown wig, and harsh character, Hunter became known to his troops—and to history—as "Black Dave." Though born in New Jersey, he had deep family roots in Virginia that, rather than instilling some sympathy toward the Confederate cause, filled him with an intense animosity toward secessionists. Graduating from West Point in 1822, Hunter resigned his commission in 1835 to seek his fortune in real estate in the booming city of Chicago. When financial success eluded him, he rejoined the army in 1841, serving as a paymaster until the outbreak of the war. In the 1850s he was assigned to Fort Leavenworth, Kansas Territory, at the height of the

David Hunter, commander of the Army of West Virginia during the Lynchburg Campaign. Known as "Black Dave," he was despised by the Confederates for the wanton destruction he wreaked upon the residents of the Shenandoah Valley. Courtesy of the National Archives.

partisan warfare over slavery that tore the region apart prior to the Civil War. During this period, he developed strong abolitionist sympathies and became a great admirer of John Brown.[2]

Hunter was commissioned a major general not long after the attack on Fort Sumter, owing to a friendship he had cultivated with the Lincolns just prior to the 1860 election. He used his rank and political connections to strongly advocate the emancipation of slaves in areas of the Confederacy occupied by the North and the enlistment of blacks in the military. His activities in this regard inspired such deep animosity in the South that the Confederate War Department issued an order that, in the event of his capture, the general would be tried and executed as a felon.[3]

In response, Hunter revealed the depth of his hatred for the rebellion and those who supported it in a communiqué so virulent that it was quickly suppressed by the Lincoln administration. Viewing the Confederacy's objective as "the plunder of the black race . . . and further degradation of ninety per cent of the white population of the South in favor of its ten percent aristocracy," he declared that the Federal government should "[hang] every man taken in arms against the United States."[4] His intemperate language demonstrated not only the violent nature of his response to secession and slavery but also his tendency toward impulsiveness regarding these issues. In the spring of 1862, he again demonstrated this propensity while serving as commander of the Department of the South, a military district encompassing occupied portions of the Confederacy. Without authority or consultation with his superiors, including the president, he declared free all of the slaves under his jurisdiction. Lincoln was as yet unprepared to take such action, considering it politically dangerous to the fragile unity of the North, and quickly repudiated Hunter's action and removed him from command. Only reluctantly did Lincoln agree a year later to appoint Hunter in place of Sigel and allow him an opportunity to redeem himself.

The men of Crook's division soon came to dislike their new departmental commander. Rutherford Hayes presciently confided to his diary that Black Dave "will come to be as odious as Butler or Pope to the Rebels and not gain our good opinion either." Captain Hastings, Hayes's adjutant, wrote, "For some reason we had very little confidence in [Hunter's] ability, and after campaigning in his immediate presence for a few days, our confidence disappeared entirely." The Confederates would be even less charitable. Brigadier General John Imboden, a West Point graduate and a cavalry commander, called him "a human hyena."[5]

At the time of Hunter's appointment, Grant was still focused on the idea of an attack in the Shenandoah both to wreak havoc on the enemy's supply lines and to weaken the Confederates at Petersburg by forcing Lee to dispatch units to defend the Valley. In furtherance of this strategy, Hunter suggested that his troops unite with Crook's at Staunton and then conduct joint operations east toward Charlottesville.[6]

But Crook at this time was far less concerned with grand strategy than with meeting the immediate needs of his men. His troops and his horses and mules needed rest, and their equipment was in dire need of repair or replacement: they were in no shape to undertake an extended campaign into central Virginia. The supplies available at Meadow Bluff were inadequate to meet his needs, particularly in the area of footwear and livestock, due to transport problems. But by May 31, Crook's 10,000 men, rested, well fed, and for the most part reequipped—shoes were still a problem—departed Meadow Bluff for Staunton. Despite the hot, sultry weather, their mood was upbeat as they welcomed the news that they were headed into the main theater of the war.[7]

Crossing the Alleghenies into the Shenandoah, Crook's Federals were harassed by Confederate guerrillas but brushed them aside. On June 6 they struck the Virginia Central Railroad and, using techniques they had perfected at Dublin, wrecked four miles of track. One squad with a creative flair and a sense of humor bent two rails in the form of a large "US," which they left standing upright beside the ruined track. Two days later the division reached Staunton, where they found that Hunter had captured the town without a fight and that a supply of badly needed shoes awaited them.[8]

Hunter's path up the Shenandoah to Staunton had been marked by fire and destruction. With evident relish, he had burned the homes and businesses of secessionists and turned his troops loose to forage in the rich fields and farmyards of the Valley. He met little real resistance until June 5 at the village of Piedmont, where he confronted a scratch Confederate force under the command of Brigadier Generals William E. "Grumble" Jones and Imboden. Outnumbered by almost two to one, the Rebels stood no chance against Hunter's army. But they put up a fierce fight, inflicting over eight hundred Union casualties before retreating south. Their departure left the road to Staunton open to Hunter's troops.

While awaiting Crook's column in Staunton, Hunter went about the business of destruction. The town had been a booming commercial center since the arrival of the railroad in the 1850s. Swelling even more as a consequence of the war, it now had a population of over 6,000 residents and boasted numerous enterprises of considerable value to the Confederacy. Staunton also served as the center for the shipment east of the agricultural bounty of the surrounding counties, becoming one of Virginia's largest military depots.[9]

In his report on the campaign, Hunter catalogued the damages he inflicted on the town, noting that he had "destroyed a large amount of public stores . . . also several extensive establishments for the manufacture of army clothing and equipments. I also had the Virginia Central Railroad entirely destroyed for several miles east and west of the town, burning all the depot buildings, shops, and warehouses." But that was only part of the story. The general permitted his troops to run rampant in Staunton, and the havoc they wreaked could not always be justified as "military necessity."[10]

Crook was appalled by the extent of the damage and the indiscipline displayed by Hunter's men. When his own troops showed an inclination to join in the mayhem, he promptly issued an order in which he expressed his disgust with the "many acts committed by our troops that are disgraceful to the command" and made his officers personally responsible for the strict enforcement of orders against looting and the destruction of civilian property. As a further measure to control indiscriminate foraging, Crook appointed regular details to supply food to his men.[11]

As a consequence of their differing approaches to military occupation, the opinions of Hunter and Crook among the Valley's citizenry were markedly different. A tale told by Richard Mauzy, editor of the *Spectator,* one of Staunton's newspapers, illustrates the point. During the occupation of the town, two of Hunter's staff officers entered the *Spectator*'s offices and forced the editor to show them his presses. Surprised that the equipment had not been hidden, one opined that the editor must not have been expecting them. He replied that he had thought General Crook would occupy the town, adding that he knew that general would not permit the shop's destruction. The following day a squad of Hunter's men returned to the newspaper and destroyed the presses, tossing type fragments into the street.[12]

Crook's prompt response to the chaos in Staunton had a sobering effect on Hunter and his staff—at least with respect to that town. Hunter finally reined in his men, posted guards to protect civilian property, and issued an order that no soldier might enter the town without a pass from his headquarters. But no amount of high-level direction could completely prevent the troops from taking advantage of the helpless population, particularly since Hunter's men, as a direct result of the general's decision to issue only minimal rations and clothing, were forced to live off the land.

While at Staunton, Hunter received a suggestion from Grant that he march via Lynchburg toward Charlottesville, following the Virginia Central and the James River and Kanawha Canal, destroying these vital Confederate supply lines to Lee's besieged army at Petersburg. He could then link up with Sheridan's cavalry, which had been dispatched on a raid from eastern Virginia against Charlottesville, following which Sheridan and Hunter would join Grant's army at Petersburg. Though Grant considered an assault on Lynchburg itself feasible, he worried that such an attack, if strongly opposed by Lee, might prevent Hunter from carrying out the more important tasks of destroying the railroad and canal. Despite his concern, he extended Hunter the latitude to take advantage of opportunities as they arose. "If on receipt of this you should be near to Lynchburg and deem it practicable to reach that point," he allowed, "you will exercise your judgment about going there."[13]

Hunter called a council of war to discuss his options. At this juncture he reposed great confidence in General Averell, now one of his cavalry commanders. When Averell advocated an attack on Lynchburg, Hunter readily agreed. The cavalryman laid out a plan calling for a strong column to move on the town by way of Lexington, home of the Virginia Military Institute. To distract attention from their objective, he proposed that General Duffié lead a feint against Charlottesville. In doing so Duffié's cavalry could destroy the Orange and Alexandria line to prevent Lee from reinforcing Lynchburg by rail. Averell concluded by proposing an ambitious thrust southward to free Union prisoners held at Danville, and even an invasion of North Carolina.

When Colonel David Strothers, Hunter's chief of staff, pulled Crook into the discussion, he found him "drier and less sanguine than either

Averell or myself." Exhibiting the commonsense approach that had served him well in the past, Crook asked what would be gained by attacking Lynchburg. Strothers responded that such a raid would draw Lee out of Richmond by threatening his western supply lines. Crook then quickly went to the heart of the issue, questioning whether their present strength was sufficient to carry out the ambitious objectives that Averell had outlined and meet the threat of forces Lee would dispatch from Petersburg. The colonel thought so, providing Grant pressed the Rebels hard enough to prevent them sending such reinforcements to the Valley. Even if Lee managed to move some of his divisions toward Lynchburg, Strothers was confident that they would be blocked by Sheridan. Crook remained skeptical. He pointed out that to move farther south meant attenuating Hunter's supply lines, requiring his troops, already underprovisioned, to live entirely off an area in which food and livestock reserves already had been depleted. He also voiced the same concern as Grant, that because of its importance, Lee would take extraordinary measures to save Lynchburg from destruction. Even if Hunter could take the town, he would not be able to hold it for long.[14]

Hunter and his staff were untroubled by the threat of Confederate reinforcements, arguing that should Lee block a Union retreat down the Valley (northward), Hunter's troops could always withdraw into West Virginia. Crook, who had already experienced the realities of such a withdrawal with inadequate supplies, was unimpressed. When he realized that his arguments failed to convince Hunter, he warned the general that if he planned to take Lynchburg, he should move without delay because Lee would act swiftly to protect it. Despite appearing to agree with this analysis, Hunter considered some delay inevitable. His men were low on ammunition, and worried that his forces would run short during the extended campaign to come, he wanted to remain in Staunton until supply trains arrived. Impatient, Crook volunteered to take Lynchburg alone, noting that *he* had plenty of ammunition and arguing that "celerity was more important than numbers or ammunition." Hunter dismissed this offer, and so the army sat in Staunton until June 10.[15]

When the Federals finally did march south, they met only scant resistance from Confederate cavalry, which attempted to delay the column long enough to allow Lee to reinforce Lynchburg. The troops easily brushed aside these attacks and continued south toward Lexington, where Hunter's arrival was awaited with considerable trepidation.

On June 11 Crook's division, marching in the van, reached the North River opposite Lexington. In an attempt to slow the Yankee advance, the Rebels had attempted to burn the only bridge for miles in either direction. They were only partially successful as enough of the structure remained above water to afford a crossing place for infantry.[16] But on the opposite bank, the Confederates had established a thin defensive line, backed up by sharpshooters stationed in the town's buildings, including some on the VMI campus, near the river's edge.

The scene—troops concentrated before a bridge overlooked by an entrenched enemy—was uncomfortably reminiscent of the situation at Rohrbach Bridge over Antietam Creek. But Crook had no intention of repeating Burnside's mistake. Rather than send his men in a frontal assault directly across the burnt timbers, he ordered one of his brigades west along the river to find a ford they could use to flank the Rebel troops out of their positions. When Hunter arrived and took in the situation, he dispatched Averell's cavalry on a similar mission in the opposite direction. Seeing that they were about to be surrounded, the Confederates hastily withdrew. The dismayed citizens of Lexington watched from behind drawn blinds as Hunter's troops, singing "John Brown's Body," marched into town.[17]

Having had several days to prepare for this moment, the town's residents had buried or otherwise hidden their valuables and anything that might incriminate them as supporters of the Southern cause. VMI cadets, perhaps sensing that they would be a special target of Hunter's wrath because of their role in defeating Sigel at New Market, had concealed their uniforms, rifles, and personal possessions in many homes about the town. They then joined the retreating Confederates, abandoning Lexington to its fate.[18]

Shortly after entering the town, Union troops began looting. It commenced harmlessly enough, with famished and thirsty soldiers approaching the doors of tidy brick homes to ask for buttermilk and fresh-baked bread. But it soon escalated into an orgy of destruction.[19]

Unlike Staunton or Lynchburg, Lexington had little strategic value. Not a transportation hub, military depot, or manufacturing center, in 1864 the town was instead a peaceful farming community surrounded by rich agricultural land. Home to some 17,000 souls—4,000 of them slaves—it included two venerable institutions of higher learning, VMI and Washington College, that latter endowed by the nation's first president.

Stonewall Jackson had lived and taught at VMI, and it was the site of his grave, a shrine for the Confederacy.

Despite its lack of military significance, Hunter regarded Lexington and its academic institutions as a personal affront, perhaps moved by VMI's prominent contributions to the secessionist cause and the fact that almost a quarter of the town's residents were enslaved. Whatever the reason, he determined to burn some of the town's most cherished buildings, including VMI, parts of Washington College, and the private residence of former Governor John Letcher, an outspoken secessionist.[20]

Crook, together with many of his officers, argued strenuously against burning many of VMI's buildings. Hayes noted in his dairy: "General Hunter burns the Virginia Military Institute. This does not suit many of us. General Crook, I know, disapproves. It is surely bad."[21] The officers thought burning the cadet barracks justified because of the students' participation in active hostilities against the Union, but the wholesale looting and burning of the library and other structures solely devoted to education disgusted them. They were particularly angered by the decision to destroy the homes of the professors, especially the residence of one academic whose brother-in-law served as an officer in the Union army.

Many in the officer corps were still imbued with chivalric notions of combat and were horrified by the idea of making war on civilians. While such idealistic concepts were soon made obsolete by the campaigns of Generals Sherman and Sheridan, at the time Hunter sacked Lexington, a significant number of army officers viewed his actions as an appalling violation of the conventions of civilized warfare. Crook later remarked in disgust that Hunter "would have burned the Natural Bridge could he have compassed it."[22]

While Hunter burned Lexington, as Crook had predicted, Lee was making an extraordinary effort to protect his supply and communications lines at Lynchburg. He dispatched Major General John C. Breckenridge with 2,000 troops to intercept and delay Hunter and another 8,000 men, almost 20 percent of the army defending Richmond and Petersburg, under Lieutenant General Jubal Early to reinforce the town itself.[23]

Early's force represented the remnants of Lieutenant General Richard Ewell's old corps, veterans of Stonewall Jackson's feared "Foot Cavalry."

A talented and aggressive officer and a clever tactician, Early was one of Lee's most highly regarded senior officers.[24] Known to his men as "Old Jube" or in better times "Old Jubilee," he had glittering eyes and a hairy face nestled atop shoulders bowed by rheumatoid arthritis, contracted during the Mexican War. These features lent him the appearance of a "malignant and very hairy spider," an image consistent with his irascible, though wily, personality. Caustic, irreverent, and a harsh disciplinarian apt to attack his subordinates with a "snarling harshness," Early was not beloved by his fellow officers but justly regarded as a brilliant and innovative field commander.[25]

To take Lynchburg, Hunter's army would have to reach it before Early. The urgency of prompt action was compounded when the Union commander learned that he could not count on Sheridan's force to block or delay the Rebels. Sheridan had abandoned his westward thrust, which was partially intended to act as a buffer against Lee's army, after clashing with Confederate cavalry at Trevilian Station, east of Gordonsville.

Crook pressed Hunter to move quickly, now regarding the destruction of Lexington as not only an act of vandalism but also an egregious waste of time. As he had previously, the general claimed to appreciate Crook's point. Nevertheless, he tarried in Lexington for three days while completing its destruction, awaiting the arrival of a shipment of ammunition from Sigel and the arrival of Duffié's cavalry, whom he presently expected to return from their feint toward Charlottesville. The Frenchman finally trotted into Lexington on the thirteenth, reporting that he had been delayed by operations that he claimed had resulted in the destruction of five miles of the Charlottesville-Lynchburg railway and the capture of seventy prisoners, seven hundred horses, and three hundred wagons. Crook, having none of it, grumpily expressed his opinion that the Frenchman's tardiness was more likely due to his penchant for pillaging.[26]

Finally, the day after Duffié's return, Hunter resumed his march toward Lynchburg, sending Crook's division ahead to destroy the James River and Kanawha Canal and lead the assault on the town. Averell's cavalry was to accompany Crook, serving as his eyes and ears in the countryside. The troops soon set about the ruination of the James River and Kanawha with such enthusiasm that in one officer's opinion, "[b]efore morning, a pollywog could not make his way in that canal."[27]

But though the canal was one of Grant's primary objectives, the time required to destroy it further delayed Hunter's advance, giving Early additional time to get his troops into the city.

On the fifteenth Crook's lead elements crossed the Blue Ridge at Peaks of Otter. As they marched through the beautiful pass, the soldiers plucked huge blooms from the rhododendrons that grew along the trail and placed them in the barrels of their rifles. Coming into camp that evening outside the agricultural center of Liberty, less than twenty-five miles from Lynchburg, the column seemed to one romantic officer "like a moving bank of flowers."[28]

But Crook was not in the mood for floral fantasies. While his troops relaxed after their hard day's march, he nervously paced the campsite. Far in the van of Hunter's army, his tents pitched in close proximity to an enemy force estimated to number 10,000 troops, he feared for his exposed flank and rear. Fortunately, the night passed quietly, and the next morning Crook's soldiers marched through Liberty, burning the Virginia and Tennessee depot and destroying some six miles of track, a column of black smoke trailing in their wake.[29]

Though Crook had worried about the slowness of Hunter's progress, in Liberty he learned that Lynchburg had not yet been strongly fortified. He also received word from Averell that the cavalry had reached the outskirts of town and had driven screening Confederate cavalry into the outer fortifications.

When Hunter heard the news as he approached Liberty, he was finally galvanized into action. He promptly ordered Crook to combine his infantry with Averell's cavalry and trap the Rebel horsemen before they could withdraw farther into the city. Hunter's men arrived on the field just in time "to witness the gallant conduct of Crook's troops driving the enemy in confusion from the field, capturing seventy prisoners and one gun." While some might have enjoyed the spectacle, it came at a personal cost to Crook. Lieutenant Cyrus Roberts, an aide with whom the general had formed a close relationship, was seriously wounded during the fighting.[30]

As darkness fell, the Kanawha Division's second brigade actually breached the outer works. But Hunter, not wanting to fight at night in hostile urban streets, lost what in hindsight would be his last opportunity to capture Lynchburg, ordering his troops to stand down until morning.

That night Crook's men camped so close to the defenses that orders were issued prohibiting campfires. The Federals bolted an unpalatable supper of "hard tack and raw bacon, washed down with water from a canteen," and lay down on their weapons to await the dawn. During the night they were repeatedly awakened by the "rumbling of trains which incessantly pulled into the railroad station, together with the beating of drums and the cheering of troops, indicating that the enemy was being reinforced by rail." Some of the sounds were made by the arrival of the remainder of Early's corps, but the majority of his men were already in Lynchburg. Most of the noise was part of a ruse by the Virginian, who had his engines run back and forth within the city throughout the night to simulate the arrival of multitudes of imaginary troops that sprang entirely from the general's fertile imagination.[31]

Dawn came with the promise of hard fighting under a relentless summer sun. Hunter soon confirmed from blacks who had fled the city that he faced a greatly reinforced Confederate force, totaling in his estimate around 20,000 men.[32] Their numbers and the fact that they had now dug in behind barricades at every point of access gave pause to the formerly confident general. Nevertheless, he was still determined to give battle.

Hunter formed his line in a three-mile arc to the southwest of Lynchburg. The field before him was broken countryside choked with thick woods and brush. From his position in the center of his line, where he placed two of his infantry divisions and artillery, the Federal commander could clearly see the strength of the Rebel fortifications and decided against a frontal assault. Instead he directed his cavalry to make a series of probes on the right and left flanks, searching for weak points in the defenses.[33]

Crook's division occupied the southern part of the Union line. At about one o'clock in the afternoon, hoping to flank the defenders and enter Lynchburg from the rear, Hunter ordered Crook to move through the thick woods around the Confederate left. Crook had advanced three or four miles before determining that such a flank attack would not be feasible. As he was returning to the division's original position, Early's troops initiated an unexpected assault on the Union left and center, their heart-stopping Rebel yells filling the air. Fortunately, Captain Henry Dupont, Hunter's young but talented artillery commander (and later author of a perceptive memoir of the 1864 Valley Campaign), had placed his guns on the field with great care. Enfilading canister fire mowed through the ranks of the Confederates, stalling the attackers and giving Crook time to hurry his men back into line to meet the renewed assault. The westerners counterattacked aggressively, driving the Rebels back to their works. One regiment, the 116th Ohio, actually beat its way over the barricades and, by liberal application of bayonet and rifle butt, entered the city streets. But alone and without support, they could not hold their position and fell back.[34]

Though Hunter had beaten back a strong Confederate attack and mounted a successful counterattack of his own, the capture of several soldiers from Ewell's II Corps confirmed in his mind Early's undoubted numerical superiority—30,000 troops according to Hunter's aide and cousin, Colonel Strothers, though Hunter later reported the number at 20,000 men. Both estimates were grossly inflated. The Federals probably outnumbered the Confederates by about a third. But Hunter, overawed by the imagined size, leadership, and quality of the troops he faced and concerned about his own shortage of supplies, most critically ammunition, decided to withdraw.[35]

The general discussed the route of withdrawal with all of his senior officers. But their unsuccessful efforts to take the city had greatly diminished his confidence in most of them. He singled out Averell for his "stupidity and conceit" and held Duffié and Brigadier General Jeremiah Sullivan, First Division commander, in equally low esteem.[36] The only general whose advice he seemed to value at the moment was Crook.

As Crook saw it, the army had two alternatives: retreat either north through the Shenandoah or northwest through West Virginia and up the Kanawha Valley, resupplying the column at Meadow Bluff. Hunter decided on the latter.[37] Though Crook had no illusions regarding the hardships a retreat through West Virginia would entail, the alternative, a march northward down the Shenandoah to the Potomac, would be more dangerous. Hunter feared that Early would use the railroad to get ahead of him and ambush his forces, which weakened by lack of ammunition and supplies, might be annihilated before they could escape the narrow confines of the Valley. Both Crook and Hunter were aware that a Union withdrawal from the Valley would remove the only force of any consequence between the Rebels and the Potomac, leaving the Shenandoah open to Early. Twice before the Confederates had used this route to invade the North. But Hunter optimistically believed that if Early tried such an attack, the Federals would be able to move quickly through West Virginia to cut him off.

The initial stages of the withdrawal were conducted after dark on the evening of June 18. Leaving a regiment of the First Division to man a picket line facing the enemy works, the remainder of Hunter's troops retreated silently into the night toward Liberty. The operation was conducted with such secrecy and haste that several units did not receive word of it, the men only discovering Hunter's intent when they found themselves alone on the battlefield. A number of wounded were abandoned because the surgeon received no word to evacuate them. Even so, at least a part of the army began the march with full bellies. Prior to their afternoon attack, Old Jube's troops had stampeded some three hundred sheep into the Union works to create a distraction. Unfazed by the rampaging ruminants, the Yankees slaughtered the lot and served them up for dinner.[38] It would be their last satisfying meal for several days.

As had been the case the previous evening, the night air carried the sounds of trains and martial music from Lynchburg, indicating to Union officers that Early was receiving additional reinforcements during the night. Dupont described the situation from the Yankees' perspective as they went into camp near Liberty in the dark hours of the morning: "With but little ammunition and less food, we now found ourselves in a hostile country several hundred miles from our base, from which we were entirely cut off, and confronted by a force of Confederate veteran troops under Early much greater than our own."[39]

The next morning a dazed Hunter appeared unable to comprehend the need to move rapidly out of Early's reach. He resumed his march only after intense prodding from Dupont, who, like Crook, appeared to have his commander's trust. Crook's division covered the withdrawal from the rear and bore the brunt of Early's harassing attacks. The men marched throughout the day and into the night, a night that Crook later described as among the most difficult he experienced during the entire war. Worn out by continuous marching and fighting over the past three weeks, the soldiers stumbled along through the darkness in a fog of exhaustion. Individuals dropped out along the road, curling up to sleep in the thick brush, too tired to have any concern for their safety. Lacking confidence in his fellow commanders, Crook felt the entire weight of responsibility for the safety of his men resting heavily on his own fatigued shoulders. Bringing up the rear and struggling to keep himself awake, the general spent long hours beating the bushes for sleeping men, knowing that if they did not get up and move, they would be snatched up by Confederate cavalry in the morning. Years later the normally good-natured officer would regretfully recall, "I had to be very cross and make myself exceedingly disagreeable, but that all failed to prevent many from falling out."[40]

Crook's reservations about his fellow senior officers appeared well founded. At dawn his men walked into an ambush that the troops marching ahead had carelessly failed to spot. Fortunately, the attack was mounted by a small party of bushwhackers and was quickly dispersed.

During the first days of the withdrawal, Hunter, in a state of shock after his failure to take Lynchburg, appeared to abdicate command. Crook, in contrast, remained cool and decisive, and other officers turned to him for guidance. After passing through Buford Gap two days out of Lynchburg, Dupont sought out Hunter for orders to continue the march. He found the commander reposing in a small cottage along the road, appearing confused and unwell, still unable to grasp the urgency of the situation. Claiming that he could not find his staff, Hunter asked the captain to take the necessary measures for continuing the march. Taking matters in hand, Dupont approached Crook, who without hesitation decided on the time and order of march.[41]

As the column progressed and Rebel activity tapered off, Hunter regained his composure—as well as his punitive attitude toward civilians. In his memoir Crook, who refrained from commenting on Hunter's failure to command during the early stages of the retreat, wrote harshly of his commander's callous treatment of local women who came to him with complaints about ravages committed against their poor farmsteads by foraging Union soldiers. With distaste, Crook watched Black Dave drive these distraught wives and mothers away with abusive shouts and threats to burn their homes.[42]

On the twenty-first, Confederate cavalry, in a last foray against the retreating Yankees, ambushed the artillery train, which contrary to Crook's advice, Hunter had concentrated in one section of the column, an action guaranteed to maximize the destructive effect of an enemy attack. The Federals lost eight cannon and thirty horses in the ambush. It did not have to happen, though: Hunter had been warned by one of the women who had approached him, but he had characteristically ignored the warning and brushed her aside.[43]

Now, though no longer threatened by the Rebels, Hunter's troops faced the same adversaries—hunger, fatigue, and difficult terrain—that had plagued Crook during his withdrawal from Dublin. But Hunter's men, unlike Crook's troops, were far less disciplined, and as a consequence suffered much more severely from lack of food. Their rations, enough for two days, had to suffice for nine, and many consumed them quickly, forcing the men to scavenge food from the poor farms along the way. When that failed, many ate tree bark.[44]

The army "reach[ed] the Kanawha Valley in a sad plight. Men were worn out from fatigue and hunger, all sadly in need of clothing. Many were barefoot." They were in such desperate straits that when they encountered a resupply column coming to their rescue, all comradeship was forgotten, and the men fell upon the rations, "quarreling like wolves." In a letter to his uncle written two days after arriving at Meadow Bluff, Colonel Hayes summed up the experience: "Our greatest suffering was want of food & sleep—I often went to sleep on my horse." By his reckoning the troops had been in the field for two months. During that time, they had marched about eight hundred miles and fought or skirmished about forty days of that time.[45] The hard campaigning had taken its toll.

CHAPTER TWENTY-THREE

Early's Raid on Washington

July 1864

When Lee ordered Early to the Shenandoah, he had given him two as-signments. The first was to attack and if possible destroy Hunter's force at Lynchburg. If successful, he was then to "move down the valley, cross the Potomac, . . . and threaten Washington City." Such an operation, Lee believed, would compel Grant to withdraw troops from Petersburg to defend the Federal capital.[1] On July 22, after breaking off his pursuit of Hunter, Early received a wire from Lee diplomatically urging him to carry out the second part of his operation. Though he had not achieved his goal of destroying Hunter's army, by driving the Federals out of the Shenandoah, he had cleared the way to carry out his second objective. On June 23, with nothing but General Sigel's ragtag command between himself and Washington, Early marched his army down the Valley Pike toward Maryland.

Were Crook and Hunter remiss in withdrawing their force into West Virginia, leaving the Valley open and Washington exposed to Early's army? Although there were those in the War Department who would have liked to hold Hunter responsible for subsequent events, General Grant was not among them. He wrote that the "want of ammunition left [Hunter] no choice of route for the return but by the way of the Gauley and Kanawha rivers."[2] Had he withdrawn north up the Valley, his army, already low on ammunition and food, would have been exposed to the threat of constant enemy attacks and cut off from sources of resupply in the North. Under these circumstances, one can speculate that the troops may well have been too weakened by the time they arrived at the Potomac to have done much to stop Early's veterans.

As it was, the Confederates moved quickly up the Valley. Sigel's troops offered minimal resistance, retreating from Martinsburg, West Virginia, north across the Potomac at the first news of Early's approach. By July 6 the entire Rebel force had crossed the river at Shepherdstown above Harpers Ferry, bypassing Sigel, and were en route to the nation's capital. For their part, myopic War Department officials, though aware that Early was on the move and faced little opposition in the Valley, remained unwilling to believe that his objective was Washington. Lincoln's chief of staff, General Halleck, and Secretary of War Stanton imagined that the Rebels intended to attack the Baltimore and Ohio Railroad, Washington's lifeline to the West. To counter this threat, they ordered Hunter to move his troops to Martinsburg.[3]

Hunter received the directive at Meadow Bluffs on July 1, only a day after his troops had completed their exhausting trek from Lynchburg. Though his men desperately needed rest and resupply, the general and most of his army embarked two days later aboard a steamer to Parkersburg en route to Cumberland, leaving Crook's division behind to guard the Kanawha Valley. Delayed by low water on the Kanawha and Ohio Rivers, Black Dave did not arrive at Cumberland until the eighth.[4] Out of communications with his superiors for that entire critical period, he was unaware that Early had crossed the Potomac two days earlier and was already in Frederick, now obviously headed for Washington rather than the Baltimore and Ohio.

Any remaining doubt as to Early's objective disappeared when elements of his army attacked Fort Stevens, one of the military posts guarding Washington, on July 12. Capturing the capital had never been a realistic objective for the relatively weak Confederate force.[5] So after encountering stiff resistance at the fort, Early withdrew from the city and crossed the Potomac back into Virginia at White's Ferry after midnight on the fourteenth.

Although the War Department hoped to intercept the Confederates before they could return to the safety of the Shenandoah, it did not believe that Hunter was the man to do it. In the department's eyes his slow progress in reaching Cumberland, his perceived refusal to communicate with Washington on a regular basis, and his failure to capture Lynchburg clearly demonstrated his lack of fitness for the task. Grant

Horatio Wright, commander of the VI Corps. His corps was one of the most reliable in the Union army throughout the Civil War. Wright himself was a competent, though not particularly inspiring, leader. Courtesy of the National Archives.

therefore ordered that Major General Horatio Wright, commander of the VI Corps, be given supreme command of all troops in pursuit of Early's forces. Considered one of the most reliable senior commanders in the Army of the Potomac, Wright had graduated from West Point second in his class, earning a position in the engineers, for which his competent but cautious nature well suited him.[6] But as he would soon demonstrate, he had neither the aggressiveness nor the independent spirit required to successfully catch a wily field commander of General Early's caliber.

Placing Wright in overall command was only part of Stanton and Halleck's plan. To ensure that Hunter's troops would be properly led in the field, they named General Crook operational commander of those forces, which effectively relegated Hunter to a desk job in Martinsburg. Faced with handing over operational control of his troops to an officer junior to him (Crook was only a brigadier) and being subordinated to a general (Wright) commissioned at a later date than himself, the offended Hunter promptly asked to be relieved of command. Only a soothing letter from Lincoln kept him from resigning his commission.[7]

While Hunter struggled to reach Martinsburg, General Crook remained with his division in Charleston tensely awaiting orders. His anxiety increased daily, fed by a constant flow of information describing Early's advance up the Valley, across the Potomac, and into Maryland. At last he received orders to proceed to Martinsburg with his division. Arriving there on July 15, he found another communiqué from the War Department instructing him to leave his men behind and report to nearby Hillsborough, West Virginia, to relieve Jeremiah Sullivan, one of Hunter's most incompetent generals, of command of the First Division. This was the first step in Crook's assumption of operational control of Hunter's forces. With the First Division, Crook was to coordinate with the VI and XIX Corps in an effort to intercept Early's army, though no one seemed to know its current location.

The troops at Hillsborough welcomed their new general. By now Crook's leadership during the Dublin raid and the Lynchburg offensive had given him the somewhat overblown reputation as "the 'Stonewall Jackson' of the Union Army," a man who—and this more accurately described him—"could be found on the skirmish line, not the telegraph office." One of his brigade commanders, Colonel Joseph Thoburn, wrote in his diary, "I am pleased with Genl. Crook and like the change."[8]

Aside from his reputation, Crook's warm welcome owed much to the fact that Sullivan's division was in complete disarray. Never one to mince words, Crook placed the entire blame squarely on its former commander. "No one knew anything about the enemy, no scouts [were] out about the country. It was sufficient to account for all this by the fact that Gen. Sullivan was in command. For in addition to his many other shortcomings, he lacked actual physical courage." Crook acted quickly, dispatching scouts to seek out the enemy. He soon learned to his dismay that Early's army had successfully eluded both his own troops and Wright's corps, slipping through a six-mile gap between the two forces. Before Crook could get his men on the road, the last of Early's rear guard had marched through Snicker's Gap, a pass in the Blue Ridge Mountains into the Shenandoah Valley.[9]

The next day, July 17, Crook joined forces with Wright's VI Corps, and together, they marched toward Snicker's Gap, still uncertain of Early's exact location. At Wright's direction, Crook ordered his cavalry through the gap to "push the rear of the enemy's column, and ascertain if possible what route they had taken."[10] They soon reported that the Confederates had already crossed the Shenandoah River at Snicker's Ford, leaving a strong force on the opposite (west) bank to discourage pursuit.

While Crook confronted Early's forces at Snicker's Ford, in Washington the War Department approved his promotion to major general. Though he had borne no great love, let alone respect, for General Hunter, the latter continued to hold Crook in high regard. On July 17 Hunter had telegraphed Secretary Stanton recommending Crook for advancement: "I consider him one of the best soldiers I have ever seen, and one of the most reliable and well-balanced of men. . . . His promotion to a superior command would be of great advantage to the public service and of very special benefit in this department." The next day Stanton accepted Hunter's recommendation. But since major generals could only be appointed to fill existing vacancies, and no such vacancies existed at present, he could only confer on Crook a brevet appointment.[11]

Though he might have found the brevet rewarding, thoughts of promotion were far from his mind as he stood with General Wright on a bluff overlooking Snicker's Ford. From their vantage point, the generals could see gray-clad troops occupying the west bank of the Shenandoah in numbers that would make a frontal assault costly. While he still did not know the location of the main body of Early's army, Crook was determined to cross the river in pursuit of the Rebels. To avoid an opposed crossing at the well-defended ford, he sent his cavalry to reconnoiter Ashby's Gap, a pass to the south, hoping that if it were unguarded, Wright's troops could cross there and come in behind the unsuspecting Rebel rear guard. But the scouts reported that Early had anticipated such a move and had blocked the gap with a strong detachment. With that option unavailable, Wright directed Crook to send Colonel Thoburn downriver (north) to cross about a mile and a half below Snicker's Ford.

Joseph Thoburn, commander of the First Division in Crook's VIII Corps. A brave and trusted leader, Thoburn was mortally wounded during the Confederate attack at Cedar Creek. Courtesy of the T. James Thoburn Collection, U.S. Army Military History Institute.

Born in County Antrim, Ireland, Joseph Thoburn had emigrated with his family to Ohio when still a child. He had been a practicing physician in civilian life and enlisted as a surgeon in a western Virginia regiment at the outset of the war. But soon he was given command of a regiment, and during the Lynchburg Campaign he had performed credibly as commander of the Second Brigade in Sullivan's division.[12] Indicative of his high regard for the colonel, Crook had elevated Thoburn to command of the First Division upon assuming operational control of Hunter's forces in the Shenandoah.

Leading his own division and a brigade from the Second Division, Thoburn quickly crossed the Shenandoah at Island Ford. There he captured several prisoners and from them learned to his consternation that an entire Confederate corps, commanded by General Breckinridge and reinforced by a division under Major General Robert Rodes, was moving rapidly to engage him. The colonel quickly dispatched a courier to Crook to inform him of this startling development while maintaining his position across the river. Thoburn's small force consisted of only 5,000 men but among them were some of the weakest elements under Crook's command, including about 1,000 dismounted cavalry and several hundred inexperienced, short-term men from Ohio and Maryland. This left him with only about 3,000 reliable troops to meet the larger, battle-hardened Confederate force approaching.[13]

The Rebels attacked in short order, initiating what became known as the Battle of Cool Spring (or Snicker's Gap). Under pressure from superior numbers, Thoburn's men soon found themselves trapped within the confines of a narrow floodplain on the west bank, their backs to the river. Some of the previously untested Union troops panicked, many breaking from the line and fleeing into the water. Only Thoburn's veterans remained steady, determined to hold off their attackers. From the bluff Crook could see that his colonel was in trouble. He urged General Wright to withdraw Thoburn back across the river. Instead Wright turned to Brigadier General James Ricketts and ordered him to reinforce the position with his division of seasoned troops from the XI Corps.[14]

By the time Crook and Ricketts descended to the riverbank, the combat opposite had become extremely heavy as increasing numbers of Southern troops moved to the attack. The river before the generals was filled with hundreds of frightened soldiers scrambling to reach the east bank and safety. The enemy showed such strength, Crook angrily wrote in his memoir, that "Gen. Ricketts declined to go to [Thoburn's] support and allowed many of my men to be sacrificed. I lost some valuable men here, murdered by incompetency or worse." For the remainder of the day, fighting from behind a stone wall that ran parallel to the river, Thoburn's remaining troops, under the colonel's staunch leadership, held off several Confederate assaults. But as night fell, in the face of mounting casualties and Ricketts's refusal to commit his men against such great odds, Crook ordered the surviving troops back across the river. Having lost over 400 men in this action, he complained bitterly to Wright of Ricketts's failure to take action, implying that it was due to a want of courage on Ricketts's part. Understanding Crook's implication of cowardice and knowing that he was badly off the mark, Wright chose to disregard the complaint.[15]

Notwithstanding Crook's insinuations, General Ricketts had an unimpeachable record of personal courage—shot four times at First Bull Run and badly injured at Antietam when his horse was shot out from under him; he would soon suffer another wound, taking a bullet in the chest. Nor had he been loath to expose his men in battle. At Monocacy only weeks before, of the 677 men killed that day, 595 were from Ricketts's division. Two weeks after the engagement at Snicker's Ford, he would be brevetted major general for gallant conduct, particularly during campaigns with Sheridan and Grant.[16] Wright recognized the absurdity of Crook's accusations in view of Ricketts's record. Furthermore, he knew that the flow of battle at the time would have made it unlikely that Ricketts's intervention would have influenced the outcome. Under the circumstances, the commander considered the general's refusal to commit his troops appropriate and Crook's assessment the result of his anger at the loss of his men.

Unfortunately, this outburst was not an isolated incident. As he rose through the ranks, Crook became increasingly less circumspect in denouncing the perceived incompetence of his fellow officers, sometimes on the field but more often in his memoirs, particularly when he thought that their actions put his men in jeopardy. These virulent outbursts, sometimes accompanied, as in Colonel Minty's case, by resort to the court-martial process, were in such marked contrast to the general's normally soft-spoken, reticent demeanor that they seemed to emanate from some inner turmoil.

Analyzing the psychological motivations of historical figures long in their graves is always suspect. But at least with respect to Ricketts, Crook's inner demons may have had their roots in a lingering insecurity that originated during his years at West Point, where westerners were sometimes the objects of scorn to the aristocratic sons of the eastern and southern establishments. These regional prejudices had become more pronounced during the years immediately preceding the Civil War and continued unabated during the war itself. At Cool Spring the VI Corps was largely composed of regiments from the East, and Ricketts himself was a New Yorker of aristocratic bearing. Perhaps Crook, the plain commander of units mostly from the West, viewed Ricketts's refusal to aid his men as yet another manifestation of an easterner's indifference to the welfare of westerners and overreacted accordingly.

On July 17, while Crook fumed and Wright puzzled over what to do next, Halleck sent a wire to Hunter, who was still nominally in command of his department. The communiqué, replete with unsubtle references to Black Dave's failure to capture Lynchburg and his decision to retreat through West Virginia, relayed Grant's decision to have Hunter pursue Early up the Valley, in the process making "all the valleys south of [the] Baltimore and Ohio road a desert as high up as possible." To emphasize the latter point, Halleck wrote, in a phrase that endures today in the hearts of the people of the Shenandoah: "He [Grant] wants your troops to eat out Virginia clear and clean as far as they go, so that crows flying over it for the balance of the season will have to carry their provender with them." "Old Brains," as Halleck was widely known, concluded his instructions with a gratuitous jab at Hunter's already bruised ego. "If compelled to fall back, you will retreat in front of the enemy toward the main crossings of the Potomac, so as to cover Washington, and not be squeezed out to one side, so as to make it necessary to fall back into West Virginia to save your army."[17]

Spurred by these insulting references, Hunter thought he saw an opportunity to demonstrate his generalship by attacking Early from the rear while the Rebels were preoccupied with Crook and Wright at Island Ford. To accomplish that objective, he ordered Colonel Hayes's brigade, which had just been transferred from the Kanawha to Martinsburg, to cross the Shenandoah to the north of the ford to hit the Confederates on their flank, trapping them between Hayes's troops and Crook's force.[18] The plan came to nothing, though. Hayes advanced to within six miles of the ford, close enough to hear cannon fire from the fighting, but after a sharp engagement at Kabletown, he withdrew upon learning that Early's entire army lay to his front.[19]

Meanwhile, Averell had moved on Winchester, endangering Early's rear and threatening his supply trains. With some infantry support, he occupied the town and attacked the Confederate rear guard. In a hot fight at Rutherford's farm outside Winchester, he skillfully managed his outnumbered Federals and won the day.

While neither engagement had much tactical significance, the presence of Averell and Hayes to his rear concerned Early sufficiently to cause him to withdraw his entire force to Strasburg, some twenty miles south of Winchester. Unfortunately, General Wright misread the reasons for this move as well as its direction, erroneously concluding that Early now intended to rejoin Lee's army at Petersburg. On July 17 the VI Corps commander declared to Halleck, "I have no doubt that the enemy is in full retreat to Richmond." Grant's original orders, as relayed to Wright, had been to pursue the Rebels only until he "[assured] himself of the retreat of the enemy toward Richmond," then to return to Washington.[20] So on July 20, in accordance with his misreading of Early's intentions, Wright withdrew the VI and XIX Corps from the Shenandoah and headed back toward Washington, confident that he was acting in accordance with Grant's wishes.

With Wright's departure, Hunter reassumed command of the entire Union presence in the Shenandoah, now reduced to two divisions of infantry, two divisions of cavalry, and some miscellaneous units, all under the field command of Crook. These were the only troops between Early and the Potomac River.

With Early gone, Crook crossed the Shenandoah River and camped near Berryville, not far from the Cool Spring battleground. His men occupied themselves reinterring the remains of the Union dead, whose bodies had been left in shallow graves by the Rebels. Though aware of his exposed position, Crook nevertheless agreed with Wright's conclusion that the Confederates were returning to Petersburg. To speed Early on his way, he planned to rest his men nearby for a couple of days "to give the enemy the impression we will not follow them, so that they may send a good portion of their command to Richmond." But, he cautioned Hunter during a July 21 visit to the general's Harpers Ferry headquarters, if the Rebels turned to attack him, "I have not forces sufficient to meet all their forces in this open valley, and my only hope is for them to divide their command."[21]

Grant also recognized this vulnerability. On the twenty-third, convinced that without Wright's troops Union forces in the Shenandoah were neither strong enough nor in shape to take on Early, he countermanded his earlier order to pursue the Confederates south. Instead he instructed Hunter to move his troops back to a defensible position along the Potomac to guard against another invasion of Maryland. Grant did not return the VI Corps to the Shenandoah as he still considered the possibility of a renewed Rebel offensive in the region to be remote. In a wire to Halleck, the general in chief opined, "Early is undoubtedly returning here [Petersburg] to enable the enemy to detach troops to go to Georgia" to oppose Sherman. But he did agree, at Halleck's urging, that until Early's intentions could be finally determined, the XIX Corps would remain in Washington rather than return to Petersburg.[22]

The only individual in the chain of command beside Halleck who appeared to believe that Early would actually attack Hunter's force was President Lincoln. He wrote to Hunter on July 23 to ask, "Are you able to take care of the enemy when he turns back upon you, as he probably will on finding that Wright has left?" The general promptly responded that, though his forces were not strong enough to hold the enemy should Early attack in full force, "[o]ur latest advices from the front . . . do not lead me to apprehend such a movement. General Crook has information, upon which he relies, that Early left his position at Berryville suddenly upon the arrival of a courier from Richmond with orders to fall back to that place [Richmond]."[23] The faith the Union generals placed in this piece of faulty intelligence would soon prove devastating.

Crook's decision to remain in the Winchester area for a couple of days gave his men a much-needed, if temporary, break and provided him with an opportunity to reorganize his troops. His command now included Sullivan's old division, inherited from Hunter; the Kanawha Division, which rejoined him at Winchester; some troops assigned to him from Sigel's old army; and two cavalry divisions under Averell and Duffié. The infantry totaled about 14,000 men on paper, but it actually numbered about 12,000 effectives, most of whom were badly in need of rest. A soldier of the Twelfth West Virginia wrote to his local newspaper describing the effect that the constant campaigning of the last three months had on the fitness of his unit. The Twelfth had begun the expedition to Lynchburg with 660 men. But, he wrote, by August 1864 they could muster only 230. "There was not a man in the regiment who did not feel pretty 'old' and debilitated." His assessment could apply to Crook's entire command.[24]

Though exhausted and of disparate and depleted units, these men represented the largest force Crook had ever led, and he now faced the daunting task of integrating them into a cohesive fighting command. Though in strength these troops would have constituted only a single moderate-sized division, Crook organized them, together with his two cavalry divisions, into a corps that he proudly christened the Army of the Kanawha, later changing the name to that used by Hunter and Sigel, the Army of West Virginia.[25] Informally known to its members as "Crook's Corps," the unit designation gave its officers and men a feeling of independence and cohesion that they had never felt as part of Hunter's command.

Crook had inherited from Sigel a brigade of Irish Americans commanded by Colonel James Mulligan. Though born in upstate New York and raised in Chicago, Mulligan was Irish to the core, a deeply religious Roman Catholic brimming with Gaelic charm and fire. By all accounts an imposing man, tall and broad shouldered, he had "large lustrous hazel eye [sic]" set in an "open Celtic face . . . surmounted by a bushy profusion of hair, tinctured with gray." He had trained as a lawyer but, at the outbreak of the war, had given up his practice and formed a brigade of Irish recruits. He and his men had been surrounded and captured after a heroic stand at Lexington, Missouri, that inspired citizens throughout the North during the first year of the war. After his release as part of a prisoner exchange, Mulligan returned to Chicago, reconstructed his brigade, and led it through two years of service in the mountains of West Virginia, battling guerrillas and guarding the Baltimore and Ohio Railroad. Wearing an emerald green shirt and scarf in battle, he was flamboyant and charismatic, commanding the adoration and undying loyalty of his men.[26]

But to Crook, Mulligan was an unknown quantity. The general preferred and trusted two other senior officers, Colonel Isaac Duval and Joseph Thoburn, whom he had seen in action and favored as division commanders. But with only two divisions, as Mulligan outranked both men by virtue of seniority, Crook would have to appoint him over one of them.

He finessed the issue by reorganizing his command into three divisions. The First Division would be led Colonel Thoburn, the Irish-born Buckeye who had proved his worth in the fighting at Cool Spring and

B 2442

James Mulligan, commander of the Third Division, Army of West Virginia. He would be mortally wounded at Second Kernstown. Had Crook listened to his advice, the defeat at Kernstown might have been avoided. Courtesy of the National Archives.

whose men regarded him as a rock in battle. The Second Division went to Duval, an adventurer with a rich romantic history. Born in Virginia, he had left home for the Far West when only thirteen years old. He became a noted scout for John Frémont, finding his way to California, it was said, using only a pocket compass. Service as an Indian agent on the Texas frontier, mining during the gold rush, and soldiering in Cuba, where he barely escaped execution by Spanish authorities, rounded out his resume. Duval had proved himself a competent and brave commander, winning Crook's approval for his conduct at Cloyd's Mountain.[27]

Crook formed the Third Division, commanded by Mulligan, around the colonel's Irish brigade. To them he added the troops he had inherited from General Sigel, mostly hundred-day men (short-term enlistments) and dismounted cavalry (horsemen who had lost their mounts and were now afoot). These were the troops that had panicked at Cool Spring, "odds and ends," Crook called them.[28] The Irishmen, he hoped, would form the backbone of the division, strengthening the weaker troops by their example.

Though Crook gave him command of a division, Mulligan did not hold his new commander in high regard. In his diary he sarcastically recorded his early impression of the general. "I'm taking Crook's measure, his name suggests it." For his part, Crook did not appear greatly impressed by the flamboyant Chicagoan. Perhaps the somewhat Calvinist general, plain of manner, speech, and dress, thought the Irish Catholic colonel too ostentatious in his apparel and form of worship and too flashy in command to be entirely trustworthy. An added reason for their mutual antipathy may have been Mulligan's political and military orientation, the polar opposite of Crook's. As an ardent Democrat, the colonel had scant use for General Grant, "an ordinary man" in Mulligan's opinion, but to Crook, a friend and patron. At the same time, Mulligan considered McClellan to be "the first soldier of the War," sharing his views on both the war and how to obtain peace.[29]

Crook's lack of confidence in his Third Division leader extended to his two cavalry commanders, Generals Averell and Duffié. His mistrust of these men, based on his assessment of Averell's performance during the Dublin raid and Duffié's during the Lynchburg operation, would have important consequences in the battle that was soon to develop around the ramshackle village of Kernstown.

CHAPTER TWENTY-FOUR

The Second Battle of Kernstown

July 24, 1864

It was apparent that Rebel troops were present in the area south of Winchester. On July 22 General Averell's cavalry, reconnoitering near Newtown, seven miles from Winchester, encountered a substantial force of Confederate infantry and cavalry that attacked and drove them back to Kernstown. General Duffié received word of the attack and sent one of his brigades to establish a picket line to hold the Rebels at bay. That evening Averell reported the engagement to Crook at his Winchester headquarters, as did Duffié.[1] Regarding both generals to be unreliable and overcautious, Crook dismissed the engagement as simply a Confederate reconnaissance in force.

At seven o'clock in the morning of the twenty-third, Duffié received information that the enemy was advancing on his picket line at Kernstown. He reported the matter to Crook, who while not entirely disregarding it, again downplayed its importance, remaining wedded to the idea that a large part of Early's army had left the Valley. Consequently, he assumed the Rebel movement represented nothing more than a rearguard action. Still, he directed Duffié to "attack and disburse" them or at least determine the "true state of affairs." Before long it would become apparent that the "true state of affairs" was that Early was probing Crook's line to ascertain its strength preparatory to an attack.[2]

Two hours later, as firing from the south became audible in Winchester, Crook ordered Colonels Mulligan, Thoburn, and Hayes to reinforce Duffié with their infantry and drive the enemy "far enough to

Alfred Duffié, commander of cavalry under Hunter and later Crook. Crook regarded him as inept, and Sheridan recommended that he be cashiered after his capture by enemy troops in the Shenandoah. Courtesy of the National Archives.

ascertain his force."[3] He also prudently protected his supply train by moving it north of Winchester.

After light skirmishing, during which they captured several Union soldiers, the Confederates retired southward in the early afternoon, a move that fit nicely into Crook's preconception of a "rear guard action to cover Early's return to Richmond." Hayes and Thoburn, whose opinions he valued, agreed with this assessment, having found the enemy gone by the time they arrived in Kernstown. Nevertheless, Crook rode down from Winchester and, accompanied by Mulligan, surveyed the ground around the village. Mulligan used the occasion to impress upon Crook his contrary opinion that by now Early must realize that Crook's small army stood alone against him and would, accordingly, go on the offensive. Though Mulligan's arguments failed to sway Crook, the general decided to reinforce Duffié's cavalry, the only force currently stationed in Kernstown, by leaving Mulligan's truncated division of 1,800 officers and men there in case the Rebels returned.[4]

Mulligan was correct. Lieutenant Colonel John S. Mosby's rangers had reported to Early that the VI and XIX Corps had departed for Washington, intelligence confirmed by Union prisoners captured on the twenty-third. With only Crook's outnumbered command between his army and the Potomac, Early determined to drive the Federals out of the Shenandoah. The forces to Crook's front were not a rear guard, but the van of the entire Army of the Valley, approximately 16,000 troops, including battle-hardened veterans who had fought with Stonewall Jackson on that very ground two years earlier. To oppose them, Crook could muster only about 14,000 men, many of them worn down by constant campaigning.[5]

Sunday, July 24, dawned sunny and warm. The Federals had no inkling of imminent danger. One soldier recorded in his diary: "We hoped we would be permitted to remain in camp all day and had made preparations accordingly. Everyone was engaged in writing letters or washing clothes."[6] But this peaceful atmosphere changed with remarkable rapidity.

In late morning Crook again received a report of heavy enemy activity in the same area as the previous day. Captain Hastings, Colonel Hayes's adjutant, noted that the rumble of cannon fire coming from that direction "seemed ominous." But according to the captain, Crook, "still relying on the information . . . that Early was well off on his way to Richmond, did not feel the necessity of immediately moving out and forming a line of battle."[7] The general continued to hold firm to the belief that the enemy's strength had been greatly exaggerated, a conviction he would be forced to abandon shortly.

Before dawn, Early's entire army had begun moving north from its base at Strasburg, twenty miles down the pike. As it marched, divisions peeled off to the east and west on routes paralleling the macadamized road, positioning themselves to attack Crook's flanks. One cavalry column bypassed Winchester, riding north and west of the town positioning itself to attack the Federals as they retreated north. Just south of Kernstown, Early halted, deploying much of his infantry in the folds of the land and in a thick forest to the south known as Barton's Woods, where they would be concealed from the enemy.[8]

On the Union side, Colonel Mulligan's division, which would soon form the center of Crook's battleline at Kernstown, had dug in on Pritchard's Hill, the high point on the battlefield and the precise location from which Union forces had held off Jackson during the First Battle of Kernstown in 1862. Around noon, observing the buildup of enemy forces to his front, the colonel sent his young brother-in-law, Lieutenant James Nugent, to Crook's headquarters to report that Early was on the field in force. Crook, irritated by the colonel's repeated (and he believed overblown) warnings, is said to have responded scornfully, "there is nothing in [Mulligan's] front but a few bushwhackers."[9]

Earlier that morning Crook had ordered Averell, who had been guarding Mulligan's left, to shift his cavalry to the south around the Rebels' right flank to strike the presumed small enemy force in its rear. Averell had been guarding Mulligan's left, and his departure now exposed the colonel's flank. Crook, though skeptical of Nugent's report, sought to correct this potential weakness in the line by dispatching Hayes's brigade to protect the Third Division's left. With Thoburn's division positioned to the rear and right of Mulligan and relatively weak cavalry detachments guarding the flanks, Hayes's arrival on the field completed the Union dispositions. A brigade of Duval's division remained in reserve.

Crook still did not realize that he faced Early's entire army. Major General John B. Gordon held the center of Early's line. To his left was Major General Stephen Ramseur's division and to his right, Brigadier General Gabriel Wharton's division of Breckinridge's Corps. Early correctly supposed that Crook was unaware of the size and composition of the Confederate force, believing it to be mainly cavalry supported by some infantry. The wily Virginian now deployed his troops to exploit this misapprehension to his advantage. At about one o'clock in the afternoon, he had Gordon push forward with a cavalry force supported by sharpshooters against the Union center, while the remainder of his infantry remained concealed in the woods. His objective was to lure Crook into taking the offensive, drawing the weaker Union army into the open fields that lay between Pritchard's Hill and Barton's Wood. Wharton and Ramseur would then emerge on the Yankee flanks and administer the drubbing Early wished to inflict in revenge for the destruction Hunter had wrought during the Lynchburg Campaign.[10]

Crook by now had come to Kernstown to better manage the engagement. But though he was on the scene, he continued to mulishly dismiss reports of the enemy's greater strength and, as Early had hoped, ordered Mulligan to leave his protected defensive position on Pritchard's Hill to drive Gordon's troops out of the fields and woods beyond. While Mulligan attacked the center, Hayes and Thoburn were to initiate assaults on the enemy's left and right flanks. With Averell coming up from the rear, they would have the Rebels in a box. It would have been a good plan had Crook really faced a numerically smaller and less determined enemy.

Just as Mulligan had feared and predicted, he met heavy resistance. While he scored an initial success—with Hayes's assistance he drove Gordon's men from the Opequon churchyard in the middle of the field—the Union triumph was short-lived. Soon thousands of Rebel infantry were pouring out of the woods and into the field, "their bands playing, flags flying." Startled Union troops and their commanders could now see that the enemy "covered a space of at least a mile from right to left." At that moment Crook must have realized his mistake. Mulligan certainly did. "There are too many for us. We will have to retreat," the colonel declared.[11]

As the Rebels drove Mulligan's troops out of the churchyard, Hayes marched to their assistance, only to find that he had walked into a trap. Wharton had moved his division under concealment of a deep ravine to a position behind some hills flanking the Valley Pike, the route that Hayes's men used to move forward. As the Federals passed beneath the brow of the hills, Wharton's men rose up and poured massed fire into their fully exposed lines. The Thirty-Sixth and Twenty-Third Ohio

Regiments took the brunt of the fusillade. One of their officers later declared, "We were broken to bits, under a most destructive fire, and with no possibility of recovering." A Virginian who witnessed the event from his hilltop position commented, "The effect was instantaneous . . . in a few moments the valley below us seemed to be a dark blue irregular moving mass." Another said that he had "never beheld as great a stampede, by as large amount of men without making some show of resistance."[12]

The temporary dissolution of Hayes's brigade as a fighting force exposed Mulligan's left to attack at the same time as Crook diverted one of Thoburn's brigades to protect the right side of the line. This maneuver opened up a gap between Thoburn's division and Mulligan's right that Gordon's men quickly exploited. Mulligan now found himself attacked from both right and left simultaneously by two veteran Rebel divisions. In the face of this Rebel firestorm, the colonel attempted to lead his battered division in an orderly retreat, but while doing so, he was wounded in the thigh. Unable to walk unaided, he was quickly surrounded by soldiers from his loyal Irish brigade, who attempted to remove him from the field under the enemy's concentrated fire. As he saw his men being shot down in a hopeless attempt to save him, Mulligan cried out, "Leave me boys, its no use sacrificing yourselves." Stubbornly they refused, but when he was struck by several more bullets, one of them inflicting a mortal wound, the colonel ordered them to save the colors and leave him on the field. Reluctantly, realizing the futility of their efforts, they obeyed, departing the field with the regimental flags but leaving their commander behind. Two days later Mulligan would die from his wounds in the Pritchard farmhouse, which the Confederates had turned into a makeshift field hospital.[13]

Observing soldiers from Hayes's and Mulligan's units in headlong flight toward Winchester, in numbers that he would later estimate at 3,000–4,000 men, Crook realized that he was beaten.[14] He did what he could to stem the panic by virtue of his calming presence and then set to work organizing an orderly withdrawal, hoping to frustrate Early's intention to capture or annihilate his army.

In this, Crook would have failed without the courageous and effective assistance of his officers. Duffié, the much-maligned cavalryman, bravely interposed his horsemen between the attacking Rebels and the remnants of Hayes's brigade, allowing the charismatic colonel time to reform his men on the brow of Pritchard's Hill and from there conduct a fighting retreat toward Winchester. For his part, Duval, who fortunately had been positioned by Crook on the right and rear of the line, was able to prevent the Confederates from hitting the army on its flank as it passed into Winchester. And lastly Thoburn, acting on orders from Crook, rapidly withdrew his men from the field in good order and marched them into Winchester, where they assumed defensive positions in preparation for the arrival of the remainder of the army.[15]

Crook devoted his energies to restoring a semblance of order and discipline among those soldiers who had panicked and fled the field, organizing a strong rear guard that retarded the Confederate pursuit. As Averell later reported, to ensure that the troops maintained their cohesion, Crook remained "constantly" in the rear during the entire retreat.[16] As a result, by the time the army reached Winchester, it was no longer a panicky mob, but a disciplined force to be reckoned with.

North of Winchester, the restored sense of order was temporarily threatened by the actions of a cavalry brigade, whose frightened warnings of an imminent Confederate attack on the supply train threw the teamsters and artillerymen into a stampede that almost resulted in the train's destruction. For a time chaos reined. Wagons and artillery caissons careened wildly along the crowded roadway, some overturning, others abandoned by their frightened drivers. But cooler heads prevailed, and Crook was able to report that, ultimately, "I got off all my artillery and wagons." Belatedly realizing the inaccuracy of this statement, he amended it to acknowledge that while some teamsters did abandon their wagons along the road, these "were destroyed so that nothing fell into the hands of the enemy."[17]

Once beyond Winchester, the Confederate pursuit lost momentum, perhaps because, as Hastings speculated, the Rebels "had many friends in town with whom they must have a word and stop for the food freely offered."[18] No longer fearful of imminent capture, the weary and beaten Federals settled into a numbing slog through a downpour that had commenced as they departed town, drenching the already bedraggled column and turning the roads to mud. At last, well after nightfall, the exhausted men stumbled into the hamlet of Bunker Hill. Without provisions for even the most marginal supper, they wrapped themselves in their wet blankets, lay down in the soupy mud, and fell into a sleep made restless by their awareness of an enemy not more than ten miles behind them.

At daybreak the men resumed their withdrawal, their stomachs empty, their spirits low, with Early's cavalry snapping at their heels. At Martinsburg confusion reigned, "our troops scattered to the four winds & no organized command." But morale was somewhat restored by an opportunity for hot coffee and bacon, the first meal for most of the soldiers since the previous morning. In the afternoon, with supply train and artillery still intact, the army withdrew across the Potomac into the safety of Maryland. Two days later they reunited with Wright's VI Corps, which had returned from Washington to reinforce Hunter in anticipation of a second invasion by Early's Army of the Valley.[19]

The defeat at Kernstown came at a bad time for the North. The bright hopes of a quick end to the war born of the spring campaign had already begun to fade on the heels of Early's attack on Washington. Now they were dashed by Crook's loss and the disasters that followed: the burning of Chambersburg, Pennsylvania, and the horrific Battle of the Crater at Petersburg. These events magnified the import of Crook's defeat and contributed to a panicky atmosphere among the population, making it appear that Lincoln was incapable of ending the war, which now might continue indefinitely unless the North agreed to peace terms dictated by the South.[20]

For George Crook, while he managed to save his army to fight another day, the battle highlighted several unfortunate aspects of his character. The general's self-assurance usually served him well. But at Kernstown, he demonstrated a propensity to turn self-confidence into arrogance and inflexibility, causing him to ignore credible evidence that failed to conform with his preconceptions. Worse, it appears that he dismissed this intelligence at least in part because of his personal dislike of the officers who brought it to him, making his behavior all the more inappropriate.[21] Though he had some cause to doubt the abilities of his cavalry commanders, Averell and Duffié, and may have been put off by Mulligan's politics and flamboyance, these were officers of long service and combat experience who were in greater proximity to the enemy than he both before and during the battle. Rightfully, their reports deserved far more consideration than Crook gave them.

A second, more persistent flaw again surfaced at Kernstown—an inability to accept responsibility for his errors. Following the battle, instead of forthrightly acknowledging the mistakes that led to his defeat, Crook attempted to shift responsibility to his subordinate commanders and, more reprehensibly, to some of his troops. In his report on the battle, written on July 27 from Harpers Ferry, he obliquely laid blame on his dismounted cavalry, Sigel's unfortunate "odds and ends." They "broke to the rear," he stated, "[at] the first fire, and all efforts to stop them proved to no avail."[22] Certainly this occurred, but it hardly spelled defeat and was an especially harsh judgment by an officer who had failed to prepare and deploy his troops to confront Early's entire army.

Nor did the general spare his mounted cavalry. In his autobiography he dismisses their efforts as "of little or no assistance" and even alleges that he had heard that Averell was drunk during the engagement, an accusation that appears to derive more from Crook's spleen than from hard evidence.[23] Actually, while some of his cavalry did panic during the retreat, producing chaos in the supply train, others effectively screened and protected the infantry during the retreat.

Crook's reckless attack on Averell's reputation, reminiscent of his allegations against Ricketts at Snicker's Gap, demonstrated a heedless disregard for his fellow officers that would make him some powerful enemies in the future.[24]

CHAPTER TWENTY-FIVE

The Bull Terrier and the Newfoundland Dog

July–August 1864

Although his army was too weak, following Kernstown, to mount another attack on Washington, Jubal Early saw opportunity in Crook's retreat into Maryland. Seeking to bring the war home to the North and further avenge Hunter's devastation of the Shenandoah, he selected Chambersburg, the prosperous Pennsylvania town targeted by Jeb Stuart two years previous, as his object lesson and Brigadier General John Mc-Causland's cavalry as his instrument of destruction. Early's instructions were clear and unequivocal: demand a tribute of $100,000 in gold—$500,000 if they wish to pay with paper currency; if they do not pay, burn the town.[1]

Easily eluding Hunter's forces, McCausland crossed the verdant Maryland countryside into Pennsylvania unopposed, reaching Chambersburg on July 30. His demand for ransom refused, his men fired the town. Over four hundred buildings were destroyed and 3,000 civilians left homeless.[2]

The sacking of Chambersburg and McCausland's subsequent ability to elude capture once more underscored the lack of coordination that had plagued Union efforts along the Potomac. The resulting angst in the North also brought home to Grant the political importance of the Shenandoah.[3] He had long known that the conquest of the Valley would seriously hamper Lee's ability to feed his troops and thereby shorten the siege of Petersburg. But now it was apparent that such a victory would revive public support for the war, restore Union morale by denying the

South its easiest invasion route to the North, and help ensure Lincoln's reelection.

In the past there had been three impediments to Union victory in the Valley: poor coordination of troop movements, inept leadership, and inadequate manpower. The lack of a coordinated strategy stemmed from the War Department's political decision to divide the region into four separate military departments, each with an independent command structure, a recipe for the chaotic and haphazard deployments that made coordination a virtual impossibility. With Lincoln's support, Grant now unified the four districts into a single department, the Middle Military Division, encompassing the entire area between the Union army's eastern and western theaters of operation.[4]

He then took on the infinitely more delicate task of identifying a competent general to command the division. Hunter would not do. Despite Grant's personal regard for the man, Black Dave's failure to take Lynchburg or to stop Early's invasion of the North, together with his latest perceived blunder in failing to prevent the raid on Chambersburg, had finally convinced the general in chief that he needed a new man for the job. Bypassing Crook, who had been so soundly defeated at Kernstown and in any event was too junior in rank and experience, Grant first suggested Major General William Franklin, whom the president rejected, and then Major General George Meade. When Meade was turned down by both the War Department and the president, he turned to Crook's old West Point roommate, Phil Sheridan. "Little Phil," as he was fondly called by his men, was now a highly successful cavalryman who had risen meteorically through the ranks since the first year of the war. Though young, he had consistently demonstrated a dogged aggressiveness in battle, most recently against Confederate cavalry in Virginia. Overcoming initial objections by the president and the War Department related to Sheridan's youth, Grant now chose him to replace Hunter.[5]

At thirty-three years of age, Sheridan now became the military commander of the newly formed Middle Military Division and its army in the field, promptly renaming it the Army of the Shenandoah. When in response to Grant's orders, Sheridan alighted from the train at Harpers Ferry to assume his new command, among the men who welcomed him was his old friend and former West Point classmate George Crook.

Sheridan and Crook, the bull terrier and the Newfoundland dog, made an unlikely pair. After three years of war, Crook showed the strain of constant campaigning. Beneath his full beard, his face had lost its youthful appearance, his features hardened into a look of stern maturity. One journalist described him as "of stalwart frame and rugged features, homely in aspect as name. . . . His hair was straight and sandy as likewise his mustache and thin beard, nose long and aquiline, somewhat of a Jewish character, while his eyes were gray and of microscopic power, as I afterwards learned. High cheek-bones and bull neck." Crook dressed casually—like his men, wearing a simple blue serge blouse, distinguished only by shoulder straps with the two stars of a major general. His pants were also of an enlisted man's cut and cloth, though he wore them tucked into high cavalry boots. His only concession to flamboyance was a white, broad-brimmed soft felt hat with braided headband, a style favored by his West Virginian troops.[6] His mode of dress reflected his character, that of a man who had long left behind the need for pretension, a practical soldier with little time or regard for meaningless protocol or ostentation.

Command had not radically altered the general's personality. His men ordinarily found him "easy going and kindly, . . . a notably keen and clear-headed man—genial, patient, low speaking and inclined to reticence, whose equanimity was rarely if ever disturbed even under the most trying circumstances."[7] Although his seemingly bland exterior often concealed strong inner emotions, outwardly at least, he was the antithesis of Sheridan, who was openly fiery, intense, combative, and often impulsive.

Phillip Henry Sheridan, the bull terrier, was three years Crook's junior, born to immigrant Irish parents in 1831. His father worked as a contractor on the construction of the National Road among other projects and was away from home a great deal. Sheridan grew to manhood, primarily under his mother's care, in Somerset, Ohio, about 150 miles east of the Crook farm outside Dayton. He would later claim to have known George Crook as a boy, but there is little evidence to that effect. Poverty forced him to exchange school for the workplace at an early age. So his formal education, like Crook's, was minimal prior to entering the academy. But Sheridan had the good fortune to clerk in a dry-goods store, where he became adept at writing, basic mathematics, and simple recordkeeping, skills that would later stand him in good stead.[8]

In 1848, filled with martial ardor as a consequence of the war with Mexico, Sheridan used a political connection made at the store to secure an appointment to West Point and probably met Crook for the first time when they boarded the same ship on Lake Erie en route to the academy. Then at West Point, though neither man mentioned it in their memoirs, the two became roommates. They subsequently formed a friendship, possibly drawn together as westerners in a student body dominated by the sons of the southern and eastern establishments.[9]

Sheridan's graduation from the academy was delayed when, in a fit of temper, he threatened a cadet officer with his bayonet, an action that resulted in a year's suspension. He ultimately graduated in 1853 and followed Crook to the Department of the Pacific. There the two officers maintained contact, though serving in widely separated assignments, and developed a bond through their shared experiences that they would renew during the war.

When the Civil War broke out, both Sheridan and Crook returned East for reassignment in the Union army. After serving briefly in several desk jobs, Sheridan like Crook saw the volunteer service as the quickest route to promotion and battlefield command. Resigning his regular-army commission, he wangled an appointment as colonel in a Michigan cavalry regiment. There his extreme aggressiveness on the battlefield soon won him rapid promotion and the attention of several powerful generals.

Physically, Sheridan did not fit the mold of the cavalry officer. Unlike the tall, strapping Crook, he stood a surprisingly diminutive five feet, five inches in height. President Lincoln unkindly described him as "a brown, chunky little chap, with a long body, short legs, not enough neck to hang him, and such long arms that if his ankles itch he can skratch [sic] them without stooping." His head was large and somewhat misshapen, making it difficult for him to keep on his hat, so he wore a distinctive porkpie that he held in his hand in battle to avoid losing it. On horseback—he favored a magnificent black horse named Rienzi presented to him by his troops—his ungainliness disappeared and he came "ablaze with enthusiasm," inspiring his men to follow his lead, often into the very jaws of death.[10] His absolute fearlessness under fire was legendary, as was his luck. Despite exposing himself with almost reckless abandon in battle after battle, he would end the war without a scratch.

Grant became an enthusiastic admirer and supporter. When told that Sheridan was awfully small for a cavalryman, the general in chief tartly replied, "You will find him big enough for the purpose before we get through with him," later comparing him to no less than Napoleon and Frederick the Great. The qualities that Grant found most endearing in Little Phil were the pugnacity that got him into so much trouble at the academy, his "magnetic quality in swaying men," and his consequent ability to get the most out of his troops on the battlefield, characteristics that would prove critical in the coming months.[11]

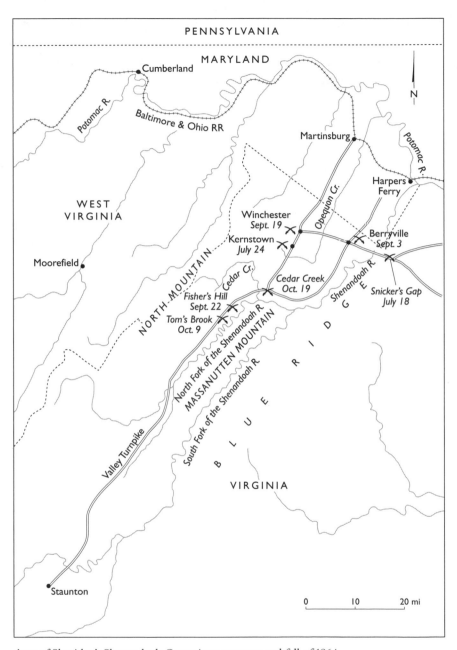

Area of Sheridan's Shenandoah Operations, summer and fall of 1864.

CHAPTER TWENTY-SIX

Campaigning in the Valley

August–September 1864

After greeting his officers at Harpers Ferry, Sheridan repaired to his new quarters and, in company with his chief engineer, Lieutenant John Meigs, pondered the best means to implement the mission Grant had given him only hours earlier. Grant's instructions had not substantially altered since he first gave them to General Hunter in July: "In pushing up the Shenandoah, . . . it is desirable that nothing should be left to invite the enemy to return. Take all provisions, forage, and stock wanted for the use of your command. Such as cannot be consumed, destroy. It is not desirable that the buildings should be destroyed—they should rather, be protected, but the people should be informed that so long as an army can subsist among them, recurrences of these raids must be expected, and we are determined to stop them at all hazards." Referring to Early's army, Grant added, "The object is to drive the enemy south; and to do this you want to keep him always in sight. Be guided in your course by the course he takes."[1]

While some in the Army of the Shenandoah considered their new general an unknown quantity, Crook and his fellow officers had no qualms about the orders under which he was to operate. Captain Hastings spoke for many when he observed, "This order conveyed the true ring, and our army felt from head all through the rank and file, that namby-pamby work of protecting the inhabitants during the growing crop season to see this crop harvested and carried away to feed Lee's army was now over, and war in earnest was to be inaugurated."[2]

For the task before him, Sheridan had at his disposal the VI Corps of the Army of the Potomac under General Wright and Crook's Army of West Virginia. The officers and men of the latter continued to refer to themselves as Crook's Corps because, as one of them wrote, "we idolized him and were always proud to carry his name." But Sheridan promptly renamed it the VIII Corps, a designation conforming to those used by the other units in the command and more in line with its modest size.[3]

In later years, writing his memoirs after his relations with Crook had cooled, Sheridan made only the briefest allusion to his former friend's role during the campaign, simply stating: "I placed implicit faith in his experience and qualifications as a general."[4] But at the beginning at least, Crook seems to have played a greater part than Sheridan later cared to admit.

While the new Union commander could certainly rely on his former classmate's experience and advice as a soldier, more importantly, in Crook this notably uncongenial and insecure man had a friend with whom he could relax after a stressful day of sparring with the enemy—and there would be many such days. Sheridan, reserved in most social situations, gravitated toward men like Crook, who were "placid and easy-going." So it was natural that he sought him out to renew their old friendship, forming the habit of "a quiet chat about old times on the frontier . . . , talking by the hour about West Point life and 'larks' on the Pacific Coast."[5] Sadly, the friendship would disintegrate under the pressure of events. But for the present, their camaraderie was invaluable to both men.

To bolster Sheridan's command, Grant sent him Brigadier General William H. Emory's XIX Corps, an unwelcome presence in the view of many veterans of the VI and VIII Corps. Captain Henry Dupont, a perceptive officer, succinctly summed up their attitude: "[The XIX Corps] lacked discipline."[6] While it contained some outstanding regiments, more often than not that corps would prove to be Sheridan's weak reed under fire.

Of significantly greater value was Grant's assignment of three brigades of crack horse soldiers, 5,000 men, the cream of the cavalry corps of the Army of the Potomac, well mounted, led by veteran officers, and fully equipped—more than half with Spencer repeating rifles. Sheridan chose Brigadier General Alfred Torbert to command his cavalry rather

Philip Sheridan and his cavalry commanders during the Shenandoah Campaign. *Left to right:* Henry E. Davies, David M. Gregg (whom Crook later replaced just prior to Five Forks), Sheridan, Wesley Merritt, Alfred T. A. Torbert, and J. A. Wilson. Courtesy of the National Archives.

than Averell, even though the latter was senior in rank, quite possibly because Crook confided to Sheridan his own reservations about the cavalryman. Though Torbert was not the most brilliant cavalry officer in the army, he was ably assisted by two outstanding division commanders, Brigadier Generals Wesley Merritt and James Harrison Wilson. Wilson would soon be succeeded by another promising cavalryman, Brigadier General George Armstrong Custer.[7] Crook was probably relieved when Sheridan melded Averell's cavalry, a legacy of Hunter's old army, into Torbert's command.

With these additions, Sheridan's fighting force now numbered at least 30,000 combat veterans, backed by another several thousand men of lesser experience guarding the rear areas. The mere act of assembling such a formidable force caused Early to hastily withdraw farther south into the Valley.[8]

Little Phil's immediate task was to drive the Army of the Valley out of the northern reaches of the Shenandoah, where their mere presence threatened to tip the coming presidential election to the antiwar Democrats. But influenced by a vastly inflated estimate of his enemy's strength, Sheridan hesitated to meet the Rebels head on and instead resorted to a war of maneuver. Soon both sides were deeply engaged in a chess game of moves and countermoves against the backdrop of the lush farms checkering the Shenandoah countryside. For seven weeks in the August and September heat, as Crook put it, "[they] backed, filled, [and] sent out reconnoitering parties."[9]

By mid-August Sheridan's army, with Crook's corps in the vanguard, was nipping at Early's heels. Avoiding a pitched battle, Union troops steadily pushed the Rebels southward to Fisher's Hill, where Early had prepared a defensive line. With his men finally poised for a climactic battle, Sheridan's plans were suddenly thrown into disarray by news that Lee had sent Lieutenant General Richard H. Anderson with 5,000 troops to Early's aid. Anderson's reported route of march would put him squarely in the rear of Sheridan's army. Heeding Grant's warning that these reinforcements would increase Early's army to 40,000 men, "too much for Sheridan to attack," Little Phil prudently retired north toward Halltown, just south of Harpers Ferry, with Early pressing his rear.[10] During the withdrawal, Crook's infantry provided support to the cavalry rear guard and bore the brunt of the fighting.

On August 18 the VIII Corps reached Berryville, a rundown market town on the south fork of the Shenandoah with an unsavory reputation for fistfights and bad whiskey.[11] Early drew his forces together in preparation for an attack. In the sweltering heat, Crook's tired westerners hastily threw up a flimsy barricade of logs, rails, and even cornstalks, bolstered with whatever dirt the soldiers could dig out of the hardened earth with mess tins, cups, and their bare hands. From behind these makeshift works, they fought off their attackers throughout the day, keeping the Rebels at bay until the remainder of Sheridan's army had retired to a defensive position at Halltown, where Crook then joined him.

After eleven days of marching and countermarching across the dusty Virginia countryside, the Army of the Shenandoah had returned to its starting point. They had gained little beyond "giving General Sheridan some practical knowledge of the country and [allowing him] to become somewhat acquainted with [the] metal of his troops."[12]

Unable to dislodge Sheridan from his fortifications, Early withdrew a few miles southwest toward Winchester, establishing his line behind the protection afforded by Opequon Creek. The Federals pushed after him, marching from Halltown to Berryville on September 3.

Not long before the sun set that evening, as the men of the VIII Corps lit their fires along the pike in anticipation of their evening meal, they suddenly heard on their right the rising crescendo of musketry coming from the lines held by the XIX Corps. Thinking that the firing indicated an attack of nerves rather than the presence of the enemy, the men at first ignored it. But soon pickets appeared in the camp to announce the approach of a substantial Rebel force. Crook ordered his buglers to sound the alarm, calling the corps to a battleline on the west side of the pike behind a stone wall. Their mouths stuffed with bacon and hardtack, the men coolly watched the enemy charging out of the sun, "yelling like devils." At this sight the XIX Corps broke, its men fleeing mindlessly through the ranks of Crook's jeering westerners. Crook's men, hardened by three years of war, held their fire until the Rebels closed to one hundred feet, then unleashed a volley into the ranks of the charging graybacks. They followed up by leaping the stone wall and driving the Southerners back in a charge that carried them almost into the Confederate defensive lines. There the Rebels held, secure in the knowledge that the gathering darkness would deter any further Union advances. Retiring to their respective lines, the two sides continued to fill the air with the crash and flare of massed musketry until late in the evening.[13]

Ironically, the bloody encounter, which cost the lives of fully 10 percent of the 1,600 Union soldiers participating in it, was not a planned attack but an accidental clash that benefited neither side. The Rebel troops who had charged Crook's position had belonged to Anderson's reinforcing column. After a month of marching and countermarching, by September 3 Early had finally concluded that Sheridan was a paper tiger and that he no longer needed these extra men and had ordered them back to Petersburg. By a stroke of astounding bad luck, as they were departing the Valley on their way from Winchester, Anderson's men unwittingly collided with the Union troops just arrived at Berryville.[14]

Though Anderson would ultimately return to Petersburg by another route, his presence in the Shenandoah continued to immobilize Sheridan for another two weeks, drawing an unaccustomed barrage of criticism from the Northern press and his superiors in Washington. But the increasing pressure to engage the enemy did not goad the general into recklessness. He heeded Grant's warning not to take on Early's reinforced command and was made doubly cautious by the injunctions he had received from Washington that a defeat could jeopardize the president's reelection. So now Sheridan refused to move until he could be sure that Anderson had left the region. To make this determination, he felt "the need of an efficient body of scouts to collect information regarding the enemy."[15]

Hunter had relied on deserters, captured Rebels, and civilian spies for intelligence on enemy activity, all with indifferent success. Sheridan up to this point had done the same, with similarly mixed results. The citizens of the Valley, for the most part hostile to the Federal presence, often provided false information to their Union occupiers. And Confederate commanders, familiar with the Union generals' reluctance to engage with less than overwhelming superiority, often used "deserters" and prisoners to spread exaggerated tales about the size and disposition of their forces. What Sheridan required was a loyal resource that could be counted on to provide accurate information.

Blazer's Scouts, the special unit that Crook had employed so effectively for reconnaissance and partisan warfare in West Virginia, was still attached to the VIII Corps. With Sheridan's approval, they had been battling Mosby's rangers and other guerrilla units that had been attacking Union supply and communication lines. Sheridan was certainly aware of their availability and experience as intelligence gatherers. Yet rather than use Blazer's men, he created a second unit of irregulars who reported directly to him rather than Crook.[16] Modeled on Blazer's Scouts, they were led by Major Henry Young of the Second Rhode Island Infantry. Naturally, they would soon be known as Sheridan's Scouts.

There is no evidence that Crook raised any objection at the time to Sheridan's failure to use Blazer's Scouts for the work, though if he had read Sheridan's 1888 memoir, he would certainly have been put out. Little Phil omitted even a passing reference to Crook's role in developing the concept of scout units. But Crook had little cause for bitterness. When he had written of Blazer's Scouts in his own memoir, he blithely claimed credit for its creation and for appointing its leader, failing to mention that the original formation of the scouts and its leadership had actually been the work of his predecessors in the Kanawha Division. Describing Sheridan's efforts, he dismissed them in a brief paragraph:

"Sheridan organized a similar force for the whole army after which I was relieved from any further service of this nature. These men of Gen. Sheridan were under Major Young. Just what they accomplished, I don't know, but they would dress at times in Confederate uniforms, and at times in our uniforms."[17]

In fact, Young's unit very quickly established its value. Within a few days the scouts unearthed an elderly black man named Tom Laws. Both intelligent (in keeping with the prejudices of the day, Sheridan preferred to describe him as "shrewd") and loyal to the Union, Laws had a Confederate pass allowing him to travel back and forth to Winchester daily, selling fresh vegetables from his wagon. If, the general speculated, he could identify someone in town to gather intelligence on Confederate troop movements, Laws would be a perfect conduit for the information. Sheridan turned to Crook for assistance because of his acquaintance with many Union sympathizers in Winchester. His friend knew just the person.[18]

Up to the time of his marriage in 1865, if one can credit his autobiography, George Crook might have resided in a monastery, so assiduously did he avoid any reference to women in his life. Only occasionally do faint clues emerge, hinting at a possible interest in the opposite sex. Like the reference in his West Point expense book to the purchase of dancing shoes, Crook's acquaintance with Rebecca Wright, the person he recommended to Sheridan, provides one such fleeting glimpse into this aspect of his life.

Wright was an earnest, twenty-six-year-old Quaker schoolmarm with dark hair and a prominent jaw, indicative, it was said, of great firmness of purpose. Though a Virginian, she was so loyal to the Union that she had lost her post at a local private school because "her pronounced Union sentiments were distasteful to the management and popular feeling of the community."[19] She now taught classes in her home to make ends meet.

Well after the war, responding to an inquiry from a writer seeking to record the incident for posterity, Crook tersely noted that he became acquainted with the lady prior to Sheridan's arrival (under what circumstances, he did not say) and was convinced of her loyalty and high character. He recalled recommending her to his friend in response to the general's inquiry whether he knew of any loyal soul in Winchester who might provide information on the Rebels. Beyond these barebones facts, he volunteered nothing. Nor does his autobiography make any reference to either Wright or the incident. But in his memoir Sheridan did provide additional details. As he tells the story, Crook furnished Wright's name, describing her as "faithful and loyal to the Government and thought she might be willing to render us assistance, but he could not be certain of this, for on account of her well-known loyalty, she was under constant surveillance," a fleeting reference indicating that Crook may have known her more than in passing.[20]

Though initially reluctant to put Wright's life in jeopardy, Sheridan eventually summoned Laws to learn whether he knew the young woman. When the old man allowed that he did, the general gave him a message wrapped in tin foil, which Laws concealed in his mouth and delivered on September 15, the occasion of his next trip into town.[21]

After receiving Sheridan's note and consulting her mother, Wright agreed to provide whatever information she could, fully aware that she could be executed if caught.[22] In a note to Sheridan, she confided that she had "no communications with the Rebels" but then provided him with a piece of information of monumental significance. The previous evening her mother had entertained a convalescing Rebel officer who had let drop the fact that Anderson's infantry and an accompanying artillery battery had just departed the Valley to rejoin Lee at Petersburg.[23]

This was precisely the information Sheridan needed. Without further delay, he began preparations to march against Early at Winchester. But as he was poised to put his plan into action, he received word that Grant, concerned about Sheridan's apparent reluctance to take the offensive, wished to see him immediately at Charlestown, just south of Harpers Ferry. The general in chief had become impatient with his subordinate's inaction and had developed a proposed plan of attack that he hoped would prod him into action. But his attitude immediately changed when the two men met. "[S]eeing that [Sheridan] was so clear and so positive in his views and so confident of success, I said nothing about [the plan] and did not take it out of my pocket." Instead he simply instructed Sheridan to "[g]o in."[24]

The meeting with Grant was on a Saturday. Sheridan intended to attack the following Monday. His plan was to move his army to Newtown, a community on the Valley Pike about six miles south of Winchester, blocking Rebel communication and supply lines to the south and thereby forcing the Confederates into a battle at a place of Sheridan's choosing. But when he received intelligence that Early had sent two of his divisions under Generals Rodes and Gordon north to attack the Baltimore and Ohio Railroad, leaving only a small force behind at Winchester, he hastily revised his timetable. Sheridan would make an immediate strike against Early's reduced forces in Winchester and then take on the two absent divisions in detail when they returned south.[25]

But Old Jube was, as usual, one step ahead of the game. Learning of Sheridan's meeting with Grant at Charlestown, he correctly assumed that it presaged an immediate Union offensive and quickly recalled Rodes and Gordon back to Winchester.[26]

CHAPTER TWENTY-SEVEN

The Battle of Opequon (Third Winchester)

September 19, 1864

For Crook's troops, camped outside Berryville on the morning of September 19, the day began well before dawn. Intermittent rain during the night had cooled the air and swept it clean of dust. The men were well rested, having remained quietly in the line since their battle with Anderson's division two weeks previous. Now eager for action, they formed ranks promptly when bugle calls broke the predawn stillness.

Stepping out smartly, they marched south along the east bank of Opequon Creek toward a ford where the Berryville-Winchester Pike crossed the stream. As the ford was some distance from their camp, they did not arrive there until an hour before noon. Filing off the road into a field of sweet-smelling clover on a rise bordering the stream, they stacked arms and stretched out on the grass to await orders.[1]

By now they were aware that a large battle was about to begin and that the VIII Corps would be held in reserve. Their immediate assignment was to guard the ford. If the attack succeeded, as Sheridan and his generals were confident it would, Crook was to lead them southwest to block the Confederates as they retreated up the Valley Pike. To make this maneuver possible, Sheridan had placed the corps three miles to the rear of the main line, too far to allow them to quickly reach the battlefield should the need arise, a decision that would prove to be one of several flaws in Little Phil's strategic plan.[2]

From the bluffs and high ground along the Opequon, Crook's men could observe the battlefield lying to the west in front of the town of

Winchester. The ground before the town formed a plateau, broken up by "occasional corn-fields and isolated pieces of woodland, and intersected with occasional lines of stone walls."[3] Behind these walls, puffs of smoke and the glint of sunlight off rifle barrels and bayonets defined the Confederate lines, extending north into an area of heavy brush and trees to a point just short of a stream flowing east and emptying into Opequon Creek—this thin blue ribbon of water, known as Red Bud Creek, would play a part in the day's drama. Behind the Rebel position, a flat open plain extended all the way to Winchester and beyond. The drifting clouds of gunsmoke, the muted sounds of cannon fire, the sporadic rattle of musketry, and the tinny bugle calls in the distance gave the scene the remote, unreal quality of a stage set.

Perhaps feeling too removed from the action, a restless Crook announced his intention to ride to Sheridan's headquarters on the battlefield. Joined by his staff and his chief of artillery, Captain Dupont, the general mounted his horse, splashed across the ford, and rode west on the Berryville road. Soon the officers entered a three-mile-long canyon through which the road—in reality little more than a country lane—passed. Upon emerging from the canyon, they joined Sheridan on a rise that afforded a panoramic view of the action.[4]

The ravine through which they rode had been used by the VI and the XIX Corps to advance to the battlefield that morning. It had steep banks covered with pines, thick underbrush, and scattered boulders. Sheridan had anticipated that the two corps would move quickly through the canyon, arriving at Winchester in time to surprise Early's force before Rodes and Gordon could rejoin it. The VI Corps, in the lead, had managed to get through the defile quickly enough, but the troops of the XIX Corps found their way blocked by General Wright's wagons and artillery. Forced off the road and onto the steep sides of the ravine, Emory's troops clamored through and around thickets of undergrowth and massive boulders, their progress hampered at every turn. As a consequence, though the XIX Corps left Berryville an hour before Crook, it did not arrive on the battlefield until noon. The delays in the canyon allowed Early to reunite his divisions in time to meet the Federal advance. Sheridan, his troops already committed by this time, had no alternative but to press the attack against his opponent's entire army.[5] His failure to anticipate delays in transiting the ravine was the second flaw in his battle plan.

By the time Crook and his small entourage entered the canyon, traffic had abated, and they made good progress, arriving at Sheridan's hilltop headquarters just as the VI and the XIX Corps were forming their battle lines. As the generals watched, Wright's divisions on the left and Emory's forces on the right briskly advanced in the direction of Winchester, crossing open fields toward the broad, wooded plateau where the Rebels lay concealed behind stone walls and in thick brush, invisible to Sheridan and his fellow officers. As the Federals entered the undergrowth, they too disappeared from view, their progress now marked by cheers and a rising crescendo of artillery and musket fire. In a short time, to Sheridan's dismay and growing anger, the left flank of the XIX Corps and men of the adjacent VI Corps division poured out of the woods, fleeing in disorder over the fields back toward the Berryville canyon. Their retreat left the right flank of the remaining VI Corps divisions unprotected. Though these troops held for the moment, Sheridan realized that they would not be able to maintain their position for long and would be forced to withdraw if attacked on their exposed flank.[6]

The exasperated general vented his rage on the fleeing troops within hearing distance, giving them "a taste of the tallest swearing they had ever heard."[7] His savage tongue-lashing actually had an effect—those men in his proximity faced about and held their position.

Then, reluctantly abandoning his original plan to use the VIII Corps as a blocking force, he turned to Crook and instructed him bring his troops forward as quickly as possible to stiffen the Emory's line. Crook sent his staff back to the Opequon to implement Sheridan's order, while he and others apparently remained for a time at their commander's side.[8] Captain Dupont was among those who remained with the generals and thus had a unique opportunity to witness the events that transpired over the next hour and record them later in his memoirs. His recollections would vary markedly from Sheridan's own account of the battle.

In later years Sheridan took credit for several critical decisions made that afternoon, decisions that others who shared the moment believed were actually attributable to his subordinates. His writings, set down in after-action reports and in his memoirs, would embitter and estrange some of his senior officers, notably George Crook, who became convinced that Sheridan robbed him of acclaim that justly should have been his.[9] But on that September day, these reports had yet to be written, and the two men, still friends and compatriots, watched the battle unfold from their position on the knoll, waiting impatiently for the arrival of Crook's troops from the Opequon.

"It was at this juncture," Sheridan would write in his report of the battle in 1866, "that I ordered a brigade of Russell's division of the VI Corps to wait till the enemy's attacking column presented its flank, then to strike it with vigor." Since the Confederate forces and the troops of the VI Corps were hidden from his view, Sheridan was in no position to order any sort of deployment. In reality, General Wright, the VI Corps commander, on his own initiative gave the order to Brigadier General David Russell for which Sheridan took credit. He instructed Russell to move his Second Division to the right to close the gap created by the precipitous flight of the XIX Corps. Russell was killed executing the maneuver. His second in command, Brigadier General Emory Upton, saved the day by leading an impromptu attack against the Confederate flank. His effort preempted a Rebel assault that probably would have broken the entire Federal line, buying time for Crook's troops to arrive on the field. In his report Wright documents this sequence of events, leaving little doubt that Sheridan's claim of credit for the order was unjustified.[10] The latter's determination to bolster his own reputation came at the expense of depriving Wright and Upton of their rightful share of recognition for the ultimate Union triumph that day. Crook would suffer similarly.

While Wright's troops engaged the Rebels before Winchester, Crook's Corps swiftly crossed Opequon Creek and entered the Berryville Gorge, marching past the disquieting sight of surgeons in bloodstained linens busily setting up their amputation tables to receive the wounded. As they entered the gorge, the men confronted a train of lurching ambulances, filled with the dead and dying, that blocked their way, forcing them onto the steep slopes. Still they managed to keep up a steady pace and traversed the ravine in about ninety minutes. Crook later reported that Sheridan then directed him to form his command to the right and rear of the XIX Corps and "look out for our right, as the enemy was reported to be moving in that direction." These orders, shouted over the din of battle, required the VIII Corps to march an additional three miles from the mouth of the ravine. As a result the troops were not in position to attack until about 2:30 that afternoon.[11]

Crook deployed Thoburn's and Duval's divisions in line of battle, Thoburn's men taking a position to the rear and right of the XIX Corps, while Duval formed up on Thoburn's immediate right. Together these men constituted the extreme right flank of the army, extending the Union line to Red Bud Run, the stream roughly marking the northern boundary of the battlefield. Crook had little faith in Emory's troops, fearing that if attacked, they would break and run as they had earlier in the day, this time carrying Thoburn's men with them. To head off this possibility, he decided to personally reconnoiter the Confederate left, hoping to find a means to flank it in a preemptive assault.[12]

Sheridan set out his own version of events in his after-action report. He claimed that after the VIII Corps had been placed into the line of battle, he joined Crook on the field and instructed him to act as a "turning column, to find the left of the enemy's line, strike it in flank or rear, break it up," adding that he "would order a left half wheel of the line of battle in support of him." But his claim was not independently confirmed. On the contrary, the accounts of Hayes and Dupont, who were with Crook at the time, fully support Crook's assertion that this plan of attack was his own.[13]

Crook's reconnoitering of the Confederate left produced immediate and interesting results. He learned that the Rebel line ended far short of where originally thought, thus making a successful flanking maneuver a distinct possibility. Crook personally executed the movement. Taking Duval's division, he led the men to Red Bud Run. Stealthily wading across the waist-high waters of the little creek, they pushed their way north through thick brush for a about a mile beyond it. Turning west, they marched parallel to the stream until, by the sound of the gunfire, they could tell that they were in the enemy's rear. Crook then halted and formed his men to face the Confederate flank in preparation for an attack.[14]

At this juncture the general paused to dispatch William McKinley, a young captain only recently added to his staff, with a message to Thoburn, instructing him to charge the enemy line as soon as he heard the Second Division attack. McKinley was then to locate Sheridan and request that the VI and XIX Corps attack westward in unison with Thoburn in support of Crook's thrust from the north.[15]

After waiting a sufficient time to allow McKinley to deliver his messages, Crook ordered the charge. Dupont described what happened next. "With a tremendous shout, which resounded along the lines of the Nineteenth Corps, our Second Division rushed forward to the charge. But at that very instant, a body of cavalry suddenly loomed up in the distance on the right flank of Duval's line of battle."[16] Fearing they were Confederates, Crook quickly turned to determine the identity of the approaching riders. To his profound relief, his keen eyes picked out the blue uniforms of Wesley Merritt's troopers.

Moving forward to meet them, Crook quickly identified Merritt's boyish face among the riders. After briefing him on the situation, he asked the young cavalry commander to strike the Confederate rear while his infantry pushed forward on the enemy front and flank. Merritt readily agreed, leaving Crook to rejoin Duval's division. To his chagrin, Crook misjudged the location of his troops and was almost captured. Riding over a ridge, he suddenly found himself about to enter the Rebel lines. He beat a hasty retreat and tried again, this time succeeding in locating Duval's men, who at that moment were in trouble.[17]

While Crook conferred with Merritt, the Second Division had continued its charge on the Confederate position, which lay on the opposite bank of Red Bud Run. But the troops found themselves abruptly confronted by an unanticipated obstacle. Between themselves and the Rebels, the run widened into a swamp about twenty-five to fifty yards in width, "filled with reeds, slimy mud and water of an unknown depth." As the shocked Yankees pulled up in disbelief, the Confederates discovered their presence, wheeled to face them, and reformed behind a stone wall facing the morass, pouring fire into the Union lines. Though Duval's disciplined soldiers stood their ground, the attack stalled as the westerners took cover and returned fire. At this moment Colonel Hayes, now a brigade commander in the division, demonstrating both courage and presence of mind, spurred his horse into the water and charged headlong at the enemy's line. Inspired by the colonel's heroic effort and prodded from the rear by General Crook and his staff, " both divisions [sic] were soon over, with the general swinging his sword, and the Rebel post was soon flanked."[18]

The hard-pressed defenders fell back, taking cover behind a series of stone walls and rail fences, steadily stiffening their resistance. Hoping to avoid a frontal assault on these makeshift works, Crook retraced his steps back to the XIX Corps, thinking to push them forward to catch the Confederates in a crossfire and drive them out of their secure positions. En route, he later recalled, he encountered General Upton, whose initiative had saved the Union line earlier in the day. Upton was beside himself with rage. General Emory had told him that his corps would not engage in an attack on the Rebel position without orders from Sheridan. After angrily accusing Emory of cowardice, Upton approached Colonel Stephen Thomas, the brigade commander on this part of the line, and repeated his request. When Thomas also refused to attack without orders from his superiors, Upton accused him too of cowardice. Upton now asked Crook to intercede. Approaching the hapless Thomas, the general informed him that he had been accused of cowardice and challenged him to disprove the accusation by making the attack.[19]

Thomas was later awarded the Medal of Honor for heroism at Cedar Creek, severely undermining the credibility of Upton's accusation. But he did have a cautious nature. While the soldiers of the Connecticut and Vermont regiments who made up his brigade volunteered to make the charge, the colonel understandably continued to maintain that he could not do so without orders from his division and corps commanders. Crook, impatient with such caution, would have none of it. "[T]his is no time to be hunting up generals," he snapped and rode off, leaving Upton and the VI Corps to press the attack alone.[20]

They did their work well. As Crook had foreseen, the simultaneous attacks on their flank and front threw the Confederate forces back on their heels. Though they fought bravely, when Merritt's cavalry hit them from the rear, the Rebels broke and ran. Only a determined rearguard action by his own cavalry allowed Early to withdraw his battered army in good order and save his guns and wagons from capture or destruction. As the sun's last rays filtered through the smoke and dust of battle, the Confederates fled south beyond Winchester, Crook's West Virginians on their heels. Only darkness compelled the exultant Union troops to break off the chase, allowing the beaten Rebels to continue their retreat unmolested.

That evening Crook and Sheridan, tired but triumphant, trotted their horses down the main street of Winchester. As they rode they were accosted by three ardently loyalist young ladies. The women expressed such unrestrained jubilation at the Federal victory that Crook, who knew them, sternly warned them to take care in publicly voicing such pro-Union sentiments. The town had changed hands so often, he feared that any secessionists who overheard them might have a further opportunity

Philip Sheridan and George Crook in Winchester after the Battle of Opequon as sketched by James Taylor. An artist for *Leslie's Illustrated News*, Taylor accompanied Sheridan's troops in the Shenandoah. This illustration shows Sheridan drafting a message to Ulysses Grant announcing his victory at Winchester, while Rebecca Wright, who spied for the Union at great personal risk, and George Crook look on. Courtesy of the Western Reserve Historical Society.

to seek revenge. Undeterred, the trio confidently retorted that Early's army had been so thoroughly whipped that the Rebels would never return to Winchester.

According to Sheridan, the two generals eventually "succeeded in calming [them] a little" and then rode on to seek a place where Sheridan could draft a telegram to Grant announcing his victory. Discounting their own advice about using discretion in Winchester, the two officers made their way to the home of Rebecca Wright, the courageous schoolmarm. The generals found her more cautious than the other ladies. Needing no prompting from Crook, she begged Sheridan to do his business and be on his way as quickly as possible lest his presence give away her role as a Union spy. The embarrassed general folded himself into a seat at a child's desk in her schoolroom and swiftly penned a message to Grant, telling him, "we had sent Early's army whirling up the valley."[21] The two officers then hastily departed.

Later that night Sheridan received word that, based on that day's action, he had been promoted to the rank of brigadier general in the regular army. After accepting his men's congratulations, he and Crook lounged by a fire, basking in the afterglow of victory. Crook chose the moment to broach a subject that had been nagging at him all evening. During the latter part of the battle, Crook's men had captured over a thousand Rebels. Unable to guard them, they were about to send them to the rear when, according to Crook, "our cavalry came up on a charge and gobbled up all the prisoners," afterward claiming credit for their capture. This seemingly minor incident and Sheridan's response would rankle over the years. It became confused in Crook's mind with the issue of credit for that day's attack on the Confederate flank and ultimately culminated in a bitter passage in his memoir.

> I complained of this [the lost prisoners] to General Sheridan who asked me to say nothing about it in my report, but that he saw the whole affair, and would give me credit for it. But instead of that he didn't write his report until after the war was over, and then instead of giving me the credit I deserved, he treated the subject something in this wise, that I was placed in a fortunate position where I could turn the enemy's flank, giving the impression that my turning the enemy's flank was part of his plan, whereas so far as I know the idea of turning the enemy's flank never occurred to him, but I took the responsibility on my own shoulders.[22]

Third Winchester, as the Confederates styled the battle, was a decisive Union victory. Early's casualties amounted to over 20 percent of his total strength, almost 4,000 men, a proportion almost as great as Chancellorsville, where Lee lost 23 percent of his infantry. It was a loss from which the Army of the Valley could not recover. Union casualties exceeded 5,000 killed, wounded, or captured. Injured men filled some twenty buildings in Winchester and spilled over into Federal hospitals at Sandy Hook and Shawnee Spring. Wright's VI Corps alone suffered 1,700 dead and wounded, while Crook's far smaller corps incurred 794 casualties.[23] But Sheridan's army could absorb these losses and, as it would prove in the days to come, remain very much an effective fighting force.

On a personal level, Crook displayed both initiative and tactical skill. Though it would not earn him the fame and advancement that would come to his commander, his performance confirmed Sheridan's faith in him and won him the respect and admiration of his troops and fellow officers. Colonel Hayes, promoted to command of Crook's Second Division—replacing Colonel Duval, who was wounded during the fighting—wrote to his uncle a week after the battle: "General Crook (who is the brains of the whole thing) with his command, turned the Rebel left and gained the victory.... General Sheridan is a whole-souled, brave man, (like Dr. Webb [the unit's surgeon and Hayes's brother-in-law]) and believes in Crook, his old class and roommate at West Point. Intellectually, he is not General Crook's equal, so that, as I said, General Crook is the brains of this army."[24] While Hayes seemed to idolize the general and customarily referred to him in such hyperbolic terms, as an experienced veteran, his opinion of Crook's role in the battle merits serious consideration.

In his own memoir, written after the war, Captain Dupont penned a more moderate assessment of the general's role at Opequon:

> [I]t frequently happens that no adequate recognition is made of the subordinate who, when unforeseen contingencies arise, possesses the rare and exceptional capacity for prompt action upon his own initiative—whose soldierly perceptions enable him to determine what ought to be done—and who fearlessly assumes the responsibility of doing it. Although the martial instincts and moral courage of such a subordinate are prime factors in determining his military merit, these are precisely the qualities which so often pass unmentioned, as in the cases of Upton and Crook at the battle of Winchester.[25]

Victory at Fisher's Hill

September 19–22, 1864

During the night of September 19, while Sheridan and Crook rested comfortably in Winchester, Early's exhausted army fled south along the Valley Pike, their way lit only by the dim starlight reflecting off the roadway's limestone surface. The march continued until noon the following day, when they at last reached fortifications they had previously prepared on Fisher's Hill, twenty miles from Winchester.

Early chose Fisher's Hill because he believed that it "was the only position in the whole Valley where a defensive line could be taken against an enemy moving up the Valley."[1] It was here that he had stopped Sheridan in his tracks a month earlier. But that was before Sheridan's army had achieved such marked superiority in numbers.

Fisher's Hill was a natural defensive position, and Early had strengthened it with extensive works constructed along its brow. The hill plugged a five-mile-wide bottleneck in the Shenandoah Valley created by the bulk of Massanutten Mountain. Squatting between the Blue Ridge and the Alleghenies from just below the town of Strasburg, Massanutten divides the Valley, in most places only about twenty miles wide, into two smaller valleys, the Main and the Luray. For its entire thirty-mile length, Massanutten provides no breaks that would allow troops to pass from one of these narrow interior valleys to the other. Fisher's Hill sits on the floor of Main Valley like a huge boulder, wedged snuggly between Massanutten on the east and North Mountain, a part of the Alleghenies, on the west. At the base of the hill's eastern slope, the Valley Pike (now U.S.

Highway 11) and the North Fork of the Shenandoah River shared the narrow opening that separates the hill from Massanutten. On the west side of the hill, Back Road, a country lane, ran along the foot of North Mountain.

The Confederates built their defenses from east to west across the four-mile width of the hill, anchored at one end by the river and on the other by the hill's steep western slope. Along this line they constructed stone and earthen works, with fortified artillery redoubts at frequent intervals. The weakness in Early's proposed defense was that casualties had so depleted his force that he no longer had enough soldiers to evenly man his works.[2] How the general deployed his meager force along his defensive line would determine the outcome of the coming engagement. In retrospect, he did not choose wisely.

Early had lookouts stationed on the peaks of Massanutten, with an excellent view of the approaches to Fisher's Hill. They would be able to spot any movement from the east against his right, giving the Confederates plenty of time to prepare for an assault from that direction. In addition, troops attacking from that direction would have to ascend an "extremely steep and precipitous" slope. These advantages made the right the strongest point on Early's line. Nevertheless, he chose to concentrate troops on that sector. He also heavily fortified his center, the place at which he believed the attack was most likely to occur. He indicated his confidence that the Union forces would be unable to breach his center by having the ammunition chests for his artillery unloaded from their caissons and placed behind the breastworks, knowing that his troops would be forced to abandon their ammunition in case of retreat.[3]

Because of his lack of manpower, Early's decision to strengthen his right and center meant that his left would be the most vulnerable point in his defense. But he did not attempt to compensate by buttressing this sector with proven troops. Rather, in a move that he never explained, he manned the left flank with some of his least-reliable troops—Brigadier General Lunsford Lomax's dismounted cavalry, whom Early had always regarded as of dubious value.[4] They were spread thinly in a line along a ridge below the crest of Fisher's Hill, facing the wooded slopes of North Mountain.

Sheridan was in no hurry to launch an attack. When he learned that Early had gone to ground at Fisher's Hill, he knew that he would have time to rest his men and plan an effective strategy to overcome the strong Rebel position. At daybreak on the twentieth, he marched his army leisurely south on the Valley Pike, arriving in the early afternoon at Cedar Creek, just north of Fisher's Hill. While his men made camp, he rode forward to view the enemy position.

The Union commander would later claim that he immediately recognized that a charge against Early's heavily fortified center would "entail unnecessary destruction of life, and, besides, be of doubtful result." So, he wrote, "I resolved on the night of the 20th to use again a turning-column against his left, as had been done on the 19th at the Opequon. To this end I resolved to move Crook, unperceived if possible, over to the eastern face of Little North Mountain, whence he could strike the left and rear of the Confederate line."[5] Though his writings were intended to leave no doubt that he had originated the strategy for the coming battle, eyewitness accounts again refute his assertion. And again, evidence points to Crook as the architect of the plan.[6]

After making his reconnaissance of Early's position, Sheridan convened corps commanders Wright, Emory, and Crook in his tent to discuss the best means to dislodge the Army of the Valley from its position and destroy it as a fighting force. Those in attendance agreed that a frontal assault would be senseless. But then, according to Crook, Sheridan suggested an attack on the enemy's right. Wright and Emory initially supported this idea, but Crook, knowing that any troop movements on that flank would be visible from Massanutten, vehemently opposed it.[7] Instead he proposed a plan of his own.

While Sheridan had been viewing Early's works from the Valley Pike, or the right side of Fisher's Hill, Crook had done some reconnoitering of his own. Riding along Back Road at the base of North Mountain, he hit upon the idea of moving his troops unseen through the thick woods that covered its slopes to a position behind the enemy's defenses. From there he would turn and envelope Early's line as he had done at Winchester. When he proposed the plan, Sheridan was dubious whether Crook's men could make such a march undiscovered; Emory and Wright shared their commander's doubts. But rather than make a final decision on the spot, Sheridan called for a meeting that evening to discuss the matter further.[8]

Crook was fully aware of his limitations as an advocate, viewing himself more as a man inclined to action than verbal expression. He also may have worried that he had too much of a West Pointer's ingrained reluctance to confront a superior officer to effectively present his case. To overcome these potential handicaps, Crook brought his division commanders, Hayes and Thoburn, neither of whom had attended the academy, to the evening meeting to argue his case. He relied on Hayes in particular, an attorney by training before becoming a volunteer officer. Highly articulate and unconstrained by a regular's deference to authority, he could be counted on to make a vigorous and persuasive case on Crook's behalf.[9]

Stealth was key to Crook's plan. Hayes, speaking for his commander, emphasized that the VIII Corps, veterans of numerous campaigns in the West Virginia hills, were famed for their ability to move about silently in the woods, earning them the sobriquet "Mountain Creepers." Further, he argued, if the assault failed, losses would be minimal, but if successful, overwhelming victory would be assured. Whether convinced by Hayes's advocacy or his continuing faith in Crook's judgment, particularly following the latter's performance at Winchester, Sheridan finally agreed to the plan.[10]

The next day Sheridan moved the VI and XIX Corps toward Fisher's Hill in a feint intended to convince Early that he planned to attack the Confederate center. Meanwhile, Crook's troops remained concealed in the woods near Cedar Creek until nightfall. Then they silently waded across the creek and, unseen by the Rebels, made a cold camp in some woods beside Back Road. At daylight, from this heavily wooded position, they could slip unobserved onto the forested slope of North Mountain.

On the morning of the twenty-second, the troops rose before dawn, refreshed by two days of relative inactivity. With Crook in the lead, they followed a succession of rock-strewn ravines toward the slope of the mountain. Rough terrain and thick stands of timber made for slow going. Nevertheless, as one soldier commented, "Crook was tramping out his detour of fourteen miles to reach Early's vulnerable flank, without arousing a single farmer or Rebel scout to carry the news of his coming to Fisher's Hill." Once on the slope of North Mountain, the general divided his men into two parallel columns for the remainder of the march. When they reached the rear of the Rebel position, this formation would enable them to make a half turn to the left and face the enemy already formed in line of battle.[11]

As they neared a point opposite Early's flank, the lead elements of Crook's columns ran into pickets from Lomax's dismounted cavalry, guarding the lower slopes of North Mountain. At the sight of the Mountain Creepers, the Rebels hurriedly withdrew, spreading the word as they fled that the woods were full of Union troops. Confederate gunners reacted by lobbing a few shells toward the abandoned position. Drawing no response, Early assumed that the pickets had merely encountered a reconnaissance patrol and took no measures to reinforce his now-endangered left.

Because of the slow going, Crook did not reach a point he judged to be beyond the enemy's flank until about three that afternoon. Giving the order to face front, "he moved steadily into the open as though on review, until his command had cleared the timber, when he faced and charged." Confederate artillery immediately opened up on them. Ignoring the shellfire, with an unearthly yell the Creepers poured down the steep slope, crossed an intervening gulch, and with the force of a thunderbolt, struck the flank of Early's line. Taken completely by surprise, the Rebels abandoned their works and beat a panicked retreat up the slope of Fisher's Hill, leaving eleven of their precious guns in Union hands. When some of his men showed a disposition to straggle, Crook, his blood fired by the attack, gathered rocks and chunked them at the laggards, making it "so uncomfortable for this rear that they tarried no longer."[12]

Reaching the crest of the hill, Crook pushed his men forward at the run. To avoid losing the momentum of the charge, he allowed no pause, either to reform the lines or to capture prisoners, regimental flags, or artillery—trophies of war so prized as measures of a unit's success in battle. Now a disordered mob of intermixed regiments, his men ran on, each soldier bent on being the first to reach the enemy. The wild stampede through the Confederate lines continued along the crest of the hill, halting momentarily only when Crook's troops met up with those of Ricketts's division and Averell's cavalry, units just completing a diversionary charge against Early's center. The Mountain Creepers by that time had covered about a mile from the point where Crook had commenced his assault.[13]

The charge resumed after only the briefest interval, the men getting their second wind. As Hayes enthusiastically described to his wife, the troops swept "down the line of works, doubling up the Rebels on each other. . . . The men rushed on, no line, no order, all yelling like madmen. Rebs took to their heels, each striving to get himself out of the way. Cannon after cannon were [*sic*] abandoned (22 captured). Thus, we rushed on until we reached their right. . . . The Rebs," he concluded," say Crook's men are devils."[14]

The victory was so total, Sheridan exulted, "I do not think that there was an army ever so badly routed." Later he would add, "The stampede was complete, the enemy leaving the field without a semblance of organization, abandoning nearly all his artillery and such other property as was in the works." Hayes put it more succinctly: "They ran like sheep." Because the battle ended so quickly, Union losses were light—about 35 killed, 415 wounded, and 6 missing.[15] Confederate killed and wounded were even lighter, usually the case with a defending force. But a telling proof of success could be found in the roughly 1,000 graybacks who either were captured or deserted under fire and, of even greater consequence, the fourteen cannon they lost.[16]

Yet in one respect, the victory fell short of Sheridan's expectations. He had hoped to eliminate Early's corps as a viable force in the Valley. To that end he had assigned the cavalry to trap the Rebels as they fled south on the pike. But his horsemen disappointed him. Inexplicably, Torbert failed to push through a weak Confederate screen in his path and instead, withdrew north to Front Royal, a move that allowed Early's army to once more slip away to fight another day. A second cavalry force under Averell gave a similarly dismal performance, and Sheridan, with brutal finality, relieved the general of command. Crook, of course, was in wholehearted agreement with his commander's decision.

While Crook and his weary men bivouacked not far from the battlefield, the VI and XIX Corps attempted to right Torbert's error. They chased Early through the night "in great confusion at times, . . . firing into each other, perhaps oftener than into the enemy." But the Confederates outlasted their pursuers. At last Sheridan called off the chase, telling his commanders, "[t]he infantry have done enough. . . . They have done nobly. I wish others had done as well."[17]

The victories at Winchester and Fisher's Hill drew fulsome praise from Lincoln, Grant, and even the naysayers Stanton and Halleck. The news acted as a tonic to Lincoln's reelection campaign and a grim foreshadowing for the Southern cause. It also turned Sheridan into a folk hero in the North.

As has been noted, Sheridan's public accounts of these battles made little reference to his corps commanders, least of all to Crook, whose tactics turned the tide at the Opequon and who authored and led the bloodless rout of Early's army from Fisher's Hill. Yet perhaps in compensation for robbing his friend of credit, in May 1866 Sheridan recommended to Secretary of War Stanton that Crook receive the brevet rank of major general in the regular army for his "gallant conduct at the battles of Opequon and Fisher's Hill." This was a rather odd request since Crook had already received that brevet rank in March 1865 as a consequence of "gallant and meritorious services in the Battle of Fisher's Hill, Virginia."[18]

CHAPTER TWENTY-NINE

The Battle of Cedar Creek

September 23–October 19, 1864

Although his army's success at Fisher's Hill drew accolades, Sheridan's task in the Shenandoah remained incomplete. Urged on by Grant, he now turned his hand to the task of ending the Valley's role as a larder for the Army of Northern Virginia.[1]

On September 26 Sheridan broke off his pursuit of Early, convinced that Old Jube's defeat would force his withdrawal from the region. Then, in compliance with Grant's instructions, he set his cavalry to work destroying the farms of the Valley, from Staunton to New Market.[2] For the next eleven days, Sheridan's infantry remained in camp while his horsemen rode across the Shenandoah, putting farms and fields to the torch. "The Burning," as the campaign became known, was executed with ruthless efficiency. Early, powerless to intervene, could only watch from afar as clouds of smoke blackened the fall sky. Ten days later Sheridan proudly summarized his accomplishments in a wire to Grant. "[T]he whole country from the Blue Ridge to the North Mountains has been made untenable for a Rebel army. I have destroyed over 2,000 barns filled with wheat, hay and farming implements; over seventy mills filled with flour and wheat; have driven in front of the army over 4,000 head of stock; and killed and issued to the troops not less than 3,000 sheep."[3]

Amid the burning, on October 3 Sheridan received shocking news. Lieutenant John Meigs, the promising young son of the quartermaster general of the U.S. Army and a much-beloved topographical officer, had been killed, shot down near Dayton, Virginia, by men Sheridan believed to be secessionist guerrillas.⁴ The enraged general ordered his aggressive cavalry commander George Armstrong Custer to put Dayton to the torch and burn every house within a five-mile radius of where the incident occurred. Custer had fired thirty houses before Sheridan cancelled the order after Colonel Thomas Wildes, one of Crook's brigade commanders, begged him to exempt the town. Wildes, like Crook and many of his officers, had serious reservations about retaliation against civilians, especially when, as he pointed out, his men had been kindly treated by Dayton's residents.⁵ Though Sheridan spared the town, he permitted Custer to continue his work in the surrounding area.

While the cavalry visited ruination on the upper Valley, Crook remained in camp a mile south of Harrisonburg, an area thick with the smoke of burning barns. Uninvolved in the destruction, his officers and men enjoyed a brief respite from the constant warfare of the past months.

During this period, his relationship with Rutherford Hayes deepened and matured. Crook had noted the colonel's competence early on, tacitly recognizing it by incorporating his old regiment, the Thirty-Sixth Ohio, into Hayes's brigade when he reorganized the Kanawha Division. Their mutual admiration and respect had grown during the Dublin Campaign and now, in the Shenandoah, ripened into friendship. On the battlefield at Winchester, Crook had given Hayes temporary command of the Second Division after Colonel Duval was wounded, and at Harrisonburg he made the promotion permanent. Proud of the recognition, Hayes wrote to his uncle, "there are five or six brigadier generals and one or two major generals sucking their thumbs in offices in Harpers Ferry and elsewhere who would like to get my command, but General Crook tells them he has all the commanders he wants and sends them back."⁶

At 5:30 A.M. on October 6, after solemnly dispatching young Meigs's body to his father in Washington, Sheridan began his army's withdrawal northward down the Valley Pike, Crook's corps in the van, followed by the VI and XIX Corps. As the Federals moved north, Sheridan charged the XIX Corps with the duty of burning the farms and fields along the pike while his horsemen continued their destructive work in outlying areas. The cavalry rode in columns that "stretched across the country from the Blue Ridge to the eastern slope of the Alleghenies, with orders to drive off all stock and destroy all supplies as it moved northward." Between Mount Crawford and Woodstock alone, they destroyed over

Rutherford B. Hayes and his staff, believed taken in April 1865. Hayes is seated in the center, bottom row. Seated to his left is his brother-in-law and regimental surgeon, Dr. Joe Webb, a close confidant and friend to both Hayes and Crook. Courtesy of the Rutherford B. Hayes Presidential Center.

seventy mills and fired two thousand barns crammed with the fall harvest. The Union officer who recorded these bleak statistics observed: "The Valley was thus desolated, partly as punishment for the frequent bushwhacking of our trains and stragglers, but mainly to prevent Early from subsisting his army in it and marching once more to the Potomac. It was a woeful sight for civilized eyes, but as a warlike measure it was very effective."[7]

The officers and men of the VIII Corps shared this view. Most, including Crook, who had burned his share of Indian villages in the Northwest, had no quarrel with what they considered a necessary act of war. In a letter to his wife, Hayes wrote: "Everything eatable is taken or destroyed. No more supplies to Rebels from this valley. No more invasions in great force by this route will be possible." And again a few days later: "[T]his valley will feed and forage no more Rebel armies. It is completely and awfully devastated."[8]

Nevertheless, these men took no delight in the destruction. While attacks on the homes and food supplies of civilian noncombatants would become a familiar feature of modern wars—and already characterized warfare against the Indians—most educated nineteenth-century Americans were sickened by the use of such tactics against a white population. James Taylor, a correspondent for *Leslies Magazine,* rode with Sheridan's men as they departed Harrisonburg. He noted an uncharacteristic grimness in their mood. Watching the "somber pillars of grimy smoke towering upwards and darkening the sky with a pall," he saw "little of that light heartedness usual among officers in lax moments on returning from a successful campaign. . . . Certainly General Crook's seriousness . . . had its weight in modifying the conversation."[9]

Sheridan's assumption that Early's departure from the Valley was imminent soon proved premature. Instead of recalling Old Jube east across the Blue Ridge, Lee decided to keep him in the Shenandoah, reinforcing the Army of the Valley with Major General Joseph Kershaw's infantry division and Brigadier General Thomas Rosser's cavalry, thus returning the army to its strength prior to Fisher's Hill.[10]

Emboldened, Early pressed Sheridan's cavalry rear guard as it moved north from Harrisonburg. On October 8 at Tom's Brook, Lomax's and Rosser's cavalry divisions, riding in advance of Early's main force, came too close to the far-stronger Union cavalry columns. Sheridan, vastly an-

noyed by the harassing Rebel presence, gave General Torbert a terse order: "whip the Rebel cavalry or get whipped." Torbert, whose reputation
had been under a cloud for his cavalry's failures at Fisher's Hill, seized
this opportunity to redeem himself. Exploiting his overwhelming numerical advantage, the following day he administered what Custer later
bragged was the most "complete and decisive overthrow of the enemy's
cavalry" of the war. His horsemen chased Rosser and Lomax twenty-six
miles from Tom's Brook to Rude's Hill. Only massed fire from Early's
infantry put a stop to the debacle.[11]

Achieving such a complete and demoralizing cavalry victory hard on
the heels of Fisher's Hill reinforced Sheridan's belief that Early's army
was finished as a force in the Shenandoah. Acting on this supposition,
he directed Wright's VI Corps to march to Front Royal and prepare to
rejoin Grant at Petersburg, while the VIII and XIX Corps went into
camp near Cedar Creek, about twelve miles north of Fisher's Hill. So
confident was he that Early no longer presented a threat that on October 13 he accepted an invitation from Secretary of War Stanton to come
to Washington for a conference on the future deployment of his army.[12]

Sheridan delayed his departure when Early sent a small force to probe
Yankee fortifications on a small knoll between Cedar Creek and Fisher's
Hill called Hupp's Hill. Though the Rebels were quickly driven back by
Union artillery, Sheridan later claimed that this skirmish caused him to
reconsider the possibility that the enemy intended to resume the offen-
sive. But when he learned that Early had withdrawn back to Fisher's Hill,
he concluded that they "could not do us serious harm from there."[13]
Nevertheless, before leaving for Washington, he took the precaution of
recalling the VI Corps from Front Royal to reinforce his lines at Cedar
Creek.

It was well that he did. Early had no intention of remaining at Fisher's
Hill. His rapidly diminishing provisions and forage left him with only
two options. He could either fall back immediately or attack. He decided to attack.[14]

In the damp, chill hour before sunrise on October 19, Captain Dupont,
Crook's chief artillery officer, awoke to a sound he at first mistook for
Union pickets chopping wood for their fires. Shaking off his predawn
torpor, he now recognized the sound as the pop of musketry coming
from his right. Hastily he pulled on his clothes and, from the entrance

to his tent, called for his orderly to fetch his horse. Standing indecisively in the thick early morning mist, the artilleryman ordered his bugler to sound "reveille." He debated whether "boots and saddles," a call to prepare for immediate action, would be more appropriate, but on reconsideration, he thought that the firing most likely came from a scheduled reconnaissance in force by the XIX Corps. So not wanting to cause undue alarm, he decided against the more alarming call.

As the captain watched the men of his battery answering roll call, "a tremendous sound of volley firing suddenly burst forth at the entrenchments on the heights above." Leaping on his horse, Dupont spurred him into a gallop toward the growing din, calling over his shoulder for his orderly to fetch his saber. He would never see either his orderly or his saber again.[15] For Dupont, the Battle of Cedar Creek had begun.

Sheridan's army had camped midway between Cedar Creek and Middletown, a hamlet of a few homes and stores aligned on both sides of the Valley Pike about three-quarters of a mile north of the creek. The three corps had pitched their tents on a north–south axis in the broken country to the east of the stream, which at that point made a series of bends in its generally southerly course before flowing into the North Fork of the Shenandoah. Though about thirty yards wide with steep banks, Cedar Creek was shallow and could easily be forded at numerous points, making it no barrier at all to an enemy assault.[16]

Crook's command anchored the Union left (its southernmost point), facing the creek. Below strength, depleted by casualties and details to other units, the VIII Corps mustered only three or four thousand effectives divided into two divisions.[17] Thoburn's First Division had dug in on a hill in a very exposed position, his line being a half to a full mile in advance of the rest of the army. With his back to a ravine, his works faced a ford on Cedar Creek at a point close to where it flows into the North Fork. In addition to his exposed position, Thoburn lacked sufficient troops to man his works along their entire length, though his lines were afforded some protection by three artillery batteries positioned by Dupont, their guns trained on the ford. Crook pointed out to Sheridan that Thoburn's line was too far back from the creek and the ground too broken for a proper defense by Thoburn's few troops. Responding to his complaint, Sheridan had Wright assign a cavalry detachment to picket the area, but he subsequently reconsidered and shifted the horsemen to patrol the army's right flank. This then left Thoburn's front without an effective early warning system, which made both Crook and his subordinate uneasy about a possible surprise attack. Crook would later blame the absence of cavalry support for his troops' inability to hold the line when the Confederates attacked, though this was a convenient oversimplification.[18]

General Emory, a veteran campaigner who apparently had excellent military instincts, shared Crook's concern, noting that "[Thoburn's position] did not command the valley in front of it." He prophetically told one of his officers, "The enemy could march thirty thousand men through that defile and [we would] not know it till they were on our left flank."[19]

In reserve and about 1,300 yards to Thoburn's rear lay Hayes's division. On a knoll separated from Thoburn by a ravine, Hayes's men were spread out in the open just east of the Valley Pike. Their position resembled a campsite more than a fortification. The earthworks to the south and east, the directions from which an enemy attack would likely come, were as yet incomplete.[20]

Sheridan's center was held by Emory's XIX Corps, entrenched on the opposite side of the pike to the north of the VIII Corps's position. Like Thoburn's men, they faced the creek. Behind Emory's lines, in a green hollow, was the limestone plantation house of Belle Grove. Sheridan had made the stately country home his headquarters, and Crook had decided to camp there with the commander's staff, which placed him over a mile away from his troops. Finally, Wright's veteran VI Corps occupied the northernmost point in the Federal encampment. They too faced the creek, which at their position bent sharply to the east. They had not completed fortifying their position, having just arrived from Front Royal.

Given his optimistic assessment of Early's intentions, Sheridan was satisfied with the deployment of his troops and turned his full attention to his meeting with Grant and the future of his Shenandoah command. On October 15 he left Wright, as senior officer, in charge during his absence and departed for Front Royal, the first stop on his journey to Washington. He was accompanied by Torbert's cavalry, which he intended to dispatch on a raid against the Virginia Central Railroad.[21]

The next morning Wright forwarded Sheridan a copy of a Rebel signal intercepted from Massanutten. The message purported to come from

Lee's army. Addressed to Early, it said that troops under James Long-street were en route to join him in an attack on the Union forces in the Valley. Sheridan correctly read the signal as a ruse. Wright took it more seriously, however, fearing that Early might be planning to attack the army's right, where his troops were camped in the open. To address these concerns, Sheridan ordered Torbert back to Cedar Creek to protect the army's flank. At the same time, he ordered Wright to strengthen his position, agreeing that, if an attack came, it would be on the open ground on the right of the line.[22] But Sheridan and Wright would be proved wrong.

Ironically, Cedar Creek would be a replay of Fisher's Hill, though in reverse. At their encampment, the Federals had left themselves vulner-able to the unexpected, just as Early had done at Fisher's Hill. And as Crook had devised a novel plan of attack for Sheridan, the advice of a clever subordinate allowed Old Jube to take advantage of the Yankees' vulnerability at Cedar Creek.

To achieve the surprise needed to overcome his disadvantage in num-bers, Early had initially planned an assault on the Union right along the lines anticipated by Sheridan and his generals. The Confederate com-mander assumed that an attack on the left, which really would be a surprise, was precluded by the sheer slopes of Massanutten. But as Crook had done on Fisher's Hill, John Gordon, one of Early's division com-manders, found a way to turn geography to his advantage.

Gordon was another of those natural soldiers who rose from the civil-ian volunteer ranks to leadership during the Civil War. He was one of only four generals to become a corps commander in the Confederate army without the benefit of a military education or extended service in the regular army. Ramrod straight and an eloquent orator, on the field of battle, he struck fire in his men. As one young soldier who served in Gordon's old brigade enthusiastically put it: "He's [the] most petti-est thing you ever did see on a field of fight. Why, it'ud put fight into a whipped chicken just to look at him."[23] Though their personalities clashed, Old Jube trusted his division commander's tactical instincts and greatly respected his martial qualities. So when Gordon, after clamoring to the top of Massanutten to spy out the Union position, came back with a plan, Old Jube listened closely to what he had to say.

The mountain air on October 13 had such a crystalline clarity that Gordon and his companions, among them the Confederacy's premiere cartographer, Captain Jedediah Hotchkiss, had been able to view the disposition of Sheridan's army in minute detail. So sharp was the view from the mountaintop that, through his glass, Gordon could see "every parapet where his heavy guns were mounted, and every piece of artillery, every wagon and tent. . . . I could see distinctly the three colors of trimmings on the jackets respectively of infantry, artillery and cavalry, and locate each, while the number of flags gave a basis for estimating approximately the forces with which we were to contend in the proposed attack."[24]

From this magnificent panorama, Gordon's mind, honed by three years of unremitting combat and assisted by Hotchkiss's cartographer's perspective, quickly encompassed the military possibilities of the situation. From the manner in which the Union forces were deployed, he clearly saw that Sheridan had assumed that it would be impractical for the Confederates to surmount the bulk of Massanutten and attack his left. Little effort had been made to build up the defenses along Sheridan's left flank, leaving it protected by only Crook's depleted and divided corps, now deprived of its cavalry screen. Gordon thought it took "no transcendent military genius" to determine that an attack on the left could roll up the Union line, exposing it to fire from the flank and rear, just as Crook's assault had overrun the Rebel defenses at Fisher's Hill. With such a flanking attack supported by a simultaneous frontal assault, a Confederate victory seemed almost assured.[25]

But an attack on the left required the Rebels to approach the Yankee flank undetected, exactly the problem Crook had to overcome in broaching his plan to Sheridan. Early approved Gordon's proposal, but only on the condition that the general find a route that would guarantee complete surprise.

On the eighteenth Gordon did just that. Scouting along the banks of the North Fork, he and Hotchkiss found a narrow path running parallel to the Shenandoah along the heavily forested lower slopes of Massanutten. The path, concealed from view, led to a ford that would allow an attacking force to cross the river unseen within a thousand yards of Thoburn's position. Dressed in the rough garb of a local farmer, the two officers strolled into the open cornfields on the east bank of the North Fork to spy out the location of the Union pickets across the river. Gordon's reconnaissance satisfied him that if three divisions departed Fisher's Hill at sundown, their way lit by a moon just past full, they could traverse the slopes of Massanutten and reach the Union lines by dawn. They could then attack the VIII Corps's left flank, while a fourth division under General Kershaw charged across Cedar Creek and hit its front. Meanwhile, to Kershaw's right, General Wharton could attack down the Valley Pike against positions held by the XIX and VI Corps. Rebel cavalry could engage the Union horsemen farther upstream, preventing them from aiding the Federal infantry.[26]

A major in the Second Ohio Cavalry later penned a description of the day before the battle in lyrical terms that have made it irresistible to any historian describing the impending engagement: "The 18th of October in the Shenandoah Valley was such a day as few have seen who have not spent an autumn in Virginia—crisp and bright and still in the morning, mellow and golden and still at noon, crimson and glorious and still at the sunsetting; just blue enough in the distance to soften without obscuring the outline of the mountains; hazy enough to render the atmosphere visible without limiting the range of sight."[27] In this idyllic weather the soldiers of the VIII Corps went about the humdrum business of camp life. The men rested contentedly. Their position appeared secure; the weather was fine; payday was imminent; new clothing had just been issued; and an unusually large mail delivery brought news from home.[28]

But among these veteran troops, there were some who refused to be seduced by the balmy Indian summer day or the belief that Early's army had, indeed, been defeated. Crook, despite the unaccustomed comfort of his Bell Grove quarters, felt a twinge of uneasiness that moved him to send a brigade commander, Colonel Thomas Harris of Thoburn's division, on a reconnaissance toward Fisher's Hill. His subsequent report to the general raised some eyebrows as he claimed that he had ridden as far as Early's camp and found it deserted. But Crook, without attempting to confirm the report, accepted it as proof that the Confederates had abandoned their fortifications and left the Valley. Subsequent events proved the inaccuracy of his assumption and indicated that the colonel had in fact only ridden as far as Hupp's Hill rather than to Fisher's Hill, where Crook had intended he go. General Wright was not as comfortable as Crook with Harris's intelligence and ordered Emory to repeat the reconnaissance to their front the following morning. But by then it would be too late. Even if Harris had proved accurate, his statement was not so definitive as to explain the failure of Sheridan's generals, including Crook, to take any additional precautions before the battle.[29]

Wright and Crook were not the only ones uncomfortable with the army's exposed deployment. Colonel Steven Thomas of the XIX Corps, the officer whom Crook and Upton had accused of cowardice at Opequon, was also nervous. To his front that afternoon, he spotted two men in civilian clothes cutting corn on Bowman's farm on the far bank of Cedar Creek. Observing them for some minutes through his field glasses, he thought their actions inconsistent with those of a simple farmer. They appeared to spend far more time looking at the Union position than at the corn. He reported their presence up the chain of command, but Wright paid little attention to it as the men were to his left, while his preoccupation was with the army's right flank. The two "farmers" were probably Gordon and Hotchkiss.[30]

Captain Dupont had a case of the jitters too. As always, his concern focused on the safety of his guns. He worried about their vulnerability on the exposed left flank. Informed that cavalry would be protecting his left, he nervously rode out in that direction to determine whether that was indeed the case. Having failed to locate any horsemen, he retired to his tent that night, his anxiety unallayed.[31]

While Dupont tossed uneasily in his tent, a wakeful Colonel Thomas prowled in front of his lines. His reconnaissance was abruptly interrupted by the crack of a rifle shot, causing him to spur his horse back to the safety of his fortified position. But uncertain that the shot had any significance and loath to disturb his men's rest, he failed to sound an alert. Not long afterward, the officer of the day for the VIII Corps stumbled on a Rebel patrol and was captured. Though Crook mentions the officer's capture in his memoir, he offers no hint as to whether the man's unexplained absence was brought to his attention before or after the battle, leaving readers to draw their own conclusions.[32] In any event, neither incident alerted his men to the impending threat.

Oblivious to danger, the Federal troops slept soundly into the predawn hours. Just before sunrise, a thick fog rolled in, muffling sound and covering the advancing Rebels with an obscuring gray cloak. The warnings of a few alert pickets who reported mysterious noises in the mist were dismissed, and the troops slept on.[33]

At five o'clock, as the eastern sky began to lighten, Crook's soldiers were abruptly jerked from their slumber by the demented sounds of the Rebel yell as a horde of scrawny men in ragged butternut and gray swooped down upon the neat rows of tents. The crack of musketry, the "wood chopping" that had aroused Captain Dupont, came from Kershaw's men, who charged across Cedar Creek and swept Dupont and the half-clad men of Thoburn's division from their blankets.

Despite the initial confusion and surprise, Crook's well-disciplined veterans offered effective resistance. A Southerner with Kershaw's Division noted, "[a]s we emerged from a thicket into the open we could see the enemy in great commotion, but soon the works were filled with half-dressed troops and they opened a galling fire upon us."[34] But the Northerners could not stand for long. Overwhelmed by surprise and terror, "[m]en, shoeless and hatless, went flying to the rear some with and some without their guns. Here and there, horses galloped at will, some bridleless, others with traces whipping their flanks to a foam."[35] The attack was so swift and unexpected that within moments Kershaw had captured seven of Dupont's precious guns and turned them against the fleeing First Division, by now halfway to Middletown. Those with slower reflexes were swiftly captured, some still in their blankets. But even in this chaos, with heroic effort Dupont extricated the remainder of his artillery and was even able to get off a few rounds at the enemy, though visibility in the fog and early morning light was close to zero. The captain acted on his own, for Colonel Thoburn, his division's commander, fell in the early moments of the attack. Mortally wounded while trying to rally his men, he was reputedly gunned down by a Confederate cavalryman who, wearing a Union overcoat, approached the unsuspecting colonel from behind and shot him in the back. Thoburn lived through the night but died the next morning.[36]

The rumble of cannon fire and the rattle of musketry reverberated across the Valley, awakening Crook and Sheridan's staff at Belle Grove and causing them "to turn out in haste and alarm." At first they thought the firing was the result of a reconnaissance in force. But as it grew in volume and came from the direction of the VIII Corps encampment, they soon realized that something far more serious was occurring. Crook, though initially shocked by the sudden and unexpected assault, recovered quickly. When a courier arrived from Hayes's Second Division, the general leapt into the saddle and dashed off in the direction of the battle.[37]

When he arrived at his troops' encampment, Crook found Hayes's division under heavy attack. Acting quickly, he rallied the men and withdrew them northward to a ridgeline about one hundred yards from the Valley Pike, forming a line facing south and reinforcing it with elements of the VI and XIX Corps. His prompt action retarded the Rebel advance and bought time for the army's supply wagons, parked on the plantation grounds, to make an orderly withdrawal. But his hastily improvised defense was soon shattered by a completely unexpected attack by Gordon's Division, which burst upon the Federals' flank from the east. The attack first hit a unit of green troops under the command of Colonel J. H. Kitching, temporarily attached to the VIII Corps. Kitching was killed, and his troops, demoralized and confused by the thick fog and gunfire that seemed to come from every direction but the north, broke and fled. Their panic spread to Hayes's veterans, and they too turned and ran with hardly any show of resistance. Their flight effectively ended the VIII Corps's participation as a unit in the battle until late in day.[38]

Colonel Thomas of the XIX Corps, once more belying Crook and Upton's accusations of cowardice, displayed great bravery during the engagement. Leading only a brigade, he interposed his men between the fleeing VIII Corps and an overwhelming Confederate force, buying precious time for the Mountain Creepers to reach safety and for the VI and XIX Corps to reform their shattered lines. He lost over a third of his men in the action. Seeing that Thomas was courageously rounding up fleeing troops and forming them into a cohesive battle line, Crook rode to his side and bestowed upon him a curt nod of approval before moving on to other duties.[39]

According to James Taylor, the *Leslie's* correspondent, it was during this action that General Wright was slightly wounded by a bullet that grazed his chin. Taylor allowed that Wright would have been killed or captured by the enemy but for the "timely efforts of General Crook . . . , who at great personal risk got the dazed general off the field." But another and more credible source, Colonel Thomas Wildes of the 116th Ohio Regiment, who was present at the time, wrote that the general was wounded while Crook was elsewhere on the field, undermining Taylor's heroic description, which if true, surely would have been reported by others.[40]

By nine o'clock the fog had burned off, leaving the sky bright and clear. The sun beat relentlessly on the Confederates, who had not eaten or rested since the previous evening. These ravenous and impoverished men, many of them barefoot and in rags, were irresistibly drawn by the sight of what in their destitute condition appeared to be lavish quantities of food, clothing, and equipment strewn about the VIII Corps camp-site. Troops peeled away from the charge, their martial ardor temporarily dampened by hunger and the temptation offered by much-needed gear—items as commonplace as a rubber ground cloth, a new blanket, or a pair of shoes. The ensuing frenzy of looting slowed the advance and drained strength from an already undermanned, and by now greatly fatigued, attacking force.[41] The resultant slackening of the Rebel assault, though brief, gave the fleeing men of the VIII and XIX Corps a chance to recover their wits, and many joined a defensive line established by Brigadier General George W. Getty of the VI Corps about a mile and a half north of Middletown. Crook formed the remnants of his VIII Corps behind Getty's left. While many individual Union soldiers joined this line, many others "drifted rearward confusedly, yet with curious deliberation . . . , none of them hurrying, but all aiming at the directest safe route to Winchester."[42]

By ten o'clock some semblance of order had been restored to the Union position. The VI Corps line, now reinforced by the soldiers of the XIX Corps and remnants of Crook's command, held steady. Torbert's cavalry protected its flanks while General Getty probed the enemy to his front, retarding their advance and buying time for stragglers to filter back to the line. This was the situation that greeted Sheridan when, a little after ten, he burst upon the scene astride his big black horse, Rienzi.

Sheridan had gone to Washington, conferred with Grant and Stanton on the future role of his army, and had returned by train to Martinsburg on the seventeenth. After a comfortable night's rest, he rode to Winchester, arriving late on the afternoon of the eighteenth. There he received word that all was quiet at Cedar Creek, twelve miles to the south, and went to bed with an easy mind. At six o'clock the following morning, he was awakened by an officer of the guard who reported the sound of artillery fire coming from the direction of the camps. Though he concluded that the firing was too irregular to connote a battle, the general remained uneasy. So after a hasty breakfast, he called for his horse and was out on the road from Winchester by about a quarter of nine, by which time the sound of artillery had become "an unceasing roar."

At Mill Creek, a mile south of Winchester, Sheridan crested a rise and was suddenly confronted with "an appalling spectacle of a panic-stricken army—hundreds of slightly wounded men, throngs of others unhurt, but utterly demoralized, and baggage-wagons by the score, all pressing to the rear in hopeless confusion, telling only too plainly that a disaster had occurred at the front." Confident that he could restore his soldiers' morale and inspire them to counterattack, he paused only long enough to gather more-complete intelligence about the situation. Then, putting spurs to Rienzi, he set out with his escort on what became his legendary ride to Cedar Creek.[43]

As the road was crowded with retreating men and wagons, Sheridan took to the fields. By his side raced a young orderly. Though mounted on a horse far smaller than the towering Rienzi, the boy managed to keep pace with the general, while the remainder of the escort trailed behind. As Sheridan dashed past retreating troops, he called out: "About face, boys! We are going back to our camps. We are going to lick them out of their boots!"[44]

Arriving on the battlefield, he passed Wright's line and galloped forward to where Getty's division and Torbert's cavalry were engaging Early's troops from behind a barricade of fence rails about three miles north of their original camp. In his memoir Sheridan would later paint his arrival in heroic colors: "Jumping my horse over the line of rails, I rode to the crest of the elevation and there, taking off my hat, the men rose from behind their barricade with cheers of recognition." According to Brigadier General Lewis Grant, one of Getty's brigade commanders, not all the cheering was for the commander. "Sheridan dashed along past our cheering men and making a quick turn rode through a break in my division, the little orderly right at his heels, then with another quick turn, he brought his horse to a standstill, the orderly turned with him and halted almost simultaneously at the proper distance behind. A general cheer went up by those who saw the incident and our men shouted as much for the little orderly as they did for Sheridan."[45]

Behind Getty's troops Sheridan saw a line of regimental colors rising over a ridgeline, "as it seemed, to welcome me." Some of those flags belonged to Hayes's division, carried by some of the sixty men who had not taken flight or who had rallied with their colonel behind Getty.[46]

Tossing out words of encouragement like bouquets to the cheering troops, Sheridan raced east in search of his corps commanders. It did not

Philip Sheridan and George Crook embracing upon the battlefield at Cedar Creek as sketched by James Taylor. Sheridan had just completed his famous ride from Winchester and arrived upon the field to find that his army had partially recovered from Jubal Early's surprise attack, rallying to halt the Confederate advance. Courtesy of the Western Reserve Historical Society.

take him long to locate Crook and Wright; the two men were conferring by the side of the pike, wrapped in their overcoats against the lingering morning chill. Sheridan exuberantly threw his arms around Crook, a gesture that, according to a bystander, brought tears to the eyes of both men. A colonel in Crook's corps recorded the following exchange between the two generals: "'Well, Crook, how is it?' he asked. 'Bad enough,' answered Crook, pointing to the remnants of his corps. 'Well, get ready now, we'll lick them out of their boots yet before night,' was Sheridan's quick reply." Then, according to Crook's orderly, who was also present, Sheridan ruined the effect by genially exclaiming, "What are you doing way back here?"[47] Turning to Wright, he shook the general's hand and, noting the bloodstains on his beard from his earlier chin wound, asked if he had been wounded. Wright indicated that it was just a scratch. Having signaled by the warmth of his greeting that no blame was to be assigned to his generals for this debacle, he got down to the business at hand.

By noon Getty had held up the Confederate advance for two hours, repelling three charges and countering with attacks of his own. Now he pulled back to the VI Corps's defensive position. With cavalry guarding its flanks, Sheridan's army now presented a strong face to the enemy.

Confronted with the solidified Union line, and aware that his own men were depleted by fatigue and their ranks thinned by looting, Early decided that it was no longer necessary to continue the fight.[48] Turning to Gordon he declared, "Well Gordon, this is glory enough for one day." The Federals, he declared, were about to abandon the field. It was time to declare victory and end the fighting. Though some of his commanders vigorously advocated pressing the attack, Early held firm. He intended to hold on to what he had gained, re-form his lines, and remove his booty from the field.[49] But this decision would cost the Confederates dearly, for it gave Sheridan precious time to carry out his own plans.

Contrary to Early's assumption, Little Phil had no thought of quitting the field. Having reorganized and strengthened his line, the Union commander stood poised to renew the battle. But Crook's corps would not play a leading role. With the exception of two of Dupont's batteries, it was in no condition to lead a counterattack, and though he continued to rely on Crook's advice, Sheridan sent the VIII Corps to the rear in reserve. He then redeployed his remaining units. The VI Corps, with the exception of Getty's division, was relatively fresh. Sheridan assigned these troops to the left of the line and the XIX Corps to the right, with Custer's and Merritt's cavalry divisions on either flank. After making his deployments, at the suggestion of one of his staff aides the general cantered, hat in hand, down the entire front of the army, giving every man a chance to see that their commander was back on the job. The review was an instant success, drawing loud cheers and stiffening his soldiers' resolve to win back the day.[50]

But Sheridan did not launch his attack immediately. Instead he cautiously delayed, worried that Longstreet's corps might have reinforced Early on the field. The delay worked to his advantage, affording an opportunity for many of Crook's scattered troops to rejoin their units. As soon as Sheridan confirmed from captured prisoners that Longstreet was not present on the field, he struck. It was almost four in the afternoon.[51]

From the crest where Wright formed his line, Sheridan watched the attack unfold. It was bloody and short. Although the Union assault initially met with stiff resistance, the Confederate lines soon broke under the pressure of superior numbers. With precision, the XIX Corps, supported by Sheridan's crack cavalry divisions and using the VI Corps as a pivot, charged in a long line, sweeping diagonally across the field like a scythe, driving the Rebels from the field. At sunset, about an hour and a half after the Union troops launched their offensive, Early's broken army retreated in confusion across Cedar Creek.[52]

Crook's artillerist, Dupont, played a prominent role in the afternoon's fighting. Throughout the morning he had saved a substantial part of the corps artillery and helped stave off repeated enemy attacks. Now as the sun sank toward the western mountains, he turned his batteries on the retreating Confederates as they massed on the pike, preparing to flee southward. The heavy shelling created panic, causing the Rebels, in their haste, to abandon the captured cannons and much of the loot they had picked up that morning. Crook would acknowledge Dupont's efforts in his official report of the battle, and as a result the artillery officer would later receive the Medal of Honor for his role in the fighting.[53]

Sheridan, in a rare display of thoughtfulness, allowed Crook's infantry divisions to redeem their honor by engaging the retreating Rebels. He wrote: "When I reached the Valley Pike, Crook had organized his men, and as I desired that they should take part in the fight, for they were the very same troops that had turned Early's flank at the Opequon and at Fisher's Hill, ordered them to be pushed forward; and the alacrity and celerity with which they moved on Middletown demonstrated that their ill-fortune of the morning had not sprung from lack of valor." With Crook at his side, the commanding general swung his cap over his head and shouted: "Forward, boys! Follow me! We'll sleep in the old camp tonight!" With a schoolboy's enthusiasm, he then led the cheering Mountain Creepers in a charge that did not end until they reached Cedar Creek.[54]

This time darkness failed to save Early's army. The Rebels were pursued hotly down the pike by Custer and Merritt's cavalry in a running battle that did not end until the Confederates were safely behind their works on Fisher's Hill. While the cavalrymen finished their work, Sheridan returned to Belle Grove and triumphantly ordered his tent pitched at the exact location of his former headquarters, the front lawn of the large manor house.

That evening he and his staff lounged beside a huge log fire built among the tents, savoring their remarkable victory and discussing various aspects of the battle. According to Crook, as the two men basked in the warmth of comradeship and shared adventure, Sheridan, in a burst of frankness and uncharacteristic modesty, turned to him and said, "I am going to get much more credit for this than I deserve, for, had I been here in the morning the same thing would have taken place, and had I not returned today, the same thing would have taken place." Whether he accurately rendered Sheridan's words or even if the general actually said them may be beside the point, for they accurately reflected the events of the day. Crook added that Sheridan's comment "made little impression on me at the time."[55] He and his fellow corps commanders and their staffs, warming their hands and egos around that fire, had already come to the same conclusion. Certainly, they agreed, Sheridan richly deserved credit for inspiring the men to heights of valor. But these officers did not believe that he had saved the day, for the Confederate attack had already come to a standstill, and the Union lines had stabilized in anticipation of a counterattack by the time he had arrived on the field.

Crook, Wright, and Emory were probably far less concerned with the credit that would accrue to Sheridan than with the blame that might fall on them for being caught so completely unawares by the Confederates. Crook in particular had good reason to fear such opprobrium since the eastern press soon ran stories attributing the surprise to the carelessness of the officers in camp at the time. These articles moved Rutherford Hayes to engage in a letter-writing campaign in defense of his commander and of the now deceased Colonel Thoburn, placing blame instead on the decision to remove the cavalry screen from Thoburn's flank and on the attenuated and undermanned condition of the VIII Corps defensive works.[56]

In later years Crook continued to argue in this vein, claiming that his corps was so severely understrength that it was unable to properly man its picket lines. This circumstance had forced him to rely on the promised cavalry as his early warning system, a duty that the horsemen failed to carry out after receiving new orders to guard Wright's corps on the Union right. But this argument does not excuse either Crook's failure to follow up on the numerous signs that the Rebels were near his lines or in hindsight his decision to establish his billet at Belle Grove, some distance away from his troops. In view of subsequent events, he could have earned a reprimand or worse for his laxness. Fortunately for him, however, as so many other Union officers failed to anticipate the attack and because the resultant battle ended in victory, his negligence attracted no censure from the army. Nevertheless, in later years an embittered Crook compared what criticism he did receive for his actions at Cedar Creek with the adulation accorded Sheridan for his famous ride, adding it to his list of grievances against his old commander. By then his discontent had fed on itself and turned his former feelings of friendship toward his former schoolmate into bitter enmity.

A year before his death, Crook returned to the battlefields of the Shenandoah for the last time. There he recalled Sheridan's admission to his staff at Belle Grove twenty-five years earlier. In the intervening decades Little Phil's ride from Winchester to Middletown, following on the heels of his decisive victories at Opequon and Fisher's Hill, had become the legendary bedrock upon which his reputation and subsequent military career had been built—a career that culminated in his appointment as commander in chief of the U.S. Army. Upon viewing the battlefield at Cedar Creek, a resentful Crook dipped his pen in acid and recorded in his diary his own judgment of events, in terms that revealed the depth of his feelings.

> After examining the grounds and position of the troops after twenty-five years which have elapsed and in the light of subsequent events, it renders Gen. Sheridan's claims and his subsequent actions in allowing the public to remain under the impressions regarding his part in these battles, when he knew they were fiction, all the more contemptible. The adulation heaped on him by a grateful nation for his supposed genius turned his head, which, added to his natural disposition, caused him to bloat his little carcass with debauchery and dissipation, which carried him off prematurely.[57]

But such thoughts were far from a younger Crook's mind that October night as he bantered easily with his commander and friend on the lawn of Belle Grove in the flickering firelight.

CHAPTER THIRTY

Mosby's Rangers

October–November 1864

Sheridan remained at Belle Grove until November 9, resting his war-weary soldiers. Though they were not required to fight or march, it was not a pleasant interlude for the troops. The weather turned dreary—cold and rainy—and their makeshift accommodations provided scant protection from the elements. Adding to the general discomfort was a pervading uncertainty about their future. Most of the men hoped that they would be going into winter quarters, performing light guard duty along the Baltimore and Ohio Railroad, but the possibility of a winter campaign lurked in the background.

Election Day, November 8, 1864, dawned drizzly and overcast. Crook, accompanied by Sheridan and Hayes, rode to the "polling place," a dilapidated wagon with a cartridge box on its bed that served as a ballot box. When the officers arrived, the troops who had been waiting patiently about the wagon to cast their vote let loose a cheer while a band assembled to entertain them broke into the "Star-Spangled Banner," a popular patriotic air at the time. Hayes wrote to his wife the following week that all three officers had voted for Lincoln, Sheridan casting the first ballot of his life. Their preference accorded with most Union troops in the field. In Hayes's division, 575 voted for Lincoln, while McClellan garnered only 98 votes. Overall, 94 percent of the entire army voted for the president in the 1864 election.[1]

The day following the election, to be closer to his base of supply at Martinsburg, Sheridan moved the army north to Kernstown, stopping at noon for a leisurely lunch. James Taylor, an inveterate sketcher, asked Crook to pose for one of his penciled portraits. The normally self-effacing general agreed, and Taylor gave him the completed sketch for a souvenir. (Unfortunately, it seems to have been lost to history.)[2]

The move to Kernstown did little to improve living conditions for the Army of the Shenandoah. Until Early's intentions could be more clearly discerned, Sheridan did not want to settle into permanent winter quarters, so the men made do with temporary shelters constructed in the open fields outside Winchester. Not long after their arrival, the temperature dropped precipitously. "Colder than any huckleberry pudding I know of!" Hayes recorded, adding that their thin linen tents afforded little in the way of protection, cutting the wind about as efficiently as "a fish seine." But when the sun shone, moods brightened, and the men occupied their time betting on frequent horse races, writing home, and endlessly speculating on their next assignment. After months of hardtack and salt pork, they now enjoyed a diet of fresh-baked bread and beef, washed down by coffee with plenty of sugar and milk. For the officers, there were even occasional feasts of oysters, lobsters, and canned peaches.[3]

During this interlude, Crook and Hayes spent an increasing amount of time together. A number of women visited the camp, including "Union young ladies" from Winchester. Hayes noted with amusement that Crook, though "fond of ladies," was "very diffident" and appeared to have made little progress on the social scene.[4]

On December 9, during the first snowfall of what would become the harshest winter of the war, Hayes received his promotion to brigadier general. Crook, in a rare public demonstration of affection and esteem, hunted up a set of his old brigadier shoulder straps and presented them to his friend. Hayes for his part mused that though the rank had been cheapened by the poor quality of men who have achieved it, he was proud to wear the star, earned for his performance during a difficult and bloody campaign and on Crook's recommendation. Just a week before, he had written to his young son regarding the naming of the boy's newly born brother. In the letter he casually mentioned that he would prefer to name him George Crook rather than his wife's rather odd choice, Bilious Cook, the name of a relative. Mrs. Hayes took the hint, and in early January 1865, a grateful Hayes responded, "I am very glad you are pleased to call the little soldier George Crook. I think it a pretty name, aside from the agreeable association."[5]

Despite the inclement weather, there was no respite from the war. Though the Army of the Valley no longer represented a real threat, Rebel partisans under Colonel John Mosby had taken up the fight. His rangers continued the hit-and-run tactics they had begun during the late summer of 1864, attacking Sheridan's supply columns and any Union troops foolish enough to stray too far from camp. In October they captured General Duffié, now one of Sheridan's cavalry commanders, who had foolishly threatened to hang any of Mosby's men that he caught. Duffié's carelessness prompted Sheridan to recommend his dismissal. "I think him a trifling man and a poor soldier. He was captured by his own stupidity," he wrote in support of his recommendation.[6] Crook, who shared Sheridan's low opinion of the man, is not known to have objected, though soon he would have cause to reconsider his position.

To counter Mosby's depredations, Crook suggested that Sheridan put Blazer's experienced scouts to the task. Sheridan had previously rejected a similar suggestion from his friend. But by mid-August, as the Rebel guerrillas became increasingly troublesome, he changed his mind. And to increase their effectiveness, he wrote the War Department: "I have 100 men who will take the contract to clean out Mosby's gang. I want 100 Spencer rifles for them. Send them to me if they can be found in Washington." The short-barreled repeaters, normally reserved for cavalry, were provided forthwith.[7]

Now impressively armed, the scouts took to the field. Blazer aimed to beat Mosby at his own game. Outnumbered three to one by Mosby's well-organized force of over 350 riders, the scouts evened the odds somewhat by confiscating the finest horses available from the Valley's secessionist farmers.[8] Well mounted, they aggressively patrolled the perimeter of Sheridan's army from dawn until well after nightfall and hunted down members of Mosby's band wherever they could be found. They were greatly aided by the good intelligence provided by local Unionists, whom Blazer sensibly treated with respect and fairness.[9]

Blazer's men fought a series of sharp engagements throughout the late summer and fall, killing forty-four guerrillas and wounding or capturing two dozen more while losing only five of their own, severely hampering guerrilla operations. Mosby's frustration reached a boiling point when Blazer bested a detachment of rangers in a skirmish near Ashby's Gap on November 16. Determined that this challenge would not go unanswered, the partisan commander ordered one of his most effective company commanders, Adolphus "Dolly" Richards, to mount two companies and "wipe Blazer out!"[10]

On the morning of the nineteenth, Blazer, with a force of about sixty-two men, was patrolling south of Charlestown on the Harpers Ferry Road. He halted at Kabletown, about a mile from a ford on the Shenandoah, to allow his men to eat their breakfast. As his scouts bolted their rations, a black child interrupted their meal to warn them that they were being watched by a large contingent of Mosby's men (later estimates ranged from 100 to 300 rangers) concealed in the woods to their rear. Aware that the partisans were in the area, having captured one the previous night, Blazer closely scrutinized the position the boy had indicated and discerned a considerable force gathered on a crest across a broad field between his men and the river. But what he could not see was an even larger body of Mosby's men concealed in a dip in the middle of the field.

Believing that he faced a detachment that at most equaled his own, the captain impulsively ordered a charge against the Rebels in the treeline. As the riders closed on the partisans, the horsemen who had hidden in the dip suddenly emerged to their front. Before the scouts could bring their Spencers into play, they found themselves locked in close combat. Mosby's men, armed with Colt revolvers, had the advantage at this distance, particularly with their superior numbers. The result was what a surviving scout described as "a nasty fight! We stood no show at all." Blazer was captured, and his scouts sustained about 50 percent casualties—killed, wounded, or captured—destroying the unit as an effective fighting force.[11]

In December, Early's troops at last took leave of the Shenandoah to rejoin Lee at Petersburg. Though Mosby remained an irritant, Early's departure marked the end of a Confederate presence in the Valley capable of threatening Washington. Sheridan now released the VI Corps, parts of the XIX Corps, and the First Division of Crook's corps to the Army of the Potomac while he established winter quarters in Winchester. On the nineteenth he ordered Crook and his Second Division to garrison Cumberland, a beautiful town nestled in a bend of the Potomac River near the West Virginia border.[12] During the winter months, the division would be responsible for guarding the Baltimore and Ohio Railroad.

Crook marched the division as far as Winchester, where on December 28, he boarded a train with his staff for the last leg to Cumberland. The remainder of his men joined him a few days later, adding their strength to Major General Benjamin "Old Ben" Kelley's division, which had been guarding the rail line alone up to this point. Upon arrival, Crook incorporated Kelley's men into his Army of West Virginia, forming three divisions: the First, under recently promoted Brigadier General Isaac Duval; the Second, under Brigadier General John D. Stevenson; and the Third, under General Kelley. The First and Third would remain in Cumberland and its environs, while the Second was assigned to Harpers Ferry.[13]

CHAPTER THIRTY-ONE

Kidnapped

December 1864–February 1865

The winter of 1864–65 was brutal. But headquartered in the Revere House, Cumberland's railroad hotel, Crook was spared most of its rigors. While the chill wind whipped snow through the streets, the attentions of the thirty-seven-year-old bachelor were focused on twenty-two-year-old Mary Dailey, the daughter of the hotel's proprietor. Though almost fifteen years younger than Crook, by the standards of the day, she was approaching spinsterhood. Contemporary photos of her have not been located, but a drawing of her in middle age shows a heavy-set, plain woman, her face set in a stern, no-nonsense expression. Despite the advance in years, it is easy to see that even as a younger woman she had been no southern belle. But the general was smitten. Perhaps moved by these alien feelings, he overcame his usual shyness sufficiently to host a ball for his officers.[1]

Wooing the daughter of a man whose family shared his pronounced secessionist sympathies was complicated. Among its pitfalls, Mary's brother, James Dailey, rode with McNeill's Rangers, one of the Rebel guerrilla bands that infested the area. James's activities posed a serious problem for the general, one that probably placed a strain on his relations with Mary's family. As department commander and protector of the railroad, it was his declared intention to rid the country of bushwhackers, a term he applied indiscriminately to McNeill's men as well as to common bandits.[2]

McNeill's Rangers was the most organized and effective partisan band operating in the mountainous region around Cumberland. The unit was originally recruited and trained by Captain John Hanson McNeill, a Missouri farmer who had first raised a militia company to fight for the Confederacy in 1861. Captured by Union forces the following year, he and his son, Jesse, escaped to western Virginia, where they then organized the rangers as a company of irregular cavalry. McNeill's men vigorously disputed the application of the label "bushwhacker," commonly used by Northern troops when referring to irregulars in the region. With some justification, McNeill considered his partisans part of the armed forces of the Confederacy rather than lawless bandits. In fact his unit was among the few guerrilla bands officially recognized by the Rebel government in Richmond as "Partisan Rangers," a legal distinction allowing them to operate as an independent yet integral part of the Confederate army. The terminology assumed practical importance since, if captured, members of the unit were entitled to prisoner-of-war status, while their less-fortunate brethren could be summarily hanged.[3]

McNeill's band, never more than 210 in number, made their headquarters in Moorefield, West Virginia, a town on the banks of the South Fork of the Potomac River only sixty miles south of Cumberland.[4] Moorefield was frequently occupied by Union troops, forcing the rangers to spend much of their time on the move among densely forested hills and hollows well suited for guerrilla warfare. Toughened by outdoor living and their fugitive existence, they harassed Federal troops, disrupted operations of the Baltimore and Ohio Railroad, and rustled livestock from the army in order to supply Confederate forces in the Shenandoah.

Just two months before Crook arrived in Cumberland, Hanson McNeill suffered a mortal wound during a raid near Mount Jackson, Virginia. Before succumbing, the partisan captain anointed Jesse, who had previously served as his father's lieutenant, as his successor in command. Though known to be a dead shot with both pistol and rifle, an accomplished horseman, and a soldier of unquestioned courage and initiative though not yet twenty-three, the younger McNeill was also hot tempered and impetuous to the point of rashness. Despite this, the rangers accepted his leadership as he had been his father's second in command.[5]

At the time of his death, Captain McNeill had been formulating a plan to kidnap General Kelley, then in command of the troops guarding the railroad, whose assignment had included operational responsibility for hunting down the rangers. Taking the task to heart, Old Ben had energetically hounded the guerrillas out of their home base on the South Fork, threatening to burn out anyone giving aid to McNeill's men. On a more personal level, Kelley had infuriated McNeill earlier in the war by attempting to arrest the partisan's wife as she was passing through Union lines to rejoin her husband after visiting family in Ohio.[6]

While immobilized by a leg injury, Jesse McNeill had ample opportunity to contemplate the feasibility of the plan following his father's death. Ultimately, after learning that Crook was headquartered in Cumberland for the winter, he decided that the benefits of bagging two generals in one raid overcame any risks involved.

After the war, surviving rangers circulated the story that Jesse was in love with General Kelley's fiancée, Mary Clara Bruce, a Cumberland belle, and that his men concocted the plan in an effort to remove a rival from the scene. But there were less frivolous reasons why the plan appealed to him. The capture of the two generals would at a stroke remove the leadership of the Department of West Virginia, boost tattered Confederate morale, and garner glory for McNeill and his men. It might also placate General Early, currently annoyed by McNeill's surreptitious recruitment of some of his best troopers.[7]

McNeill vetted the plan with Sergeant John Baptist Fay. Fay had been in the Confederate army since 1861 and before the war had resided in Cumberland. Jesse's father had first turned to the sergeant for advice when he came up with the idea of kidnapping Kelley. Like many of the rangers, Fay was an intelligent and literate man.[8] He knew that the exploit would not be easy to carry off. Cumberland was filled with Federal troops, and a crack cavalry regiment, the Twenty-Second Pennsylvania, was stationed at New Creek, West Virginia, only twenty-eight miles west of town. Yet the sergeant was enthusiastic about the plan.

Success required that Fay first reconnoiter the town. He had visited his home several times since the war began, on one occasion spending a week in Cumberland undetected. He was confident he could slip in and out at will, though well aware of the risks involved. While McNeill remained in Moorefield preparing for the raid, the sergeant surreptitiously entered the town. From Rebel sympathizers, plentiful in this border region, he identified the number and location of the picket posts and learned the details about the hotels where the generals slept. Fay's intelligence allowed McNeill to set a date for the raid: February 20, 1865. As a final precaution Fay agreed to return to Cumberland the day before to ensure that conditions had not changed.[9]

On the nineteenth, as the temperature plummeted, Fay left Moorefield at nightfall accompanied by Cephas Ritchie Hallar, a teenager from Missouri, a two-year ranger veteran, and a man "of well tested fidelity and courage." Riding throughout the night, the two rangers arrived at a ford on the Potomac just outside Cumberland by early morning. Crossing the ice-encrusted river, they sought out the house of a Confederate sympathizer and confirmed that the situation remained unchanged. Then turning their horses south once more, they rode to the small town of Romney, halfway between Moorefield and Cumberland. From there Hallar pushed his reluctant mount into a blinding snowstorm to report to McNeill, who was on his way from the rangers' base.[10]

By early evening on the twentieth, McNeill's force of sixty-three riders, rangers and a sprinkling of regular cavalry from the Seventh and Eleventh Virginia Regiments, had received Hallar's report and joined Fay at Romney.[11] After the briefest rest, only enough time to feed the horses and gulp down the meager rations that would constitute their only meal that day, McNeill and his men set out on the final stage of their journey. Though it had stopped snowing, the temperature had dropped once more, causing an icy surface to form over the slushy roadway. In the darkness the horses' hooves broke through the crust with unnerving cracks that rang out like pistol shots.

The raiders' path took them over twenty miles of wind-scoured ridges and across snow-filled mountain hollows. In places the men dismounted and pushed through the drifts to make a path for their laboring horses. Well before dawn they crossed Nobley (Knobley) Mountain and soon reached the Potomac. Then, at a hairpin bend in the river, they saw Cumberland on the opposite bank. Before entering the town, though, McNeill paused to confirm that General Crook was still there.[12]

At about 2 A.M. the Rebels forded the Potomac just west of town and emerged from the woods onto the old National Road leading into Cumberland. For some of the men, this was the first inkling they had of their objective. Moments later they encountered their first Union pickets. McNeill had taken the lead, his sergeants, Joseph Vandiver, Joseph

Kuykendall, and Fay, at his side. The rest of the column, under Lieutenant Isaac Welton, second in command, followed close behind. It was still several hours before dawn, but the starlight reflecting off the powdery snow enabled the men to see clearly for short distances. By this ghostly illumination, they spotted a shadowy figure standing in the roadway a few hundred yards to their front. Seeing unknown riders approach, the man issued a sharp challenge, "Halt, who comes there?" As Fay later recalled: "We responded, 'Friends from New Creek.' [The picket] then said, 'Dismount one, come forward, and give the countersign,' when, without a moment's warning, McNeill , putting spurs to his horse, fired a pistol at the man's head. We had nothing to do but to follow rapidly and secure the picket, whom we found terribly alarmed at the peculiar conduct of his alleged friends."[13]

The rangers quickly subdued the two remaining sentries. Pressing a pistol to the head of one, they attempted to learn the countersign that would allow them to proceed into Cumberland unmolested. The pistol made no impression. But when one of the rangers threw a rope over a tree limb, fitted a noose over the frightened man's head, and hauled him into the air, it produced a sudden change of heart. Lowered to the ground, he gasped out the countersign: "Bull's Gap."[14]

Taking the three shaken sentries captive, the column moved off at a brisk trot to the second picket post—five Ohio men "snugly ensconced in a shed-like structure, engaged in a friendly game of cards, and with a blazing log fire in their front." Their guns were stacked in a far corner of the shed, and before they could move, the raiders surrounded them and seized their weapons. As taking any more prisoners with them was plainly impractical, they ordered the Ohioans to flee for their lives, spurring their departure with claims that a much larger attacking force was close at their heels.[15]

McNeill's men proceeded unmolested down the town's main road, Baltimore Street, to the hotels where the generals were billeted, riding at a sedate pace so as not to arouse the suspicions of the small groups of soldiers patrolling the streets. Flickering light from the fires around which these men huddled was too dim to reveal the gray uniforms the riders wore under their stolen Union great coats. To perfunctory challenges from sleepy guards, they identified themselves as a detachment of the Twenty-Second Pennsylvania, the cavalry unit stationed at New Creek. No one attempted to question them further, and the riders con-

Benjamin Kelley, commander of the garrison guarding the Baltimore and Ohio Railroad. He and Crook were kidnapped from their Cumberland, Maryland, hotels in February 1865 by McNeill's Rangers. Courtesy of the National Archives.

tinued boldly down the center of the road. A few of the Rebels, in a show of bravado, even hummed a few bars of "Yankee Doodle" as they passed.[16]

The two hotels where the generals slept were not far apart. The raiders drew up in double formation along the curb, the head of their column in front of the Revere House, where Crook was quartered, and its rear by the Barnum House, where Kelley reposed.

McNeill had selected two squads to capture the generals. The first, led by Sergeant Kuykendall, an unflappable veteran, was assigned to take Kelley. Having at one time been held prisoner by the general, Kuykendall could readily identify him. In his squad was an ambitious and impetuous private named Sprigg Lynn, who also knew Kelley. Without waiting for the others, Lynn pushed his way into the hotel and rushed up the darkened staircase to be first to reach the general. In his haste he entered the wrong room, awakening Major Thayer Melvin, Kelley's adjutant. The confusion was quickly resolved, and a nervous and irate Kelley and Melvin were forced to dress at gunpoint and led hurriedly down into the street.

At the Revere House, Sergeant Vandiver, described by Fay as "a man of imposing size and figure, fond of dress and full of self-assertion," led the squad assigned to capture Crook. The men found the front door to the hotel locked but gained entry by rousing the porter. After he opened the door, the badly frightened young man was cowed into revealing Crook's room number—46. Establishing its whereabouts with the help of a former hotel clerk turned ranger, the Rebels charged up the stairs, among them Mary Dailey's brother, James.[17]

A sharp rap on his door roused Crook from a sound sleep. Three o'clock on a frigid February morning seemed hardly a time to expect visitors. But the general felt no uneasiness, secure in the knowledge that he was surrounded by an estimated 7,000 Federal troops.[18] Drowsily, he responded to the knock, "Who's there?" The reply—"A friend"—aroused no suspicion. But when he bid the knocker to enter, Crook was rudely jolted out of his complacency by the appearance of a large man in a Confederate uniform shining a lantern on the general's startled face. As soon as Vandiver stepped through the doorway in response to Crook's summons, he drew himself up to his full, impressive height and pompously intoned: "General, I am General Rosser of Fitzhugh Lee's Division. We have captured the city and you are my prisoner." Though temporarily dumbfounded by this declaration, Crook recovered quickly and accepted the situation "with much grace and cheerfulness." He later confided to Fay, "Vandiver was such a looking man as I supposed General Rosser to be, and I took him at his word."[19]

The rangers had their generals, and as a bonus they seized their prisoners' unit colors from the hotels.[20] Their horses exhausted, the weary

Rebels now faced the daunting challenge of getting their prisoners out of Cumberland and through sixty miles of Union-occupied territory to Moorefield. From there they would have to ride an additional ninety miles through ice and snow to deliver their captives to General Early at his camp in Harrisonburg, Virginia. With Union troops snapping at their heels, to reach Moorefield McNeill's column would have to run a gauntlet between the Twenty-Second Pennsylvania at New Creek and Sheridan's men at Winchester, only sixty miles to the east.

To prevent Cumberland's garrison from alerting these forces, Fay, Hallar, and a third ranger rode to the nearby telegraph office and cut the line. While they were doing so, other raiders called at the livery stable and liberated eight additional mounts, three to relieve their own fatigued horses from the additional weight of three prisoners and the other five to prevent their use by the Federals. The horses taken included Phillipi, a stallion presented to General Kelley by his troops after defeating Rebel forces at a West Virginia town of the same name.[21] For Kelley, it was a final insult.

Following the Chesapeake and Ohio towpath out of town, the raiders successfully passed one picket post. Approaching a second, they heard a sentry ask his sergeant whether he should shoot. Vandiver, feigning anger, shouted: "If you do, I will place you under arrest. This is General Crook's bodyguard, and we have no time to wait. The Rebels are coming, and we are going to meet them." Overawed by Vandiver's tone, the pickets allowed the rangers to pass, while the apoplectic Kelley bleakly growled, "Don't that beat hell!"[22] Four miles from Cumberland, the echoing boom of a cannon behind them announced that their audacity had been discovered. Yankee troops were in pursuit.

Incredibly, Crook seemed to enjoy himself immensely. Realizing that Rosser's troops had not overrun the town as Vandiver had claimed, and secure in the knowledge that his kidnapping would not affect the outcome of the war, he had the carefree air of a boy playing hooky. For the first time in three years of combat, the responsibility for the lives and safety of large numbers of troops had been lifted from his shoulders. And as a general, he was confident that he would soon be released in a prisoner exchange. His good humor was only slightly dampened by the discomfort of riding a bony cavalry nag bareback at the pace set by the fleeing Rebels. Seeking relief, he turned to the ranger riding at his side and asked if a saddle could not be obtained. When the man responded that he did not know where one could be found, Crook joked, "Take one from the first Yank you meet and tell him General Crook ordered you to take it."[23] He soon had his saddle.

As his captors bluffed their way past more two picket posts, Crook could not resist teasing General Kelley, who justifiably regarded the whole affair as humiliating. McNeill, talking his way past yet another Union guard, jokingly complained about Kelley. "Don't you think he is a regular old granny whenever he hears there are a few Johnnies about." The guard tartly replied, "Yes I do, every time I am put on outpost duty in such weather." The response drew a chuckle from Crook, who jabbed Kelley with his knee. At a second post McNeill, continuing his banter, declared to the sentries, "I wish that General Grant would remove Granny Kelley from Cumberland, and put Crook in his command." The officer in charge agreed, whereupon Crook guffawed and punched the sulking Kelley appreciatively on the leg.[24]

South of Romney, about eighteen miles from Moorefield, the column sighted a large force of Federal cavalry approaching rapidly from behind. McNeill threw a rear guard across a winding stretch of road, and the pursuers immediately backed off, confronted by what they feared was a superior force.

McNeill had entertained hopes of staging a grand entrance at Moorefield with his captives. But two miles north of town, he saw a long blue line, moving fast on a parallel course on the opposite side of the river, clouds "of vapor from the panting horses extend[ing] back in a long level line like the smoke of an express train."[25] It was the Twenty-Second Pennsylvania from New Creek, racing toward Moorefield in the hope of intercepting the raiders. With their fresh horses and superior numbers, they would succeed if McNeill's men continued on their present course.

But the rangers knew the area too well. As General Crook glanced over his shoulder and regretfully murmured, "Oh! So near, and yet so far," the column peeled off the road and into the woods, following a path that led them in a wide circle around the town. Soon they crossed the Winchester road only minutes before Sheridan's troops and, as winter darkness closed upon them, made camp in a concealed gorge seven miles to the south. Their pursuers closed their trap on an empty town. As night fell, the Federals gave up the chase. McNeill's men had ridden in intense cold and snow for twenty-four hours almost without break on a 120-mile circuit across rough country. Now, exhausted and hungry, they bivouacked on the cold ground, their "only sentinels . . . the shining stars."[26]

The next morning a small squad of rangers was detailed to deliver the captives to General Early's headquarters. They made thirty-nine miles that day, spent another cold night on the trail, and the following morning arrived at Harrisonburg, where the two generals became Old Jube's reluctant guests at a local establishment. As the generals stiffly dismounted, Crook turned to his captors and cheerfully remarked, "Gentlemen, this is the most brilliant exploit of the war."[27]

The two Union generals had by now been on the road for three days, covering 154 miles on horseback. To spare them further hardship, Early pressed an old stagecoach into service to transport them to Staunton, where they boarded a train that would carry them to Richmond's infamous Libby Prison.[28]

On February 24 General Lee sent a message to Secretary of War John Breckinridge. Referring to the kidnapping, he allowed that "McNeill and his party deserve much credit for this bold exploit." Perhaps more valued by the rangers was the praise tendered by their peer, Colonel John Mosby. Meeting the generals and their guards aboard the train that carried Crook and Kelley to Richmond, the famous partisan commander extended his congratulations to McNeill's men. "You boys have beaten me badly," he said. "The only way I can equal this is to go into Washington and bring out Lincoln!"[29]

Over the ensuing days, Secretary of War Stanton eagerly sought to make an example of both Crook and Kelley by mustering them out of the service for gross negligence in allowing themselves to be captured. But Grant was equally anxious to have Crook back at the front. Despite the secretary of war's efforts to block Crook's release, the commanding general prevailed. Crook, Kelley, and Major Melvin were exchanged for Confederate general Isaac Trimble, captured at Gettysburg, and a guarantee from Grant to upgrade the treatment of several captured rangers being held at Fort McHenry outside Baltimore.[30]

On March 11, not quite three weeks after their capture, the three Union officers boarded a flag-of-truce steamer, together with between five hundred and six hundred wounded Yankee prisoners, and headed down the James River from Richmond toward Union lines. Released on parole, the officers were ordered to return to their homes to await the official notice of exchange that would allow them to return to their units. Two days later Crook received word that he had been awarded the brevet rank of brigadier general in the regular army for meritorious service during the campaign of 1864; on the same day he became a brevet major general in the regular service for his role at Fisher's Hill.[31]

The issue of gross negligence on Crook's part, which Stanton had raised, has never been examined. Most accounts of the generals' kidnapping were written by veterans of McNeill's Rangers or their relatives. Quite naturally they did not dwell on Union errors that facilitated the exploit but rather on the skill and boldness of the partisans.

General Kelley was responsible for the security of the town and so technically would bear responsibility had charges of negligence been brought.[32] Yet Crook, as overall commander of the garrison, was entitled to his share of the blame. In fact he had received intelligence prior to the raid of a gathering of horsemen, assumed to be Rosser's men, at Moorefield, the known headquarters of the rangers. He had thought enough of the information to pass it on to Sheridan the day before the kidnapping. But Sheridan chose to ignore Crook's message, agreeing with the assumption that it applied to Rosser's men, who had reportedly just disbanded for the remainder of the winter.[33] Crook then let the matter drop without informing Kelley or taking any other precautions, though he could have alerted and strengthened his guard posts or sent out patrols along the river. Instead he turned in for the night, snug in his hotel room, surrounded by his troops, and comfortable in his belief that the enemy was on his last legs. Like General Dwight Eisenhower just prior to the Battle of the Bulge and the Hessians at Trenton, he relied on weather and terrain to protect him. But—as with Eisenhower and the Hessians—a determined and skillful enemy exploited Crook's inattention. Unfortunately, rather than acknowledge his mistake, Crook once again looked to point the finger elsewhere, in this instance at an "ignorant Dutchman who happened to be on picket and gave [the rangers] the countersign."[34]

For his part, McNeill also missed an opportunity, but hardly due to negligence. Three future presidents, Rutherford Hayes, William McKinley, and James Garfield, in addition to two division commanders in Crook's VIII Corps, were also in Cumberland that night. Had McNeill managed to bag this array of celebrities, McNeill surely would have earned more prominent mention than a mere line in one of Lee's dispatches.[35]

As it was, the Rebel triumph was short-lived. Following Lee's surrender in April, McNeill and his men remained at large for some weeks, loath to turn in their arms and accept defeat. Finally, on May 8, after some negotiation, the rangers agreed to surrender to a company of Union cavalry. They met on the South Branch, the forces on opposite sides of the river. A small detachment of nervous Federals crossed over to accept the ranger's weapons. McNeill's men cast a number of firearms to the ground, for the most part ancient muskets more suited for museum display than combat. But they retained their captured Union carbines, saddles, and equipment and defied the Federals to retrieve them. The Yankees, far outnumbered by the guerrillas, did not push their luck and rode off, leaving the rangers to savor their final moment of triumph before returning to their homes and families, leaving the war behind.[36]

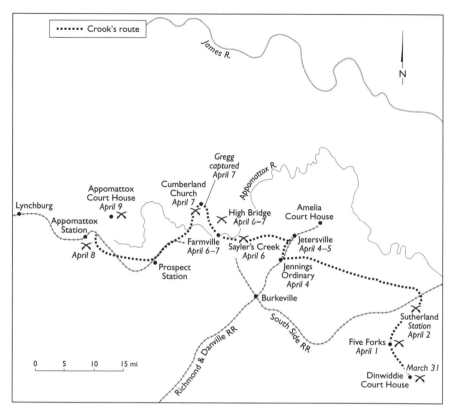

Crook's Route during the Appomattox Campaign, April 1865.

CHAPTER THIRTY-TWO

Commander of Cavalry in Grant's Army

March 1865

Scarcely a week after his release from Libby Prison, Crook received orders returning him to active duty. He optimistically reported to General Grant for his next assignment as his brevet promotions had led him to believe that he had emerged unscathed from the fiasco of his capture. But the meeting with Grant did not go as he had hoped. Instead of returning him to the VIII Corps, Grant wanted Crook to head the cavalry element of Meade's Army of the Potomac. It was a more modest appointment than might appear at first glance. Grant had stripped the once-powerful cavalry arm of Meade's army of two of its three divisions to reinforce Sheridan in the Shenandoah. All that remained was a single division made up of three brigades, a total of some 3,300 men. Crook thought the assignment disappointing, unsuited to his rank and experience. But attempting to put a good face on it, he wrote to Hayes that he suspected that it was only temporary pending his return to a reconstituted VIII Corps.[1]

His supposition may have been correct. Less than a week later, Halleck wired Grant recommending Crook for the command of the reformed corps. The general in chief appeared to lean in that direction, responding, "I may be able to send Crook back soon."[2] But rapidly altering circumstances would prevent whatever plans Grant had for him from coming to fruition.

Leaving the future to take care of itself, Crook remained concerned about how his present duties would be perceived by his fellow officers and the public. Up to now he had treated the kidnapping lightly. But following his release and reassignment, he recognized that some might view the circumstances of his capture as a dereliction of duty and his removal from command of the Department of West Virginia a well-deserved punishment. He may have been aware that Stanton had advocated cashiering him for "gross negligence" after his capture.[3] And he certainly recalled Sheridan's contemptuous appraisal of General Duffié after he fell into Mosby's hands—"a trifling man and a poor soldier."

To salve his pride and save face, he prevailed upon Grant to permit him to resume his old post briefly, even if only for a day, to publicly demonstrate that he was not out of favor. Grant agreed to the proposal, sending the order to Colonel Edward Townsend, the assistant adjutant general, instead of through normal channels.[4] As a result the War Department was unaware of Crook's temporary appointment and, of course, did not inform Major General Winfield Scott Hancock, the current commander of the Department of West Virginia.

Hancock, hero of Gettysburg, was a man with strong political connections to the Democratic Party and a keen sense of military protocol. He found Crook's assignment to his department, of which he only became aware upon the latter's arrival in Cumberland, highly offensive. As soon as he made this discovery, Hancock dashed off an angry telegram to Halleck from his Winchester headquarters, informing the army's chief of staff that he had just been told of Crook's claim to departmental command. As he hotly pointed out, he had been duly named to that post by the president of the United States. Absent official notice of Crook's reassignment to that position, Hancock considered the general's assumption of command an inexcusable usurpation of authority. To set the matter right, he told Halleck, "I have ordered him to . . . report at Frederick, Maryland, in arrest, and will prefer charges against him as soon as practicable."[5] Unperturbed, Crook, who had received a copy of the telegram, comfortably established himself in Cumberland and waited for his superiors to resolve the flap that he and Grant had created.

Hancock's wire to Halleck, followed by a barrage of others, including one charging Crook with "a gross breach of discipline," created a stir in Washington. No one wished to anger Hancock because of his powerful political connections. Stanton, still annoyed with Crook, sent a scathing message to Grant on the twenty-second asserting that Crook's behavior had led the secretary of war to question the "propriety of giving him a command so important as that of your cavalry." Of course, Stanton hedged, he would approve any course the general in chief decided to pursue.[6] In this instance Grant ignored Stanton's concerns.

Placating messages flowed into Hancock's office—from Halleck, the Adjutant General's Office, and even Lincoln, who weighed in with soothing words and copies of Grant's original order to Crook. Hancock, calmed by the attention he received and by the assurances that Crook's assignment to Cumberland was only a temporary expedient, withdrew his arrest order, disingenuously claiming that his actions had only been the logical result of the application of military principles.[7] Now that things had been cleared up, he reassured one and all, there would be no delay in returning Crook to Grant.

While the generals and the politicians did their administrative dance, Crook happily allowed himself to be entertained by General Hayes at his camp outside Cumberland and probably paid court to Mary Dailey. Though he affected indifference to the stir he had created, more likely he enjoyed it immensely. Responding to Hancock's expressions of outrage, he unapologetically wired the general's chief of staff: "Understand . . . that Major General Hancock was unaware of my being reassigned to the command of this department. I transmit herewith the order under which I yesterday assumed command." The following day, under orders to report to Grant at City Point, Crook departed Cumberland. Before boarding the train, though, he took one last parting shot at Hancock. With tongue firmly in cheek, he penned a general order from "Head-quarters, Department of West Virginia, Cumberland, March 22, 1865," relinquishing command of the department and revoking all orders and actions he had taken "since assuming command."[8]

The substance of Crook's meeting with his commander at City Point was not recorded. But Grant had weightier matters on his mind than a spat between two of his generals. His forces had besieged Petersburg for over a year, and all indications were that the Army of Northern Virginia could not hold out much longer. The general's focus was not so much on capturing Petersburg, though its capitulation would hand him Richmond. His objective remained the defeat of Lee's army, which he believed would end the war. If Petersburg fell, the Army of Northern Virginia would be forced out of its trenches into the open, where the Union's overwhelming strength could, if properly deployed, guarantee victory in the field.

The only circumstance that could wreck his strategy, a possibility that had kept Grant "sleeping with one eye open and one foot out of bed for many weeks," was that the wily Lee would slip out of Petersburg, lead his army south to join Joe Johnston's command in North Carolina, and form a united front against General Sherman, a series of events that could prolong the war for at least another year. To forestall that eventuality, Grant planned to attack Lee at Petersburg as soon as possible. He only delayed to await the arrival of Sheridan's cavalry from the Shenandoah and for the roads, now rain-fed rivers of red mud, to dry out enough to allow his troops to move.[9]

The original plan called for an attack on Petersburg by the infantry corps of the Armies of the Potomac and James, supported by Crook's cavalry. Sheridan's horsemen, the largest body of mounted troops in the Union army, were not to take part. Instead they were to ride south into North Carolina to unite with Sherman and finish off Johnston.

When Little Phil got wind of the part Grant planned for him, he hurried to City Point to press his objections. Dismayed at the idea of missing out on what he saw as the real center of action, the climactic battle against Lee's army, he was determined to change his commander's mind. Arriving on March 26, he went straightaway to the general in chief's tent and rapidly briefed him on the Shenandoah campaign. Then, after giving Grant a few moments to squeeze in an explanation of his coming offensive, Sheridan emotionally drove home his argument that he ought to participate in the attack on Lee's army rather than join Sherman in North Carolina.

After his subordinate had exhausted his emotional energy, Grant good-naturedly agreed to revise the plan in accordance with Sheridan's arguments. He had no trouble doing so as he had only devised the original assignment as cover against criticism should Lee's army escape. His revised orders gave Sheridan a key role in the coming battle that carried with it independent command over the entire cavalry force, including Crook's division. The general's immediate assignment would be to occupy a crucial crossroads known as Five Forks southwest of Petersburg on the Confederate's flank and rear. Grant believed that Sheridan's presence there would force Lee to withdraw troops from his center to meet this challenge, thereby weakening his lines at Petersburg. Grant would then hit the vulnerable center, drive the Confederates from their trenches into the open, and destroy them with his stronger force.[10]

Philip Sheridan and his commanders during the Appomattox Campaign. *Left to right:* Wesley Merritt, Sheridan, Crook, James W. Forsythe (Sheridan's chief of staff), and George A. Custer. After defeating the Confederacy, these men later would play significant roles in defeating the western Indians. Courtesy of the National Portrait Gallery.

Though Crook's new command remained technically part of Meade's Army of the Potomac, Grant's plan called for him report to Sheridan rather than to Meade for the duration of the campaign. Brigadier General Merritt, who was junior in seniority to Crook, currently had overall command of the two other cavalry divisions of Sheridan's force. These divisions, led by Brigadier Generals Thomas Devin and George Custer, had fought under Sheridan in the Shenandoah campaign. Merritt, Custer, and Devin were reputedly the most aggressive and experienced cavalry commanders in the Union army. Having Crook report directly to Sheridan permitted Merritt to continue in command of his two divisions and left Crook in command of only his own division. This rather awkward arrangement seems to have been based on Sheridan's conviction that Merritt and his two division commanders functioned smoothly as a team rather than on any doubts about Crook's competence.[11]

Crook's division had previously been commanded by Major General David Gregg, an officer of noted competence who had served with distinction in the Peninsula Campaign, at Chickamauga and Gettysburg, and was much esteemed by his men. Sheridan greatly valued Gregg's abilities and had been disappointed to learn of his abrupt resignation in February 1865 to take up farming in Delaware for reasons that were never made clear.[12]

The division was comprised of three brigades, each headed by experienced cavalrymen who had all served under Gregg. Brigadier General Henry Davies, a New Yorker and graduate of Columbia University, commanded the First Brigade. A lawyer by training, he was one of the few officers in the volunteer cavalry to achieve the rank of general, a tribute to his military abilities and longevity of service. The Second Brigade was led by Brigadier John Irvin Gregg, a cousin of David Gregg. "Long John," as he was known to his men, had commanded his Pennsylvania troopers in the field since the beginning of the war. He had a brash personality and a reputation as a hard fighter. Brigadier General Charles Smith had charge of the Third Brigade. A quiet, steady soldier from the state of Maine, his brigade included the only Ohio regiments in the division.[13]

Crook's situation as commanding officer of the Second Division contrasted markedly with his former commands, which had been characterized by strong bonds of trust and confidence built carefully over time between himself and his troops. He had never served with any of the officers or men of the division and now had less than a week to get to know them and earn their respect before going into battle. To complicate matters, he had doubts about their aggressiveness in combat, suspecting that their long service might have eroded their fighting spirit. For their part, the officers and men were equally unsure of Crook, knowing little of his character and ability.[14] An already difficult situation may have been exacerbated by the fact that the brigade commanders, and almost all of their regiments, were easterners, veteran soldiers of the Army of the Potomac. Considering themselves members of the most elite unit in the Union army, officers and men alike may well have looked down on the unassuming general from the west who had served much of the war well away from eastern Virginia, which they regarded the most important theater of action. Crook's authority was further compromised by the command structure that Sheridan imposed on him. Though he was to report directly to the cavalry commander, Sheridan made it known that on occasion he might give orders directly to Crook's brigade commanders, conveying the impression that he wished to keep Crook on a tight rein and did not completely trust him in his new role as a cavalry commander.

During the coming days, under these trying circumstances, Crook would have his work cut out for him. Though he never eluded to it, this period must have severely tested his leadership abilities and self-confidence.

On March 27 Crook's division joined Sheridan's command at Hancock's Station outside Petersburg. The men, who had been "somewhat blue" at the outset, anticipating a tough campaign under an unknown commander, were greatly cheered to learn that they would once again be serving with Little Phil. Two days later, on a cold and cheerless morning, the cavalry broke camp. Moving southwest around the siege lines of Petersburg, they headed for a village that occupied an intersection of farm roads known locally as Dinwiddie Court House, "a half dozen unsightly houses, a ramshackle tavern propped up on two sides with pine poles, and the weather-beaten building that gave official name to the cross-roads."[15] The importance of this unprepossessing hamlet lay in its location—about five miles to the south and west of Lee's right flank on a road that ran directly to Sheridan's objective, the more important crossroads at Five Forks, about twelve miles away. Union occupation of Five Forks would deny the Army of Northern Virginia access to the South Side and Danville Railroads, its supply line and potential escape route to North Carolina. As Grant had foreseen, Lee could not afford to leave Sheridan's presence there unchallenged.

As soon as he became aware of the direction of Sheridan's march, Lee scraped together a force of 6,000 infantry and three divisions of Confederate cavalry, estimated at about 5,500 men, from his already thinly spread forces around Petersburg and dispatched them to prevent the Federals from occupying Five Forks. Commanded by Major Generals George Pickett and Fitzhugh Lee, Robert E. Lee's cavalryman nephew, these troops would be facing Sheridan's 13,000 horsemen.[16]

But Sheridan had access to reinforcements, and the Confederates did not. Grant had initially promised him an infantry corps if he needed it. The cavalry commander now requested the VI Corps, whose reliability in combat he knew to be beyond question. But as Grant planned to use the VI Corps to assault Petersburg, he instead agreed to send the V Corps. Sheridan was not happy with the choice. Though its commander, Major General Gouverneur Warren, had distinguished himself at Gettysburg, Sheridan doubted his zest for combat.[17]

The weather had not been cooperative to either side. No one who participated in the ensuing campaign omitted mention of the incessant rain and the awful mud. Though March 29 dawned overcast but dry, a succession of rainy days had left the red-clay roads "in a frightful state," and the numerous streams crisscrossing the area had overflowed their banks. Horace Porter, a member of Grant's staff, exaggerated only slightly when he wrote that "whole fields had become beds of quicksand in which horses sank to their bellies, wagons threatened to disappear altogether, and it looked like the bottom had fallen out of the roads."[18]

Despite the glutinous mud and the rain-swollen streams, two exhausted divisions of cavalry, led by Crook and Devin, struggled into Dinwiddie Court House by 5 P.M. It had stopped raining earlier that afternoon, but after the still-sodden troops arrived at the crossroads, the deluge resumed. Sheridan, who rode in later that evening, appropriated the local tavern as his headquarters, leaving his troops to hunker in the mud, their pickets watching the roads the enemy might use to gain access to town. During the night, the rain became torrential. Some of the more enterprising of the cavalrymen pulled boards from an old barn to make a platform over the mud. But most, having neither wood nor tents, simply endured the downpour under the meager protection offered by their sodden blankets, burning fence rails at a prodigious rate to keep warm.[19] Finally, in the dreary predawn haze, they emerged blearily like swamp creatures from the primal ooze to receive their orders for the coming day.

In preparation for the attack on Five Forks that Sheridan planned to initiate that day, Little Phil divided Crook's command. Davies's brigade would follow Devin's division in a reconnaissance in force up the road toward the crossroads. Crook, riding with Gregg's brigade, remained at Dinwiddie guarding the Boydton Plank Road, a corduroy farm lane running to the northeast. If Fitzhugh Lee's cavalry managed to move that day to join Pickett's infantry, which already occupied Five Forks, it would be along this road. The presence of Gregg's brigade was intended to block their way, forcing them to make a wide detour around the Union position in order to reach the vital crossroads. Crook's third brigade (Smith's) was held in reserve "for use in any direction required."[20]

Crook must have regarded himself as lucky not to have to move on this particular morning. With the additional precipitation that had fallen overnight, the roads had become, in General Porter's words, "sheets of water, and it looked as if the saving of that army would require the services, not of a Grant, but of a Noah."[21] Grant apparently agreed and sent a message calling off offensive operations until the rains ceased and the roads became passable.

But Sheridan would have none of it. Convinced that the weather should not be allowed to interfere with his attack, he mounted Breckenridge, his strongest horse, and pushed through the viscous mud to army headquarters some miles away to convince the general once more to change his mind. In the face of Sheridan's combativeness, Grant withdrew his order, saying simply, "We will go on," and immediately sent orders to the V Corps to prepare to join Sheridan at Five Forks. On his way back to Dinwiddie, Little Phil called at Warren's headquarters to impress upon him the importance of the infantry's presence on the battlefield. To Sheridan the New Yorker appeared despondent about the prospects of the coming battle, raising warning signals in the cavalry commander's mind about the quality of support he could expect when the fighting started.[22]

Upon his return to Dinwiddie, Sheridan learned that Rebel infantry had encountered Devin's probe on the road outside Five Forks and engaged. As Devin's force was badly outnumbered and Sheridan was not yet prepared for a full-scale battle, he sent word to the division commander to withdraw back toward Dinwiddie. The fighting ended at sundown, with Devin's division dug in about two miles away from the crossroads.[23]

The next morning, the last day of March, Sheridan mounted his offensive. Davies's brigade was again assigned to support Devin's division, this time in an assault along the main road. Crook, with his remaining two brigades, would move toward Five Forks on a converging route that more or less paralleled Devin's line of attack. Unknown to Sheridan or Crook, Pickett was marching his infantry down this same road in an effort to circle the Federal left flank and attack Sheridan from behind. This put the two forces on a collision course.

When they eventually clashed, Crook's two brigades, Smith's in particular, mounted a stiff resistance. Ordinarily, in a confrontation between cavalry and infantry, the horsemen would break off and flee the field. But at Dinwiddie, fighting on foot and armed with repeating carbines, the Union cavalry held their ground and staved off Pickett's advance for three hours, until at last running short on ammunition and seriously outnumbered, they conducted an orderly withdrawal back toward the court house. Their determined resistance bought time for the remainder of Sheridan's forces to retreat to a defensive position just outside Dinwiddie, where they stopped Pickett's attack in its tracks.

Much of the fighting that day had been borne by Crook's three brigades, and they incurred the heaviest casualties, losing about one-third of their effective force. Despite these losses, Sheridan was delighted with the performance of his entire command. In his report of the day's events, he cited "Generals Crook, Merritt, Custer, and Devin, [who] by their courage and ability, sustained their commands and executed the rapid movements of the day with promptness and without confusion."[24] If Little Phil had harbored doubts about Crook's effectiveness, they were beginning to evaporate.

Though Sheridan enthused that "he has had one of the liveliest days in his experience, fighting infantry and cavalry with cavalry only," he had not lost sight of the predicament in which the day's action had left him. Hemmed in by Pickett and Fitzhugh Lee and now cut off from Grant's army, he soberly dispatched a message to the lieutenant general acknowledging: "[Pickett] is too strong for us. I will hold on to Dinwiddie Court-House until I am compelled to leave." The subtext of his message could not have been clearer. Now was the time to reinforce the cavalry with the promised infantry corps. Grant responded in a dispatch that evening that Warren was on his way.[25]

That evening, Pickett's men captured two soldiers from the V Corps who had strayed into Confederate lines. Their presence alerted the Virginian to the fact that Warren was now en route to Dinwiddie. Pickett immediately withdrew his forces from their exposed position near the crossroads and, under cover of night, retreated toward fortifications he had begun to prepare at Five Forks.

When Sheridan discovered this, he determined to attack the Rebels while they were still in the open.[26] Based on Grant's assurances that Warren's troops would arrive at Dinwiddie by midnight, he initially intended to launch his offensive at 3 A.M. When Warren failed to arrive at the appointed time, Sheridan irritably revised the plan, sending a dispatch to the V Corps commander asking that he redirect his march to catch Pickett on his flank just to the south of Five Forks, a move that would trap the Rebels between Sheridan's cavalry and Warren's infantry.

As the sky lightened and the sun burned off the early morning fog, Sheridan, in anticipation of Warren's arrival, ordered Merritt's two divisions to set out for Five Forks as planned, leaving Crook's Second Division, not yet fully recovered from the previous day's heavy fighting, to guard his rear at Dinwiddie. Crook would thus miss one of the final important battles of the war, a circumstance that he seemed to accept with uncharacteristic equanimity.

Delayed by muddy roads, the advance elements of the V Corps did not begin to trickle in to the environs of Five Forks until about 8 A.M., and it was almost noon before Warren himself finally arrived.[27] Despite their tardiness, his corps performed well in the ensuing battle, which finally began in the late afternoon. While the V Corps hammered the Confederate right, Sheridan's cavalry struck their left, eventually flanking and then routing the entire enemy force.

But Warren moved too slowly to suit Sheridan. Though victory was complete and the infantry general had personally displayed great courage on the field, Sheridan summarily relieved him after the battle, citing his failure to "exert himself to inspire [his men]." Humiliated, Warren resigned his commission as major general of volunteers, reverting to the rank of major in the regulars. In later years, under criticism for ruining this good soldier's career, Sheridan expanded his rationale for relieving

Warren, adding that he had considered himself gravely threatened by Lee's army to his rear and felt a want of confidence in having the general as a corps commander in such dangerous circumstances.[28]

Though his handling of the Warren affair demonstrated Sheridan's volatility and vindictiveness, no one, not even Crook, could gainsay his military achievements in the Five Forks operation. Sheridan's strategic grasp of the situation, his willingness to argue his case with his commanding general, and his aggressive pursuit and defeat of the enemy burnished a reputation already glowing in the reflected light of his victories at Opequon and Fisher's Hill and his famous ride to rally the troops at Cedar Creek. The coming week would only add further luster to his name.

Though Crook's role in the campaign had been primarily defensive, he had handled his troops with sufficient competence to dispel most doubts about his fitness as a commander. But absent from the main engagement at Five Forks and sidelined over the next few days in guarding the army's supply train, his relatively passive role stood in marked contrast to the prominent part he had played in the Shenandoah campaign. Then Crook had served as Sheridan's confidant and advisor and had been constantly in the forefront of the fighting. Consigning him to guard duty during and immediately after Five Forks appears to have been a deliberate choice on Sheridan's part, perhaps motivated either by a desire to give the division a brief respite after the heavy fighting of the previous two days or by continuing doubts about Crook's fitness to command cavalry.

CHAPTER THIRTY-THREE

The Final Struggle

April 2–9, 1865

In the predawn darkness of April 2, Crook's troopers, still bivouacked on the muddy grounds around Dinwiddie Court House, awakened to a steadily growing rumble to the northeast. With grim satisfaction, they recognized the significance of the thunder and flickering light that lit the early morning sky. The pyrotechnics did not signal yet another gathering storm, but the beginning of the artillery barrage that preceded Grant's final offensive against Petersburg. The fighting at Dinwiddie and Pickett's route at Five Forks had fatally depleted the Confederate defenses around the city. In doing so it had set the stage for the climactic battle now in progress, a battle timed to preempt any counteroffensive Lee might have been tempted to mount against Sheridan's rear.

With the exception of Gregg's brigade, which joined Merritt in pursuit of Pickett, Crook's Second Division did not participate in the fighting. "Badly handled," as Crook put it, in the previous day's fighting, his men remained near Dinwiddie with Sheridan's supply train.[1] But they soon learned that after a day of bitter combat the outer works protecting Petersburg had fallen, and by sunrise the following day, the city had surrendered. Lee's army, its supply lines cut and its defenses breached, had evacuated during the night. Richmond's defenses had collapsed a few hours later, and President Jefferson Davis and his government had fled southward, leaving behind only the remnants of General Ewell's corps and a few fragmentary units as a rearguard. Even this small contingent would soon withdraw from the city to reunite with Lee at a prearranged rendezvous at Amelia Court House.

Despite the loss of the Confederate capital and the overwhelming display of Union might, Lee's sense of commitment and honor compelled him to continue the struggle. With an intact army still numbering some 25,000 veterans—though at the moment strung out between Richmond and Petersburg—he clung to the hope of eluding Grant's army and striking out for the Richmond and Danville Railroad. From there, if luck held, the Army of Northern Virginia would follow the tracks south to the Virginia–North Carolina border and join Joseph Johnston's Army of Tennessee in its fight against Sherman. Lee still held out hope that the combined armies might defeat Sherman and then turn to take on Grant.[2] This unlikely scenario depended on The ability of the Army of Northern Virginia to reach the rail line before Federal forces could cut them off. Unencumbered by a supply column, Lee was confident that he had the mobility to outrun any pursuit.

But Grant did not intend to allow Lee's forces to elude him to fight another day. He had worked too hard and shed the blood of too many of his men to let this opportunity escape him. And his highly energized, numerically superior force shared his commitment. Euphoric in victory, these war-weary veterans were now convinced that, as Crook put it, "the end of the war was near at hand, and that the Confederate army was in its last throes."[3]

Grant expected Lee to make a stand at Amelia Court House in order to keep the Richmond and Danville line open for his escape southward. He directed Sheridan, supported by Meade's infantry, to pursue the Rebels and prevent this from happening. With luck, they would slow the Confederate retreat sufficiently to allow Major General Ord's slow-moving but powerful Army of the James, en route from Petersburg, to insert itself between Lee and the Danville road.[4]

The pursuit, in which Crook now would have a key role, played out along the length of the rain-swollen Appomattox River, a muddy ribbon of water snaking fifty miles across central Virginia from Appomattox Station eastward to Richmond before eventually emptying into the James. Two railroads, the Richmond and Danville, Lee's planned escape route, and the South Side Railroad, etched a sprawling "X" across the Appomattox, each spanning the river at different points. The Danville line slashed northeast to southwest, while the South Side ran more or less due west from Petersburg, crossing the Danville track at Burkeville, about midway between Richmond and Appomattox Court House, before continuing on to Lynchburg. Both armies headed for Burkeville. If Lee could reach it before the Yankees, who marched along the convergent South Side tracks, he would have a clear run south. If the Federals arrived first, they could bottle up Lee in central Virginia and put an end to his flight. Though his forces moved more slowly than the Rebels, Grant relied on the fact that Lee's troops would have a longer distance to travel. The Danville line ran in a broad arc that would force them to cross the Appomattox twice to get to Amelia Court House. The South Side track, which Sheridan and Ord would follow, was twenty miles shorter and required no river crossings.

Lee's army marched from Petersburg for a day and into the night on empty bellies and little rest, their spirits buoyed only by the promise of provisions at Amelia, where they expected to be resupplied by rail. But when they reached the sleepy hamlet at noon on Tuesday, they found that the expected 350,000 rations had not arrived. In the confusion of the hasty evacuation, trains were dispatched from Richmond carrying caissons, artillery ammunition, and harnesses, but not a scrap of food or forage. Unwilling to proceed without food for his men, Lee called a halt to permit his troops to forage for provisions and to await the arrival of Ewell's 6,000 troops. But obtaining sufficient provender from the surrounding countryside proved impossible. The farms in the area had been stripped for some time to feed Lee's besieged army, leaving neither food nor fodder to fill his supply wagons or the bellies of his men. Their rations consisted of a few sassafras buds and the occasional ear of parched corn discovered in odd corners of the harvested fields surrounding the town.[5]

As Lee rode toward Amelia, Sheridan moved out of Five Forks on April 2, using his cavalry to clear away the remnants of Pickett's troops and Fitzhugh Lee's horsemen. The Army of Northern Virginia was starting to disintegrate. "[H]undreds and hundreds of prisoners, armed and unarmed, fell into our hands, together with many wagons and five pieces of artillery," Sheridan would later recall.[6] Crook's three brigades formed a part of Sheridan's mounted force, but of the three, only Gregg's saw any action. While Merritt and Custer pursued Confederate horsemen northwest along the road to Namozine Church, Crook and his remaining brigades found themselves once again in the rear of the column guarding the wagons.

The following day was more of the same. Sheridan and Meade continued to push toward Amelia, marching between the South Side Railroad and the Appomattox on a direct route to Burkeville. Merritt's cavalry rode in the van, and Meade's V and VI Corps Infantry slogged along some distance to their rear. Crook's division remained in the rear of the force, guarding the supply wagons.[7] Grant, riding with the slower Army of the James, followed the tracks of the South Side line, parallel to, but to the rear of, Sheridan's forces.

In the cold drizzle of April 4, Crook, whose division had seen no action since March 30, finally received orders that would send him back into the thick of the fray. Neither Lee nor Grant knew the exact location of the other's army. But Grant believed that the Confederates had gathered at Amelia preparatory to driving south to Burkeville. Sheridan agreed and positioned his horsemen in between Amelia and Burkeville to block the anticipated Rebel movement. With cavalry alone, Sheridan knew that he could not prevent Lee from reaching his objective but hoped that his mere presence would induce the Confederates to surrender. If not, Sheridan could at least put a up a good fight, delaying Lee long enough for Meade and the bulk of his infantry to arrive. Sheridan now needed to verify the Rebels' presence in Amelia. Meanwhile, he had to begin to deploy his men as a blocking force.[8]

With these objectives in mind, he ordered Merritt to reconnoiter to the northeast while he led a small detachment of cavalry and elements of the V Corps north to Jetersville, a village lying about midway between Amelia and Burkeville on the Danville line. In this respectable little hamlet of perhaps a dozen homes, a store or two, a post office, and of course a railroad depot, he directed his men to prepare their defenses.[9]

While Sheridan dug in at Jetersville, Crook's division moved to its assigned position as a backup force, blocking the railroad farther south at another rural depot with the evocative name Jennings Ordinary. Crook had barely arrived there when he received a dispatch from Sheridan ordering him to Jetersville as quickly as possible. Little Phil had intercepted a courier carrying a message from Lee's commissary general asking that 300,000 rations be dispatched to Burkeville for the army, which the message indicated was in Amelia. From the contents of the dispatch,

Sheridan confirmed not only the location of Lee's troops but also an approximation of their number. This information led him to summon both Crook and Merritt to join him at Jetersville immediately. Crook hastily complied. Arriving in the early evening, he promptly put his division to work, throwing up fence-rail barricades in anticipation of an imminent attack that, fortunately, failed to materialize that night.[10]

The next morning, while Sheridan's troopers waited anxiously behind their makeshift fortifications, Lee, still in Amelia, stood somberly in a continuing drizzle, watching the last of his forage wagons return empty from the countryside. He knew that he could not remain here without provisions, and while he lingered, his lead over Grant diminished, and with it his chances of escape. Ewell's corps had arrived the previous night, thus removing the last reason to delay his departure. So with Longstreet in the van, Ewell in the middle, and Gordon's Valley veterans serving as rear guard, positions each would maintain throughout the march, Lee resumed his retreat south along the rail line toward Burkeville.[11]

But he had tarried too long. Five miles outside Amelia (about a mile north of Jetersville), his forward elements encountered Sheridan's pickets. Unsure of what he faced, Lee ordered skirmishers to push the pickets out of the way but quickly discovered that they were only the vanguard of a much larger force. By now Meade's infantry had arrived in Jetersville and had reinforced Sheridan's thin line. The tables had turned. Lee now faced an army substantially stronger than his own famished and worn-out troops could handle. Cut off from Burkeville and his route south, he made a last desperate attempt to escape the trap that Grant had laid for him, turning off the railroad and heading west across the countryside toward Farmville on the South Side line. There he hoped to be resupplied from Lynchburg before continuing south to North Carolina.[12]

Again Sheridan correctly assessed Lee's intention. To confirm his conclusion, he ordered Crook to send Davies's brigade to reconnoiter in the direction of Farmville. As Davies rode around the flank of the Southern army, he encountered a large supply train, accompanied by artillery and four hundred Rebel cavalry, moving west toward Farmville, just as Sheridan had predicted. Spotting the Federal cavalrymen, the column's escort wheeled one of their guns around to bear on the pursuing horsemen, who without pause, charged through an intervening swamp and seized the artillery piece before the desperate gunners could get off a shot. Driving off the badly outnumbered escort, they attacked the now unguarded wagon train, stretched out along several miles of roadway. While the bulk of Davies's force roamed the flanks of the train to guard against rescue, three or four hundred of the exuberant Union troopers swept down on the wagons, setting fire to their canvas tops and, with their sabers, beating the terrified teamsters off the wagon boxes. Soon the air filled with the pop of igniting ammunition and clouds of acrid black smoke. Capturing cartloads of equipment and supplies, they destroyed the remaining wagons and ammunition on the spot.[13]

The Confederates had no intention of absorbing this shocking loss without a fight, particularly as the captured booty included the personal effects of high-ranking Confederate officers, among them, Fitzhugh Lee. In an effort to recapture the wagons, Lee's entire cavalry corps charged Davies's single brigade, forcing its hasty withdrawal back toward Jetersville. As the Federals neared the town, driving the captured wagons before them, Crook rode out of the hamlet at the head of his remaining brigades and drove off Lee's cavalry, saving Davies's prize intact for a delighted Sheridan.[14]

The location and direction of the supply train confirmed for the cavalry commander that Lee had turned his army toward Farmville. But General Meade, already resentful of Sheridan, refused to accept his assessment. Suffering from a severe gastrointestinal ailment that caused him considerable discomfort and made him even more irascible than usual, Meade dismissed Sheridan's theory. He adamantly refused to commit his infantry to a joint offensive aimed at cutting off Lee before he could reach Farmville, insisting that the Confederates were withdrawing back toward Amelia to make their stand. Sheridan, unwilling to back down, promptly dispatched one of his scouts to Grant, requesting that he overrule Meade.[15]

The general in chief received Sheridan's message after dark. Rather than wait for morning to reply, he promptly mounted his horse and rode to Jetersville with a small escort to resolve the issue. Arriving at about 10:30 P.M., he met with the two generals in the log cabin Sheridan had appropriated for his headquarters. Grant agreed with Sheridan's plan of action and sharply reminded Meade that the army should be trying to get ahead of Lee instead of following him. But he gave Meade an opportunity to prove that he was right, directing him to march on Amelia with the V and VI Corps at first light.[16]

Sheridan, his force once again reduced to a cavalry command by the removal of the infantry units, refused to accompany Meade on a venture he considered a fool's errand. Acting on his own reading of the situation, on the morning of April 6, he dispatched Merritt and Crook toward Farmville to find and intercept the Confederates.[17] Selecting his old friend for this dangerous mission indicates that any doubts Sheridan might have had about his fitness to command cavalry had now been resolved.

Crook and his troopers enthusiastically embraced their mission. Men and officers alike sensed that they were about to break the backbone of the rebellion and were participating in a historic "chase for final victory and triumph." General Meade, however, was furious. By sending the cavalry on a mission in a direction away from the infantry's route of march, Sheridan had effectively deprived the Army of the Potomac of its eyes and ears. To Meade, no act more clearly exemplified the little Irishman's selfishness and conceit.[18] But while the general may have correctly read Sheridan's character, Crook soon confirmed that his friend had been right about Lee.

The men of the division were in high spirits, and the weather made the ride toward Farmville enjoyable. With the sun shining after so many days of rain, the roads began drying out, the air was now clear and fresh, and the trees on either side of the road were tinged with green, heralding the coming of spring. At times as they moved across high ground, the Union troopers had flickering glimpses of Lee's supply wagons through the trees in the distance, indicating that their columns were moving along parallel routes.[19]

Gradually, the distance between the two columns narrowed as their paths converged. Not far from Farmville, Crook, his division in the lead with Merritt close behind, came in such close proximity to Lee's force that he succumbed to the temptation to probe the enemy's strength. He found the supply train heavily guarded by a division of General Anderson's corps, a force too strong for him to take on alone. Hoping to at least slow it down, he mounted repeated flank attacks on the column, which forced Anderson to halt frequently to fight off his attackers. These delays caused the Rebel division to lose contact with Longstreet's corps, to its front, opening a gap in Lee's line of march.[20]

While Crook slowed the supply train, Custer's division rode parallel to the Rebel column, seeking out a vulnerable point to attack. Before noon his troopers found the gap between Longstreet and Anderson just as the beleaguered wagons crossed Sayler's Creek, a marshy stream wandering north across the Confederate line of march. Joined by Merritt and Crook, the three cavalry divisions now swept down on the train, demolishing several hundred wagons, taking many prisoners, and capturing sixteen cannon.[21] More importantly, the Yankee thrust isolated not only the supply wagons but also Ewell's entire corps, some 6,000–8,000 men who had been marching at the rear of the train. These troops were now cut off from the protection of Longstreet's infantry, the strongest unit in Lee's army.

Ewell's command had been followed by Gordon's corps, which served as the army's rear guard. The two corps together would have been too powerful for the Union cavalry to attack. But at this juncture, Ewell became separated from Gordon. While Merritt and Crook engaged the wagon train, Gordon's troops had come under fire from Federal infantry. Ewell heard the sounds of this engagement and realized that the enemy was now behind as well as in front of him. Fearing for the safety of his wagons and believing that he had discovered a shortcut to the Appomattox River and safety, he sent his train off on a side road to the northwest while his infantry continued to follow Longstreet's line of march. Unfortunately, he neglected to inform Gordon of this. The latter arrived at the fork in the road and turned right behind the wagons, assuming that the infantry had marched in that direction too. Ewell's troops thus lost their rear guard.[22]

Though Sheridan's cavalry alone was still not strong enough to take on Ewell's force, they had sufficient muscle to hold the Confederates in place until Meade arrived. The latter, responding to an urgent message from Sheridan, sent his II and VI Corps to the scene with an alacrity that belied his sour mood at having to acknowledge that the cavalry commander had correctly predicted Lee's whereabouts.

To prevent Ewell's corps from escaping, Crook planted his division squarely in their path. With two of his brigades fighting dismounted, as they often did during this campaign, and the third mounted, Crook's cavalry swarmed like angry bees all along the Confederate front and right, while Merritt's men attacked along Crook's right.[23] The fierceness of their combined assaults and the heavy fire from the troopers' Spencer carbines held the Rebels until the Union infantry arrived.

At one point in the fighting, Crook's mounted troopers, many of whom rode mules, charged the breastworks the Rebels had hastily thrown up but were repelled by heavy fire. The general, seeing so many empty saddles among the returning mules, feared the worst. But with relief he soon discovered that the animals had bolted toward the enemy lines as soon as they came under fire, and the men, unable to turn them, had wisely abandoned their saddles. One young trooper, later identified as William Richardson of the Second Ohio, had an entirely different experience. Unable to jump off in time, he was carried by his mule over the breastworks into the enemy position. In the confusion he rode straight through their lines to Sheridan, who at the time was busily deploying Meade's infantry in Ewell's rear. The young man's deed earned him a brief moment of recognition and a sentence in Sheridan's memoirs. He was the only soldier on the field able to provide his commander with information regarding the disposition of both his own cavalry and the Confederate units, intelligence the general found invaluable in deploying the infantry as they joined the battle.[24]

The appearance of Meade's men dramatically altered the balance of power. Ewell now found himself confined in the narrow swampy valley of Sayler's Creek, trapped between two strong infantry corps on one end and two cavalry divisions on the other, with additional Union horsemen on his flanks. The valley's slopes were covered with thick brush, making escape all but impossible for the majority of Ewell's troops. Despite the hopelessness of their situation, the Rebels battled with a savagery graphically recorded by one Confederate officer involved in the fight.

[Q]uicker than I can tell it, the battle turned into a butchery and confused melee of brutal personal conflicts. I saw numbers of men kill each other with bayonets and the butts of muskets, and even bite each other's throats and ears and noses, rolling on the ground like wild beasts. . . . I had cautioned my men against wearing [captured] Yankee overcoats, especially in battle, but had not been able to enforce the order perfectly, and almost at my side I saw a young fellow of one of my companies jam the muzzle of his musket against the back of the head of his most intimate friend, clad in a Yankee overcoat, and blow his brains out.[25]

But such ferocity could not overcome the odds, and Ewell, eventually recognizing the futility of the struggle, surrendered his corps. Near sundown, General Lee mounted a bluff overlooking the battlefield. Witnessing a scene of utter chaos, he exclaimed, "My God! Has the army been dissolved?" Thinking to bolster his commander's flagging morale, a determined officer responded, "No, General, here are troops ready to do their duty."[26]

But there were not many such souls left, and those remaining had been reduced to a terrible state. While the exigencies of the Confederate retreat made accurate estimates of Rebel losses problematic, one author has noted that "close to 7,700 men of the Confederacy" were rendered "hors-de-combat" at Sayler's Creek.[27] These casualties—killed, wounded, captured, and missing—represented almost one-third of the troops that had begun the retreat from Petersburg on April 2. The severity of this loss was enhanced by the capture of eight generals, including Ewell, Kershaw, and Lee's own son, Custis. Among the remaining Rebel soldiers were many so wracked by hunger and exhaustion that they could hardly be expected to participate effectively in the fighting. Yet most were not ready to abandon the cause, their gritty faith exemplified by their cries as General Lee rode past them: "It's General Lee! Uncle Robert! Where's the man who won't follow Uncle Robert?" Few, it seemed, were ready to admit the truth of General Ewell's bitter exclamation at Sayler's Creek: "Our cause is lost. Lee should surrender before more lives are wasted."[28]

That evening an exultant Sheridan, sensing that the end was near, penned a dispatch to Grant at Burkeville. "If the thing is pressed," he wrote, "I think that Lee will surrender." Grant relayed the message to Lincoln at City Point, where the president anxiously awaited the outcome of the campaign. With characteristic simplicity, Lincoln replied, "Let the thing be pressed."[29]

Sheridan assigned Merritt to push the pursuit, while Crook and Custer flushed the remnants of Ewell's division from their hiding places in the brush surrounding the battlefield under the cold light of an almost full moon. Disgruntled by what he regarded as the perfidy of his fellow officers, Crook later sourly complained that Custer had claimed a lion's share of the honors, including seven generals, fifteen pieces of artillery, and thirty-one battle flags.[30] But at the time, Crook had little opportunity to brood on the boy general's greed, for Sheridan soon had him back on the trail of Lee's retreating army.

Lee did not linger near Sayler's Creek. After witnessing the demise of Ewell's corps, he hastily gathered his remaining troops and marched them through the night toward Farmville, hoping to put the Appomattox between his remaining forces and Grant's army. If the requested provisions had arrived, and if his men could cross the river in time, perhaps they could still escape the rapidly closing Union net and make it to Lynchburg.

But crossing the Appomattox effectively funneled Lee's army into a narrow seven-mile-wide corridor between the James and the Appomattox Rivers shaped, one Confederate officer thought, like a jug lying on its side.[31] The way north was barred by the James, its bridges burned and its banks lined with Union infantry. To the south lay the Appomattox, its muddy waters all that now separated Lee's exhausted troops from the bulk of Grant's army. To his rear, Crook's cavalry followed by the hard-marching men of Horatio Wright's VI Corps pressed the Confederates inexorably toward their only exit, the neck of the jug and its mouth, the rural hamlet of Appomattox Court House. Lee's only remaining option was to reach the town and its nearby depot on the South Side line before Grant used Sheridan as a cork to seal the Army of Northern Virginia's fate.

Extreme fatigue afflicted both pursuers and pursued. But on the morning of April 7, Crook's men, though they had marched and fought and marched again without respite, drew new energy from the obvious signs of the Army of Northern Virginia's disintegration strewn along on the road to Farmville. On all sides the unburied corpses of dead Rebels intermingled with discarded equipment, ammunition, and the twisted bodies of dead and dying horses, clearly signaling that the end was very near.[32]

Having outdistanced their supply trains as they rode forward, the Yankee cavalry foraged for food at the farms that dotted a landscape spared so far from many of the ravages of war. After almost four years of fighting, Crook's men were as skilled as Sherman's bummers at living off the land and had no scruples about taking what they wanted from secessionist farmers. Hardened to civilian suffering by the long campaign, Crook noted without censure that his men pursued final victory with "provisions tied to their saddles, . . . ham, . . . chickens, ducks, geese, turkeys, etc. etc." When they engaged the enemy, as they now did with increasing frequency, their living contraband would escape, filling the fields with fluttering fowl and presenting, Crook thought, "a most ludicrous spectacle."[33]

Riding toward Farmville, Crook encountered Major General Andrew Humphreys's combined II and III Corps, marching in the same direction. Leaving the road to the infantry, Crook led his cavalrymen through the countryside along a parallel route. When Humphreys branched off toward High Bridge, hoping to capture the railway span that crossed the river at the town to which the bridge gave its name, Crook continued on toward Farmville, driving off Confederate units attempting to burn bridges along the road.[34] Arriving opposite the town, a thriving tobacco depot of fifteen hundred souls, he found the Confederates had already crossed to the north bank of the Appomattox and were in the act of burning the only bridge at this point on the river. Though he failed to save the span, Crook entered the town by means of a nearby ford.[35]

Once across the river at Farmville, with Gregg's brigade in the lead, the division rode north. Approaching Buckingham Court House at about four o'clock that afternoon, Gregg's scouts sighted a body of Confederate horsemen, troopers of Rosser's cavalry division, riding herd on a supply train in the rear of Lee's army. Whether Gregg's judgment was clouded by fatigue or he was simply overconfident, he attacked without waiting for the remainder of the division to come up. Unknown to him, a second division of Rebel cavalry under Brigadier General Thomas Munford had been riding parallel to Rosser's men concealed by a ridge to Gregg's left flank. Seeing Union cavalry flashing by, Munford promptly charged. The unexpected attack hit the Union troopers hard. Hemmed in by a stout rail fence along both sides of the road, they tried to retreat back the way they had come only to find their way blocked by a Union supply train advancing behind them. Frightened by the sudden appearance of Confederate cavalry, the teamsters tried to turn their wagons and mules in the narrow roadway, creating a panic that spread to Gregg's troopers.[36]

Recounting the incident years later, Crook claimed that he found the pell-mell retreat of the brigade "unaccountable," asserting that Munford had less than a hundred men with him. He was even more perplexed to find that in their flight, Gregg's men were "deliberately discharging their revolvers into their comrades ahead of them." Evidently still contemptuous of Gregg despite the intervening years, Crook chose to ignore the surrounding circumstances, the suddenness of the attack, the unexpected number of the enemy, the pack train blocking the road, and most frightening, a sudden and devastating twelve-gun artillery salvo that opened up on the Union horsemen as they fled into the roadway.[37]

Crook's lingering resentment stemmed from the reality that, whether explicable or not, the precipitous flight of Gregg's men endangered the entire division. Fearing that the stampeding cavalrymen and teamsters might spread panic to the rest of his command unless promptly brought under control, Crook had galloped to the head of the fleeing column. Waving his sword and clutching at the reins of the troopers' horses in an effort to face them about, he became so absorbed in his effort that he soon found himself in the very rear of his division with Rebel horsemen coming straight at him. His egress blocked by the fences on either side of the roadway, Crook managed a last-minute escape by wheeling his horse through a fortuitous gap he found just as the enemy closed in. His luck continued to hold when his artillery, positioned in the field in which he now found himself, fired into the pursuing Rebels, discouraging further pursuit. But Gregg was not so lucky. Crook snidely commented that the brigade commander was "a heavy man, and riding a small horse, [he] couldn't keep up with his men" and so was captured by Munford's cavalry. General Gordon, who later spied the disconsolate officer walking in a line with other Union prisoners, asked him whether he would prefer a mount. Though appreciative of the offer, Gregg declined, "preferring to share the fate of his men"—a gesture that might have substantially improved Crook's jaundiced view of him had he been aware of it.[38]

While Crook skirmished with Lee's cavalry, Sheridan arrived at Prince Edward Court House, southwest of Farmville, where he positioned Merritt's division to block any effort by the Confederates to thrust southward toward the Richmond and Danville line. Thus far Sheridan's instincts had proved impeccable, and they did not fail him now. Word of Crook's fight north of the river now convinced him that Lee had abandoned his plan to join Johnston and instead was redirecting his army west toward Lynchburg.[39] To counter this move, he prepared to redeploy his cavalry on the Lynchburg road in order to delay the Confederates long enough for the powerful infantry units marching hard behind him to catch up and press the "thing" to its conclusion. Preparatory to executing this maneuver, he assembled his cavalry force at a small depot on the South Side Railroad called Prospect Station, not far from Appomattox Court House.

If Crook had any plans to rescue Gregg, he was forced to abandon them on receiving orders from Sheridan to withdraw to the Prospect Station rendezvous. In the early morning hours of April 8, he reached the depot, where he found a small cavalry division under the command of Brigadier General Ranald Mackenzie awaiting him. Mackenzie, who in the next decade would achieve fame as an Indian fighter in Texas, had been borrowed by Sheridan from the Army of the James to reinforce Crook's command. Little Phil himself arrived at Prospect Station with Merritt's division at dawn, having camped down the road the previous night.[40]

Union scouts reported sighting the Confederate army pushing west along a path that would soon bring it to the Appomattox depot, where Lee hoped the supplies from Lynchburg would be waiting. Responding to this information, Sheridan had just ordered the cavalry in pursuit when a figure, oddly clad in Confederate gray, galloped up to the column and demanded to be taken to General Sheridan. Fortunately, before any of the nervous troopers could shoot the man down, he was recognized by a number of the general's staff officers as Sergeant Jim White of Major Young's scouts. After recovering his breath, the sergeant reported the presence at the Appomattox depot of several trains loaded with the supplies Lee had requested.[41] The bulk of the Confederate force had not yet reached the station, so the trains were only lightly guarded. Recognizing the opportunity, Sheridan immediately dispatched Merritt, with Crook's and Devin's divisions on his flanks, to capture the supplies.

At 2 P.M. Custer's men, in the van of Merritt's column, galloped into the depot ahead of Lee's advance guard and seized the trains. They then went to work ripping up the tracks to the west of the station to prevent any cars from returning to Lynchburg. While the cavalrymen wrecked the line, Custer's scouts discovered one of the lead elements of Lee's army, a large artillery unit, camped north of the depot. The Federals immediately attacked it, beginning an engagement that lasted well into the night. The fighting effectively prevented Lee from gaining access to the depot and the desperately needed supplies that now lay just beyond his reach.[42]

Crook's men arrived at the depot at dusk and were startled to hear the chug and whistle of an approaching engine and, strangely, the sounds of raucous cheering. As the train clattered slowly up to the tired cavalrymen, one of Custer's men leaned out of the cab and shouted that the general had captured three trainloads of supplies. "Pitch in, boys," he called, and the eager troopers clamored aboard the cars to claim their prizes: clothing, including a priceless shipment of clean underwear, various provisions, and forage for their horses.[43]

That evening, Lee was bottled up at Appomattox Court House, about four miles to the north of the depot, with the entire Union cavalry, including Crook's division, to his front. Far into the night, following Sheridan's orders, the Federal horsemen harassed the enemy force, allowing the played-out Confederates no rest.

A triumphant Sheridan, convinced that he had at last brought Lee to his "last ditch," relayed the news to Grant and requested that the infantry, in this case troops under Major Generals Ord and John Gibbon, hurry forward for the kill. Crook's 2,000 troopers had ridden hard all day. But unlike the other divisions, they had done little fighting and were still relatively fresh. Sheridan now ordered them to deploy on the Lynchburg road with instructions to "resist the enemy with all [their] power" until the infantry could reach the battlefield.[44]

Sheridan's orders were necessarily vague because at this point Lee's intentions could only be surmised. The Rebel commander himself would only formulate his last desperate gambit for escape that evening at a council of war held with his senior commanders. Only then would he declare that his army's only hope lay in breaking out of the bottleneck at dawn, before Grant's infantry arrived on the scene, and then force its way west along the Lynchburg road. To that end, he ordered Fitzhugh Lee's cavalry to strike at the flanks of Sheridan's command, while Gordon's infantry, with Longstreet's corps in reserve, attacked the center of the line.

Anticipating the direction of Lee's attack, if not its specifics, Crook decided to place Smith's brigade, which had been the last to arrive in camp that night, across the Lynchburg road as near as possible to the Rebel lines. They were to be the canary in the coal mine, while the rest of the division remained in the rear in reserve to await the Rebel push. Crook's instructions to Smith that evening were characteristically concise: "Sheridan thinks General Lee is in a tight place, and may try to get out tonight by the Lynchburg Pike; he wants me to look out for him, and I guess you better go."[45]

At 9 P.M. Smith's troopers, who had just turned in, were rudely ousted from their warm blankets and given the curt order to "saddle and pack, and be ready to move out at once." Though grumbling that this was "shoving" it a bit, the men obediently moved out down the road toward Appomattox Court House, marching silently through a landscape of destruction lit by the flickering firelight cast off by burning wagons. Occasionally exchanging fire with Rebel pickets, they reached their forward position without serious opposition.[46]

Facing an enemy of superior numbers, Smith deployed his three regiments and an accompanying battery of 3-inch guns along a ridge. He had decided on a position only a half mile from the Rebel encampment in order to give his troopers as much room for maneuver to their rear as possible. So close were they to Lee's camp that they could hear "the Rebel teamsters in the valley below parking their wagons, with oaths and imprecations savoring of tired horses and wearied angry men." Noiselessly, under the dim illumination of the stars, Smith's weary troopers constructed breastworks across and at right angles to the road, using fence rails and as much dirt as they could dig up with sharpened sticks, the only tools at hand. Then, lying down in the cold dirt without blankets, they dozed fitfully on their arms, waiting for Lee to make his move.[47]

From their embattled position, the Confederates looked out upon the hundreds of Union campfires, winking like fireflies, announcing more clearly than words that the full strength of Sheridan's cavalry now lay athwart Lee's path to Lynchburg. A pall of defeat descended on the Rebel camp. With hardly more than 8,000 effectives to throw into battle against the tens of thousands in Grant's army, Lee indeed had reached his "last ditch." He made it known to his senior officers that if Union infantry arrived on the field before his men could break out past Sheridan's cavalry, he would have no alternative but to surrender.

April 9, Palm Sunday, dawned fresh and cool. Wisps of fog lingered over the fields in the damp early morning air. As the sky brightened, the ragged Confederates, veterans of a hundred campaigns, rolled stiffly out of their blankets, nibbled at the bread crusts and parched corn that composed their breakfast, and checked their weapons for the last time. Then, forming into a broken line stretching almost a mile from northwest to southeast, the remnants of Gordon's infantry and Fitzhugh Lee's cavalry settled down to wait for the bugle call that would send them forward.

While the Confederates formed their battle lines, Sheridan deployed his forces in the cool dawn in preparation for what he hoped would be the final engagement of the war. Devin and Custer were assigned to the center, covering Smith's position from the rear. Crook placed the remainder of his division so that Mackenzie's brigade-sized division protected his left flank while Davies's brigade reconnoitered the enemy's right. Gregg's brigade, now commanded by Colonel Samuel B. M. Young, was stationed close to Smith's rear in reserve.[48] Smith's troopers, unaware of the surrounding deployments, crouched behind their makeshift barricades, feeling very much alone.

At about 6:30 A.M. the Confederates moved on Smith's works. Instructed to hold on as long as possible, the brigade put up a stout resistance. His troopers, armed with seven-shot Spencers and sixteen-round Henry rifles, unleashed such a strong, persistent fire on the attackers that the Rebels were unable to budge them by direct assault.[49] As a consequence, Gordon's infantry wasted more than two hours maneuvering about the field in an attempt to flank Smith's barricades before advancing once more in a head-on attack. The delay proved fatal.

By 9 A.M., under renewed assaults by a combination of Confederate infantry and Fitzhugh Lee's horse soldiers, Smith's men, though reinforced by other elements of Sheridan's command, were unable to hold any longer against Gordon's numerically superior troops. As they grudgingly gave ground in a slow and orderly withdrawal, they heard an excited cry: "Keep up your courage, boys; the infantry is coming right along—in two columns—black and white—side by side—a regular checker-board." Still, for what seemed like an hour, though it was probably no more than a few minutes, Smith's battle-weary troopers continued to fight alone. But then, as they retreated up a long rise of land toward a fringe of trees crowning the crest of a ridge, they suddenly found themselves passing through a line of tired but grimly eager black troops pressing toward the front. To the Rebels, who had seemed to be on the verge of breaking through the Union lines, it was as if a theater curtain had suddenly parted, "disclosing a long line of blue clad infantry bearing down on them."[50]

These troops, soldiers of the all-black XXV Corps, were the lead element of Ord's Army of the James. Crook's men withdrew through their ranks, "the enemy in force so close [behind us] that we could possibly do good no longer."[51] As they did so, the white troopers turned to cheer the dusty, footsore freedmen who had come into battle after twenty hours on the march and now pushed forward against the massed Confederates without the slightest hesitation.

No longer actively involved in the fighting, Crook and several other officers seized the opportunity to observe for the first time black troops in battle. Months earlier the general had expressed to Hayes his interest in the performance of "darks," as he called them, of whom he had heard much but never observed in action. Now he had the chance to indulge his curiosity. Sending his staff to reorganize his scattered command, he turned about and accompanied the black troops as they pitched into the enemy. This grandson of a Maryland slaveholder later described the experience with a mixture of wonder and naiveté. "They looked like so many crows, they were so black," he marveled, adding, "[t]hey marched up in splendid order and although some of them were knocked over, they showed no flinching."[52] The memory of the courage and discipline of these black troops never left him. In later years on the frontier, unlike some of his fellow officers, he never hesitated to rely on black regiments, the so-called Buffalo soldiers, in confrontations with the Indians on the plains and deserts of the West.

With Union infantry now on the field in strength, the Confederate position became untenable. Gordon sent a message to Lee acknowledging, "I have fought my corps to a frazzle."[53] After somberly digesting the Georgian's words, Lee turned to an aide and pronounced his epitaph for the Army of Northern Virginia: "There is nothing left me but to go and see General Grant, and I had rather die a thousand deaths." The war had all but ended.

The actual meeting between Grant, clothed in the muddy and rumpled uniform he had worn for several days, and Lee, impeccably attired for the occasion, took place in the parlor of the modest, two-story brick farm home of Wilmer McLean. In 1861, in one of the many ironies of the war, this same Virginia farmer had removed his family from Manassas to Appomattox Court House for safety after coming under fire at Bull Run during one of the opening skirmishes in the first major battle of the war. Now he played unwilling host to the meeting that for all intents and purposes would end the conflict.

Sheridan attended the surrender, participating in the orgy of looting that Union officers indulged in following the departure of the two commanding generals—personally grabbing the table that Grant had used to sign the surrender document (which he later gives to Custer as a present for his young wife). Though Crook had been present at the McLean House during preliminary meetings with the Confederates, he did not loiter about the home during Grant's negotiations, preferring to remain with his troops awaiting the outcome.[54]

In his memoir Crook failed to record his thoughts on the occasion. But there is little doubt that he shared the emotions expressed by a soldier of the First Maine Cavalry, who wrote: "Is the fighting over? Can it possibly be that the end of marching and fighting, of hardship and exposure, of dull pickets and duller camp duty has come? And their thoughts at once return to their homes and they think, 'If this only could be true.'"[55]

The war was indeed over. While other Confederate armies remained in the field in North Carolina and in the West, over the next several days, they too surrendered. The four years of violence and bloodshed were at an end.

CHAPTER THIRTY-FOUR

Afterward

April 1865–January 1866

At first light on April 10, the Union cavalry, short of forage for its mounts, was forced to depart Appomattox for Petersburg, and so missed the ceremonial surrender of Lee's army that it had worked so hard to bring about. That evening the soldiers camped at Nottaway Court House, a small depot on the South Side Railroad east of Burkeville. There they remained for several days, awaiting orders, recuperating from the campaign, and enjoying the fine spring weather. They spent these hours tending to clothing and equipment badly neglected during the hectic pursuit of Lee's army and speculating on their future. A pervasive sense of contentment settled over the camp, the troopers secure in their belief that the war was all but over.[1]

They were still in Nottaway on the evening of the fifteenth, when a dispatch arrived bringing word of Lincoln's assassination. (Crook called it a "massacre," a not inappropriate term used on the western frontier to denote the slaughter of innocents.) Their first reaction was denial. Sheridan dismissed the news as a "canard." Of course, it was not, and "[s]trong and hardy men, commanders, too, . . . bent in tears among their comrades." A mood of grief and anger soon communicated itself through the entire Union army, though Crook recorded none of this in his account.[2]

A new, more vindictive administration now took up the task of putting a final end to the conflict. When Sherman negotiated a peace with General Johnston on the same terms that Grant had offered Lee at Appomattox, a vengeful Stanton rejected the agreement as too soft, and the cavalry was put on alert in case of trouble.

Upon receipt of the news of Lincoln's death, Sheridan had gone to Washington for consultations, leaving Crook in charge of the cavalry, which was redeployed to Petersburg to await orders. There Sheridan rejoined his command and on April 25 led the cavalry, including Crook's division and the VI Corps, south toward Danville to reinforce Sherman's army in case of need. Crook's men had just crossed the Dan River near the Virginia–North Carolina border when Sheridan received word that Johnston had surrendered on Stanton's terms and that Union forces were being recalled to Petersburg.[3]

Trust and confidence continued to characterize relations between Crook and Sheridan. And on May 6 Little Phil once again placed his old roommate in charge of the cavalry corps before departing for Washington for discussions with Grant.[4]

Crook fulfilled his last duties to his cavalry command by reporting to General Meade at Fairfax Court House for instructions concerning a grand review of the entire army to take place on May 23 in Washington. But on the date of the review, General Merritt, not Crook, led the cavalry troops of the Army of the Potomac down Pennsylvania Avenue. Never one for pomp and circumstance, only days before the review, Crook took leave to visit his family in Ohio and so did not participate in the celebration.[5]

The review was planned as a grand show of military might, involving thousands of veterans representing every corps in Mr. Lincoln's army. One can only speculate at the thoughts and memories that might have run through Crook's mind had he led his horsemen down the avenue at the trot, dressed in columns of four, eyes turned toward the reviewing stand erected days earlier in front of the White House. They were a magnificent sight, the sun glinting off polished leather and the glossy coats of their mounts, filling the air with the clatter of shod hooves, the blare of bugles, and the jangle of sabers. Would he have smiled at the antics of Custer, whose long blond hair streamed behind him while he attempted to regain control of his horse as it galloped wildly along the parade route?[6]

On June 27 Crook was relieved of command of the Cavalry Corps, Department of Washington and ordered to return to his place of residence, reporting to the adjutant general of the army for further orders.[7]

George Crook in the uniform of a major general, 1865. When compared to the image of him from 1863, one can see how the war had aged the young officer. Courtesy of the National Archives.

He waited for the War Department's decision in a state of suspended animation, certain that he would be allowed to return to the regular army, but when, at what rank, and in what capacity remained unclear. Finally, after a seemingly interminable two-month delay, the department contacted him. For the time being Crook was to remain in the volunteers with the rank of major general and report to the Department of North Carolina, one of several administrative commands created to facilitate the military occupation of the South during Reconstruction. There he would serve under the department's chief officer, Major General John Schofield, as commander of the District of Wilmington, eight counties strung out along the Atlantic Coast around Cape Fear.

As he was not expected to report to Wilmington until September, he spent the intervening weeks completing his courtship of Mary Dailey, the daughter of the proprietor of the Revere House in Cumberland.[8] The general never publicly discussed his courtship. But that only freed the various newspapers of the day, eager for sensational revelations to boost their readership, to speculate on improbable but romantic scenarios. Most of their tales revolved, not surprisingly, around Crook's kidnapping, owing to Mary's father's ownership of the Revere House and the fact that her brother, James, rode with the kidnappers. In 1883 the *Washington Chronicle* published a story alleging that James had swooped down and captured Mary and George while the general had been visiting her home "behind Rebel lines." According to this storyline, their romance had developed during their shared captivity.[9] A different but equally spurious story was advanced in a letter to the editor that appeared in a Springfield, Massachusetts, paper in 1901. The letter alleged that Crook had been kidnapped at James's instigation. As the general was courting Mary, James thought it would be a fine joke on his sister to grab her fiancé. Claiming to have almost been taken prisoner himself while courting a southern lady, the writer had reached the bizarre conclusion that Confederates often made a practice of kidnapping Yankees who romanced their women.[10] Still another journalistically inspired fantasy had Crook marrying Mary Dailey as a gallant gesture intended to quash rumors that she had somehow been involved in his abduction. And one source even averred that the two fell in love while Mary nursed the general back to health after he had been gravely wounded in battle.[11] None of these stories squared with the facts, but they most certainly helped sell newspapers.

Though the details of Crook's courtship are obscure, he was obviously successful. On August 26 he wrote a terse and, considering the circumstances, remarkably unsentimental note to his friend Rutherford Hayes. Datelined Baltimore, where he spent his brief honeymoon, the note read: "I was duly married on the morning of the 22nd instant and arrived here the same day and am feeling as happy as could be expected of one who has so suddenly changed his past. She joins me in sending our kindest regards to yourself and Webb."[12] The grudging tone of the brief epistle certainly could be read to imply that Crook's was a marriage born of convenience rather than romance and as proof that he was a cold and austere husband.

Historians have found support for this thesis in the scant attention Crook gave his wife in his autobiography, a fact that Martin Schmitt, editor of his autobiography, thought "not accidental." In one of his few references to his spouse, Crook wrote of his courtship and marriage in a single unrevealing sentence: "I was married on August 22, 1865," a reference so meager that it does not even include his bride's name. Some have surmised that this was because she apparently played such a minor role in his career.[13] But it is far more likely that Crook excluded her from his memoir for the same reason that he made no mention of his parents or siblings—because he believed that his private life was and should remain just that, private.

Imbued with her own sense of privacy and Victorian rectitude, Mary too eschewed public displays of affection and is rumored to have destroyed the general's letters upon his death to protect the privacy of their relationship.[14] Yet in the years following his fatal heart attack, she maintained a correspondence with a longtime aide, John Bourke, that belies the image of a cold and uncaring husband. Her letters reflect a genuine and deep sense of loss and sorrow at his passing. A month after the general's death, she wrote of her hopes for an early death, confessing, "I shall gladly welcome the hour that will take me to my noble dead." That fall, her grief still unassuaged, she wrote, "Life is so sad to me and the longing for the sound of the voice that is still overwhelms me." And a year following his death, "[e]very hour of my life is filled with the memories of his good deeds, noble unselfishness and tender care." In the winter of 1891, on reading Bourke's recently released *On the Border with Crook,* she wrote to tell him how it recalled "so much that was filled with pain and joy! How happy we were in those days." And she confessed, "I would like to find a little ease for the constant unrest and true yearning for the touch of a vanished hand."[15]

In truth the circumstances of the general's frontier service often compelled the Crooks to reside apart. While they shared his first assignment to the West following the war, living through a harsh Idaho winter in a structure more reminiscent of a tent than a cabin, they were frequently apart thereafter.[16] His campaigns would last for weeks at a time, summer and winter. During these periods, Mary would remain at post with almost no word about her husband's welfare. As she grew older, driven by loneliness, the stress of frontier life, and her dislike of the extreme winters on the Great Plains, she made it her custom to return to Maryland to stay with her family through the winter months and into late spring.

Even on those occasions when they resided together, their interests diverged, as was often the case during an era when gender roles were so uncompromisingly defined. He preferred the "masculine" pastimes—hunting, fishing, yarning, and playing cards with his male friends—while she gravitated toward the more traditional "feminine" interests offered by the formal social events organized by a nineteenth-century officer's wife—socials, teas, and dances.

The couple would never have children. But in the warm relationships that Crook cultivated with Webb Hayes, son of Rutherford Hayes, and some of the young officers under his command, one can sense a real longing for children of his own. Azor Nickerson, a longtime aide, paints a picture of the usually stern and stoic general "rolling on the floor of his parlor with a pair of chubby, childish hands alternately pulling his hair and whiskers, while a favorite dog was tugging away at the tails of his army blouse; and it would have been difficult to decide which was enjoying the romp more, the man, the child, or the dog."[17] One can only presume that he would have been a loving, though frequently absent, father.

As a newlywed, Mary accompanied her husband on his assignment to Wilmington. Though today the city is a well-known seaside resort on the North Carolina coast, in 1865 it was not an easy place to begin married life. The town had been partially burned by retreating Confederates very late in the war. Food was scarce and sanitary conditions ghastly. The streets and homes were overcrowded with an unhealthy mix of several thousand impoverished refugees, both white and black; half-starved and disease-ridden Union soldiers newly released from Confederate prisons; and destitute Confederate veterans, many of them maimed. Order was tenuously maintained by black troops commanded by white officers and civilian police, the latter in many instances little more than armed thugs.[18]

In his autobiography Crook mentions none of this. Nor does he delve into the duties that occupied him during the four months of his assignment in Wilmington. His reticence in referring to this period is unsurprising. Like many Union officers, Crook found administering the occupation of the South to be a distasteful and alien experience. Deaf to the subtle complexities of Southern culture and racial politics and ill equipped to deal with the resurgent white power structure's campaign to suppress the aspirations of the newly freed slave population, he did not handle the situation well.

His brief stint in command coincided with a period of extreme racial tension. Former slaves, backed by the federally created Freedman's Bureau, eagerly sought to take advantage of their newfound freedom. Most chose to farm small landholdings received from the government, carved out of the expropriated or abandoned plantations formerly owned by secessionist planters. Not unreasonably, they expected that they would be free to claim the bounty of their hard labor and the political and social advantages enjoyed by their white neighbors. Instead they were met by white resistance at every turn.

The army's role in this struggle often depended on the sympathies of the local officer in charge. The first commander of the Wilmington District had been Brigadier General Joseph Hawley. The son of a Connecticut father and a North Carolina mother, he was an ardent abolitionist and supporter of the Radical cause who used the authority of the Freedmen's Bureau to support the conversion of abandoned plantations into forty-acre farms distributed to former slaves willing to work them. Not surprisingly the *Wilmington Journal* editorialized about Hawley, "no government official who has ever been in command [of the] South has rendered himself so objectionable to the Southern people by his extreme Radical views and his utter disregard of the feelings and conditions of the White population."[19] As the Johnson administration was not supportive of the efforts of the Freedmen's Bureau, Hawley did not last long in the job and was replaced in late June 1865 by a member of his staff, Brigadier General John Worthington Ames.

Although Ames had commanded the Sixth U.S. Colored Infantry during the war, he was a conservative whose sympathies lay more with the white aristocracy than with the freedmen. Wilmington society readily embraced such officers. As one city paper declared, "The true soldier, whether they wore the grey or the blue, are now united in their opposition . . . to a negro government and negro equality." Ames restored full governing authority to the white power structure of the city and to its courts, taking the army out of the business of local government. Wilmington officials responded by introducing what was termed the "Black Code," a system of regulations designed to maintain freedmen in a state of inferiority and servitude. The system was enshrined in law the following year by the conservative-dominated North Carolina legislature.[20]

While Ames represented the apex of military authority in Wilmington, his power rested upon the blue coats of the Federal occupation force, many of whom were drawn from the black regiments that had served in the war. Predictably, these men were outraged by the arrogant repression of the freedmen that they encountered daily on the streets of the city. Their intervention in racial incidents occasionally turned violent, thoroughly frightening the white population, always alert to the danger of black insurrection. Warning that "we are sitting on a volcano, the general eruption is likely to occur at any time," in July city officials unsuccessfully petitioned Ames for the immediate removal of all black troops from the district.[21]

On August 1 the inevitable occurred. A white policeman became embroiled in a fracas with a black soldier. The black population was aroused, and a riot ensued. The next morning the entire police force and the city administration resigned to protest the perceived lack of support they had received from the army. Ames promptly restored them to power, giving them increased control over policing functions in the district. More shockingly, he allowed local police carte blanche in dealing with black Union troops. The police, aided by newly formed militia companies armed with repeating rifles, began the process of disarming the district's black citizens and enforcing the Black Code. By December 1865 there were eight white militia companies in the District of Wilmington, each commanded by former Confederate officers and each dedicated to the violent suppression of black aspirations.[22]

When Crook replaced Ames as district commander on September 7, almost immediately he found himself thrust into this maelstrom of racial strife. He would prove to be no activist in the freedmen's cause. Absent a commitment to either abolitionist ideals or white supremacy, his guiding principle became military policy. Under the Johnson administration, that policy was to get the army out of the business of civilian affairs, though supposedly remaining alert for any egregious acts of racial discrimination. Crook articulated his understanding of his military duty in a letter to a police captain who requested military action to enforce the Black Codes in a civil case involving a freedman: "It is not the policy of the military authority to interfere in private matters of difference between citizens when without manifest injustice the case can await the adjudication of a proper civil authority." His naiveté as to what constituted "manifest injustice" in the context of black-white relations in the South became immediately evident when he went on to suggest that in deciding minor disputes between parties, "the mode you report of selecting jurors by lot from the police to hear and determine the issue is as good as any other." But within weeks his grasp of the situation had improved. To a local magistrate he wrote, "[w]henever evidence is excluded from a civil court on account of the color of the witness it at once becomes a proper subject for military interference." He then curtly ordered the judge to report immediately to headquarters the reasons for his failure to turn over a case to the military after his court refused to consider testimony from a black witness.[23]

Though naturally inclined to protect the rights of freedmen, Crook's concern definitely took a back seat to his overriding interest in preserving law and order. He was far less worried about the increasing oppression of the black population than by the perceived threat of an impending black uprising.

He had been thoroughly briefed on the riots of the previous August. Now rumors abounded that the increasingly restive freedmen planned an insurrection on January 1, 1866, to mark the third anniversary of the Emancipation Proclamation. To prevent such an eventuality from occurring, the local paper reported: "It is [General Crook's] wish that the citizens shall form themselves into companies for volunteer service in case of emergency. He will furnish them with arms and ammunition and military aid and sustain them with the entire power of his command."[24] The paper accurately reported Crook's intentions. If a black insurrection occurred, he was prepared to put it down and, if necessary, rely on the white population to help him do it. Though he did make a halfhearted effort to be evenhanded in his management of the situation, his actions reflect a misplaced reliance on the good faith of local authorities.

As Emancipation Day drew close, he issued a series of directives designed to promote the rights of white citizens to protect themselves, again unwisely relying on the discretion of local law enforcement. On December 16 he authorized a rural police captain to seize weapons from freedmen and use them to arm white volunteers, provided, "you are well satisfied that the freedmen have any immediate plan on foot." And he continued, "arrest and forward to this headquarters any person without regard to color who makes treasonable or insurrectionary speeches within your jurisdiction." Finally, he explicitly granted the police the authority, under limited circumstances, to enlist local white civilians in the suppression of blacks, "[s]hould you have sufficient reason to fear an uprising of the freedmen at any time and feel that your company is not large enough [to] meet the emergency."[25]

Five days later Crook issued an order headed, "Without regard to color!" The exclamation point may have indicated that he was beginning to have doubts about the impartiality of the local police. But if so, the contents of the order hardly reflect it. The new directive required the seizure of federally provided arms by county police captains and their redistribution to local police. It could only have referred to weapons in the hands of freedmen, for the government did not distribute arms to former Confederates. Similarly, he decreed that all arms belonging to persons "disturbing the peace or likely to disturb the peace" were to be confiscated and redistributed to the police. And finally, all persons making treasonable or seditious speeches with the purpose of disturbing the peace and harmony of the community were to be arrested and sent to district headquarters to be dealt with by the military.[26] The effect of the order in the hands of local authorities was to disarm the black population and provide grounds for their arbitrary arrest.

January 1, 1866, came and went without incident. At that point Crook must have realized that he had been manipulated by the white establishment who had used the threat of black insurrection to more firmly reestablish their grip on power. There is some evidence that at this time the general may have been moved to restore some measure of equity to the system. On January 4, learning that the police had used the pretext of insurrection to appropriate mules and horses belonging to black farmers, he issued an order requiring them to turn in all such confiscated live-stock to the government for return to their rightful owners.[27]

But on January 15, after only four months in Wilmington, Crook received notice that his service in the volunteers, and with it his role in the military occupation of the South, had ended.[28] He was now a civilian for the first time since his entry into West Point thirteen years earlier, consigned to limbo until the War Department decided what role, if any, he would play in the much-truncated peacetime army.

Epilogue

How does one assess George Crook's overall performance in the Civil War? Unquestionably, his value as an officer was much appreciated by his superiors. There is ample evidence to that effect, both stated and implied. Aside from recommendations for promotions, which carried Crook from captain in the regular army to major general of volunteers and corps commander in three and a half years of war, the dispatches and battle reports of his superiors are replete with accolades. On more than one occasion, generals requested his transfer to their commands in recognition of his special skills and reliability. Even after Crook's embarrassing capture by McNeill's Rangers, Grant considered his value to the war effort of sufficient importance to override the objections of Secretary of War Stanton and secure his release from a Confederate prison so that he could participate in the final campaign of the war. Finally, and of no small significance, Crook earned four brevets for meritorious service during the course of the conflict.

But does his role in the war stand the test of time? John Waugh, in his book chronicling the West Point class of 1846, which included both Stonewall Jackson and George McClellan, established a list of criteria by which to measure an officer's greatness. Applying them to these two famous generals, he found Jackson great and McClellan wanting.[1] Although used to measure greatness, Waugh's criteria are really the attributes by which any officer might be judged. An examination of

Crook's record against these standards yields a well-rounded picture of his performance—the good, the bad, and the ugly.

According to Waugh, the first essential attribute of military greatness is an absolute will to succeed no matter the obstacles. Crook's character was suffused with an ingrained determination to achieve the goals he set for himself, a quality he probably inherited from his pioneering father. His drive first became evident at West Point in his struggles with academia, continued to exhibit itself in his early operations against Indians in the Redwood country of California, and was exhibited again and again during the war. An exception, notable because it was unusual, was his performance at Antietam, where after failing to find Rohrbach Bridge, he simply gave up on his planned assault. But his conduct on that occasion was to a large degree offset by his leadership during subsequent battles and campaigns as he became more comfortable with the responsibilities of command.

Waugh also postulates that a great leader must exhibit cool judgment under stress and in the face of the unexpected. For the most part, Crook possessed this characteristic in abundance. He was uncommonly brave and unflappable in combat, in most cases directing his troops calmly and rationally under fire. On occasion, however, overcome with the heat of battle, his heedless courage could become a liability. Particularly in his early days on the frontier, there were instances when, in the presence of the enemy, he lost all perspective and endangered his own safety— and by extension that of his men—through his recklessness. At Cloyd's Mountain, during the Dublin raid, he demonstrated that he had not entirely overcome this youthful exuberance. Though holding the rank of general, he needlessly accompanied his troops on a wild charge against an entrenched enemy position, risking his life and with it, the success and safety of his command.

In the adrenalin-charged atmosphere of combat, Crook, normally taciturn and good natured, was also subject to outbursts of temper, evidence of a further lack of self-control. His record includes instances where he tongue-lashed fellow officers in the midst of battle for real or imagined shortcomings. These harsh and sometimes grossly unjustified outbursts, which on occasion developed into longstanding grudges, were destructive and demoralizing. Later in his career, when this tendency occurred more frequently, it became divisive. Yet one should note that Sheridan, whom some might consider a truly great general, was subject to more-frequent and devastating tantrums.

Waugh writes that great generals ought to have an accurate knowledge of the battlefield environment, normally a function of intelligence gathering and analysis, at which Crook excelled. Based on his experience on the Pacific Coast, he realized the importance of familiarity with both the terrain and the habits of his elusive adversaries. Adapting these lessons during the Civil War and in his later career, he became famous for his innovations in the organization and deployment of scouts as intelligence gatherers.

Though ordinarily able to assimilate intelligence and act accordingly, there were instances when his stubborn nature interfered with his use of the data reported. At several critical junctures during the war, he refused to credit information brought to him because it either did not fit with his preconceived ideas of the dispositions and intentions of the enemy or came from a source he mistrusted, sometimes without justification. Crook's rigidity and consequent refusal to heed the intelligence on such occasions had negative consequences at Antietam and even more so at Kernstown and Cedar Creek.

Waugh also attaches critical importance to an officer's ability to formulate a plan of action that anticipates exigencies and the flexibility to alter that plan in the face of changed circumstances. This standard implies a broad strategic sensibility at a level of command that Crook never attained. Yet the general demonstrated superior tactical skills both in the field and in the design of battle plans that he proposed to his superiors. Crook had an intuitive feel for terrain and was skilled at reading enemy deployments. This proficiency enabled him to devise and implement tactics that secured victories from Lewisburg to Fisher's Hill and to alter deployments during the course of battle to meet unexpected exigencies. His tactical abilities hinted at the potential for similar talents in the area of strategic planning, but his subordinate role throughout the war provided little opportunity to develop them. As mentioned above, his stubbornness did hint at a degree of inflexibility that does not accord with Waugh's standards.

A great general furthermore must possess an intuitive knowledge of the enemy, as Lee knew McClellan. In his years as an Indian fighter, much of Crook's success would be attributed to his deep understanding of the Indian. During the Civil War, his performance in this area was less consistent. On those occasions when he had independent command, Crook sometimes proved prescient. His pursuit of General Wheeler in Tennessee and his tactics during the Dublin raid speak to a high order of insight into his opponents' intentions. And the predictions he made regarding enemy movements during the Lynchburg Campaign were usually on the mark, though General Hunter sometimes chose to disregard them. Yet he had little luck forecasting Jubal Early's designs in the Shenandoah. But then again, few did.

Waugh's great general requires the charisma to stir his men by example. Crook's qualities as a motivational leader were not such as to arouse his men to a fever pitch in battle. In that respect, he was no Sheridan. But his quiet, confident, self-reliant personality; his willingness to lead by example; and his competence and personal courage inspired his troops and instilled in them a willingness to follow him in battle. Furthermore, his character, coupled with his obvious concern for the welfare of his soldiers and his willingness to share their hardships, created a deep bond of loyalty between them and their commander. This attachment accounts for the professionalism of Crook's Ohio regiment—and later the entire VIII Corps—and the willingness of his men to endure the harsh conditions to which they were often exposed.

A final criterion for Waugh's great general is success in battle. Though victorious in almost every action in which he led his men, Crook was usually subordinate to others who controlled the overall disposition of troops and took credit for victory. So his achievements obviously would never reach the level of importance of a Sheridan or Sherman. Nevertheless, he contributed greatly to the Union's success in several key battles, though in smaller and less publicized arenas.

In sum, though he exhibited areas of weakness and made several telling mistakes during the war, there can be no doubt that overall Crook established a fine record of leadership and achievement. Thus in July 1866 he was disappointed and angry when the army offered him the rank of major in command of the Third Infantry Regiment. He pointed out to his superiors, who included his former comrades in arms Grant and Sheridan, that the appointment would leave him inferior in grade to two men who had served as his subordinates in the cavalry during the closing days of the war, both of whom had been promoted to colonel.

Certain that his experience and four brevet promotions deserved greater consideration, he asked that the decision be reviewed. Reconsidering, the War Department awarded Crook the rank of lieutenant colonel and ordered him to report to Fort Boise, Idaho Territory, as commander of the Twenty-Third Infantry.

In Idaho, as he had in California and Oregon, he "got interested after the Indians."[2] They in turn would become the focus of the remainder of his life and career. And on the western frontier, where he would spend the twenty-four years left to him, Crook's tenacity, leadership, and tactical sense would combine with his unparalleled knowledge of the Indian and the wilderness to elevate him to a level of competence and recognition that had eluded him during the Civil War. But that is a story for another book.

Notes

PROLOGUE

1. "Death of Gen. Crook," *Oakland (Md.) Republican*, 29 Mar. 1890.

2. Ibid.; "Gen. Crook Buried," *New York Times*, 25 Mar. 1890.

3. Telephone interview with John Grant, May 2001. Grant is an Oakland historian and longtime resident; his grandfather knew General Crook.

4. "Death of Gen. Crook," *Oakland (Md.) Republican*; Washington, *Diaries*; e-mail exchange with John Grant, 17 18 May 2001.

5. "Save the Oakland Railroad Station," http://www.oaklandmd.com/train/main .html (accessed 8 May 2001).

6. Davis, "Glades Hotel," 180; Glades Hotel Register, 29 July 1880, 1 Aug. 1882, Oakland Historical Society; "Reverse Arms Burial of General Crook at Oakland," *Dayton Daily*, 25 Mar. 1890.

7. "Crook as a Hunter," *Chicago Daily InterOcean*, 5 Apr. 1890; Bourke, *On the Border*, 490.

8. Bourke, *On the Border*, 486–87.

9. "Death of Gen. Crook," *Oakland (Md.) Republican; New York Times*, 25 Mar. 1890.

10. "Death of Gen. Crook," *New York Times*, 22 Mar. 1890; *New York Times*, 25 Mar. 1890.

11. Bourke, *On the Border*, 489.

12. Ibid.; "Body of One of Ohio's Greatest Soldiers Being Borne across the Country to Maryland for Interment," *Dayton Daily*, 24 Mar. 1890.

13. Bourke mentions only Walter as being present, stating that the only other surviving brother, Charles, the youngest, was too ill to attend. None of the newspapers reporting on the funeral noted Charles's presence; however, an article in the *Chicago Daily InterOcean* mentions the presence of "brothers" in the funeral car en route to Oakland. Bourke, *On the Border*, 489; *Daily InterOcean*, 5 Apr. 1890.

14. *New York Times*, 25 Mar. 1890; Schmitt, *Crook, His Autobiography*, xix.

15. *New York Times,* 25 Mar. 1890; "Crook Crest Revisited," *Oakland (Md.) Republican,* 17 Mar. 1977.

16. John Bourke to Charles Scribner, 8 Jan. 1891, quoted in Schmitt, *Crook, His Autobiography,* 301.

17. This diary is found in the Crook/Kennon Papers, U.S. Military History Institute, Carlisle, Pa.

18. Schmitt, *Crook, His Autobiography,* xvii; McGeary, "My Search for General George Crook," 289–306.

CHAPTER 1. ON THE OHIO FRONTIER

1. George Crook to Daniel Farrington, 20 June 1883, Charles B. Gatewood Papers, Arizona Historical Society Library, Tucson. The birthdate 28 September 1828 is given in Schmitt, *Crook, His Autobiography,* xx; Crook's obituary, *The New York Times,* 22 Mar. 1890, and Howe, *Historical Collections of Ohio,* 294. A descendant of the Crook family also indicated that this date is given in the Crook family Bible, now in the custody of the Ohio Genealogy Society. But Crook's gravestone at Arlington National Cemetery lists his birthdate as 9 September 1830; Headquarters of the Army, General Order No. 33, dated March 22, 1890, the official War Department notice of his death, gives 23 September 1829; and the program for the Military Order of the Loyal Legion of the United States memorial service (undated) gives 8 September 1830. Some newspapers reporting on Crook's death gave other dates, all of which fall within the 1828–30 range and give September as the month of his birth.

2. Tax List of Baltimore Co., 1783, Heads of Families, First Census of the United States, 1790, MSA S 1437, Maryland Historical Society, Baltimore, 38; Conover, *Centennial Portrait,* 922–23. For the names of Thomas Crook's parents, see Record of Deaths, Probate Court, Montgomery County, 30 June 1876, Ohio Department of Vital Records, Dayton, 28.

3. Schmitt, *Crook, His Autobiography,* xx.

4. Conover, *Centennial Portrait,* 922–23. Records of Thomas's service in the Baltimore militia have been lost or destroyed. Schmitt's introduction to the autobiography states: "he served in a militia company of Baltimore in 1813, thought to be 'Capt. Hazelet's company, engaged in the defense of Fort McHenry at the time the British frigate, *Belvidere,* captured and destroyed the East Town packet near the mouth of the Petapsco.' Shortly thereafter, he took sick and was discharged." Schmitt gives no source for these statements other than a reference to Thomas's "sworn record." *Crook, His Autobiography,* xx. Fort McHenry was not attacked until after Thomas was discharged from the militia; from that I have deduced that he helped construct its defenses.

5. Underwood, *Fifty Families,* 115.

6. Conover, *Centennial Portrait,* 922; "The Late Thomas Crook," *Dayton Daily,* 11 July 1875; Deed, 1814, William Vanderslice to Thomas Crook, Sec. 34, T2, R 8, Deed Book D, Montgomery County, Department of Vital Records, Dayton, 64–66.

7. Schmitt, *Crook, His Autobiography,* xv. Thomas's various land acquisitions are recorded in Deed Books K, M, N, O, U, and Z, Montgomery Co. His will left the farm, "340 acres, more or less," to his son Charles. Record of Deaths, Probate Court, Montgomery Co.; also see Conover, *Centennial Portrait,* 922. A Dayton paper noted that the original home was burned by vandals in 1959. "Crumbling Monument to Fighter," *Dayton Daily News,* 30 Aug. 1959.

8. Conover, *Centennial Portrait,* 922; "Late Thomas Crook."

9. Conover, *Centennial Portrait,* 922, 923.

10. Faragher, *Daniel Boone,* 311. The church operated in accordance with the deed for many years until the brethren apparently tired of its use by other sects. In April 1872 a mob they were suspected of organizing tore down the building and stole the materials, some of which were said to have been used to construct a saloon in a nearby county. Brown, *Montgomery County,* 87, 826; Drury, *City of Dayton and Montgomery County,* 869.

11. Conover, *Centennial Portrait,* 922.

12. "Crook as a Hunter," pt. 2, *Chicago Daily InterOcean,* 5 Apr. 1890; Bourke, *On the Border with Crook,* 111.

13. Brown, *Montgomery County,* 326; Bourke, *On the Border with Crook,* 109; interview with Capt. Charles King, in Russell, *Campaigning with King,* 43. See also Schmitt, *Crook, His Autobiography,* 167–68.

14. Conover, *Centennial Portrait,* 923; Computerized Heritage Association, *Miami Valley Genealogical Index;* Record of Deaths, Probate Court, Montgomery Co., vol. 18, p. 28; Brown, *Montgomery County,* 326. The exact date of his mother's death was 9 February 1844. Conover, *Centennial Portrait,* 923.

15. Conover, *Centennial Portrait,* 1252–53.

16. Ibid. For more on Simon Kenton, see Eckert, *The Frontiersman.*

17. Lyman W. V. Kennon, Diary, 1886–90, George Crook/Lyman W. V. Kennon Papers, U.S. Army Military History Institute, Carlisle, Pa.

18. Schmitt, *Crook, His Autobiography,* xxii.

19. Stanley, *American General,* 31.

CHAPTER 2. WEST POINT

1. Sheridan, *Memoirs,* 1.

2. *Washington Chronicle,* 1 July 1883.

3. Grant, *Memoirs,* 11.

4 *Washington Chronicle,* 1 July 1883.

5. Edgar, *Pioneer Life in Dayton and Vicinity,* 249.

6. Milo G. Williams to Robert C. Schenck, 23 Dec. 1847, Applications to West Point, Microfilm Application File 79, National Archives, Washington, D.C., 688–165; Schenck to Colonel Totten, chief engineer, West Point, 21 Dec. 1847, ibid.

7. Schenck to Pres. James Polk, 15 Mar. 1848, ibid.; Schmitt, *Crook, His Autobiography,* xxiii.

8. Though Sheridan makes no mention of encountering Crook on this trip, Stanley, in his memoir, records the presence of both young men and gives a detailed account of the journey. *American General,* 44.

9. Ibid.

10. For a detailed description of a new cadet's arrival at West Point, see Tidball, "Getting through West Point," 5–7.

11. Stanley, *American General,* 45; Schmitt, *Crook, His Autobiography,* xxiii.

12. George Crook, Cadet Expense Book, Crook/Kennon Papers, U.S. Military History Institute, Carlisle.

13. Tidball, "Getting through West Point," 9–10.

14. See also Newhall, *With Sheridan in the Final Campaign,* 5; Hutton, *Phil Sheridan and His Army,* 5; O'Connor, *Sheridan,* 33. Though Sheridan does not mention it in his memoirs, Rutherford Hayes, who served in the Civil War with both Sheridan and Crook, wrote that the two were roommates, whether initially or at some time after their first year he does not

say. Rutherford Hayes to Uncle Sardis [Birchard], 26 Sept. 1864, Hayes Papers, Rutherford B. Hayes Memorial Library, Rutherford B. Hayes Presidential Center, Fremont, Ohio. Charles King, who served with Crook on the frontier and became a close friend, wrote after the general's death, "They [Sheridan and Crook] were assigned to different companies at first, but eventually roomed together in the gloomy old barracks." "Major General George Crook," 5. Crook as usual had nothing to say on the subject.

15. Morrison, *Best School in the World,* 66; Bourke, *On the Border with Crook,* 111.

16. Morrison, *Best School in the World,* 61.

17. Hathaway, "Recollections of Sheridan as a Cadet," 2.

18. Smith, "West Point and the Indian Wars," 48.

19. Mahan, "Composition of Armies," 24 Mar. 1836, quoted in ibid., 49–51.

20. Smith, "West Point and the Indian Wars," 43.

21. U.S. War Department, Conduct Rolls of the U.S. Military Academy, 1848–52, RG 94, National Archives, Washington, D.C.; Sheridan, *Memoirs,* 6.

22. War Department, Conduct Rolls; Morrison, *Best School in the World,* 84.

23. Utley, *Frontiersmen in Blue,* 22.

24. "Death of General Crook," *New York Times,* 22 Mar. 1890; War Department, Conduct Rolls.

25. Crook, Cadet Expense Book, May 1851.

26. War Department, Conduct Rolls, 1852.

27. Ambrose, *Duty, Honor, Country,* 155.

28. See "Books Issued to Cadets by Special Permission of the Superintendent, 1850–52," U.S. Military Academy Library, West Point, N.Y.

29. Schmitt, *Crook, His Autobiography,* xxiii.

CHAPTER 3. AN ENTIRELY NEW EXPERIENCE

1. George Crook, Manuscript B, Crook/Kennon Papers, U.S. Military History Institute, Carlisle, Pa. [hereafter cited as Crook, Ms. B], 1; Schmitt, *Crook, His Autobiography,* 3. Crook wrote at least three drafts of his autobiography, all contained in the Crook/Kennon Papers at the U.S. Military History Institute. The first (Ms. A), 12 pages in length, appears to have been written sometime between 1873 and 1881. The second (Ms. B), is 55 pages long and was probably written between 1881 and 1885. And the third, believed to be the draft published by Schmitt, is 451 pages and dated Fort Bowie, May 18, 1885. Crook gives the date of his departure from Governors Island as December 4 in Ms. B; he corrected this date in his final manuscript, "to about the fourth of November."

2. Schmitt, *Crook, His Autobiography,* 3.

3. Utley, *Frontiersmen in Blue,* 42.

4. Crook, Ms. B, 1.

5. Grant, *Memoirs,* 98–99. For a description of the trip across the isthmus, see Sheffield, "Reminiscences," 52–59.

6. Schmitt, *Crook, His Autobiography,* 4.

7. Ibid.

8. Ibid.

9. Ibid., 5.

10. Crook, Ms. B, 3.

11. Stout, *Nicaragua,* 159.

12. Crook, Ms. B, 3; Schmitt, *Crook, His Autobiography,* 6.

13. Crook, Ms. B, 3.

14. Ibid.; Sheffield, "Reminiscences," 58; Schmitt, *Crook, His Autobiography,* 21; Army Appropriations Act, 9 Stat. 508 (Sept. 28, 1850), quoted in Utley, *Frontiersmen in Blue,* 31; ibid., 36. See also Schmitt, *Crook, His Autobiography,* 6n3, and 20.

15. Secretary of War, *Annual Report* (1853), 96; quoted in Utley, *Frontiersmen in Blue,* 39; Schmitt, *Crook, His Autobiography,* 7.

16. Crook, Ms. B, 4.

17. Schmitt, *Crook, His Autobiography,* 6.

CHAPTER 4. ASSIGNMENT TO FORT HUMBOLDT

1. Schmitt, *Crook, His Autobiography,* 8, 9n8; Strobridge, *Regulars in the Redwoods,* 42.

2. Schmitt, *Crook, His Autobiography,* 8.

3. Crook, Ms. B, 4.

4. Sherry L. Smith, *The View from Officer's Row: Army Perceptions of Western Indians* (Tucson: University of Arizona Press, 1990), 3. For a discussion of the gap between officers and men, see Don Rickey Jr., *Forty Miles a day on Beans and Hay* (1963; repr., Norman: University of Oklahoma Press, 1976), 63–72; and Utley, *Frontiersmen in Blue,* 40.

5. Schmitt, *Crook, His Autobiography,* 9.

6. Strobridge, *Regulars in the Redwoods,* 22. For a detailed account of the devastation wrought on the Native American culture of California during the gold rush, see Secrest, *When the Great Spirit Died.*

7. For more on military attitudes toward the Indians over the course of the nineteenth century, see Smith, *View from Officer's Row.*

8. U.S. Senate, *Report of the Secretary of War,* 33rd Cong., 1st. sess., 1853, S. Exec. Doc. 1, 2:691.

9. Division of the Pacific, General Order No. 2, 20 Jan. 1853, cited in Schmitt, *Crook, His Autobiography,* 8n8; Strobridge, *Regulars in the Redwoods,* 48.

10. Strobridge, *Regulars in the Redwoods,* 48–49; Irvine, *History of Humboldt County,* 60.

11. Schmitt, *Crook, His Autobiography,* 10.

12. Irvine, *History of Humboldt County,* 59–60; Hoopes, *Lure of the Humboldt Bay Region,* 102–103.

13. Hoopes, *Lure of the Humboldt Bay Region,* 101.

14. Crook, Ms. B, 5.

15. Bourke, *On the Border with Crook,* 110; Schmitt, *Crook, His Autobiography,* 11; Leigh H. Irvine, *History of Humboldt County, California, with Illustrations Descriptive of its Scenery* . . . (San Francisco: Wallace W. Elliot, 1881), 64.

16. Raphael and House, *Two Peoples, One Place,* 112–13.

17. Crook, Ms. B, 5–6.

18. Strobridge, *Regulars in the Redwoods,* 53.

19. Ibid., 62.

CHAPTER 5. FORT JONES

1. Crook, Ms. B, 6.

2. Schmitt, *Crook, His Autobiography,* 16.

3. Sutton and Sutton, *Indian Wars of the Rogue River,* 74; editorial, *Yreka Herald,* June 1853.

4. Bancroft, *Works,* 318. For further details on the treaty signing, see Sutton and Sutton, *Indian Wars of the Rogue River,* 89–99.

5. E. A. Schwartz, *The Rogue River Indian War and its Aftermath, 1850–1980* (Norman: University of Oklahoma Press, 1997), 60–68.

6. Crook, Ms. B, 10.

7. Schmitt, *Crook, His Autobiography,* 14; *Shasta Courier,* 3 Sept. 1855.

8. Schmitt, *Crook, His Autobiography,* 17. For an example of Patten's poetry, see "Come, Let Us Die Like Men," available online at Representative Poetry Online, Selected Poetry of George Washington Patten (1808–1882), 2004, http://tspace.library.utoronto.ca/html/1807/4350/poem3210.html (accessed 30 Nov. 2010). For an example of his military writings, see George Washington Patten, *Artillery Drill* (New York: J. W. Fortune, 1863).

9. Schmitt, *Crook, His Autobiography,* 31; Strobridge, *Regulars in the Redwoods,* 70.

10. Schmitt, *Crook, His Autobiography,* 19. Judah's correspondence with the adjutant general's office at Benicia for this period is found in Department of the Pacific, Letters Received, Records of U.S. Army Continental Commands, RG 393, National Archives [hereafter referred to as Dept. of the Pacific, LR]. Allegations of drunkenness on duty and incompetence dogged Judah throughout his career. During the Battle of Resaca outside Atlanta in 1864, his gross incompetence caused his corps to suffer casualties rivaling the losses of the famous Light Brigade of the Crimean War; Judah was removed from command. Rich Wallace, "Area Men Die, Hurt in Useless Battle," p. 3, 1997, Shelby County Ohio Historical Society, http://www.shelbycountyhistory.org/schs/archives/civilwararchives/resacacwarp3a.htm.

11. Secrest, *When the Great Spirit Died,* 211. For a description of Judah's skills in dealing with the Indians, see Strobridge, *Regulars in the Redwoods,* 93–95.

12. Judah to Dept. of the Pacific, Mar., Sept. 1854; Apr.–May 1855, Fort Jones, Returns from Military Posts, 1800–1916, M617, National Archives, roll 560.

13. Crook to various offices, 1854–58, Dept. of the Pacific, LR,.

14. Judah to Major Cross, 21 Aug. 1855, Consolidated Correspondence File, Fort Jones, 1855–56, Dept. of the Pacific, LR.

15. Schmitt, *Crook, His Autobiography,* 21. Crook was accompanied on these hunts by John Bell Hood, and the two men "formed a warm attachment to one another." Hood, *Advance and Retreat,* 6.

16. Citizens of Cottonwood to Judah, 14 Jan. 1854, Dept. of the Pacific, LR.

17. Schmitt, *Crook, His Autobiography,* 18. In his report of the incident, Judah spelled the militia captain's name "Greiger." Judah to Wright, 21 Jan. 1854, Dept. of the Pacific, LR. The *Yreka Herald* spelled it "Geiger." "The Present Indian Difficulties," *Yreka Herald,* 4 Feb. 1854. No source mentions the officer's first name, which remains unknown.

18. Schmitt, *Crook, His Autobiography,* 18.

19. Ibid., 19.

20. Crook, Ms. B, 8; Schmitt, *Crook, His Autobiography,* 19.

21. Schmitt, *Crook, His Autobiography,* 19.

22. Judah to Wright, 21 Jan. 1854, Dept. of the Pacific, LR; Schmitt, *Crook, His Autobiography,* 19–20.

23. Schmitt, *Crook, His Autobiography,* 10; Judah to Wright, 21 Jan. 1854.

24. Smith to Wright, 31 Jan. 1854, Dept. of the Pacific, LR.

25. Sutton and Sutton, *Indian Wars of the Rogue River,* 111.

26. Ibid.; Smith to Wright, 31 Jan. 1854; Crook, Ms. B, 9.

27. "The Present Indian Difficulties," *Yreka Herald,* 4 Feb. 1854.

28. Schmitt, *Crook, His Autobiography,* 20; Hoopes, *Lure of the Humboldt Bay Region,* 111; Strobridge, *Regulars in the Redwoods,* 72, 92–95.

29. Strobridge, *Regulars in the Redwoods,* 73; Schmitt, *Crook, His Autobiography,* 21.

30. Schmitt, *Crook, His Autobiography,* 21. Hood claimed to have received $1,000 in gold as a result of the enterprise. *Advance and Retreat,* 7.

31. O'Donnell, *Arrow in the Earth,* 243–44.

CHAPTER 6. EXPLORING THE COUNTRY AND THE WILLIAMSON-ABBOT EXPEDITION

1. Strobridge, *Regulars in the Redwoods,* 120.

2. Cover letter to secretary of war, in Abbot, *Report,* 2; ibid., 60.

3. Schmitt, *Crook, His Autobiography,* 52; Abbot, *Report,* 61, 63.

4. Sheridan, *Memoirs,* 22–23.

5. Ibid., 24.

6. Abbot, *Report,* 65, 71. Crook would continue to pursue his interest in Indian languages and, together with some of his fellow officers, eventually would submit several brief monographs on the Indian languages of the Pacific Northwest to the Smithsonian, where they now reside. See Crook, Manuscripts on Indian Languages in the Pacific Northwest, 84–86, 209, National Anthropological Archives, Smithsonian Institution, Washington, D.C. See also George Gibbs, "Observations on the Coast Tribes of Oregon," NAAMS, 196–99, National Anthropological Archives, Smithsonian Museum Support Center, Suitland, Md.

7. Sheridan, *Memoirs,* 24; Abbot, *Report,* 101.

8. For a detailed account of the Yakima War, see Glassley, *Indian Wars of the Pacific Northwest,* 109–42.

9. Abbot, *Report,* 106.

10. Abbot, "Reminiscences of the Oregon War of 1855," 439; Sheridan, *Memoirs,* 29.

11. Abbot, "Reminiscences," 440.

12. Walsh, *Indian Battles along the Rogue River,* 1; Sutton and Sutton, *Indian Wars of the Rogue River,* 151.

13. Sutton and Sutton, *Indian Wars of the Rogue River,* 152.

14. Robbins, "Journal of the Rogue River War," 345; Utley, *Frontiersmen in Blue,* 182.

15. Crook, Ms. B, 11.

16. Abbot, *Report,* 107.

17. Abbot, "Reminiscences," 440.

18. Schmitt, *Crook, His Autobiography,* 27.

19. Abbot, "Reminiscences," 441.

20. Schmitt, *Crook, His Autobiography,* 27.

21. For Crook's version of the events as compared to another witness, see Schmitt, *Crook, His Autobiography,* 27–29, including footnotes 22 and 29.

22. Abbot, *Report,* 108.

23. Ibid., 110.

24. Judah to Townsend, adjutant general, 21 Jan. 1856, Dept. of the Pacific, LR.

CHAPTER 7. INDIAN REMOVAL AND THE ROGUE RIVER WAR

1. Judah to Townsend, 13 Dec. 1855, Dept. of the Pacific, LR; Strobridge, *Regulars in the Redwoods,* 127.

2. Fort Jones, Oct. 1852–June 1858, Feb. 1856, Returns from U.S. Military Posts, M617, National Archives, roll 560.

3. O'Donnell, *Arrow in the Earth,* 252–53.

4. Utley, *Frontiersmen in Blue,* 183.

5. Schmitt, *Crook, His Autobiography,* 31; O'Donnell, *Arrow in the Earth,* 252–53.

6. Utley, *Frontiersmen in Blue,* 184; Schmitt, *Crook, His Autobiography,* 31.

7. Schmitt, *Crook, His Autobiography,* 32.

8. Ibid.

9. Ibid.

10. For an account of the battle, see Glassley, *Indian Wars of the Pacific Northwest,* 105–106.

11. Schmitt, *Crook, His Autobiography,* 33.

12. Walsh, *Indian Battles along the Rogue River,* 17; Sutton and Sutton, *Indian Wars of the Rogue River,* 261, 283.

CHAPTER 8. CAMPAIGNING IN THE PIT RIVER VALLEY

1. Judge A. M. Rosborough to Judah, n.d. (received c.10 Feb. 1857), Dept. of the Pacific, LR.

2. Secrest, *When the Great Spirit Died,* 238–42.

3. *Yreka Union Extra,* 7 Feb. 1857.

4. Judah to Mackall, 8 Feb. 1857, Dept. of the Pacific, LR; undated endorsement, ibid.; Judah to Mackall, 31 May 1857, ibid.; Strobridge, *Regulars in the Redwoods,* 144; Secrest, *When the Great Spirit Died,* 246.

5. Schmitt, *Crook, His Autobiography,* 35–37.

6. Ibid., 35, 36; Judah to Mackall, 31 May 1857.

7. Judah reported receipt of Gardiner's message in ibid.

8. Schmitt, *Crook, His Autobiography,* 35, 36. Crook and other officers often used the term "rancheria," a Spanish word originally applied to Indian settlements in California and later in the Southwest, indiscriminately in reference to any Indian village.

9. Crook's aide John G. Bourke later wrote, "[Crook's] senses became highly educated; his keen, blue-gray eyes would detect in a second and at a wonderful distance the slightest movement across the horizon." *On the Border with Crook,* 111.

10. Schmitt, *Crook, His Autobiography,* 37.

11. Judah to Mackall, 31 May 1857; Schmitt, *Crook, His Autobiography,* 37.

12. While Crook recalled that Judah had left him with only sixteen men, the captain's written order to Crook assigned him twenty-five men of his company for the purpose of "protecting travel upon the road between Shasta and Yreka as well as the ferry at this point." Schmitt, *Crook, His Autobiography,* 37; Judah to Crook, 27 May 1857, Dept. of the Pacific, LR.

13. Judah to Crook, 27 May 1857.

14. Crook, Ms. B, 13.

15. Ibid., 13, 14. His ability to pass himself off as a miner indicates that Crook had already adopted his trademark habit of wearing rough civilian dress while in the field.

16. Ibid., 14.

17. Ibid. Crook frequently used language that today would be considered demeaning or racist to describe Indians—terms like "buck," "squaw," and "savage." Such words, all too common on the frontier in Crook's day, were often intended to denote the inferior and even

subhuman nature of the Indian. Though Crook never viewed Indians as racially inferior, as many of his contemporaries did, he did share their belief that Indian culture and lifestyles were inferior to that of whites. His use of these terms may have reflected this belief, or more likely, it may be a simple reflection of their common usage in his time and place.

18. Schmitt, *Crook, His Autobiography*, 39.

19. Ibid.

20. Secrest, *When the Great Spirit Died*, 248; Schmitt, *Crook, His Autobiography*, 40.

21. Schmitt, *Crook, His Autobiography*, 40.

22. Ibid.

23. Crook to Judah, 12 June 1857, Fort Jones, Dept. of the Pacific, LR.

24. Schmitt, *Crook, His Autobiography*, 41; Judah to Mackall, 14 June 1857, Dept. of the Pacific, LR. Crook wrote in his autobiography that Judah attempted to accompany Dryer but got drunk and "fell by the wayside." Schmitt, *Crook, His Autobiography*, 41.

25. Judah to Dryer, Order No. 24, 13 June 1857, Dept. of the Pacific, LR.

26. Crook, Ms. B, 15.

27. Schmitt, *Crook, His Autobiography*, 40–41.

28. Dryer to Judah, 6 July 1857, Dept. of the Pacific, LR.

29. Ibid.; Schmitt, *Crook, His Autobiography*, 42. The Modocs would later effectively use the lava beds to stand off the army in an uprising in 1873.

30. Dryer to Judah, 6 July 1857. Crook sarcastically commented that Dryer and the doctor were "anxious to return to their flesh pots." Schmitt, *Crook, His Autobiography*, 42. This was both an unkind and inaccurate comment. The doctor had departed five days previously, and Dryer was responding to a direct order from Judah.

31. Schmitt, *Crook, His Autobiography*, 45; Crook to Judah, 8 July 1857, Dept. of the Pacific, LR.

32. Strobridge, *Regulars in the Redwoods*, 147; Gardiner to Mackall, [12?] July, 18 Aug. 1857, Dept. of the Pacific, LR.

33. Strobridge, *Regulars in the Redwoods*, 147–48; Crook to Judah, 8 July 1857, Fort Jones, Dept. of the Pacific, LR; Judah to Gardiner, 20 June 1857, Fort Crook, ibid.

34. Judah to Gardiner, 11 July 1857, Fort Jones, Dept. of the Pacific, Letters Sent, Records of U.S. Army Continental Commands, RG 393, National Archives [hereafter cited as Dept. of the Pacific, LS]; Judah to Crook, 11 July 1857, ibid.

35. Gardiner to Mackall, 15 July 1857, Dept. of the Pacific, LR.

36. Mackall to Judah, 24 Oct. 1857, Dept. of the Pacific, LS.

37. Schmitt, *Crook, His Autobiography*, 47.

38. Crook to Gardiner, 4 Aug. 1857, Fort Crook, Dept. of the Pacific, LR.

39. Crook, Ms. B, 19.

40. Mackall to Gardiner, 6 Aug. 1857, Dept. of the Pacific, LS.

41. Gardiner to Mackall, 11 Aug. 1857, Dept. of the Pacific, LR.

42. Ibid.; Strobridge, *Regulars in the Redwoods*, 150–52.

43. Strobridge, *Regulars in the Redwoods*, 150–52.

44. Gardiner to Mackall, 11 Aug. 1857.

45. *Sacramento Union*, 1 Sept. 1857, quoted in Secrest, *When the Great Spirit Died*, 251.

CHAPTER 9. FORT TER-WAW

1. Schmitt, *Crook, His Autobiography*, 54.

2. Mackall to Crook, 10 Sept. 1857, Dept. of the Pacific, LS.

3. Crook, Ms. B, 20.
4. Crook to Mackall, 21 Oct. 1857, Dept. of the Pacific, LR.
5. Ibid.
6. McBeth, *Lower Klamath Country,* 38; Schmitt, *Crook, His Autobiography,* 55. The site, abandoned in June 1862 due to perennial flooding, is now on private land in the Klamath River Indian Reservation and is unmarked. McBeth, *Lower Klamath Country,* 40–41.
7. Crook, Ms. B, 21; Schmitt, *Crook, His Autobiography,* 56–57.
8. Schmitt, *Crook, His Autobiography,* 57; Crook, Ms. B, 21.
9. Crook to Mackall, 21 Nov. 1857, Dept. of the Pacific, LR; Crook to Raines, 11 Dec. 1857, ibid.
10. Crook to Mackall, 25 Dec. 1857, ibid.; Schmitt, *Crook, His Autobiography,* 57.
11. Sheridan, *Memoirs,* 50.
12. Crook, Ms. B, 21.
13. Schmitt, *Crook, His Autobiography,* 68–69.
14. Crook, Ms. B, 21–22; Schmitt, *Crook, His Autobiography,* 69.
15. Schmitt, *Crook, His Autobiography,* 70–71; Crook, Ms. B, 21–22.
16. George Crook, "Address to the Graduates of the U.S. Military Academy, Class of 1884," delivered at West Point, N.Y., 1884, quoted in Leonard, "Reluctant Conquerors," 3.
17. Crook, Ms. B, 22.

CHAPTER 10. THE COEUR D'ALENE WAR

1. For more on Garnett, see Guie, *Bugles in the Valley.*
2. Strobridge, *Regulars in the Redwoods,* 171; Schmitt, *Crook, His Autobiography,* 58n5.
3. Schmitt, *Crook, His Autobiography,* 59.
4. Guie, *Bugles in the Valley,* 115, 118; Crook, Ms. B, 22; Schmitt, *Crook, His Autobiography,* 59.
5. Utley, *Frontiersmen in Blue,* 203.
6. Schmitt, *Crook, His Autobiography,* 60; Guie, *Bugles in the Valley,* 120.
7. Schmitt, *Crook, His Autobiography,* 60–61; Crook, Ms. B, 23–24.
8. Crook, Ms. B, 24.
9. Schmitt, *Crook, His Autobiography,* 63; Crook, Ms. B, 25.
10. Schmitt, *Crook, His Autobiography,* 63; Crook, Ms. B, 25.
11. Schmitt, *Crook, His Autobiography,* 64; Crook, Ms. B, 26.
12. Schmitt, *Crook, His Autobiography,* 65.
13. Guie, *Bugles in the Valley,* 124–25.
14. Schmitt, *Crook, His Autobiography,* 68.

CHAPTER 11. RETURN TO FORT TER-WAW

1. Schmitt, *Crook, His Autobiography,* 68, 78.
2. George Crook, Order No. 9, 20 Feb. 1859, Order Book, Camp Lincoln (Ter-Waw), 1857–61, Records of U.S. Army Continental Commands, 1821–1920, RG 393, National Archives.
3. Crook to Mackall, 30 Nov. 1859, Letter Book, Fort Ter-Waw, Nov. 1858–Oct. 1859, ibid.
4. Smithsonian Institutions, Washington, D.C., Staff, *Catalogue to Manuscripts at the National Anthropological Institution Archives, National Museum of Natural History* (Washington, D.C.: Cengage Gale, 1975), 471.

5. Crook to Col. D. C. Buell, Indian agent, 27 June 1859, Letter Book, Fort Ter-Waw.

6. Crook to Mackall, 20 July 1859, ibid.

7. George Crook, Order No. 27, 12 July 1859, Order Book, Camp Lincoln (Ter-Waw); Crook to Mackall, 20 July 1859, Letter Book, Fort Ter-Waw.

8. Crook to Mackall, 30 Aug. 1859, Letter Book, Fort Ter-Waw.

9. Crook to Mackall, 23 Sept. 1859, ibid.

10. Schmitt, *Crook, His Autobiography*, 78.

11. Crook, Ms. B, 28.

CHAPTER 12. A TRIP EAST

1. Schmitt, *Crook, His Autobiography*, 78–79.

2. Ibid.

3. Crook, Ms. B, 42.

4. Ibid., 29.

5. Cox, *Military Reminiscences*, 206.

6. "Crook as a Hunter," *Chicago Daily InterOcean*, 5 Apr. 1890.

7. Order No. 70, 25 Dec. 1860, Order Book, Camp Lincoln (Ter-Waw); Schmitt, *Crook, His Autobiography*, 81.

8. Crook, Ms. B, 31.

9. Bourke, *On the Border with Crook*, 112.

10. Schmitt, *Crook, His Autobiography*, 82.

CHAPTER 13. A COLONEL IN THE VOLUNTEERS

1. Schmitt, *Crook, His Autobiography*, 84; Crook, Ms. B, 31.

2. Schmitt, *Crook, His Autobiography*, 83.

3. Crook, Ms. B, 31.

4. Warner, *Generals in Blue*, 422–23.

5. Schmitt, *Crook, His Autobiography*, 84.

6. Ibid.

7. Ibid., 84–85.

8. Horton and Tevervaugh, *History of the 11th Regiment*, 261.

9. Reid, *Ohio in the War*, 233; Schmitt, *Crook, His Autobiography*, 85.

10. Crook, Ms. B, 32.

11. Reid, *Ohio in the War*, 233; Schmitt, *Crook, His Autobiography*, 86.

12. Williams, *Hayes of the 23rd*, 30–38; John T. Booth Papers, Ohio Historical Society, Columbus, 180, quoted in Stephenson, *Headquarters in the Brush*, 17.

13. Reid, *Ohio in the War*, 233; Cunningham and Miller, *Report of the Ohio Antietam Battlefield Commission*, 88.

14. Schmitt, *Crook, His Autobiography*, 85–86.

15. Stephenson, *Headquarters in the Brush*, 17.

16. Cox, *Military Reminiscences*, 205.

17. Reid, *Ohio in the War*, 233; Booth Papers, quoted in Cunningham and Miller, *Report of the Ohio Antietam Battlefield Commission*, 83. Crook mistakenly recalled the disease that ravaged his men as typhoid. Schmitt, *Crook, His Autobiography*, 86.

18. Schmitt, *Crook, His Autobiography*, 86–87. Briefly, early in the war, the Confederacy nominally incorporated all guerilla units into its army under what was known as the Partisan

Ranger Act. But with a few exceptions, such men proved impossible to control, and their excesses became such an embarrassment to the Southern high command that the authorities disowned all but a few select units. See Stephenson, *Headquarters in the Brush,* 6–7.

19. Stephenson, *Headquarters in the Brush,* 87; Kempfer, *Salem Light Guard,* 38.

20. Reid, *Ohio in the War,* 233; Schmitt, *Crook, His Autobiography,* 87.

21. Schmitt, *Crook, His Autobiography,* 88.

22. Crook, Ms. B, 32; War Department, *War of the Rebellion,* 12(3):84 (hereafter cited as OR; all references are to series 1 unless otherwise indicated].

CHAPTER 14. LEWISBURG

1. Jacob Cox, "West Virginia Operations under Frémont," in Johnson and Buel, *Battles and Leaders,* 2:278.

2. Warner, *Generals in Blue,* 97–98.

3. Cox to Crook, 28 Apr. 1861, OR, 22(3):113.

4. Crook to Cox, 16 Apr. 1861, ibid., 57.

5. Crook to Bascom, 16 Apr. 1861, OR, 24:84.

6. Cox, "West Virginia Operations under Frémont," 279.

7. Cox, *Military Reminiscences,* 219.

8. Stutler, *West Virginia in the Civil War,* 180. Although some have stated that Heth was a classmate of Crook at the academy, Heth was in the class of 1847, while Crook was in the class of 1852. Benjamin, "Gray Forces Defeated in Battle of Lewisburg," 24–35.

9. Stutler, *West Virginia in the Civil War,* 178; Kempfer, *Salem Light Guard,* 62.

10. Lang, *Loyal West Virginia,* 183; Benjamin, "Gray Forces Defeated in Battle of Lewisburg," 25; Schmitt, *Crook, His Autobiography,* 90.

11. Schmitt, *Crook, His Autobiography,* 90; Benjamin, "Gray Forces Defeated in Battle of Lewisburg," 25. Though Heth's men may have been raw recruits, Lewisburg was also the first time the Thirty-Sixth had seen combat.

12. Schmitt, *Crook, His Autobiography,* 90–91.

13. "Report of Lieut. Col. Melvin Clarke, Thirty-sixth Ohio Infantry," 23 May 1862, OR, 12(1):808; Crook to Bascom, 24 May 1862, OR, 12(1):807; Schmitt, *Crook, His Autobiography,* 90.

14. Kempfer, *Salem Light Guard,* 67.

15. Crook to Bascom, 24 May 1862.

16. Ibid.; Cox to Crook, 24 May 1862, OR, 12(1):805; Stutler, *West Virginia in the Civil War,* 182.

17. Schmitt, *Crook, His Autobiography,* 90–91n.

18. Crook to Bascom, 25 June 1862, OR, 12(1):430–31.

19. Cox to Crook, 21 June 1862, ibid., 418.

20. Crook to Cox, 26 June 1862, ibid., 436.

CHAPTER 15. THE SECOND BATTLE OF BULL RUN

1. Cox, *Military Reminiscences,* 223; Schmitt, *Crook, His Autobiography,* 92.

2. Cox, "West Virginia Operations under Frémont," in Johnson and Buel, *Battles and Leaders,* 2:281.

3. Schmitt, *Crook, His Autobiography,* 92.

4. Ibid., 93; John Pope, "The Second Battle of Bull Run," in Johnson and Buel, *Battles and Leaders,* 2:489.

5. Schmitt, *Crook, His Autobiography,* 93, 95.

CHAPTER 16. SOUTH MOUNTAIN AND ANTIETAM

1. Robert E. Lee to Jefferson Davis, 3–9 Sept. 1862, OR, 19(2):590–603; Edwin Bearss, "Introduction," in Priest, *Before Antietam,* 8; Sears, *Landscape Turned Red,* 66–67; Foote, *Civil War,* 1:662.

2. Cox, *Military Reminiscences,* 268; Priest, *Before Antietam,* 9.

3. Priest, *Before Antietam,* 94.

4. Cox, *Military Reminiscences,* 272.

5. Priest, *Before Antietam,* 96.

6. See Sears, *Landscape Turned Red,* 66–67.

7. Cox, "Forcing Fox's Gap and Turner's Gap," in Johnson and Buel, *Battles and Leaders,* 2:585; Cox, *Military Reminiscences,* 277–78.

8. Williams, *Hayes of the 23rd,* 25, 43; Cox, *Military Reminiscences,* 278.

9. Cox, "Forcing Fox's Gap and Turner's Gap," 2:585.

10. Foote, *Civil War,* 1:676.

11. Ibid., 586; Cox, *Military Reminiscences,* 280.

12. Priest, *Before Antietam,* 134.

13. Cunningham and Miller, *Report of the Ohio Antietam Battlefield Commission,* 88.

14. Sears, *Landscape Turned Red,* 140. Cox wrote that Reno was "shot down by an enemy posted among the rocks and trees." "Forcing Fox's Gap and Turner's Gap," 2:589. But an eyewitness stated that the shot that mortally wounded Reno was fired accidentally by a startled soldier of the Thirty-Fifth Massachusetts Regiment. The bullet glanced off Reno's scabbard and struck him in the chest below the heart. A. H. Wood, "How Reno Fell," *National Tribune,* 6 July 1885, quoted in Priest, *Before Antietam,* 216

15. Schmitt, *Crook, His Autobiography,* 96; Jacob Cox, South Mountain report, 20 Sept. 1862, OR, 19(1):460.

16. Jacob Cox, "The Battle of Antietam," in Johnson and Buel, *Battles and Leaders of the Civil War,* 2:630, 631.

17. Pierro, *Maryland Campaign,* 196.

18. Toney, "Attack and Defense of Burnside's Bridge," 5; Sears, *Landscape Turned Red,* 260.

19. Cox, "Battle of Antietam," 632n. Ezra Carman's study indicates that McClellan's engineers had reported a ford, but that when Brig. Gen. Isaac Rodman went to cross at that spot on the day of the battle, he discovered the location wrongly represented, the ford actually being a mile farther away over rough terrain. Pierro, *Maryland Campaign,* chap. 21.

20. Toney, "Attack and Defense of Burnside's Bridge," 6.

21. Cunningham and Miller, *Report of Ohio Antietam Battlefield Commission,* 89; Schmitt, *Crook, His Autobiography,* 97.

22. Schildt, *Ninth Corps at Antietam,* 100; Faust, *This Republic of Suffering,* 120–21.

23. Cox, "Battle of Antietam," 2:632; Schmitt, *Crook, His Autobiography,* 97.

24. Schmitt, *Crook, His Autobiography,* 97.

25. Cox, "Battle of Antietam," 2:648.

26. Sears, *Landscape Turned Red,* 261–62.

27. It is generally accepted that Burnside did not receive his orders until ten o'clock. Cox, in his battlefield report written the week after the battle, said it was delivered at nine o'clock, but he subsequently repudiated this. Confederate general Robert Toombs, based on his perception, also thought the attack occurred at nine, but both Burnside and McClellan in their original reports give the time as ten o'clock. See ibid., 353–57.

28. Ibid., 632–33; Priest, *Antietam: The Soldier's Battle,* 308.

29. Schmitt, *Crook, His Autobiography,* 97.

30. Lyman J. Jackson, South Mountain and Antietam report, 20 Sept. 1862, OR 19(1):473.

31. George Crook, South Mountain and Antietam report, 20 Sept. 1862, OR, 19(2):471–72; Schmitt, *Crook, His Autobiography,* 98; George Crook to John T. Booth, 19 Dec. 1887, in Cunningham and Miller, *Report of the Ohio Antietam Battlefield Commission,* 92.

32. Cox, "Battle of Antietam," 2:632–33; Cox, *Military Reminiscences,* 342; Pierro, *Maryland Campaign,* 334.

33. Crook, South Mountain and Antietam report, 472.

34. Toney, "Attack and Defense of Burnside's Bridge," 8; Pierro, *Maryland Campaign,* 333.

35. Toney, "Attack and Defense of Burnside's Bridge," 8.

36. Pierro, *Maryland Campaign,* 334; Toney, "Attack and Defense of Burnside's Bridge," 8.

37. Toney, "Attack and Defense of Burnside's Bridge," 8.

38. Ibid.; Cox, "Battle of Antietam," 2:651.

39. Pierro, *Maryland Campaign,* 336.

40. Sears, *Landscape Turned Red,* 314, 317; Catton, *Terrible Swift Sword,* 451–52.

41. McClellan to Halleck, 18 Sept. 1862, OR, 19(2):322; Schmitt, *Crook, His Autobiography,* 100.

42. Headquarters, IX Army Corps, General Order No. 2, 1 Oct. 1862, OR, 51(1):874.

43. Crook to Halleck, 10 Oct. 1862, OR, 19(2):62; Marcy to Crook, 10 Oct. 1862, ibid., 63.

44. For details of the Chambersburg raid, see Thomas, *Bold Dragoon,* 175–80. See also Marcy to Crook, 12 Oct. 1862, OR, 19(2):73.

45. Schmitt, *Crook, His Autobiography,* 101.

CHAPTER 17. THE ARMY OF THE CUMBERLAND

1. Cozzens, *No Better Place to Die,* 14, 26–27.

2. Rosecrans to Wright, 20 Nov. 1862, OR, 20(2):75.

3. Wright to Rosecrans, 20 Nov. 1862, ibid., 76.

4. Daniel, *Days of Glory,* 226; Wright to Granger, 20 Jan. 1863, OR, 20(2):343; Rosecrans to Wright, 29 Jan. 1863, OR, 23(2):22.

5. Cullum to Wright, 20 Jan. 1863, OR, 20(2):342; Cist, *Army of the Cumberland,* 141; Crook to Goddard, 5 Mar. 1863, OR, 23(2):110. See also Daniel, *Days of Glory,* 231.

6. Foote, *Civil War,* 2:664–65.

7. Schmitt, *Crook, His Autobiography,* 101; Crook to Garfield, 27 Mar. 1863, OR, 23(2):179; Crook, Ms. B, 37.

8. Kempfer, *Salem Light Guard,* 106.

9. Crook, Ms. B, 37.

10. General Order No. 3, 30 June 1863, OR, 23(1):411–13.

11. Ibid., 10.

12. Daniel, *Days of Glory,* 265–67; Cist, *Army of the Cumberland,* 155–56; Cottrell, *Civil War in Tennessee,* 87.

13. Foote, *Civil War,* 2:668; Daniel, *Days of Glory,* 232; Schmitt, *Crook, His Autobiography,* 102–103. Wilder's men were so committed to the Union cause that when the army refused to arm them with highly effective seven-shot Spencer carbines, they had used their own funds to procure them.

14. Daniel, *Days of Glory,* 274.

CHAPTER 18. IN COMMAND OF CAVALRY AND THE CHATTANOOGA CAMPAIGN

1. OR, 23(2):580; Warner, *Generals in Blue,* 511–12; Stanley, *American General,* 140. Stanley scornfully referred to Turchin "as a dumpy, fat Russian with short legs" who could not ride a horse, considering him "a perfectly cold blooded foreigner—he did not care a fig what became of me or the few troops who followed me."

2. Cottrell, *Civil War in Tennessee,* 187.

3. Cist, *Army of the Cumberland,* 177–84; Daniel, *Days of Glory,* 287–88.

4. Crook, reports, 8, 29 Sept. 1863, OR, 30(1):917–18.

5. Schmitt, *Crook, His Autobiography,* 104; Stanley to Garfield, 14 Sept. 1863, OR, 30(3):637. Crook made a half-hearted attempt to correct his misrepresentation in the memoir, stating that on the morning of September 21, he "found" that Mitchell had replaced McCook as commander of the First Division and "was also in command of the [Cavalry] corps." Schmitt, *Crook, His Autobiography,* 105.

6. Schmitt, *Crook, His Autobiography,* 103; Daniel, *Days of Glory,* 298–99.

7. Daniel, *Days of Glory,* 304.

8. Stanley, *American General,* 149; Rosecrans, report, 14 Sept. 1863, OR, 30(1):54; Mitchell to Garfield, 15 Sept. 1863, ibid., 653; Cottrell, *Civil War in Tennessee,* 92.

9. Schmitt, *Crook, His Autobiography,* 105; Mitchell to Garfield, 20 Sept. 1863, OR, 30(1):140–41.

10. Stanley, *American General,* 139. Crook and Stanley were not far off the mark in their assessments of Mitchell's abilities and character. After the war the general became governor of New Mexico Territory, where "he failed to take his duties either seriously or with dignity . . . affronted the [legislature] by leaving Santa Fe . . . and absenting himself for . . . months without explanation." W. A. Kelcher, *Violence in Lincoln County, 1869–1881* (Albuquerque: University of New Mexico Press, 1957) 5, cited in Warner, *Generals in Blue,* 329.

11. Schmitt, *Crook, His Autobiography,* 105–106; Crook, report, 29 Sept. 1863, OR, 30(1):918–19.

12. Crook, Ms. B, 39; Schmitt, *Crook, His Autobiography,* 106. Mitchell's report states: "The enemy attacked the forces at the various fords in strong force, and after severe fighting succeeded in effecting a crossing, but gained but little ground afterward, for they were stubbornly resisted at every step and finally gave up the attempt." OR, 30(1):893.

13. Cottrell, *Civil War in Tennessee,* 92; Cist, *Army of the Cumberland,* 220–23.

14. Schmitt, *Crook, His Autobiography,* 106–107; Cist, *Army of the Cumberland,* 227.

15. Mitchell, report, OR, 30(1):894; Crook, Ms. B, 40; Schmitt, *Crook, His Autobiography,* 107.

CHAPTER 19. THE WHEELER RAID

1. Cist, *Army of the Cumberland,* 230–31.

2. George H. Thomas, report, 24 Nov. 1863, OR, 30(2):664; George Crook, report, 5 Nov. 1863, ibid., 681.

3. Crook, report, 5 Nov. 1863, ibid., 681.

4. Schmitt, *Crook, His Autobiography,* 109.

5. Crook, report, 5 Nov. 1863, OR, 30(2):685, 686; Joseph Wheeler, report, 30 Oct. 1863, ibid., 724. In view of subsequent events, it is ironic that it was Colonel Minty who probably suggested the saber charge. Minty had used this tactic several months previously against Wheeler's men at Shelbyville, earning his troopers the nickname "The Saber Brigade." He is said to have learned it while serving in the British army in West Africa. See Wittenberg, "Robert H. Minty," http://civilwarcavalry.com.

6. Robert Mitchell, report, 20 Oct. 1863, OR, 30(2):669–70.

7. Crook, Ms. B, 42; Crook, report, 5 Nov. 1863, OR, 30(2):686.

8. Crook, report, 5 Nov. 1863, OR, 30(2):687.

9. Ibid.

10. Ibid., 668; Schmitt, *Crook, His Autobiography,* 111.

11. See General Court-Martial, Case of Col. R. H. G. Minty, Fourth Reg. Michigan Vol. Inf., Court-Martial Case Files, Records of the Office of the Judge Advocate General, RG 159, National Archives, Washington, D.C. [hereafter cited as Minty Court-Martial].

12. See Crook, report, 5 Nov. 1863, OR, 30(2):687.

13. Reply of the Judge Advocate, Trial Testimony, Minty Court-Martial.

14. Ibid.

15. General Mitchell ordered Col. Edward M. McCook's division to ride toward Unionville. Crook's division was directed to pursue the enemy on the Farmingdale Road, which ran at right angles to McCook's route. Hence it is unlikely that Minty would have any doubt as to which road he was to follow. See Mitchell, report, 20 Oct. 1863, OR, 30(2):669–70.

16. Ibid., 670.

17. Crook, report, 5 Nov. 1863, ibid., 687.

18. Reply of the Judge Advocate, Trial Testimony, Minty Court-Martial.

19. General Order No. 36, 28 Feb. 1864, Minty Court-Martial.

20. Crook, report, 5 Nov. 1863, OR, 30(2):687.

21. Ibid., 688; Thomas, report, 24 Nov. 1863, ibid., 665; William S. Rosecrans, congratulatory order, 19 Oct. 1863, ibid., 667.

CHAPTER 20. BLAZER'S SCOUTS

1. Rutherford Hayes to Uncle Sardis [Birchard], 7 Feb. 1864, Rutherford B. Hayes Papers, Rutherford B. Hayes Library, Fremont, Ohio.

2. "Report of Capt. C. Regnier Commanding Steamer *Levi,*" 10 Feb. 1864, OR, 33:110–11; Wilson, *Hayes of the Twenty-third,* 166; Hayes to Uncle Sardis, 7 Feb. 1864. Hayes would be considerably less flippant when General Crook found himself in the same situation a year later. See chapter 31.

3. Schmitt, *Crook, His Autobiography,* 114.

4. Stephenson, *Headquarters in the Brush,* 21–28.

5. Ibid., 36–37.

6. Ibid., 60–61, 63.

7. Ibid., 62.

8. See ibid., 212–13.

CHAPTER 21. THE DUBLIN RAID

1. Quoted in Fuller, *Generalship of U. S. Grant,* 211–12.

2. Warner, *Generals in Blue,* 447–48; McManus, *Battle of Cloyds Mountain,* 1–2.

3. Grant to Sigel, 29 Mar. 1864, OR, 33:765.

4. McManus, *Battle of Cloyds Mountain,* 2.

5. Grant to Sigel, 29 Mar. 1864.

6. Grant to Sigel, 17 Apr. 1864, OR, 33:828; McManus, *Battle of Cloyds Mountain,* 4.

7. McManus, *Battle of Cloyds Mountain,* 4–5.

8. Russell Hastings, "Personal Recollections," Hastings File, Rutherford B. Hayes Library, Rutherford B. Hayes Presidential Center, Fremont, Ohio; Rutherford B. Hayes, diary, 28 Apr. 1864, Rutherford B. Hayes Papers, ibid. [hereafter cited as Hayes Diary].

9. McManus, *Battle of Cloyds Mountain,* 8–9.

10. Hayes to his mother, 1 May 1864, Hayes Papers.

11. Hastings, "Recollections," 29 Apr. 1863; McManus, *Battle of Cloyds Mountain,* 9.

12. Duncan, *Lee's Endangered Left,* 45; Hastings, "Recollections," 3 May 1864; McManus, *Battle of Cloyds Mountain,* 13.

13. McManus, *Battle of Cloyds Mountain,* 12. See also Stephenson, *Headquarters in the Brush,* 88–91.

14. Rutherford B. Hayes, "Battle of Cloyds Mountain," transcript of interview with J. Q. Howard, 1896, Hayes Library, 4; McManus, *Battle of Cloyds Mountain,* 18.

15. McManus, *Battle of Cloyds Mountain,* 15.

16. Arthur, "Dublin Raid," 4.

17. McManus, *Battle of Cloyds Mountain,* 25; Duncan, *Lee's Endangered Left,* 57.

18. Hastings, "Recollections," 9 May 1864.

19. Duncan, *Lee's Endangered Left,* 56; McManus, *Battle of Cloyds Mountain,* 25.

20. Crook estimated the distance from the mountain to the Confederate breastworks at three-quarters of a mile. Crook, report, 23 May 1864, OR, 37(1):10.

21. McManus, *Battle of Cloyds Mountain,* 23, 25; Crook, report, 23 May 1864, OR, 37(1):11.

22. McManus, *Battle of Cloyds Mountain,* 26.

23. Arthur, "Dublin Raid"; McManus, *Battle of Cloyds Mountain,* 32.

24. Hastings, "Recollections," 9 May 1864; Hayes, "Battle of Cloyds Mountain," 5.

25. Williams, *Hayes of the 23rd,* 177–88; McManus, *Battle of Cloyds Mountain,* 39.

26. Arthur, "Dublin Raid."

27. Hastings, "Recollections," 9 May 1864.

28. Duncan, *Lee's Endangered Left,* 66.

29. Crook, report, 23 May 1864, OR, 37(1):12; Schmitt, *Crook, His Autobiography,* 115–16; Duncan, *Lee's Endangered Left,* 65, 66.

30. Hastings, "Recollections," 10 May 1864; James A. Wilson, "51st Virginia Regiment," *West Virginia History* 29 (1968), 111, quoted in Duncan, *Lee's Endangered Left,* 67; ibid., 68; Hayes Diary, 10 May 1864. Hayes claimed that he understood that the bridge was out of use for six weeks. Hayes, "Battle of Cloyds Mountain," 7.

31. See Duncan, *Lee's Endangered Left,* 69.

32. Crook, report, 23 May 1864, OR, 37(1):12.

33. Hastings, "Recollections," 12 May 1864.

34. Williams, *Hayes of the 23rd,* 185; Hayes Diary, 15 May 1864; William Averell, report, 28 May 1864, OR, 37(1):42.

35. Hastings, "Recollections," 16 May 1864; Hayes Diary, 17 May 1864.

36. Crook, report, 23 May 1864, OR, 37(1):13; Hayes to his wife, 19 May 1864; Hayes to Uncle Sardis, 19 May 1864.

37. Diary of Sgt. Edward Davis, 9 May 1864, quoted in Duncan, *Lee's Endangered Left,* 63; Crook, report, 23 May 1864, OR, 37(1):12–13; Cozzens, "Fire on the Mountain," 73.

38. R. B. Wilson, "The Dublin Raid," in *G.A.R. War Papers* (Cincinnati, n.d.), 1:107; Hastings, "Recollections," 8 Apr. 1864.

39. Williams, *Hayes of the 23rd,* 187.

CHAPTER 22. THE LYNCHBURG CAMPAIGN

1. Crook, report, 7 July 1864, OR, 37(1):120; Grant to Halleck, 19 May 1864, ibid., 485.

2. Duncan, *Lee's Endangered Left,* 138–41.

3. Miller, *Lincoln's Abolitionist General,* 124.

4. Quoted in ibid., 124.

5. Hayes Diary, 12 June 1864; Hastings, "Recollections," 30 May 1864; Wittenberg, *Little Phil,* 33.

6. Duncan, *Lee's Endangered Left,* 143; Miller, *Lincoln's Abolitionist General,* 168.

7. Crook, report, 7 July 1864, OR, 37(1):120; Hastings, "Recollections," 31 May 1864.

8. Hastings, "Recollections," 6, 9 June 1864; Crook, report, 7 July 1864, OR, 37(1):120.

9. Duncan, *Lee's Endangered Left,* 190.

10. Hunter, report, 8 June 1864, OR, 37(1):96.

11. James L. Botsford, General Orders, Second Infantry, 8 June 1864, ibid., 607.

12. Mauzy, "Vandalism by General Hunter," 50–53, quoted in Duncan, *Lee's Endangered Left,* 195–96.

13. Grant to Hunter, 6 June 1864, OR, 37(1):598.

14. Eby, *Virginia Yankee,* 250, 250n.

15. Ibid., 250–51.

16. Ibid., 253.

17. Hastings, "Recollections," 11 June 1864; Duncan, *Lee's Endangered Left,* 216.

18. Pendleton, "Hunter's Sack of Lexington," 175.

19. Ibid., 176.

20. Washington College narrowly missed destruction. Yankee troops looted and vandalized the school, stealing or defacing most of the books in its library, and packed wood shavings into its rooms preparatory to firing the buildings. At this point one of the school's trustees intervened, arguing that the college was founded largely through the efforts of President Washington, whose bust adorned the main building. Strothers agreed to spare that building out of respect for the Founding Father but carted off the bust. It wound up in Wheeling, West Virginia, where it remained until Strothers, who became adjutant general of Virginia after the war, ordered it returned to Lexington years later. Eby, *Virginia Yankee,* 256–57.

21. Schmitt, *Crook, His Autobiography,* 117; Hastings, "Recollections," 12 June 1864. See also Dupont, *Campaign of 1864 in the Valley,* 69; and Hayes to Wife, 12 June 1864, Hayes Papers.

22. Hastings, "Recollections," 12 June 1864.The reference is to a natural stone bridge not far from Lexington that some officers went out of their way to see on the march to Lynchburg.The quote is found in Sorrel, *Recollections of a Confederate Staff Officer*, 275.

23. Duncan, *Lee's Endangered Left*, 249, 256.

24. In May, Lee had considered him as a temporary replacement for Longstreet after the latter had been wounded at the Wilderness. Freeman, *Lee's Lieutenants*, 672.

25. Duncan, *Lee's Endangered Left*, 261; Freeman, *Lee's Lieutenants*, 83. In 1879 Crook, who had briefly met Early during the war, sought him out for a visit at his home in Lynchburg. Hoping for cheerful reminiscences, instead he found Early "as bitter and virulent as an adder. He has no use for the Government or the northern people, boasts of his being unreconstructed and that he won't accept a pardon for his Rebellious offenses." George Crook, diary, 6 Jan. 1879, Crook/Kennon Papers, U.S. Military History Institute, Carlisle, Pa.

26. Eby, *Virginia Yankee*, 258; Schmitt, *Crook, His Autobiography*, 117. Strothers agreed with Crook after seeing Duffié draw from his pocket "a package containing millions in Confederate money" and proudly announce, "Eh bien, General, I gob all dis monnoie. I gob wagos, by gar. I gob de whole administration of Staunton." Eby, *Virginia Yankee*, 258.

27. Hastings, "Recollections," 14 June 1864.

28. Ibid., 15 June 1864.

29. Eby, *Virginia Yankee*, 262; Duncan, *Lee's Endangered Left*, 242.

30. Eby, *Virginia Yankee*, 264; Schmitt, *Crook, His Autobiography*, 117. Roberts would recover and serve with Crook throughout the war and into Reconstruction. He later rejoined the general in the 1880s during the campaign against Geronimo and remained with him up to the date of his death. Crook's special fondness for him can be inferred from the fact that, though he infrequently mentions his aides in his memoir, the general makes specific reference to Roberts's injury in describing this campaign.

31. Hastings, "Recollections," 17 June 1864; Dupont, *Campaign of 1864 in the Valley*, 75; Duncan, *Lee's Endangered Left*, 273.

32. Hunter, report, 8 June 1864, OR, 37(1):100.

33. Duncan, *Lee's Endangered Left*, 275–77.

34. Crook, report, 7 July 1864, OR, 37(1):121; Dupont, *Campaign of 1864 in the Valley*, 78; Duncan, *Lee's Endangered Left*, 280–81; Eby, *Virginia Yankee*, 265–66; G. L. Early, *I Belonged to the 116th*, 101–102.

35. Miller, *Lincoln's Abolitionist General*, 202; Hunter, report, 8 June 1864, OR, 37(1):100; Dupont, *Campaign of 1864 in the Valley*, 83.

36. Hunter to Grant, 6 Dec. 1864, OR, 37(2):366; Duncan, *Lee's Endangered Left*, 292–93; Schmitt, *Crook, His Autobiography*, 120.

37. Schmitt, *Crook, His Autobiography*, 118.

38. Eby, *Virginia Yankee*, 266; Duncan, *Lee's Endangered Left*, 285, 287.

39. Eby, *Virginia Yankee*, 266; Dupont, *Campaign of 1864 in the Valley*, 83.

40. Eby, *Virginia Yankee*, 267; Schmitt, *Crook, His Autobiography*, 118, 119.

41. Dupont, *Campaign of 1864 in the Valley*, 85–86.

42. Schmitt, *Crook, His Autobiography*, 120.

43. Ibid.; Dupont, *Campaign of 1864 in the Valley*, 87.

44. Dupont, *Campaign of 1864 in the Valley*, 90–91.

45. Schmitt, *Crook, His Autobiography*, 121; James M. Comly, diary, 25–30 June 1864, Comly Notebooks, Ohio Historical Society, Columbus, quoted in Williams, *Hayes of the 23rd*, 201; Hayes to Uncle Sardis, 30 June 1864.

CHAPTER 23. EARLY'S RAID ON WASHINGTON

1. Jubal A. Early, "Early's March to Washington in 1864," in Johnson and Buel, *Battles and Leaders,* 4:493; Lee, report, 19 July 1864, OR, 37(1):346.

2. Pond, *Shenandoah Valley in 1864,* 78–79n1; Grant, *Memoirs,* 460. Early was skeptical of Grant's defense of Hunter, finding it incredible that the latter would embark on such an important campaign with an insufficient supply of ammunition. J. Early, *Memoir,* 50n.

3. J. Early, *Memoir,* 495; Halleck to Grant, 1 July 1864, OR, 37(2):4.

4. Hunter to Stanton, 15 July 1864, OR, 37(2):340.

5. J. Early, *Memoir,* 492.

6. Williams, *Hayes of the 23rd,* 208; Grant to Halleck, quoted in Pond, *Shenandoah Valley in 1864,* 71; Warner, *Generals in Blue,* 575–76.

7. Hunter to Adjutant General, 15 July 1864, OR, 37(2):341; Special Order No. 126, 15 July 1864, ibid., 342; Hunter to Stanton, 15 July 1864, ibid., 339–40; Eby, *Virginia Yankee,* 279; Lincoln to Hunter, 17 July 1864, OR, 37(2):365.

8. Special Order No. 126; James Abraham to brother, 30 June 1864, James Comly Papers, Ohio Historical Society, Columbus, quoted in Patchan, *Shenandoah Summer,* 38; Thomas Thoburn, *Hunter's Raid, 1864* (Thomas Beer, 1914), 21, quoted in ibid., 44.

9. Schmitt, *Crook, His Autobiography,* 122; Crook, report, 12 Oct. 1864, OR, 37(1):287.

10. Crook, report, 12 Oct. 1864, OR, 37(1):287.

11. Hunter to Stanton, 17 July 1864, OR, 37(2):365; Stanton to Hunter, 17 July 1864, ibid., 365–66.

12. Patchan, *Shenandoah Summer,* 64; Eby, *Virginia Yankee,* 244n1.

13. Patchan, *Shenandoah Summer,* 67.

14. Schmitt, *Crook, His Autobiography,* 122.

15. Ibid.; Crook, report, 12 Oct. 1864, OR, 37(1):287; Patchan, *Shenandoah Summer,* 81.

16. Warner, *Generals in Blue,* 403–404.

17. Halleck to Hunter, 17 July 1864, OR, 37(2):366.

18. Hayes to his wife, 17 July 1864, Hayes Papers.

19. For a description of this operation, see Patchan, *Shenandoah Summer,* 105–109.

20. Wright to Halleck, 17 July 1864, OR, 37(2):368–69; Halleck to Hunter, 17 July 1864, OR, 37(1):366.

21. Patchan, *Shenandoah Summer,* 154; Crook to Hunter, 22 July 1864, OR, 37(2):417.

22. Pond, *Shenandoah Valley in 1864,* 85; Grant to Halleck, 22 July 1864, OR, 37(2):422.

23. Lincoln to Hunter, 23 July 1864, OR, 37(2):423; Hunter to Lincoln, ibid. 423–24.

24. Williams, *Hayes of the 23rd,* 217; Letter, *Wheeling Intelligencer,* 16, Aug. 1864.

25. Stackpole, *Sheridan in the Shenandoah,* 149.

26. *New York Times,* 28 Sept. 1861; Patchan, *Shenandoah Summer,* 164, 166; Williams, *Hayes of the 23rd,* 216.

27. Patchan, *Shenandoah Summer,* 133–34, 160; Williams, *Hayes of the 23rd,* 218.

28. Schmitt, *Crook, His Autobiography,* 123.

29. Diary of Col. James A. Mulligan, quoted in Nash, "Colonel James A. Mulligan," 40B, 41B; Patchan, *Shenandoah Summer,* 166.

CHAPTER 24. THE SECOND BATTLE OF KERNSTOWN

1. Bonnell, *Sabres in the Shenandoah,* 120; Alfred N. Duffié, report 28 July 1864, OR, 37(1):322; Patchan, *Shenandoah Summer,* 169.

2. Duffié, report, 28 July 1864, OR, 37(1):322; Patchan, *Shenandoah Summer*, 172; Farrar, *Twenty-Second Pennsylvania Cavalry*, 291.

3. Patchan, *Shenandoah Summer*, 178.

4. Ibid., 178, 179; Earley, *I Belonged to the 116th*, 120.

5. Farrar, *Twenty-Second Pennsylvania Cavalry*, 291; Earley, *I Belonged to the 116th*, 121; Patchan, *Shenandoah Summer*, 264.

6. Ezra Walker, Diary of July–Sept. 1864, U.S. Army Military History Institute, Carlisle, quoted in Earley, *I Belonged to the 116th*, 121.

7. Hastings, "Recollections," 24 July 1864.

8. Patchan, *Shenandoah Summer*, 182; Pond, *Shenandoah Valley in 1864*, 96, 190.

9. Pond, *Shenandoah Valley in 1864*, 185; Nash, "Colonel James A. Mulligan," 40. Nash does not provide her source for Crook's conversation with Nugent. Her study, a master's thesis, evidences a deep attachment to her subject. As the source for this incident is not given, its credibility is difficult to evaluate.

10. Patchan, "Shenandoah Valley," 44.

11. Farrar, *Twenty-Second Pennsylvania Cavalry*, 298.

12. James Comly Journal, Ohio Historical Society, Columbus, quoted in Patchan, *Shenandoah Summer*, 213; Augustus Forsberg memoirs, Forsberg Papers, Washington and Lee University, Lexington, quoted in ibid., 214; F. G. Shackelford, "My Recollections of the War," *The Nicholas Chronicle*, 14 Sept. 1895, quoted in ibid.

13. Patchan, *Shenandoah Summer*, 222–24.

14. Crook, report, 16–26, 27 July 1864, OR, 37(1):286.

15. Farrar, *Twenty-Second Pennsylvania Cavalry*, 297; Isaac Duval, report, 23–25 July, 13 Sept. 1864, OR, 37(1):310; Thoburn to AAG Botsford, 7 Aug. 1864, ibid., 293.

16. William W. Averell, report, 8 July–3 Aug. 1864, ibid., 328.

17. Crook, report, 27 July 1864, ibid., 286, Farrar, *Twenty-Second Pennsylvania Cavalry*, 279; Patchan, *Shenandoah Summer*, 242.

18. Hastings, "Recollections," 24 July 1864.

19. Duncan, *Alexander Neil and the Last Shenandoah Campaign*, 55; Patchan, *Shenandoah Summer*, 254; Pond, *Shenandoah Valley in 1864*, 107.

20. Patchan, *Shenandoah Summer*, 258; Thomas and Hyman, *Stanton*, 324; Fuller, *Generalship of U. S. Grant*, 305; McFeely, *Grant*, 180, Patchan, *Shenandoah Summer*, 311.

21. Patchan, *Shenandoah Summer*, 259.

22. Crook, report, 27 July 1864, OR, 37(1):286.

23. Schmitt, *Crook, His Autobiography*, 123.

24. For an extended analysis of Crook's shortcomings at Kernstown, see Patchan, *Shenandoah Summer*, 258–67.

CHAPTER 25. THE BULL TERRIER AND THE NEWFOUNDLAND DOG

1. Stackpole, *Sheridan in the Shenandoah*, 90.

2. Porter, *Campaigning with Grant*, 270. Grant gives a more modest estimate of "300 families left homeless." Grant, *Memoirs*, 468.

3. Sandburg, *Storm over the Land*, 285; Williams, *Lincoln and His Generals*, 327.

4. Williams, *Lincoln and His Generals*, 326–27; Pond, *Shenandoah Valley in 1864*, 112; Sheridan, *Memoirs*, 254.

5. Stackpole, *Sheridan in the Shenandoah*, 165; Grant, *Memoirs*, 468–71; Williams, *Lincoln and His Generals*, 328–29; Sheridan, *Memoirs*, 254.

6. J. Taylor, *Sketchbook,* 122.

7. Dupont, *Campaign of 1864 in the Valley,* 135.

8. Sheridan, *Memoirs,* 1–3.

9. Hutton, *Phil Sheridan and his Army,* 5. In a letter to his uncle during the 1864 Shenandoah Campaign, Hayes describes Sheridan as believing in Crook, "his old class & room-mate at West Point." Hayes to Uncle Sardis [Birchard], 26 Sept. 1864, Hayes Papers.

10. Lincoln quoted without attribution in Hutton, *Phil Sheridan and his Army,* 2; Wittenberg, *Little Phil,* 18; Williams, *Hayes of the 23rd,* 230.

11. Morris, *Sheridan,* 1; Wittenberg, *Little Phil,* xv.

CHAPTER 26. CAMPAIGNING IN THE VALLEY

1. Sheridan, *Memoirs,* 256; Grant to Hunter, 5 Aug. 1864, quoted in ibid., 255.

2. Hastings, "Recollections," 7 Aug. 1864.

3. Ibid., 26 Aug. 1864; Williams, *Hayes of the 23rd,* 233.

4. Sheridan, *Memoirs,* 259.

5. Newhall, *With Sheridan in the Final Campaign,* 4–5.

6. Dupont, *Campaign of 1864 in the Valley,* 112.

7. Morris, *Sheridan,* 186; Sheridan, *Memoirs,* 258–59; Stackpole, *Sheridan in the Shenandoah,* 153.

8. Stackpole, *Sheridan in the Shenandoah,* 154.

9. Schmitt, *Crook, His Autobiography,* 124.

10. Grant to Halleck, 12 Aug. 1864, OR, 43(1):43.

11. J. Taylor, *Sketchbook,* 69.

12. Hastings, "Recollections," 21 Aug. 1864.

13. Ibid., 3 Sept. 1864.

14. Pond, *Shenandoah Valley in 1864,* 144.

15. Sheridan, *Memoirs,* 273, 275; Stackpole, *Sheridan in the Shenandoah,* 174.

16. Sheridan, *Memoirs,* 275.

17. Schmitt, *Crook, His Autobiography,* 135.

18. Sheridan, *Memoirs,* 276.

19. Bonsal and Sheridan, *Loyal Girl of Winchester.* This source is a bound pamphlet containing a short biography of Wright and letters from Sheridan, Crook, and others to her, which was reprinted by the Library of Congress in 1888 by order of Pres. Rutherford Hayes. A copy may be found in the Rare Book Room, Library of Congress.

20. Crook to Col. Theodore Bean, 26 Sept. 1886, in ibid.; Sheridan, *Memoirs,* 276.

21. Sheridan, *Memoirs,* 276.

22. Wright made this assertion in a letter to James Taylor in February 1895. See J. Taylor, *Sketchbook,* 355.

23. Sheridan, *Memoirs,* 277.

24. Grant, *Memoirs,* 474. After the war Sheridan wrote to Wright informing her of the importance of the information she had provided and presented her with a silver watch as a memento of her contribution to the war effort. In 1868, as a further reward for her service, she received a job at the Treasury Department. See Bonsal and Sheridan, *Loyal Girl.*

25. Sheridan, *Memoirs,* 280.

26. Ibid.

CHAPTER 27. THE BATTLE OF OPEQUON

1. Hastings, "Recollections," 19 Sept. 1864.

2. Ibid.; Dupont, *Campaign of 1864 in the Valley,* 108; Morris, *Sheridan,* 197.

3. Lincoln, *Life with the Thirty-Fourth Massachusetts,* 353.

4. Dupont, *Campaign of 1864 in the Valley,* 109. Contemporary sources give contradictory accounts of where Crook and Sheridan were at this time during the battle. The accounts of Colonel Hayes and Captain Hastings place the two men with the VIII Corps on the east bank of the Opequon. Hayes to Uncle Sardis [Birchard], 28 Sept. 1864, Hayes Papers; Hastings, "Recollections," 19 Sept. 1864. But Crook and Dupont stated that while they had been with Sheridan, their position was on a rise about three miles forward of the creek at the western end of the canyon. Schmitt, *Crook, His Autobiography,* 126; Dupont, *Campaign of 1864 in the Valley,* 109. Sheridan also recalled that he had passed through the canyon with the VI Corps and observed the battle from the rise. I have chosen to accept Crook and Dupont's version as it makes more sense in the context of the battle and Sheridan's personality, for the general would want to be as far forward as feasible. I believe that Hayes's and Hastings's versions resulted from the confusion of the day. For an extended discussion of this point, see Williams, *Hayes of the 23rd,* 254.

5. See Dupont, *Campaign of 1864 in the Valley,* 108; and DeForest, *Volunteer's Adventure,* 175. In fairness to Sheridan, he seems to have anticipated problems with the ravine and instructed his generals to send all wagons that would "inconvenience the quick movement of troops" to Harpers Ferry the day before the battle. Wright seems to have ignored this order. See Pond, *Shenandoah Valley in 1864,* 158n1.

6. For an exceptionally clear description of this phase of the battle, see Williams, *Hayes of the 23rd,* 250–52.

7. J. Taylor, *Sketchbook,* 359–60.

8. Sheridan, *Memoirs,* 293. Neither Crook nor Dupont are precise on this point. Crook recalled that his staff officers were "dispatched to hurry up" his troops to the front. Schmitt, *Crook, His Autobiography,* 126. From Dupont's narrative one can infer that he too remained with Sheridan, awaiting the arrival of the VIII Corps on the field. *Campaign of 1864 in the Valley,* 113. T. Harry Williams asserts that it was highly improbable that Crook would leave the battlefield to return through the ravine to fetch his corps. *Hayes of the 23rd,* 255.

9. Schmitt, *Crook, His Autobiography,* 127.

10. Sheridan, report, 3 Feb. 1866, OR, 43(1):47; Wright, report, 18 Oct. 1864, ibid., 150.

11. Hastings, "Recollections," 19 Sept. 1864; Crook to Lt. Col. Kingsbury, AAG, 17 Oct. 1864, OR, 43(1):361; Schmitt, *Crook, His Autobiography,* 117.

12. Crook, report, 19 Sept., 17 Oct. 1864, OR, 43(1):361; Schmitt, *Crook, His Autobiography,* 126.

13. Sheridan, report, OR, 43(1):47; Sheridan, *Memoirs,* 293; Dupont, *Campaign of 1864 in the Valley,* 121; Hastings, "Recollections," 19 Sept. 1864. Hayes described the movement, stating that Crook "is the brains of the whole thing." Hayes to Uncle Sardis, 26 Sept. 1864. T. Harry Williams has argued that Sheridan was too much of an aggressive commander to have placed Crook opposite the extreme left of the enemy line without intending that he make an enveloping attack, further commenting that Crook merely executed the attack "with great competence." Williams, *Hayes of the 23rd,* 257–88. But Eric Wittenberg does not agree with this assessment. He concluded that "Crook had proposed the flank attack that helped carry the day at Third Winchester." Wittenberg, *Little Phil,* 106. In his draft memoir,

Crook himself asserts that Sheridan had ordered him to support the XIX Corps "when I made the flank[ing] movement before mentioned without orders or Gen. Sheridan's knowing anything about the move until it was all over." Crook, Ms. B, 51.

14. Hastings, "Recollections," 19 Sept. 1864; Hayes to his wife, 21 Sept. 1864. See also Williams, *Hayes of the 23rd,* 258.

15. Dupont, *Campaign of 1864 in the Valley,* 120. McKinley was one of two future presidents under Crook's command.

16. Ibid., 121–22.

17. Ibid, 121–23.

18. Hastings, "Recollections," 19 Sept. 1864; Hayes to his wife, 21 Sept. 1864.

19. Schmitt, *Crook, His Autobiography,* 128.

20. Ibid., 127–28, 128n4; DeForest, *Volunteer's Adventure,* 187. This account is at variance with Crook's draft memoir, in which he wrote that Thomas ordered his troops forward, but moments later Crook saw that "[Thomas's] men were again in a flopped position." Ms. B, 50. In DeForest's account, he notes that two regiments of the XIX Corps did charge but were abruptly halted on orders from Colonel Thomas. The men then resumed the charge and carried it to a successful conclusion. *Volunteer's Adventure,* 187.

21. Sheridan, *Memoirs,* 294, 295; J. Taylor, *Sketchbook,* 372–75.

22. Schmitt, *Crook, His Autobiography,* 127.

23. Sears, *Chancellorsville,* 442; Stackpole, *Sheridan in the Shenandoah,* 404; Wert, *From Winchester to Cedar Creek,* 102.

24. Hayes to Uncle Sardis, 26 Sept. 1864.

25. Dupont, *Campaign of 1864 in the Valley,* 128.

CHAPTER 28. VICTORY AT FISHER'S HILL

1. J. Early, *Memoir,* 98.

2. Ibid., 76, 98. Estimates of the opposing forces following Opequon vary. According to Edward Stackpole, Early faced Sheridan's 37,000 men with only 17,000 troops defending Winchester. *Sheridan in the Shenandoah,* 404. Counting the aggregate losses of each side in that battle, at Fisher's Hill Sheridan would have had 32,000 men against Early's 13,000.

3. J. Early, *Memoir,* 77; Dupont, *Campaign of 1864 in the Valley,* 134; Sheridan, *Memoirs,* 300.

4. J. Early, *Memoir,* 98.

5. Sheridan, *Memoirs,* 299–300.

6. See Dupont, *Campaign of 1864 in the Valley,* 134; and Hayes to wife, 23 Sept. 1864, Hayes Papers.

7. Schmitt, *Crook, His Autobiography,* 129, 130. On Wright and Emory, see Hayes to wife, 24 Sept. 1864, Hayes Papers.

8. Williams, *Hayes of the 23rd,* 267.

9. Lang, *Loyal West Virginia,* 333–34; Dupont, *Campaign of 1864 in the Valley,* 134.

10. Lang, *Loyal West Virginia,* 334n.

11. DeForest, *Volunteer's Adventure,* 195; Crook, Ms. B, 52.

12. Farrar, *Twenty-Second Pennsylvania Cavalry,* 385; Schmitt, *Crook, His Autobiography,* 131; J. Early, *Memoir,* 100.

13. Schmitt, *Crook, His Autobiography,* 131; Lincoln, *Life with the Thirty-Fourth Massachusetts,* 366–67; Pond, *Shenandoah Valley in 1864,* 177.

14. Hayes to wife, 28 Sept. 1864, Hayes Papers.

15. Sheridan to Grant, 23 Sept. 1864, OR, 43(2):152; Sheridan, *Memoirs,* 301; Rutherford B. Hayes, "Battle of Fisher's Hill," Hayes Papers. Again, the Union figures vary. For example, Edward Stackpole lists 52 killed, 456 wounded, and 19 missing. George Pond lists 43 killed, 410 wounded, and 6 missing. See Stackpole, *Sheridan in the Shenandoah,* 406–408 (Table 3); and Pond, *Shenandoah Valley in 1864,* 269 (App. C).

16. Wert, *From Winchester to Cedar Creek,* 128. Sheridan reported to have captured sixteen cannon. Sheridan to Grant, 23 Sept. 1864. For his part, Early stated that Union forces only captured eleven guns. J. Early, *Memoir,* 100. These conflicting claims are understandable given the disproportionate importance attached to artillery and regimental colors at the time. The loss of either to Confederates was regarded as a stain on the honor of a unit. Conversely, the capture of either could earn a Union soldier the Medal of Honor.

17. DeForest, *Volunteer's Adventure,* 196.

18. Sheridan to Stanton, 2 May 1866, Sheridan Papers, Library of Congress; Cullum, *Biographical Register,* 330; Schmitt, *Crook, His Autobiography,* 136n2.

CHAPTER 29. THE BATTLE OF CEDAR CREEK

1. See Grant to Sheridan, 26 Aug. 1865, OR, 43(1):916.

2. For a map showing the full extent of the destruction, see Heatwole, *The Burning,* 66.

3. Sheridan to Grant, 7 Oct. 1864, OR, 43(2):30.

4. Meigs was actually killed by regular Confederate troops of the Tenth Virginia Cavalry, scouts who wore oil clothes over their uniforms because of the rain and so were not immediately recognizable as soldiers. Ben Shaver, the trooper who fired the fatal shot, later claimed he did so after being fired on by Meigs. Unions soldiers riding with Meigs countered that, without provocation, Shaver shot Meigs twice in the head while riding by his side pretending to be a Federal trooper. See J. Taylor, *Sketchbook,* 434–39. John Heatwole accepts Shaver's account as entirely credible. See *The Burning,* 90–93.

5. Heatwole, *The Burning,* 90–94; Wert, *Winchester to Cedar Creek,* 145.

6. Hayes to Uncle Sardis [Birchard], 27 Sept. 1864, Hayes Papers.

7. Sheridan, *Memoirs,* 310; Heatwole, *The Burning,* 183–84; DeForest, *Volunteer's Adventure,* 197.

8. Hayes to wife, 2, 10 Oct. 1864, Hayes Papers.

9. J. Taylor, *Sketchbook,* 441, 444.

10. J. Early, *Memoir,* 104.

11. Pond, *Shenandoah Valley in 1864,* 203–205; Wert, *Winchester to Cedar Creek,* 165–66.

12. Sheridan, *Memoirs,* 312–13.

13. Ibid., 313–14.

14. J. Early, *Memoir,* 107.

15. The orderly, Pvt. Charles Tucker, was captured and died in captivity in Salisbury, N.C. See Dupont, *Campaign of 1864 in the Valley,* 153–54.

16. Williams, *Hayes of the 23rd,* 289; Pond, *Shenandoah Valley in 1864,* 222.

17. Schmitt, *Crook, His Autobiography,* 132; Crook to Col. J. W. Forsyth, 7 Nov. 1864, OR, 43(1):365.

18. Schmitt, *Crook, His Autobiography,* 132, 134.

19. DeForest, *Volunteer's Adventure,* 203.

20. Ibid., 206; Wert, *From Winchester to Cedar Creek,* 170; Whitehorne, *Battle of Cedar Creek,* 7.

21. Sheridan, *Memoirs,* 314.

22. Ibid., 314–15. These pages in Sheridan's memoir include the texts of "Longstreet's" message, Wright's cover note to Sheridan of October 16, and Sheridan's reply of the same date.

23. Lewis, *Guns of Cedar Creek,* 105; Freeman, *Lee's Lieutenants,* 41 (quote).

24. Gordon, *Reminiscences,* 334.

25. Ibid., 334–35.

26. Lewis, *Guns of Cedar Creek,* 123–24; J. Early, *Memoir,* 109.

27. Nettleton, "How the Day Was Saved at the Battle of Cedar Creek," 265, quoted in Lewis, *Guns of Cedar Creek,* 143. Nettleton's description is also quoted in Whitehorne, *Battle of Cedar Creek,* 10; and Wert, *From Winchester to Cedar Creek,* 174.

28. Williams, *Hayes of the 23rd,* 287.

29. Stevens, "Battle of Cedar Creek," 194; DeForest, *Volunteer's Adventure,* 203. See also Lewis, *Guns of Cedar Creek,* 140; and Williams, *Hayes of the 23rd,* 292.

30. Carpenter, *Eighth Vermont Volunteers,* 207–208.

31. Dupont, *Campaign of 1864 in the Valley,* 152.

32. Carpenter, *Eighth Vermont Volunteers,* 208; Schmitt, *Crook, His Autobiography,* 133.

33. Stevens, "Battle of Cedar Creek," 197.

34. Dickert, *History of Kershaw's Brigade,* 447–48.

35. Ibid.

36. Dupont, *Campaign of 1864 in the Valley,* 156; Stevens, "Battle of Cedar Creek," 199; Farrar, *Twenty-Second Pennsylvania Cavalry,* 429; J. Taylor, *Sketchbook,* 488.

37. Crowninshield, *Battle of Cedar Creek,* 16. Crowninshield, who was on Sheridan's staff and hence was at Belle Grove, asserts that Wright was camped elsewhere but came to head-quarters immediately after the firing commenced. Emory had camped with his corps.

38. Stevens, "Battle of Cedar Creek," 201, 200; Crowninshield, *Battle of Cedar Creek,* 18.

39. Carpenter, *Eighth Vermont Volunteers,* 211; DeForest, *Volunteer's Adventure,* 76. Carpenter states that Colonel Thomas informed Crook that he had taken the liberty of borrowing some VIII Corps troops to help hold the line and that the general nodded his assent. *Eighth Vermont Volunteers,* 219.

40. J. Taylor, *Sketchbook,* 489; Wildes, *One Hundred and Sixteenth Ohio Infantry,* 90.

41. In his memoir Early notes that at this point in the battle, he "discovered a number of men in the enemy's camps plundering" and that it was subsequently reported to him "that a great number were at the same work." J. Early, *Memoir,* 115. But Dickert, who also observed the looting, pointed out, "their wants were few, or at least that which they could carry, so they grabbed a slice of bacon, a piece of bread, a blanket, or an overcoate, and were soon again following up the enemy." Dickert, *History of Kershaw's Brigade,* 449.

42. Lewis, *Guns of Cedar Creek,* 236; DeForest, *Volunteer's Adventure,* 214–16.

43. Sheridan, *Memoirs,* 322–23.

44. DeForest, *Volunteer's Adventure,* 222.

45. Sheridan, *Memoirs,* 329; J. Taylor, *Sketchbook,* 502.

46. Sheridan, *Memoirs,* 330; Stevens, "Battle of Cedar Creek," 220.

47. Wildes, *One Hundred and Sixteenth Ohio Infantry,* 91; J. Taylor, *Sketchbook,* 507. Taylor gives his source for this encounter as A. O. Perkins, one of Crook's orderlies.

48. J. Early, *Memoir,* 115–16. See also Freeman, *Lee's Lieutenants,* 757. On the question of looting, historians disagree whether it really had a debilitating effect on Early's troop strength. See, for example, Lewis, *Guns of Cedar Creek,* 258–59; and Williams, *Hayes of the 23rd,* 306.

49. Gordon, *Reminiscences,* 341; J. Early, *Memoir,* 116.

50. Pond, *Shenandoah Valley in 1864,* 237; Stevens, "Battle of Cedar Creek," 225; Sheridan, *Memoirs,* 331. Sheridan notes that Crook endorsed his plan for a counterattack. Sheridan, *Memoirs,* 330.

51. Stevens, "Battle of Cedar Creek," 228; Sheridan, *Memoirs,* 332.

52. Wert, *From Winchester to Cedar Creek,* 236.

53. Dupont, *Campaign of 1864 in the Valley,* 172–73, 176; Crook to Forsythe, 7 Nov. 1864, OR, 43(1):366.

54. Sheridan, *Memoirs,* 332–33; J. Taylor, *Sketchbook,* 519.

55. Schmitt, *Crook, His Autobiography,* 134.

56. Hayes to Gen. B. R. Cowan, 25 Oct. 1864, Hayes Papers; Hayes to Maj. John Gould, 10 Jan. 1884, ibid.

57. George Crook, diary, 26 Dec. 1889, Crook/Kennon Papers, U.S. Military History Institute, Carlisle.

CHAPTER 30. MOSBY'S RANGERS

1. Hayes to his wife, 13 Nov. 1864, Hayes Papers; J. Taylor, *Sketchbook,* 545–46; Hayes Diary, 9 Nov. 1864; James M. McPherson, *Battle Cry of Freedom: The Civil War Era* (1988; repr., New York: Ballantine Books, 1989), 688.

2. J. Taylor, *Sketchbook,* 553.

3. Hayes Diary, 23 Nov. 1864; Hayes to his wife, 6 Dec. 1864, Hayes Papers.

4. Hayes to mother, 6 Dec. 1864, Hayes Papers.

5. Hayes to wife, 9 Dec. 1864, ibid.; Hayes to James Webb (son), 30 Nov. 1864, ibid.; Hayes to wife, Jan. 5, 1865, ibid.

6. Sheridan to Halleck, 27 Oct. 1864, OR, 43(1):35.

7. Wert, *Mosby's Rangers,* 202, Sheridan to Auger, 20 Aug. 1864, OR, 43(1):860.

8. Wert writes that Mosby had "at least 1,900 men" under his command from January 1863 to April 1865. But he also notes that the number who rode with Mosby at any given time did not exceed 350 at any one time during this period. *Mosby's Rangers,* 73–74.

9. Ibid., 203.

10. Richard Blazer, report, 24 Oct. 1864, OR, 43(1):615–16; Wert, *Mosby's Rangers,* 252.

11. This account is based on Wert, *Mosby's Rangers,* 254–58; and Stephenson, *Headquarters in the Brush,* 167–82. Of the 63 men in Blazer's unit who went into the fight, 19 were killed and 16 captured. Stephenson, *Headquarters in the Brush,* 179. Blazer was sent to Libby Prison in Richmond and was exchanged in February 1865. Ibid., 202.

12. Sheridan, *Memoirs,* 338.

13. Hayes Diary, 2 Jan. 1865.

CHAPTER 31. KIDNAPPED

1. Hayes to his wife, 12 Feb. 1865, Hayes Papers.

2. Schmitt, *Crook, His Autobiography,* 131. As to the pro-secessionist activities of Mary's father, see note 6 below.

3. Vandiver, "Two Forgotten Heroes," 405–407.

4. Bright, "McNeill Rangers," 355; Fay, "Capture of Major-Generals Crook and Kelley," 107.

5. Bright, "McNeill Rangers," 352; Vandiver, "Two Forgotten Heroes," 354, 412.

6. Vandiver, "Two Forgotten Heroes," 354; Bright, "McNeill Rangers," 355. According to one source (the son of one of the rangers), McNeill's wife eluded her pursuers and safely made her way to her husband's headquarters in Moorefield with the aid of Mary Daily's father. Vandiver, "Two Forgotten Heroes," 413.

7. Thomas and Williams, *History of Allegany County,* 397; J. William Hunt, Across the Desk, *Cumberland Evening Times,* 25 May 1947. Still another reason for the raid, advanced by W. D. Vandiver, is that it would secure two hostages who could be exchanged for two rangers previously captured by Kelley's forces. "Two Forgotten Heroes," 413–14.

8. Fay, "Capture of Major-Generals Crook and Kelley," 107; Felix Robinson, "Two Big Ones That Didn't Get Away," news clipping, Oakland Historical Society, Oakland, Md. After the war Fay became an attorney and the editor of the *Mountain Democrat,* a local newspaper. And at the urging of his old comrades, he would write an account of the Cumberland raid, which would become a major source of information about the kidnapping.

9. Fay, "Capture of Major-Generals Crook and Kelley," 107, 108; Duffey, *Two Generals Kidnapped,* 6.

10. Fay, "Capture of Major-Generals Crook and Kelley," 108; Duffey, *Two Generals Kidnapped,* 8.

11. Fay, "Capture of Major-Generals Crook and Kelley," 108; Duffey, *Two Generals Kidnapped,* 8. Unknown to the raiders, they almost missed Crook. The day before, Sheridan had ordered him to report to Winchester to confer about Confederate troop movements in the Valley. Crook embarked that morning by train only to find that the Rebels had cut the tracks not far out of town. Frustrated, he returned to his headquarters and turned in early in his customary room at the Revere. Sheridan to Crook, 20 Feb. 1865, OR, 48(2):607; Hunt, Across the Desk, 24 Feb. 1957.

12. Duffey, *Two Generals Kidnapped,* 8. According to Fay, the rangers followed a trail that ran north along the base of the mountain. "Capture of Major-Generals Crook and Kelley," 108.

13. Spalding, "Confederate Raid on Cumberland," 34; Fay, "Capture of Major-Generals Crook and Kelley," 109.

14. Spalding, "Confederate Raid on Cumberland," 35.

15. Fay, "Capture of Major-Generals Crook and Kelley," 109; Spalding, "Confederate Raid on Cumberland," 35.

16. Spalding, "Confederate Raid on Cumberland," 36.

17. Entry into the two hotels is best described by Fay, who was there, and Duffey, who also had a role in the raid. See Fay, "Capture of Major-Generals Crook and Kelley," 110; and Duffey, *Two Generals Kidnapped,* 10–11.

18. For an extended analysis of the number of Federal troops actually in Cumberland that night, see Bright, "McNeill Rangers." After considering a number of sources, Bright concludes that about 7,000 troops were in the town and its immediate environs that night. Ibid., 364.

19. Fay, "Capture of Major-Generals Crook and Kelley," 110. There are several versions of the dialogue at the scene; Fay's seems the most credible.

20. Duffey, *Two Generals Kidnapped,* 12.

21. Spalding, "Confederate Raid on Cumberland," 36–37; Fay, "Capture of Major-Generals Crook and Kelley," 110; Vandiver, "Two Forgotten Heroes," 416.

22. Fay, "Capture of Major-Generals Crook and Kelley," 111; Vandiver, "Two Forgotten Heroes," 416.

23. Thomas and Williams, *History of Allegany County,* 393; Duffey, *Two Generals Kidnapped,* 13.

24. Unidentified item, J. C. Saunders Papers, Potomac State School of W.Va. University, Keyser, W.Va., quoted in Bright, "McNeill Rangers," 364.

25. Duffey, *Two Generals Kidnapped,* 14.

26. Duffey, *Two Generals Kidnapped,* 14. See also Vandiver, "Two Forgotten Heroes," 417.

27. Duffey, *Two Generals Kidnapped,* 16.

28. Ibid.

29. Lee to Breckenridge, 21 Feb. 1865, OR, 46(1):471–72; Duffey, *Two Generals Kidnapped,* 16.

30. Stanton to Grant, 21 Feb. 1865, OR, 46(2):608; Hayes to Uncle Sardis [Birchard], 24 Mar. 1865, Hayes Papers; *Maryland Historical Magazine,* 41:258.

31. Schmitt, *Crook, His Autobiography,* 136n2. Regarding the release of Crook and Kelley, see Grant to Stanton, 10 Mar. 1865, quoting *Richmond Examiner,* OR, 46(2):914. On the conditions of parole, see Grant (AAG Bowers), Special Order No. 50, 14 Mar. 1865, ibid., 966. Also see Schmitt, *Crook, His Autobiography,* 304.

32. Hayes to his wife, 21 Feb. 1865, Hayes Papers.

33. Crook to Sheridan, 20 Feb. 1865, OR, 46(2):606; Sheridan to Crook, 20 Feb. 1865 ibid.

34. Schmitt, *Crook, His Autobiography,* 135.

35. Hunt, Across the Desk, 24 Feb. 1957.

36. Maxwell and Swisher, *History of Hampshire County,* 687–89.

CHAPTER 32. COMMANDER OF CAVALRY IN GRANT'S ARMY

1. Crook to Hayes, 20 Mar. 1865, Crook Letter Book, Hayes Library.

2. Halleck to Grant, 21 Mar. 1865, OR, 46(3):170; Grant to Halleck, ibid.

3. Stanton to Grant, 21 Feb. 1865, OR, 46(2):608.

4. Hayes to Uncle Sardis [Birchard], 24 Mar. 1865, Hayes Papers ; Grant to Townsend, 18 Mar. 1865, OR, 46(3):28. One can speculate that Grant's failure to notify the War Department was not inadvertent but a ploy to bypass Stanton, who most certainly would have objected.

5. Hancock to Halleck, 21 Mar. 1865, OR, 46(3):69; Morgan to Crook, 21 Mar. 1865, ibid., 72.

6. Hancock to Townsend, 22 Mar.1865, ibid., 82; Stanton to Grant, 22 Mar. 1865, ibid., 72.

7. See Lincoln to Hancock, Halleck to Hancock, Hancock to Lincoln, and Hancock to Halleck, all 22 Mar. 1865, ibid., 81–83.

8. Crook to Morgan, 21 Mar. 1865, ibid., 69, 85.

9. Horace Porter, "Five Forks and the Pursuit of Lee," in Johnson and Buel, *Battles and Leaders,* 4:708; Grant, *Memoirs,* 524–25.

10. Grant, *Memoirs,* 530–31, 532; Sheridan, *Memoirs,* 355.

11. Sheridan, *Memoirs,* 359–60; Longacre, *Cavalry at Appomattox,* 34.

12. Warner, *Generals in Blue,* 188. One historian alleges that Gregg's resignation was due to his despising Sheridan, a circumstance the general never reduced to writing. See Castner, "Saga of Brigadier General David McMurtie Gregg."

13. Longacre, *Cavalry at Appomattox,* 34.

14. Crook to Hayes, 28 Mar. 1865, Crook Papers, Hayes Library; Tobie, *First Maine Cavalry,* 385.

15. Tobie, *First Maine Cavalry,* 386; Sheridan, *Memoirs,* 362.

16. Longacre, *Cavalry at Appomattox,* 36; Freeman, *Lee's Lieutenants,* 776.

17. Grant, *Memoirs,* 332; Longacre, *Cavalry at Appomattox,* 77.

18. Sheridan, *Memoirs,* 361; Porter, "Five Forks and the Pursuit of Lee," 709.

19. Sheridan, *Memoirs,* 362; Tobie, *First Maine Cavalry,* 386.

20. Sheridan, *Memoirs,* 363.

21. Porter, *Campaigning with Grant,* 427.

22. Sheridan, *Memoirs,* 365.

23. Longacre, *Cavalry at Appomattox,* 63; Foote, *Civil War,* 3:869.

24. Longacre, *Cavalry at Appomattox,* 75; Sheridan to Grant, 16 May 1865, OR, 46(1):1103.

25. Porter, *Campaigning with Grant,* 711; Sheridan to Grant, 31 Mar. 1865, OR, 46(3):381; Grant to Sheridan, ibid.

26. Sheridan, *Memoirs,* 371.

27. Longacre, *Cavalry at Appomattox,* 86–87.

28. Field Order, 1 Apr. 1865, OR, 46(3):420; Sheridan to Grant, 16 May 1865, ibid., 46(1):1105; Sheridan, *Memoirs,* 378; Morris, *Sheridan,* 377. A court of inquiry later convened at Warren's request found Sheridan's action unjustified and cleared Warren's name. But their judgment came too late. Warren died, still under a cloud, three months before the investigation was completed.

CHAPTER 33. THE FINAL STRUGGLE

1. Schmitt, *Crook, His Autobiography,* 137.

2. Freeman, *Lee's Lieutenants,* 786; Longacre, *Cavalry at Appomattox,* 107. Lee's troop strength is taken from W. Taylor, *Four Years with General Lee,* 188. Taylor was Lee's adjutant and is considered an exceptionally reliable resource.

3. Schmitt, *Crook, His Autobiography,* 137.

4. Grant to Sheridan, 3 Apr. 1865, OR, 46(3):528.

5. Davis, *To Appomattox,* 190, 193; Longacre, *Cavalry at Appomattox,* 126–27.

6. Sheridan, *Memoirs,* 380.

7. Longacre, *Cavalry at Appomattox,* 116.

8. Sheridan, *Memoirs,* 380.

9. Longacre, *Cavalry at Appomattox,* 124.

10. Ibid.; Sheridan, *Memoirs,* 381; Charles H. Smith, report, 15 Apr. 1865, OR, 46(1): 1157–58.

11. Davis, *To Appomattox,* 213–14.

12. Longacre, *Cavalry at Appomattox,* 129, 132.

13. Henry R. Davies, report, 14 Apr. 1865, OR, 46(1):1145; Sheridan, *Memoirs,* 381–82.

14. Sheridan, *Memoirs,* 382; Davies, report, 14 Apr. 1865, OR, 46(1):1145.

15. Sheridan, *Memoirs,* 382; Grant, *Memoirs,* 546.

16. Porter, *Campaigning with Grant,* 455–56; Grant, *Memoirs,* 546; Sheridan, *Memoirs,* 383.

17. Sheridan, *Memoirs,* 383.

18. Tobie, *First Maine Cavalry,* 413; Longacre, *Cavalry at Appomattox,* 138.

19. Tobie, *First Maine Cavalry*, 414.

20. Calkins, *Thirty-Six Hours*, 5.

21. Sheridan, *Memoirs*, 383.

22. Freeman, *Lee's Lieutenants*, 794; Calkins, *Thirty-Six Hours*, 8.

23. Sheridan, *Memoirs*, 384.

24. Schmitt, *Crook, His Autobiography*, 138; Sheridan, *Memoirs*, 384.

25. Robert Stiles, *Four Years under Marse Robert* (New York: Neale, 1903), 333, quoted in Calkins, *Thirty-Six Hours*, 13.

26. Lee's statement is quoted in, among others, Davis, *To Appomattox*, 261. Its source has been ascribed to Maj. Gen. William Mahone, the officer who replied to Lee's anguished utterance. Longacre, *Cavalry at Appomattox*, 156, 219n37.

27. Calkins, *Thirty-Six Hours*, 20. Edward Longacre puts the number of captured at 6,000 troops. *Cavalry at Appomattox*, 155.

28. W. Taylor, *Four Years with General Lee*, 188; Calkins, *Thirty-Six Hours*, 20; John E. Cooke, *Life of General Robert E. Lee* (New York: D. Appleton, 1887), 455, quoted in Davis, *To Appomattox*, 262; Ewell quoted in Foote, *Civil War*, 3:919.

29. Sheridan, *Memoirs*, 389.

30. G. A. Custer, report, 15 Apr. 1865, OR, 46(1):1132; Schmitt, *Crook, His Autobiography*, 139.

31. Brig. Gen. E. P. Alexander quoted in Davis, *To Appomattox*, 307.

32. Tobie, *First Maine Cavalry*, 418.

33. Schmitt, *Crook, His Autobiography*, 139.

34. Humphreys failed to secure the railroad bridge but managed to cross the river on a nearby wagon bridge. Longacre, *Cavalry at Appomattox*, 160; Foote, *Civil War*, 3:922.

35. Tremain, *Last Hours of Sheridan's Cavalry*, 173–77. Tremain served as an aide-de-camp to Crook during this campaign.

36. Ibid., 194–95; Longacre, *Cavalry at Appomattox*, 164–65.

37. Tremain, *Last Hours of Sheridan's Cavalry*, 194–95; Longacre, *Cavalry at Appomattox*, 139–40; Calkins, *Thirty-Six Hours*, 53.

38. Schmitt, *Crook, His Autobiography*, 139; Gordon, *Reminiscences*, 430.

39. Sheridan, *Memoirs*, 389.

40. Ibid., 390.

41. Sheridan, report, 15 May 1865, OR, 46(1):1109.

42. Tremain, *Last Hours of Sheridan's Cavalry*, 217.

43. Tobie, *First Maine Cavalry*, 423.

44. Sheridan, report, 15 May 1865, OR, 46(1):1109; Schmitt, *Crook, His Autobiography*, 140.

45. Tobie, *First Maine Cavalry*, 424.

46. Ibid., 423. Tremain wrote that Crook's men did not take their positions on the Lynchburg road until a little before dawn, having first had a few hours rest. At that time they relieved Devin's division, which had guarded the road during the night. Tremain, *Last Hours of Sheridan's Cavalry*, 241–42.

47. Tobie, *First Maine Cavalry*, 424, 437; Longacre, *Cavalry at Appomattox*, 181.

48. Tremain, *Last Hours of Sheridan's Cavalry*, 239–43.

49. Longacre, *Cavalry at Appomattox*, 186.

50. Tobie, *First Maine Cavalry*, 125; Tremain, *Last Hours of Sheridan's Cavalry*, 427.

51. Schmitt, *Crook, His Autobiography*, 140.

52. Ibid. Earlier, Hayes had written: "[Crook] has become a convert to negro soldiers. Thinks them better than a great part of the sort we are now getting." Hayes Diary, 12 Feb. 1865.

53. Gordon, *Reminiscences,* 438.

54. Morris, *Sheridan,* 258; Tremain, *Last Hours of Sheridan's Cavalry,* 322.

55. Tobie, *First Maine Cavalry,* 427.

CHAPTER 34. AFTERWARD

1. Tremain, *Last Hours of Sheridan's Cavalry,* 266–77.

2. Schmitt, *Crook, His Autobiography,* 141; Sheridan, *Memoirs,* 399; Tremain, *Last Hours of Sheridan's Cavalry,* 279. Sheridan wrote that the news came by telegraph. *Memoirs,* 399. Henry Tremain says it was delivered by "dispatch from the War Department." *Last Hours of Sheridan's Cavalry,* 278–80.

3. Tremain, *Last Hours of Sheridan's Cavalry,* 280–96.

4. Ibid., 296; General Forsythe, orders, 1 May 1865, OR, 46(3):1061.

5. OR, 46(3):1177; Tremain, *Last Hours of Sheridan's Cavalry,* 316–17; Schmitt, *Crook, His Autobiography,* 141.

6. Tremain, *Last Hours of Sheridan's Cavalry,* 310, 319.

7. Special Orders no. 336, 27 June 1865, OR, 46(3):1300.

8. At least one source speculates that Crook was already engaged to Mary at the time he was kidnapped. See Maxwell and Swisher, *History of Hampshire County,* 679.

9. "General George Crook," *Washington Chronicle,* 1 July 1883. This story was repeated as fact by Carrie Adell Strahorn in a book on the travels she and her husband took to promote the Northern Pacific Railroad. Strahorn believed this story even though she had stayed with the Crooks in Omaha while the general was commanding the Department of the Platte. The couple apparently never shared with her the real facts of their courtship. Strahorn, *Fifteen Thousand Miles by Stage,* 181–82.

10. The author of the letter was one Henry Goddard of Baltimore, who claimed to know the Crook family. Goddard wrote that he based his information on conversations with a Mrs. Markland, Crook's sister-in-law, following Mary's death. He was probably the originator of the story that the couple became engaged on the evening before his capture. While this story may be apocryphal, the two certainly had developed a relationship by that time. A desire to see Mary may have been one motive behind Crook's stubborn insistence on visiting Cumberland after his release from Libby Prison prior to joining his cavalry division. "Civil War Incident," *Springfield (Mass.) Republican,* 16 May 1902.

11. Howe, *Historical Collections of Ohio,* 564; "Gen. Crook Won Southern Belle," *The Chicago Tribune,* 21 Mar. 1890, republished in *Prescott Weekly Courier,* 18 Jan. 1930. The latter story has the general wounded after his release from Libby and proposing to Mary three times before she accepted.

12. Crook to Hayes, 26 Aug. 1865, Crook Correspondence, 1864–June 1883, Rutherford Hayes Library, Fremont, Ohio.

13. Joseph C. Porter, "Foreword," in Schmitt, *Crook, His Autobiography,* xiii; ibid., 141, 306.

14. See McGreary, "My Search for General George Crook," 296.

15. Mary Crook to John Bourke, 5 Apr., 13 Oct. 1890, 8 Mar., 10 Nov. 1891, Bourke Papers, RG 2955, Nebraska Historical Society, Lincoln.

16. Their accommodations during that winter were described in a pamphlet prepared

by Crook's staff on the occasion of his dog's demise. See *In Memoriam of "Jim," died Nov. 21, 1874,* Box 10–2, ibid.

17. Azor H. Nickerson, "Major General George Crook and the Indians, a Sketch," Crook/Kennon Papers, U.S. Military History Institute, Carlisle, 31.

18. Evans, *Ballots and Fence Rails,* 36–45.

19. Warner, *Generals in Blue,* 219; Evans, *Ballots and Fence Rails,* 55–56; *Wilmington Journal,* 7 Apr. 1868, quoted in ibid., 58.

20. Evans, *Ballots and Fence Rails,* 64, 66–67; *Wilmington Weekly Journal,* 13 July 1865, quoted in ibid., 65.

21. *Wilmington Herald,* 10 July 1865, quoted in ibid., 76.

22. Ibid., 80–81.

23. Headquarters, Dist. of Wilmington, to Capt. A. C. [illegible], 17 Oct. 1965, Dist. of Wilmington, Dept. of Va. and N.C., Letters Sent, Records of U.S. Army Continental Commands, 1821–1920. RG 393, vol. 178, National Archives; Crook to Justice Connelly, 17, 19 Oct. 1865, ibid.

24. *Wilmington Dispatch,* 27 Nov. 1865, quoted in Evans, *Ballots and Fence Rails,* 130.

25. Crook to Capt. [illegible], 6 Dec. 1865, Dist. of Wilmington, Letters Sent.

26. Circular by command of Maj. Gen. Crook from AAG Rhoades, 11 Dec. 1865, ibid.

27. Seizing draft animals was an important part of the white power structure's campaign to reduce freedmen to servitude since it deprived blacks of not only their means to work their land but also their means of transportation. See Evans, *Ballots and Fence Rails,* 72–73.

28. For Crook's complete service record, see Military Order of the Loyal Legion of the United States, Circular 20, no. 122, Cincinnati, 25 Oct. 1888, M567, National Archives. It gives 15 January 1866 as the termination date for Crook's service in Wilmington and the date he was mustered out of the volunteer service.

EPILOGUE

1. Waugh, *Class of 1846,* 516–17.

2. Schmitt, *Crook, His Autobiography,* 144.

Bibliography

MANUSCRIPTS

Arizona Historical Society Library, Tucson.
    Charles B. Gatewood Papers.
Library of Congress, Washington, D.C.
    Phillip Sheridan Papers.
Maryland Historical Society, Baltimore.
    Tax List of Baltimore County, 1783, Heads of Families. First Census of the United States, 1790. File MSA S 1437.
National Anthropological Archives. Smithsonian Institution, Washington, D.C.
    George Crook. Manuscripts on Indian Languages in the Pacific Northwest, 84–86, 209.
National Archives, Washington, D.C.
    Applications to West Point. Microfilm Application File 79.
    Conduct Rolls of the U.S. Military Academy, 1848–52. Records of the Adjutant General's Office, 1762–1984. Record Group 94.
    Court-Martial Case Files, Records of the Office of the Judge Advocate General. Record Group 159.
    Department of the Pacific, Letters Received. Records of U.S. Army Continental Commands, 1821–1920. Record Group 393.
    Department of the Pacific, Letters Sent. Records of U.S. Army Continental Commands, 1821–1920. Record Group 393.
    District of Wilmington, Department of Virginia and North Carolina. Letters Sent, March 1865–February 1866. Records of U.S. Army Continental Commands, 1821–1920. Record Group 393, vol. 178.
    Fort Ter-Waw Letter Book, November 1858–October 1859. Records of U.S. Army Continental Commands, 1821–1920. Record Group 393.
Nebraska Historical Society, Lincoln.
    John G. Bourke Papers. Record Group 2955.
        Anonymous. *In Memoriam of "Jim," Died Nov. 21, 1874.*

Oakland Historical Society, Oakland, Md.
    Glades Hotel Register.
Ohio Department of Vital Records, Dayton.
    Deed Books D, K, M, N, O, U, and Z, Montgomery County, 1814–34.
    Record of Deaths. Probate Court, Montgomery County.
Ohio Historical Society, Columbus.
    John T. Booth Papers.
Potomac State School of West Virginia, Keyser.
    J. C. Saunders Papers.
Rutherford B. Hayes Library, Rutherford B. Hayes Presidential Center, Fremont, Ohio.
    George Crook Papers.
    Russell Hastings. "Personal Recollections." Hastings File.
    Rutherford B. Hayes. "Battle of Cloyds Mountain." Transcript of an interview with J. Q.
        Howard, 1896.
    Rutherford B Hayes Papers.
Special Collections, U.S. Military Academy, West Point.
    "Books Issued to Cadets by Special Permission of the Superintendent, 1850–52." U.S.
        Military Academy Library.
    Dennis H. Mahan. "Composition of the Armies." 24 March 1836. Textbook Collection,
        unbound folio T355.6.
    John C. Tidball. "Getting through West Point." 1895.
U.S. Military History Institute, Carlisle, Pa.
    Crook/Kennon Papers.
        George Crook. Cadet Expense Book.
        George Crook Diary.
        Lyman W.V. Kennon Diary.
        Azor H. Nickerson. "Major General George Crook and the Indians, a Sketch."

PUBLISHED DOCUMENTS

Abbot, Henry L. *Report of Henry L. Abbot, Corps of Topographical Engineers upon Explorations for a Railroad Route, from the Sacramento Valley to the Columbia River, Made by Lieutenant R. S. Williamson, Corps of Topographical Engineers, Assisted by Lieut. Henry L. Abbot, Corps of Topographical Engineers.* 33rd Cong., 2nd sess., 1857. S. Exec. Doc. 78. Vol. 6.
Cunningham, D., and W. W. Miller. *Report of the Ohio Antietam Battlefield Commission.* Springfield, Ohio: Springfield Publishing, 1904.
Military Order of the Loyal Legion of the United States, Circular 20, no. 122, Cincinnati, Oct. 25, 1888. M567, National Archives, Washington, DC.
Stevens, Hazard. "The Battle of Cedar Creek." *Civil War Papers of the State of Massachusetts Military Order of the Loyal Legion of the United States.* Vol. 1. Boston: F. H. Gilson, 1900.
U.S. Senate. *Report of the Secretary of War.* 33rd Cong., 1st sess., 1853. S. Exec. Doc. 1.
U.S. War Department. "General Order No. 33." Washington, D.C., 1890.
———. Order Book Camp Lincoln (Fort Ter-Waw), California, 1857–1861. Washington, D. C.
———. *The War of the Rebellion: A Compilation of the Official Records of the Union and Confederate Armies.* 130 vols. Washington, D.C.: Government Printing Office, 1881–98.

ARTICLES AND PAMPHLETS

Abbot, Henry L. "Reminiscences of the Oregon War of 1855." *Journal of the Military Service Institution of the United States* 40, no. 162 (November–December 1909): 436–42.

Arthur, E. C. "The Dublin Raid." *Ohio Soldier* 2 (January 5–April 13, 1889).

Benjamin, J. W. "Gray Forces Defeated in Battle of Lewisburg." *West Virginia History* 20, no. 1 (October 1958): 24–35.

Bonsal, Rebecca Wright, and Philip Sheridan. *The Loyal Girl of Winchester, September 1864.* 1888. Reprint ordered by Rutherford B. Hayes, Library of Congress.

Bright, Simeon M. "The McNeill Rangers: A Study in Confederate Guerilla Warfare." *West Virginia History* 12, no. 4 (July 1951): 338–87.

Castner, Charles Schuyler. "The Saga of Brigadier General David McMurtie Gregg." *Historical Review of Berks County* (Winter 1993–94). Available online at Historical Society of Berks County, Pennsylvania, http://www.berkshistory.org/articles/general-gregg.html (accessed December 2010).

Cozzens, Peter. "Fire on the Mountain." *Civil War Times Illustrated* 36, no. 5 (Oct. 1997): 61–72.

Davis, J. M. "The Glades Hotel." *The Glades Star* (1953): 180. Copy in files of the Garrett County Historical Society, Oakland, Md.

Duffey, J. W. *Two Generals Kidnapped—A Race for a Prize.* 3rd ed. Washington, D.C.: J. W. Duffey, 1927.

Fay, John B. "The Capture of Major-Generals Crook and Kelley." *Blue and Gray* (n.d.): 107–12.

Hathaway, John L. "Recollections of Sheridan as a Cadet." Paper delivered at Sheridan Memorial Meeting, U.S. Military History Institute, Carlisle, October 3, 1888.

Hunt, J. William. Across the Desk (recurring column). *Cumberland Evening Times,* 1947–57.

King, Charles. "Major General George Crook, United States Army: A Paper Read before the Commandery of Wisconsin, Military Order of the Loyal Legion of the United States, 1 April 1890." War Papers no. 6. Milwaukee: Burdick, Armitage, and Allen, 1890.

Leonard, Thomas C. "The Reluctant Conquerors: How the Generals Viewed the Indians." *American Heritage Magazine* 27, no. 5 (August 1976): 34–41.

Mauzy, Richard. "Vandalism by General Hunter, 1864." *Augusta Historical Bulletin* 14 (1978): 50–53.

McBeth, Frances Turner. *Lower Klamath Country.* 1950. Reprint. Crescent City, Calif.: Crescent City Printing, 1993.

McGreary, George D. "My Search for General George Crook, the Interrupted Autobiography, and the Mystery of the Missing Papers." *Journal of the Arizona History* 41 (June 2000): 289–306.

Nash, Sister May Eleanor. "Colonel James A. Mulligan, Chicago's Hero in the Civil War." Masters thesis, St. Louis University, 1929.

Patchan, Scott. "The Shenandoah Valley, July 1864." *Blue and Gray Magazine* 23, no. 3 (Summer 2006): 6–22, 42–50.

Pendleton, Rose. "General David Hunter's Sack of Lexington." Edited by Charles Turner. *Virginia Magazine of History and Biography* 83 (April 1975): 173–83.

Robbins, Harvey. "Journal of the Rogue River War." *Oregon Historical Quarterly* 34, no. 4 (December 1933).

Sheffield, Delia B. "Reminiscences of Mrs. Delia B. Sheffield." *Washington Historical Quarterly* 15, no. 1 (January 1924): 49–62.

Smith, Thomas. "West Point and the Indian Wars." *Military History of the West* 24, no. 1 (Spring 1994): 22–55.

Spalding, Basil William. "The Confederate Raid on Cumberland in 1865." *Maryland Historical Magazine* 36 (1940): 33–38.

Toney, B. Keith, "'Dying as Brave Men Should Die': The Attack and Defense of Burnside's Bridge." *Civil War Regiments* 6, no. 2 (1998).

Vandiver, W. D. "Two Forgotten Heroes—John Hanson McNeill and His Son Jesse." *Missouri Historical Review* 21 (1927): 404–19.

Wallace, Rich. "Area Men Die, Hurt in Useless Battle." Shelby County Historical Society, 1997. http://www.shelbycountyhistory.org.

BOOKS

Ambrose, Stephen. *Duty, Honor, Country: A History of West Point.* Baltimore: Johns Hopkins University Press, 1966.

Bancroft, Hubert Howe. *The Works of Hubert Howe Bancroft.* Vol. 30, *The History of Oregon: Vol. 2, 1848–1883.* San Francisco: History Company, 1888.

Bonnell, John C. *Sabres in the Shenandoah: The 21st New York Cavalry, 1863–1866.* Shippensburg, Penn.: Burd Street, 1996.

Bourke, John G. *On the Border with Crook.* 1891. Rev. ed., New York: Time-Life Books, 1980.

Brown, R. C., et al., comps. *History of Montgomery County, Ohio.* Chicago: W. H. Beers, 1882.

Calkins, Chris M. *Thirty-Six Hours before Appomattox: The Battles of Sayler's Creek, High Bridge, Farmville, and Cumberland Church.* Farmville, Va.: Farmville Herald, 1980.

Carpenter, George W. *History of the Eighth Vermont Volunteers.* Boston: Deland and Barta, 1886.

Catton, Bruce. *Terrible Swift Sword.* Vol. 2 of *Centennial History of the Civil War.* Garden City, N.Y.: Doubleday, 1963.

Cist, Henry M. *The Army of the Cumberland.* 1882. Reprint, Edison, N.J.: Castle, 2002.

Conover, Frank. *Centennial Portrait and Biographical Record of the City of Dayton and of Montgomery County, Ohio.* Dayton: A. W. Bowen, 1897.

Cottrell, Steve. *Civil War in Tennessee.* Gretna, La.: Pelican, 2001.

Cox, Jacob. *Military Reminiscences of the Civil War.* New York: Charles Scribner's Sons, 1900.

Cozzens, Peter. *No Better Place to Die: The Battle of Stones River.* Urbana: University of Illinois Press, 1991.

Crowninshield, Benjamin W. *The Battle of Cedar Creek: A Paper Read before the Massachusetts Historical Society, Dec. 8, 1879.* Cambridge, Mass.: Riverside, 1879.

Cullum, George Washington. *Biographical Register of the Officers and Graduates of the United States Military Academy at West Point, N.Y., from its Establishment, Mar. 16, 1802, to the Army Reorganization of 1866–67.* Vol. 2, *1841–1867.* New York: D. Van Nostrand, 1868.

Daniel, Larry. *Days of Glory: The Army of the Cumberland, 1861–1865.* Baton Rouge: Louisiana State University Press, 2004.

Davis, Burke. *To Appomattox: Nine April Days, 1865.* New York: Rinehart, 1959.

DeForest, John William. *A Volunteer's Adventures: A Union Captain's Record of the Civil War.* Edited by James H. Croushore. New Haven, Conn.: Yale University Press, 1946.

Dickert, D. August. *History of Kershaw's Brigade.* Newberry, S.C.: Elbert H. Aull, 1899.

Drury, August Waldo. *History of the City of Dayton and Montgomery County, Ohio.* Vol. 2. Chicago and Dayton: S. J. Clarke, 1909.

Duncan, Richard R., ed. *Alexander Neil and the Last Shenandoah Campaign: Letters of an Army Surgeon to His Family, 1864.* Shippensburg, Pa.: White Mane, 1996.

Duncan, Richard R. *Lee's Endangered Left: The Civil War in Western Virginia, Spring of 1864.* Baton Rouge: Louisiana State University Press, 2004.

Dupont, Henry A. *The Campaign of 1864 in the Valley of Virginia and the Expedition to Lynchburg.* New York: National American Society, 1925.

Earley, Gerald L. *I Belonged to the 116th: A Narrative of the 116th Ohio Volunteer Infantry during the Civil War.* Bowie, Md.: Heritage Books, 2004.

Early, Jubal A. *A Memoir of the Last Year of the War for Independence, in the Confederate States of America, Containing an Account of the Operations of his Commands in the Years 1864–1865.* 1866. Reprint, Columbia: University of South Carolina Press, 2001.

Eby, Cecil D., Jr., ed. *A Virginia Yankee in the Civil War: The Diaries of David Hunter Strothers.* Chapel Hill: University of North Carolina Press, 1959.

Eckert, Allan W. *The Frontiersman: A Narrative.* 1967. Reprint, Ashland, Ky.: Jesse Stuart Foundation, 2001.

Edgar, John H. *Pioneer Life in Dayton and Vicinity.* Dayton: United Brethren Publishing House, 1896.

Evans, W. McKee. *Ballots and Fence Rails: Reconstruction on the Lower Cape Fear.* Chapel Hill: University of North Carolina Press, 1966.

Faragher, John Mack. *Daniel Boone: The Life and Legend of an American Pioneer.* New York: Henry Holt, 1992.

Farrar, Samuel Clarke. *The Twenty-Second Pennsylvania Cavalry and the Ringgold Battalion, 1861–65.* 1911, Reprint, Pittsburgh: New Warner, for the Twenty-Second Pennsylvania Ringgold Cavalry Association, 2009.

Faust, Drew G. *This Republic of Suffering: Death and the American Civil War.* New York: Alfred A. Knopf, 2008.

Foote, Shelby. *The Civil War: A Narrative.* 3 vols. New York: Random House, 1958.

Freeman, Douglas Southall. *Lee's Lieutenants: A Study in Command.* 1943. Reprint, 3 vols. in 1, New York: Scribner, 1998.

Fuller, Col. J. F. C. *The Generalship of U. S. Grant.* 1929. Reprint, New York: Da Capo, 1991.

Glassley, Ray H. *Indian Wars of the Pacific Northwest.* 1953. 2d ed. Portland: Binfords & Mort, 1972.

Gordon, John B. *Reminiscences of the Civil War.* 1903. Reprint, New York: Time Life Books, 1981.

Grant, Ulysses S. *Personal Memoirs of U. S. Grant.* 1885. Reprint, New York: Da Capo, 1982.

Guie, H. Dean. *Bugles in the Valley: Garnett's Fort Simcoe.* Portland: Oregon Historical Society, 1977.

Heatwole, John L. *The Burning: Sheridan in the Shenandoah Valley.* Charlottesville, Va.: Howell, 1998.

Hood, John Bell. *Advance and Retreat: Personal Experiences in the United States and Confederate States Armies.* 1880. Reprint, New York: Da Capo, 1993.

Hoopes, Chad L. *Lure of the Humboldt Bay Region.* Dubuque: William C. Brown, 1966.

Howe, Henry. *Historical Collections of Ohio.* Rev. ed., 2 vols. in 1. Cincinnati: C. J. Krehbiel, 1908.

Horton, J. H., and S. Teveraugh. *A History of the 11th Regiment.* Dayton: S. J. Shuey, 1866.

Hutton, Paul Andrew. *Phil Sheridan and His Army.* 1985. Reprint, Lincoln: University of Nebraska Press, 1994.

Irvine, Leigh H. *History of Humboldt County.* Los Angeles: Historical Record Company, 1915.

Johnson, Robert U., and Clarence C. Buel, eds. *Battles and Leaders of the Civil War.* 4 vols. 1888. Reprint, Secaucus, N.J.: Castle, 1990.

Kempfer, Lester L. *The Salem Light Guard, Company G, 36th Ohio Volunteer Infantry, Marietta, Ohio, 1861–1865.* Chicago: Adams, 1973.

King, Capt. Charles. *Campaigning with Crook.* 1890. Reprint, Norman: University of Oklahoma Press, 1989.

Lang, Theodore F. *Loyal West Virginia from 1861 to 1865.* Baltimore: Deutsch Publishing, 1895.

Lewis, Thomas A. *The Guns of Cedar Creek.* New York: Harper and Row, 1988.

Lincoln, William S. *Life with the Thirty-Fourth Massachusetts Infantry in the War of Rebellion.* Worcester, Mass.: Press of Noyes, Snow, 1879.

Longacre, Edward G. *The Cavalry at Appomattox: A Tactical Study of Mounted Operations during the Civil War's Climactic Campaign, March 27–April 9, 1865.* Mechanicsburg, Pa.: Stackpole, 2003.

———. *Mounted Raids of the Civil War.* Lincoln: University of Nebraska Press, 1994.

Maxwell, Hu, and H. L. Swisher. *History of Hampshire County, West Virginia, from its Earliest Settlement to the Present.* Morgantown: A. Brown Boughner, 1897.

McFeely, William S. *Grant: A Biography.* New York: W. W. Norton, 1981.

McManus, Howard R. *The Battle of Cloyds Mountain: The Virginia and Tennessee Railroad Raid.* Lynchburg: H. E. Howard, 1989.

McPherson, James M. *Battle Cry of Freedom: The Civil War Era.* 1988. Reprint, New York, Ballantine, 1989.

Miller, Edward A. *Lincoln's Abolitionist General: The Biography of David Hunter.* Columbia: University of South Carolina Press, 1997.

Morris, Roy, Jr. *Sheridan: The Life and Wars of General Phil Sheridan.* 1992. Reprint, New York: Vintage Books, 1993.

Morrison, James L., Jr. *The Best School in the World: West Point, the Pre–Civil War Years, 1833–1866.* Kent, Ohio: Kent State University Press, 1986.

Newhall, Frederick C. *With Sheridan in the Final Campaign against Lee.* 1866. Reprint, Baton Rouge: Louisiana State University Press, 2002.

O'Connor, Richard. *Sheridan, the Inevitable.* 1953. Reprint, New York: Konecky and Konecky, 1993.

O'Donnell, Terrence. *An Arrow in the Earth: General Joel Palmer and the Indians of Oregon.* Portland: Oregon Historical Society Press, 1991.

Patchan, Scott C. *Shenandoah Summer: The 1864 Valley Campaign.* Lincoln: University of Nebraska Press, 2007.

Pierro, Joseph, ed. *The Maryland Campaign of September 1862: Ezra A. Carman's Definitive Study of the Union and Confederate Armies at Antietam.* New York: Routledge, Taylor, and French, 2008.

Pond, George E. *The Shenandoah Valley in 1864.* 1883. Reprint, Wilmington, N.C.: Broadfoot, 1989.

Porter, Horace. *Campaigning with Grant.* 1897. Reprint, Lincoln: University of Nebraska Press, 2000.

Priest, John M. *Antietam: The Soldier's Battle.* Shippensburg, Pa.: White Mane, 1989.

———. *Before Antietam: The Battle for South Mountain.* Shippensburg, Pa.: White Mane, 1992.

Raphael, Ray, and Freeman House. *Two Peoples, One Place.* Eureka, Ohio: Humboldt County Historical Society, 2007.

Reid, Whitlaw. *Ohio in the War.* Vol. 2. Cincinnati and New York: Moore, Wilstach, and Baldwin, 1868.

Robinson, Charles. *General Crook and the Western Frontier.* Norman: University of Oklahoma Press, 2001.

Russell, Don. *Campaigning with King.* 1964. Reprint, Norman: University of Oklahoma Press, 1989.

Sandburg, Carl. *Storm over the Land.* 1939. Reprint, Saybrook, Conn.: Konecky and Konecky, 1995.

Schildt, John W. *The Ninth Corps at Antietam.* Chewsville, Md.: Self-published, 1988.

Schmitt, Martin. *General George Crook, His Autobiography.* 1946. 2d ed. Norman: University of Oklahoma Press, 1960.

Sears, Stephen. *Chancellorsville.* Boston: Houghton Mifflin, 1996.

———. *Landscape Turned Red: The Battle of Antietam.* 1983. Reprint, Boston: Mariner, 1993.

Secrest, William B. *When the Great Spirit Died: The Destruction of the California Indians, 1850– 1860.* Sanger, Calif.: Quill Driver Books/Word Dancer Press, 2003.

Sergent, Mary Elizabeth. *They Lie Forgotten: The U.S. Military Academy, 1856–1861.* Middletown, N.Y.: Prior King, 1986.

Sheridan, Philip Henry. *Personal Memoirs of P. H. Sheridan.* 1888. Reprint, New York: Da Capo, 1992.

Sorrel, G. Moxley. *Recollections of a Confederate Staff Officer.* 1905. Reprint, New York: Konecky and Konecky, 1994.

Stackpole, Edward J. *Sheridan in the Shenandoah.* 1961. 2nd edition, Harrisburg, Pa.: Stackpole Books, 1992.

Stanley, David Sloan. *An American General: The Memoirs of David Sloan Stanley.* Santa Barbara, Calif.: Narrative, 2001.

Strahorn, Carrie Adell. *Fifteen Thousand Miles by Stage.* Vol. 1. 1911. Reprint, Lincoln: University of Nebraska Press, 1988.

Stephenson, Darl L. *Headquarters in the Brush, Blazer's Independent Union Scouts.* Athens: Ohio University Press, 2001.

Stout, Peter F. *Nicaragua: Past, Present, and Future.* Philadelphia, John E. Potter, 1859.

Strobridge, William F. *Regulars in the Redwoods: The U.S. Army in Northern California 1852– 1861.* Spokane: Arthur H. Clark, 1994.

Stutler, Boyd B. *West Virginia in the Civil War.* Charleston, W.Va.: Education Foundation, 1966.

Sutton, Dorothy, and Jack Sutton, eds. *Indian Wars of the Rogue River.* Grants Pass, Ore.: Josephine County Historical Society, 1969.

Taylor, James E. *The James E. Taylor Sketchbook: With Sheridan Up the Shenandoah Valley in 1864; Leaves from a Special Artist's Sketchbook and Diary.* Dayton: Western Reserve Historical Society, 1989.

Taylor, Walter H. *Four Years with General Lee.* 1877. Reprint, New York: Bonanza Books, 1962.

Thomas, Benjamin F., and Harold M. Hyman. *Stanton: The Life and Times of Lincoln's Secretary of War.* New York: Alfred A. Knopf, 1962.

Thomas, Emory M. *Bold Dragoon: The Life of J. E. B. Stuart.* New York: Harper and Row, 1986.

Thomas, James W., and T. J. C. Williams. *History of Allegany County, Maryland.* Vol. 1. Cumberland, Md.: Glisson T. Porter, 1923.

Tobie, Edward P. *History of the First Maine Cavalry, 1861–1865.* Boston: Press of Emery and Hughes, 1887.

Tremain, Henry E. *Last Hours of Sheridan's Cavalry: A Reprint of War Memoranda.* New York: Bonnell, Silver, and Bowers, 1904.

Underwood, Nancy Chambers, comp. *Fifty Families, a History.* Dallas: N.p., 1978.

Utley, Robert M. *Frontiersmen in Blue: The United States Army & the Indian, 1848–1865.* 1967. Reprint, Lincoln: University of Nebraska Press, 1991.

Walsh, Frank K. *Indian Battles along the Rogue River, 1855–56.* 1972. Reprint, North Bend, Ore.: Te-Cum-Tom Publications, 1996.

Warner, Ezra J. *Generals in Blue: Lives of the Union Commanders.* 1964. Reprint, Baton Rouge: Louisiana State University Press, 1992.

Washington, George. *The Diaries of George Washington.* 1925. Reprint, New York: Houghton Mifflin, 1971.

Waugh, John C. *The Class of 1846.* New York: Time Warner Books, 1994.

Wert, Jeffry D. *From Winchester to Cedar Creek: The Shenandoah Campaign of 1864.* Carlisle, Pa.: South Mountain, 1987.

———. *Mosby's Rangers.* New York: Simon and Shuster, 1990.

Whitehorne, Joseph W. A. *The Battle of Cedar Creek.* Washington, D.C.: Center for Military History, U.S. Army, 1992.

Wildes, Thomas F. *Record of the One Hundred and Sixteenth Ohio Infantry Volunteers in the War of Rebellion.* Sandusky, Ohio: I. F. Mack and Bros., 1884.

Williams, T. Harry. *Hayes of the 23rd.* 1965. Reprint, Lincoln: University of Nebraska Press, 1994.

———. *Lincoln and His Generals.* New York: Alfred A. Knopf, 1952.

Wittenberg, Eric J. *Little Phil: A Reassessment of the Civil War Leadership of General Philip H. Sheridan.* Foreword by Jeffry D. Wert. Dulles, Va.: Potomac Books, 2002.

NEWSPAPERS

Chicago Daily InterOcean
Chicago Tribune
Cumberland (Md.) Evening Times, 1947–1957
Dayton Daily News
Dayton Daily
National Tribune
New York Times
Springfield (Mass.) Republican
Oakland (Md.) Republican
Washington Chronicle
Wheeling Intelligencer
Wilmington (N.C.) Dispatch
Wilmington (N.C.) Herald
Wilmington (N.C.) Journal
Yreka (Calif.) Herald

ELECTRONIC SOURCES

Computerized Heritage Association. *Miami Valley Genealogical Index.* Miami County, Ohio: FoxPro, 1998.

Save the Oakland Railroad Station. http://www.oaklandmd.com/train/main.html.

Shelby County Ohio Historical Society. Civil War Home Page, http://www.shelbycounty history.org/schs/archives/civilwararchives/homepagecwara.htm.

Wittenberg, Eric. "Robert H. Minty," March 28, 2007. Rantings of a Civil War Historian, www.civilwarcavalry.com.

Acknowledgments

Originally conceived as a thinly veiled excuse to indulge my lifelong interest in the history of the Old West, this project soon took on a life of its own. Like the counter on a Ouija board, it began leading me in unexpected directions. As it developed in fits and starts, I found that I was meeting people, discovering institutions, and visiting places that would never have entered my life had I not chosen to make this journey. So my deepest debt of gratitude is to George Crook, who set me on this road. Having said that, I must also acknowledge the more immediate contributions of many others along the way.

Very shortly after I began researching Crook's life, I realized that, as an amateur historian and first-time author, I would not be able to do it alone. From the outset I wanted the story to interest and entertain. The dry, dispassionate voice I had learned in law school and adopted during thirty years in government practice seemed particularly ill suited to that end. In the hope of developing a more accessible writing style, I enrolled in the nonfiction-writers program at Johns Hopkins's Krieger School of Arts and Sciences. Under the guidance of the program's director and veteran journalist, David Everett, and Mary Collins, an inspired member of the teaching staff, writing became an unexpected delight. Soon I even began to believe that I might produce a publishable book.

Writing can be a lonely exercise, and after completing the Hopkins program, I missed the positive reinforcement, the knowledgeable critiques, and simply the companionship of other writers. That particular problem resolved itself after I retired to my longtime summer residence on Martha's Vineyard. The island is home to a profusion of writers and would-be writers, many of whom have organized into writers' groups. The two groups that I joined were initiated and nurtured by Cynthia Riggs, an indefatigable island institution, who herself had begun a successful second career as a mystery writer only a few years earlier. To her and the writers she mentors, my thanks for creating a secure space where I could share my work and receive the supportive criticism and encouragement that propelled me toward completion of this project.

Writing is a joy, but in the case of nonfiction, it is not so much an art form as a vehicle for conveying knowledge. Locating and distilling the knowledge needed to tell Crook's story proved my greatest challenge, especially as the general seemed to have devoted a good deal of energy to concealing the more personal aspects of his life. Additionally, my limited budget and scanty formal academic training in history (dating from college in the 1960s) made the task no easier.

Such a meager background in historical research and analysis made it difficult to navigate the maze of public archives, libraries, universities, museums, and local historical sites and societies where the needed facts lay hidden. So I am infinitely grateful for the dependable assistance provided by a veritable army of historians, both amateur and professional, and librarians and archivists. Unfortunately, most of my contacts with these individuals were all too brief, as locales for the research were usually far from home, and my travels were undertaken on a tight schedule. But happily those who work in these disciplines are generally a welcoming and helpful lot, willing and even eager to take time out of busy schedules to respond to the inquiries from an unknown and inexperienced researcher.

Among the historians, I was most impressed by those employed by the National Park Service, a generally unheralded cadre of experts charged with the responsibility of preserving and interpreting the history of the various locales to which they have been assigned. Moved by enthusiasm for their subject matter, they make history come alive in their personal presentations and in the numerous books they have written on many of the lesser-known aspects of American history.

While most of these NPS historians may not remember me, they made an indelible impression, and their contributions are found throughout this book. Robert Utley, the dean of early western history; Ed Bearss;

Neil Mangum; Robert Krick; Paul Hedren; and Jerome Greene—all past or present NPS employees—are but a few whose influence appears in these pages. I am eternally grateful to them for the depth of their expertise and their willingness to share as well as their encouragement in my efforts. Such affirmations are especially important when writing about a figure whose name usually evokes a blank stare or at best a wary, "the name sounds familiar, but I can't quite place it." Under such circumstances, meeting and talking with individuals who have not only heard of George Crook but also recognize his importance to the history of the frontier West has been welcome refreshment in a parched landscape.

While professional historians provided advice, direction, and a sense of participation in a greater whole, libraries, archives, and historical societies made available the documentation that composed the body of research resulting in this book. The Library of Congress and the National Archives are, of course, the mother lode for researchers, and I was drawn back to them again and again. To their knowledgeable and helpful staffs, whom I am afraid will have to remain nameless, my thanks for guiding this bewildered researcher through the labyrinth of books, original documents, reports, and letters in their collections.

For Crook's personal papers, such as they are, the U.S. Military History Institute, located in the historic town of Carlisle, Pennsylvania, is the primary repository, and its librarians proved vital. My thanks to the men and women who manage this vast holding of military history, especially to one unnamed librarian who, in defiance of bureaucratic imperatives, allowed me to swap a typescript I made of a handwritten draft of Crook's autobiography for a complete photocopy of the diary the general kept during the 1880s.

I found many additional materials in smaller libraries, both public and private, well off the beaten path. With only limited time available, I could not have succeeded in this project without the help of their small, often overworked and largely volunteer staffs, who unearthed documents for me, some of which I had not even known existed. In libraries and museums from Maryland to California, their diligence contributed substantially to the completion of this book. John Grant of the Oakland (Maryland) Historical Society, who took the time to drive me around the beautiful town and impart factual nuggets not otherwise available; Beth DiGustino of the Allegany County (Maryland) Library; Nancy Horlacher of the Dayton and Montgomery Country (Ohio) Public

Library; Nan Card of the Rutherford B. Hayes Presidential Library in Fremont, Ohio; and Alan Aimone and Sheila Biles of the U.S. Military Academy Library, will have to stand as representatives of a long list of such dedicated and kind individuals. And I would be seriously remiss if I failed to mention the help I received from my own incomparable West Tisbury Free Public Library and its wonderful staff, including Beth Kramer, Colleen Murray, Laura Coit, and Steve Klebs.

In the course of my research, I had occasion to correspond with some of George Crook's descendants. Carolyn Lawson and Alexander Kennedy in particular were most generous in providing additional information. I hope someday to meet them and explore their family connections more completely.

Every author owes a debt of gratitude to his or her publisher. In my case I was fortunate to meet Bob Clark, University of Oklahoma Press, at a symposium on Western history at Fort Robinson, Nebraska. He was interested in George Crook and my efforts to write about him. But he gently suggested that my manuscript, which had grown to 1,200 pages, might be somewhat problematical for a publisher, given Crook's limited stature; one of about 350 pages might be of greater interest. Though temporarily immobilized by the idea of pruning my work down to such a bare nubbin, I ultimately suggested a single volume covering Crook's life through the Civil War, with the potential for a second book to complete the general's story. Bob's reply—basically to "go for it"—was all the encouragement I needed. Then when this volume was finally completed, he shepherded it through the many-layered procedures of academic-press approval.

My thanks, too, to Kevin Brock and Steven Baker, my editors who diligently guided me through the production phase of the project and cleaned up my prose, corrected my citations, and forced me to add historical details I might otherwise have omitted, and to Bill Nelson for capturing part of Crook's story on maps.

I must also acknowledge my family and friends who stood by me in my obsessive journey through Crook's life and continued to express polite interest in how the book was coming along well after they must have stopped believing that I would ever complete it. Those friends who took a more active role were Mike Weaver, who introduced me to the Hopkins writing program; Frank Bucholz, whose genealogical investigations into the Crook family proved of great value; Mark Winston, who patiently accompanied me on a tour of the Appomattox campaign and read my drafts; and Juris Jurjevics, who gave me valuable advice on how to approach the world of publishing. Finally my thanks go to my wife, Anita, and wonderful children, Zachary and Danielle, who continued to encourage me despite long absences during which I wrote, researched, and traveled on project-related expeditions to obscure corners of the United States.

Index